黒鷺死体宅配便
the KUROSAGI corpse delivery service

story
EIJI OTSUKA

art
HOUSUI YAMAZAKI

original cover design
BUNPEI YORIFUJI

translation
TOSHIFUMI YOSHIDA

editor and english adaptation
CARL GUSTAV HORN

lettering and touch-up
IHL

DARK HORSE MANGA

contents

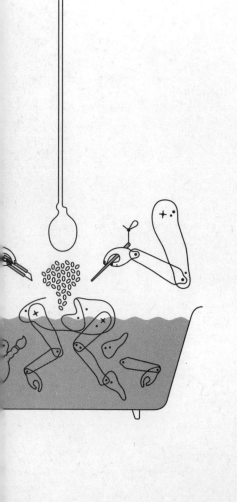

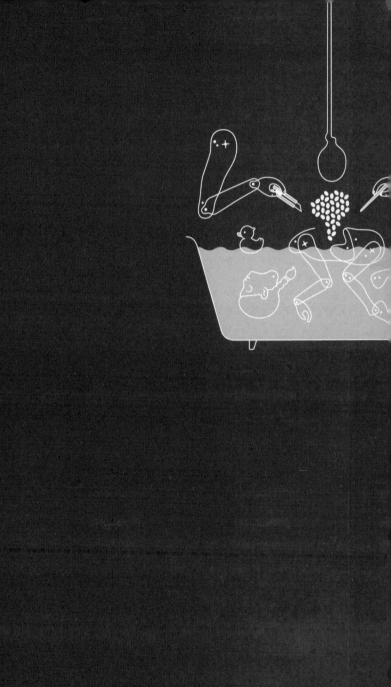

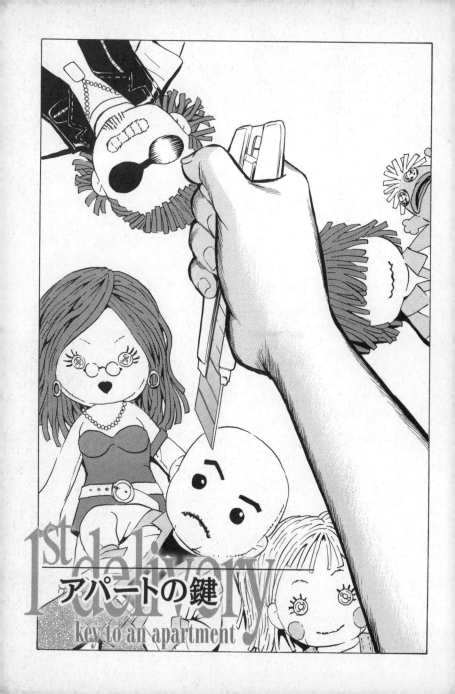

1st delivery
アパートの鍵
key to an apartment

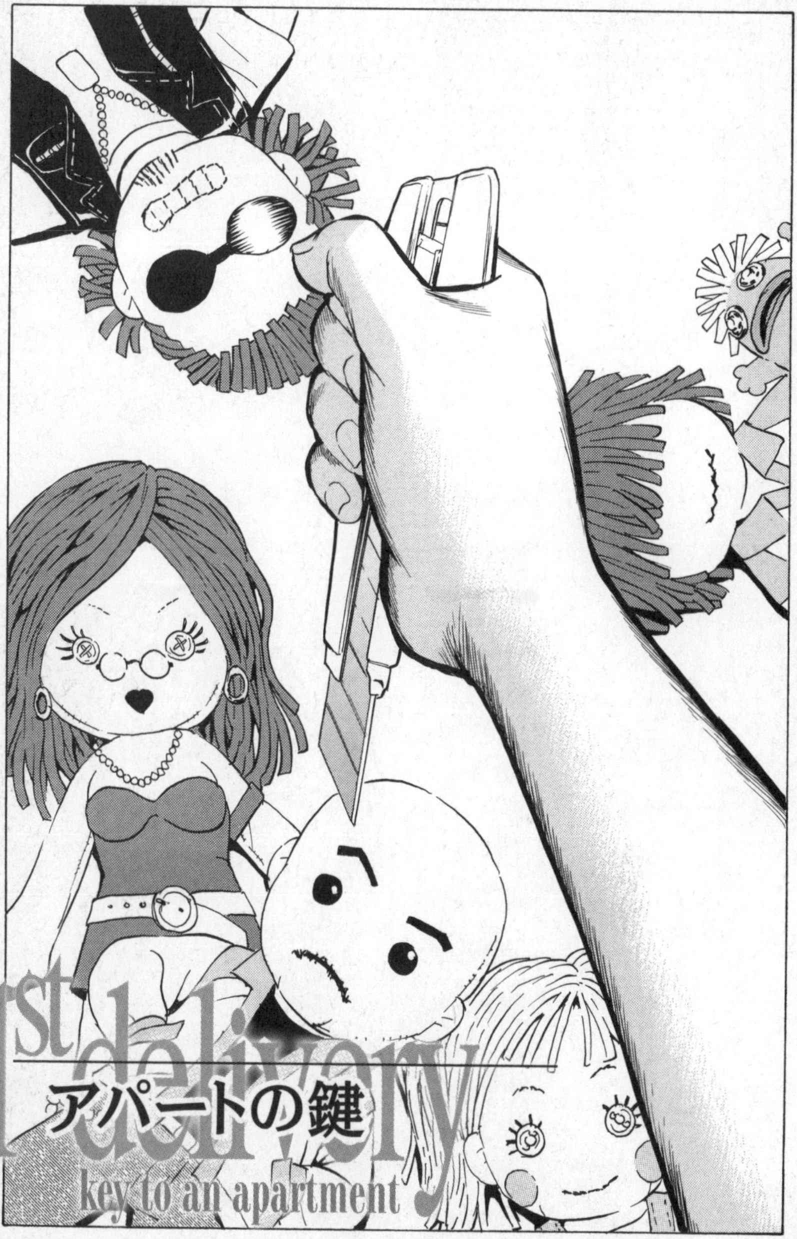

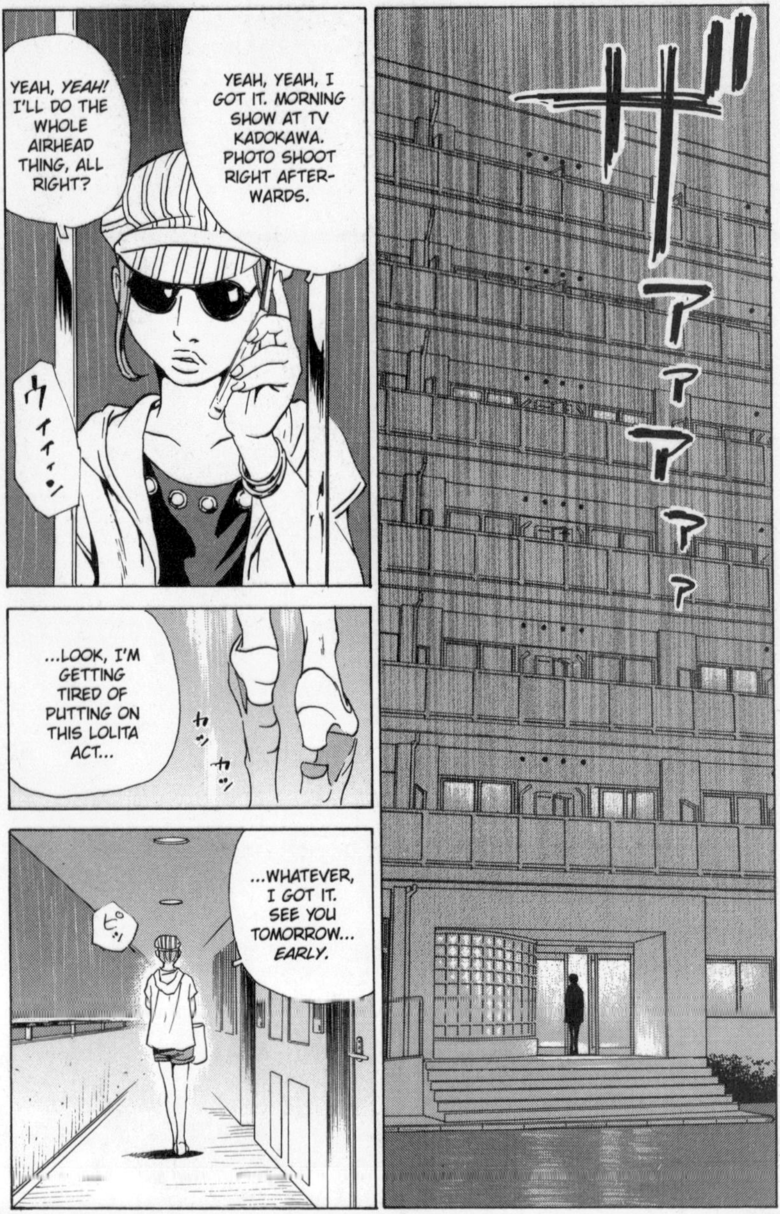
ザァァァァァ
YEAH, YEAH, I GOT IT. MORNING SHOW AT TV KADOKAWA. PHOTO SHOOT RIGHT AFTER-WARDS.
YEAH, *YEAH!* I'LL DO THE WHOLE AIRHEAD THING, ALL RIGHT?
ウィィィン
...LOOK, I'M GETTING TIRED OF PUTTING ON THIS LOLITA ACT...
カッ
カッ
...WHATEVER, I GOT IT. SEE YOU TOMORROW... *EARLY.*
ピッ

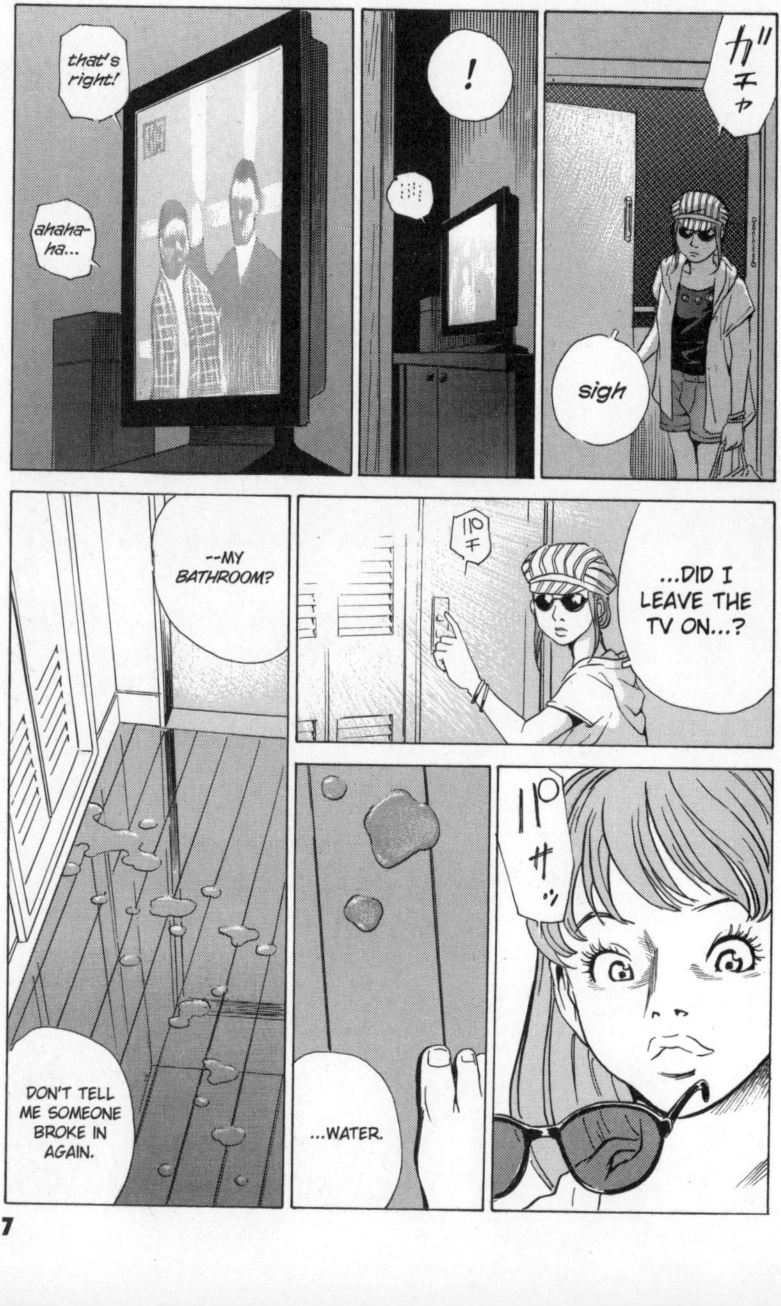

ガチャ
sigh
!
that's right!
ahaha-ha...
パチ
...DID I LEAVE THE TV ON...?
パサッ
...WATER.
--MY BATHROOM?
DON'T TELL ME SOMEONE BROKE IN AGAIN.

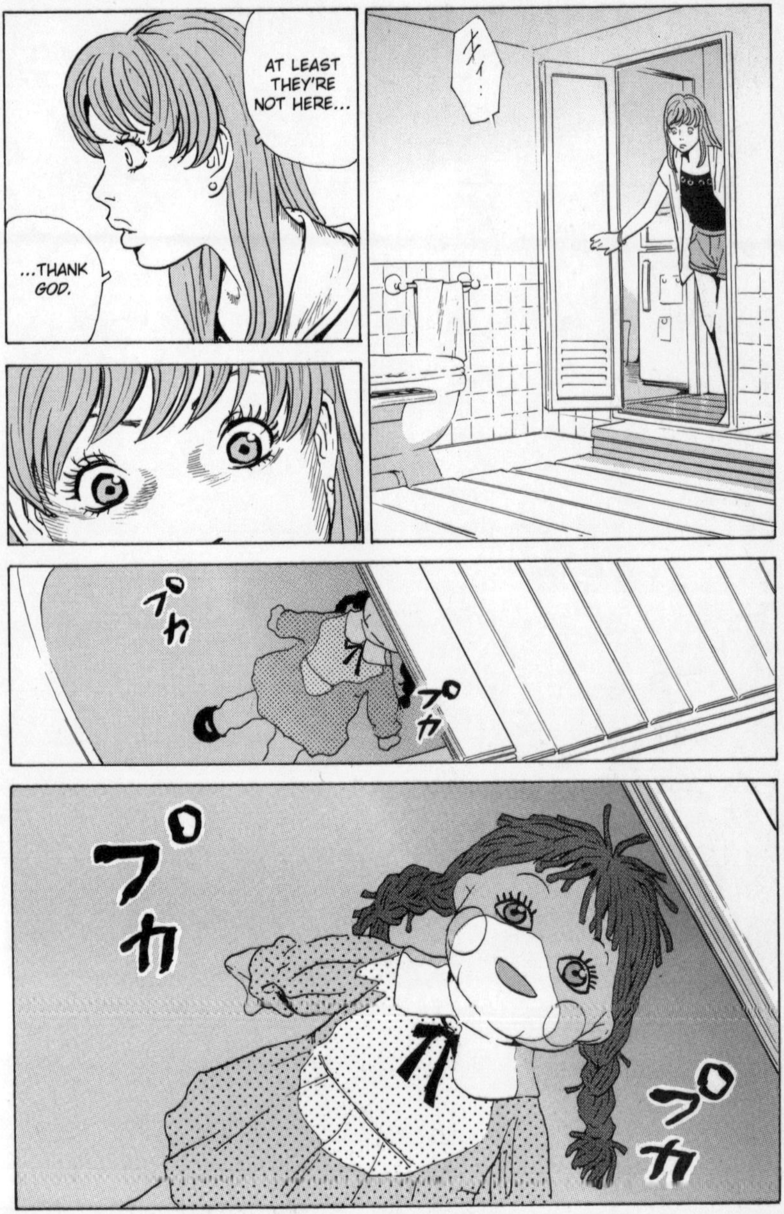
キィ…
AT LEAST THEY'RE NOT HERE...
...THANK GOD.
プカ
プカ
プカ
プカ

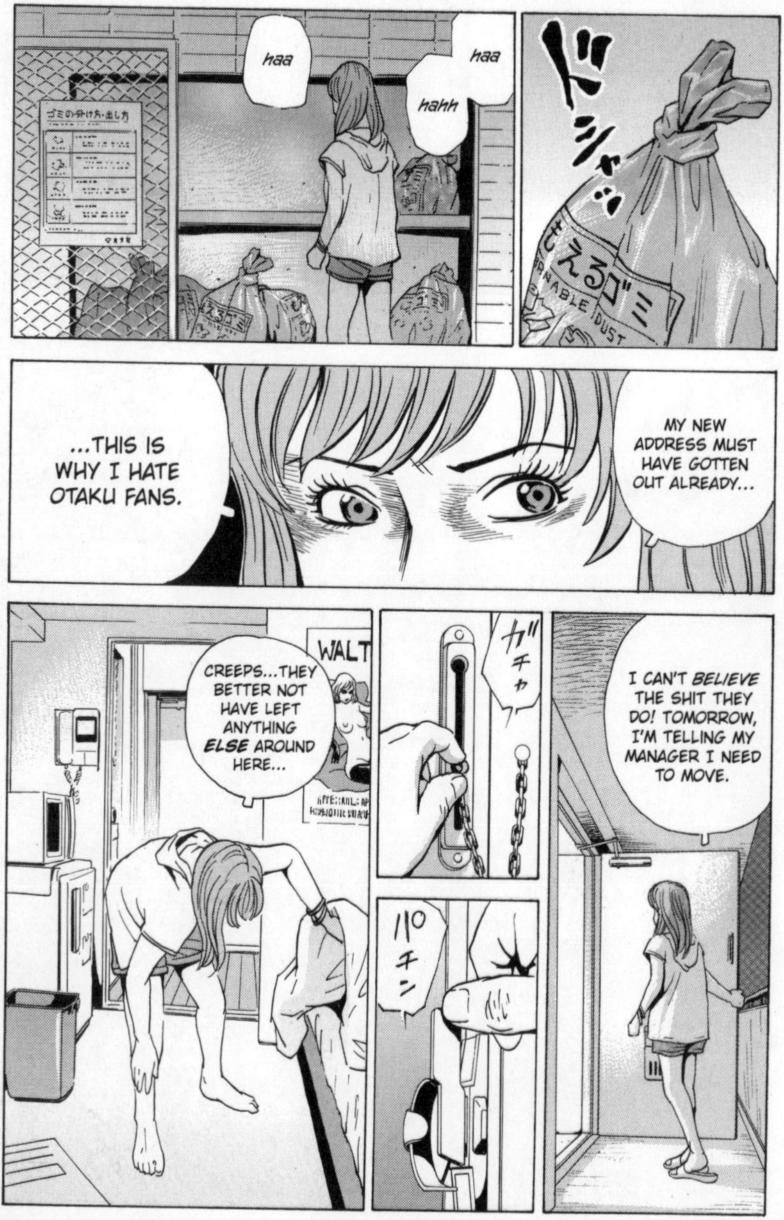
ドシャッ
もえるゴミ
haa
hahh
haa
ゴミの分け方・出し方
MY NEW ADDRESS MUST HAVE GOTTEN OUT ALREADY...
...THIS IS WHY I HATE OTAKU FANS.
I CAN'T *BELIEVE* THE SHIT THEY DO! TOMORROW, I'M TELLING MY MANAGER I NEED TO MOVE.
ガチャ
パチン
WALT
CREEPS...THEY BETTER NOT HAVE LEFT ANYTHING *ELSE* AROUND HERE...

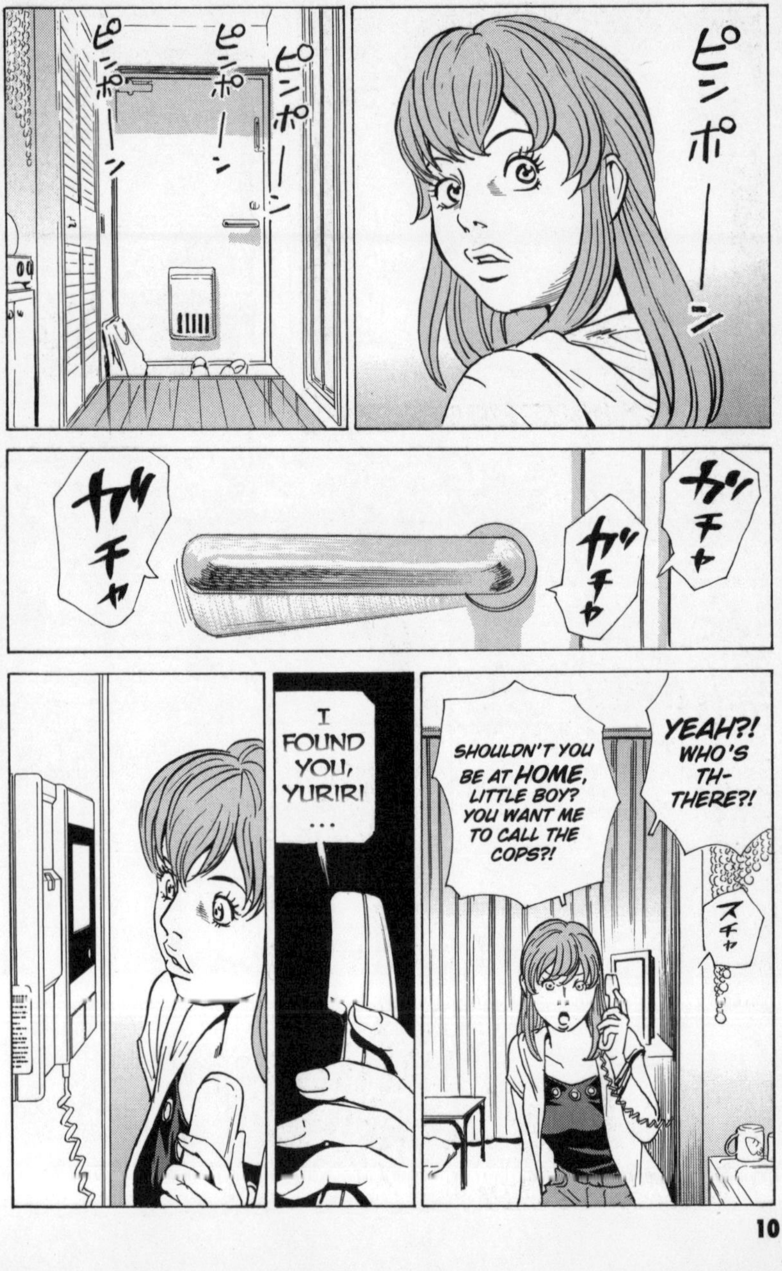

ピンポーーン
ピンポーン
ピンポーーン
ピンポーン
ガチャ
ガチャ
ガチャ
YEAH?! WHO'S TH- THERE?!
SHOULDN'T YOU BE AT HOME, LITTLE BOY? YOU WANT ME TO CALL THE COPS?!
スチャ
I FOUND YOU, YURIRI ...

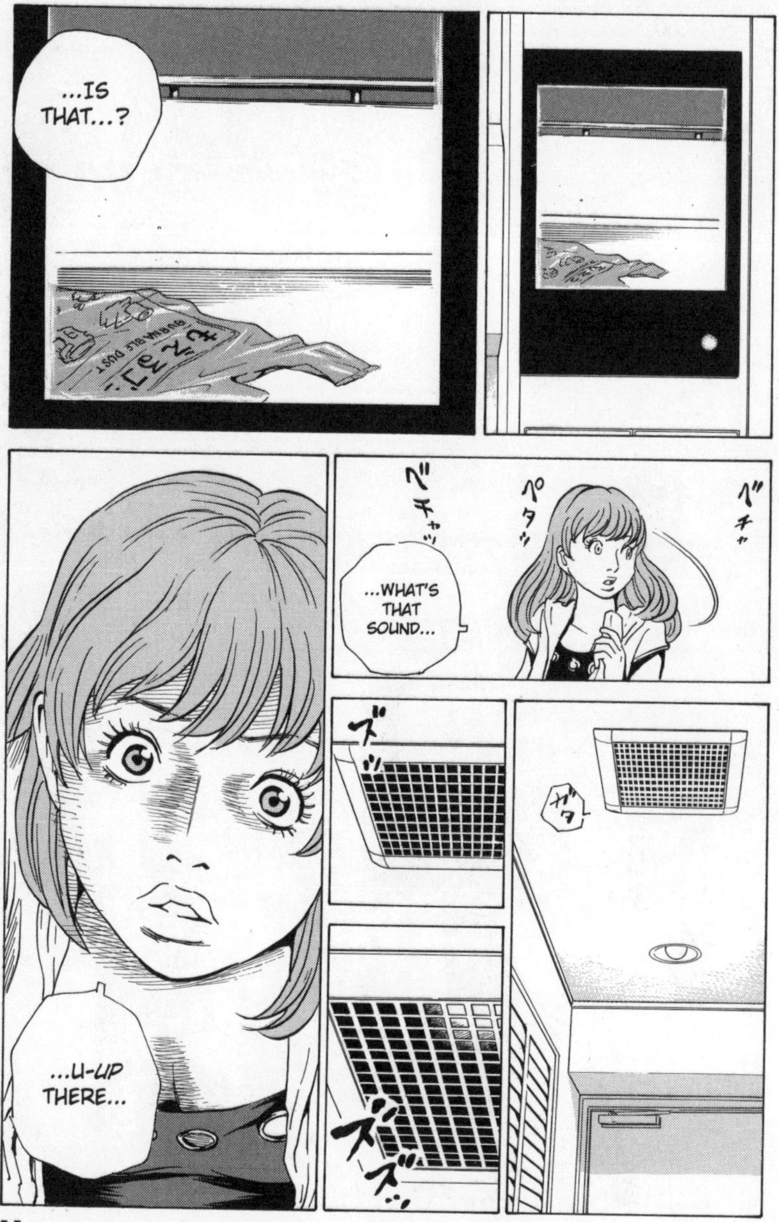
...IS THAT...?
ベチャ
ペタッ
ベチャッ
...WHAT'S THAT SOUND...
ガタ
ズッ
ズズズッ
...U-UP THERE...

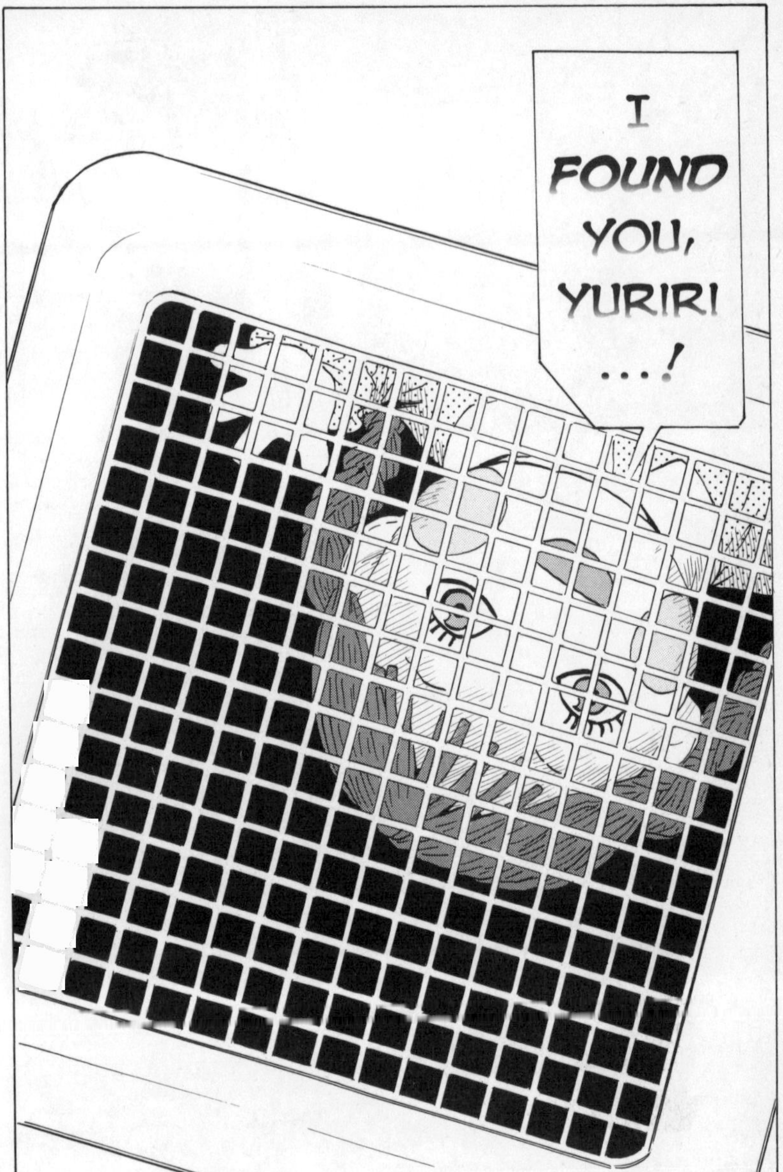
I FOUND YOU, YURIRI ...!

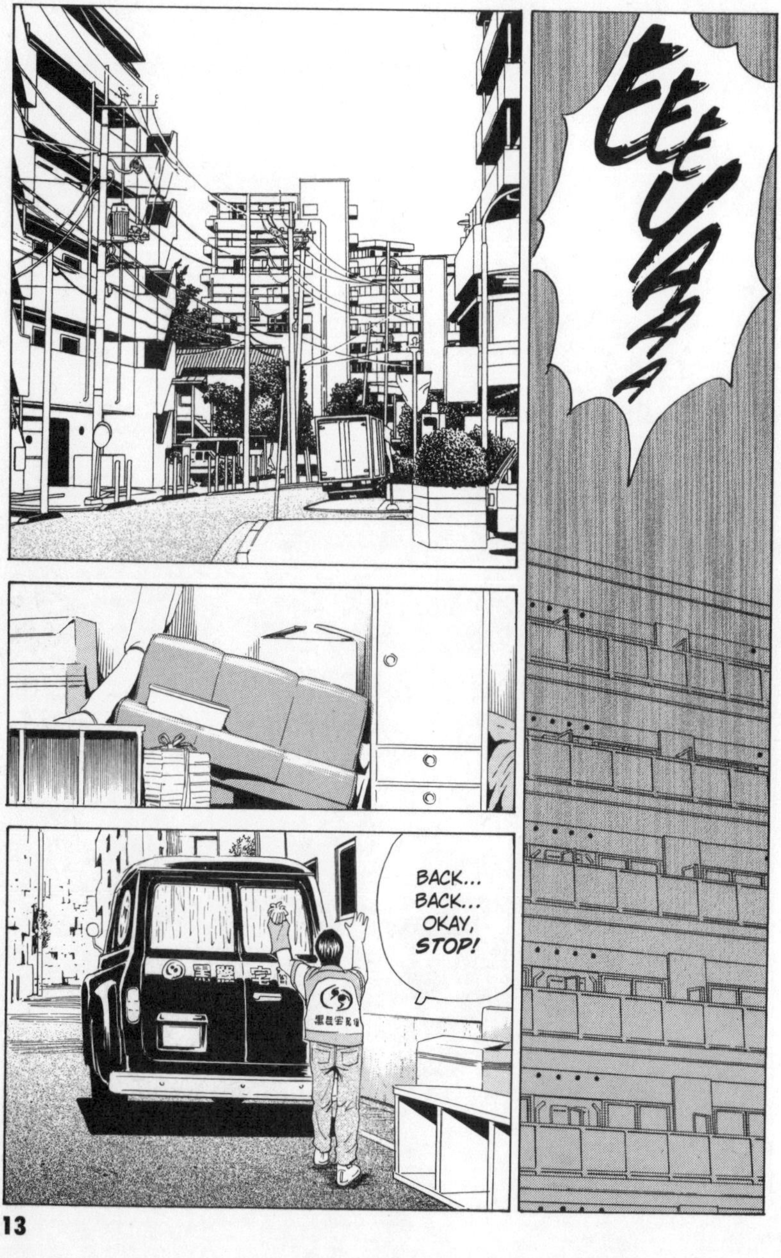
EEEYAAA
BACK... BACK... OKAY, STOP!

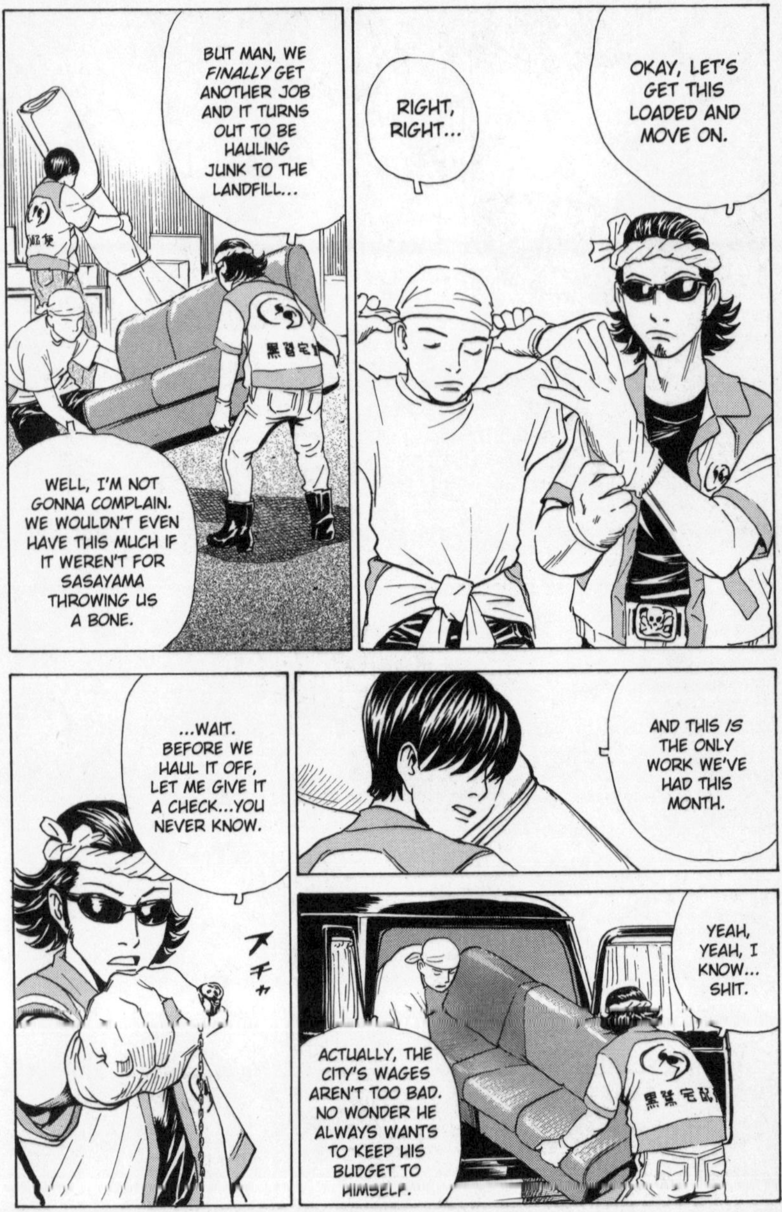
OKAY, LET'S GET THIS LOADED AND MOVE ON.
RIGHT, RIGHT...
BUT MAN, WE *FINALLY* GET ANOTHER JOB AND IT TURNS OUT TO BE HAULING JUNK TO THE LANDFILL...
WELL, I'M NOT GONNA COMPLAIN. WE WOULDN'T EVEN HAVE THIS MUCH IF IT WEREN'T FOR SASAYAMA THROWING US A BONE.
AND THIS *IS* THE ONLY WORK WE'VE HAD THIS MONTH.
YEAH, YEAH, I KNOW... SHIT.
ACTUALLY, THE CITY'S WAGES AREN'T TOO BAD. NO WONDER HE ALWAYS WANTS TO KEEP HIS BUDGET TO HIMSELF.
...WAIT. BEFORE WE HAUL IT OFF, LET ME GIVE IT A CHECK...YOU NEVER KNOW.
カチャ

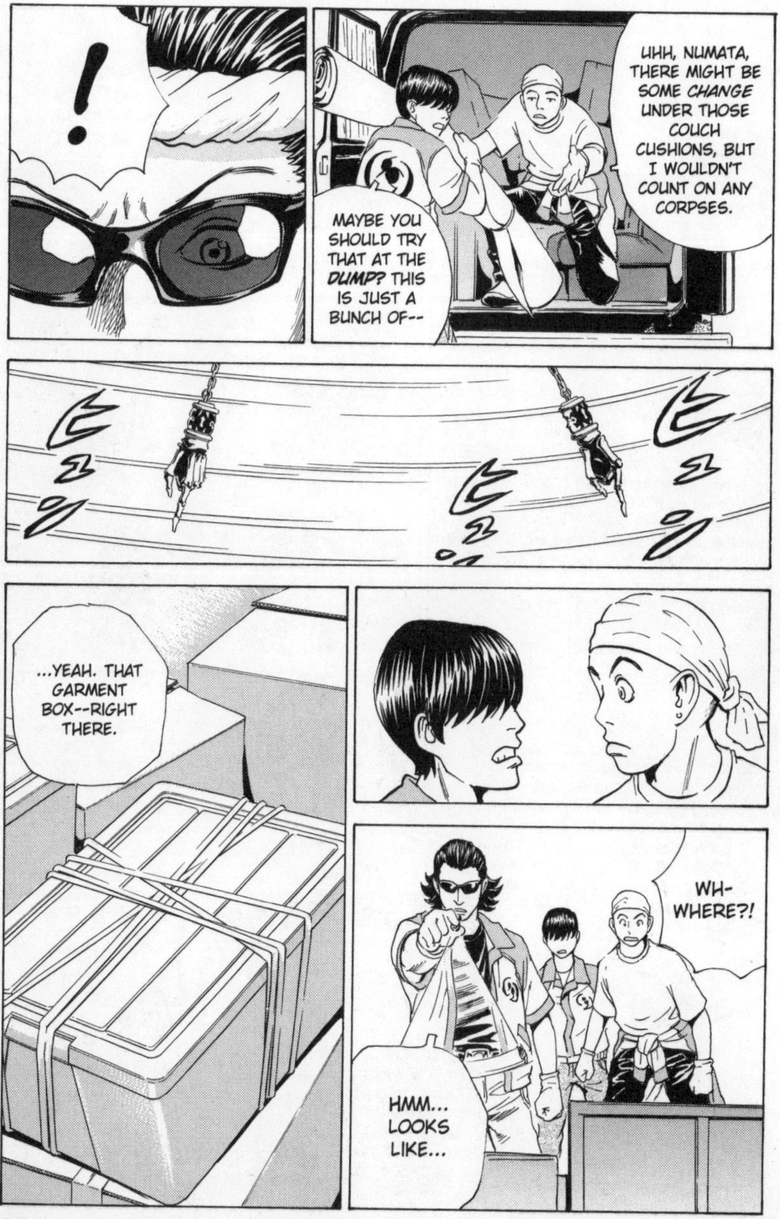
UHH, NUMATA, THERE MIGHT BE SOME CHANGE UNDER THOSE COUCH CUSHIONS, BUT I WOULDN'T COUNT ON ANY CORPSES.
MAYBE YOU SHOULD TRY THAT AT THE DUMP? THIS IS JUST A BUNCH OF--
!
WH- WHERE?!
HMM... LOOKS LIKE...
...YEAH. THAT GARMENT BOX--RIGHT THERE.

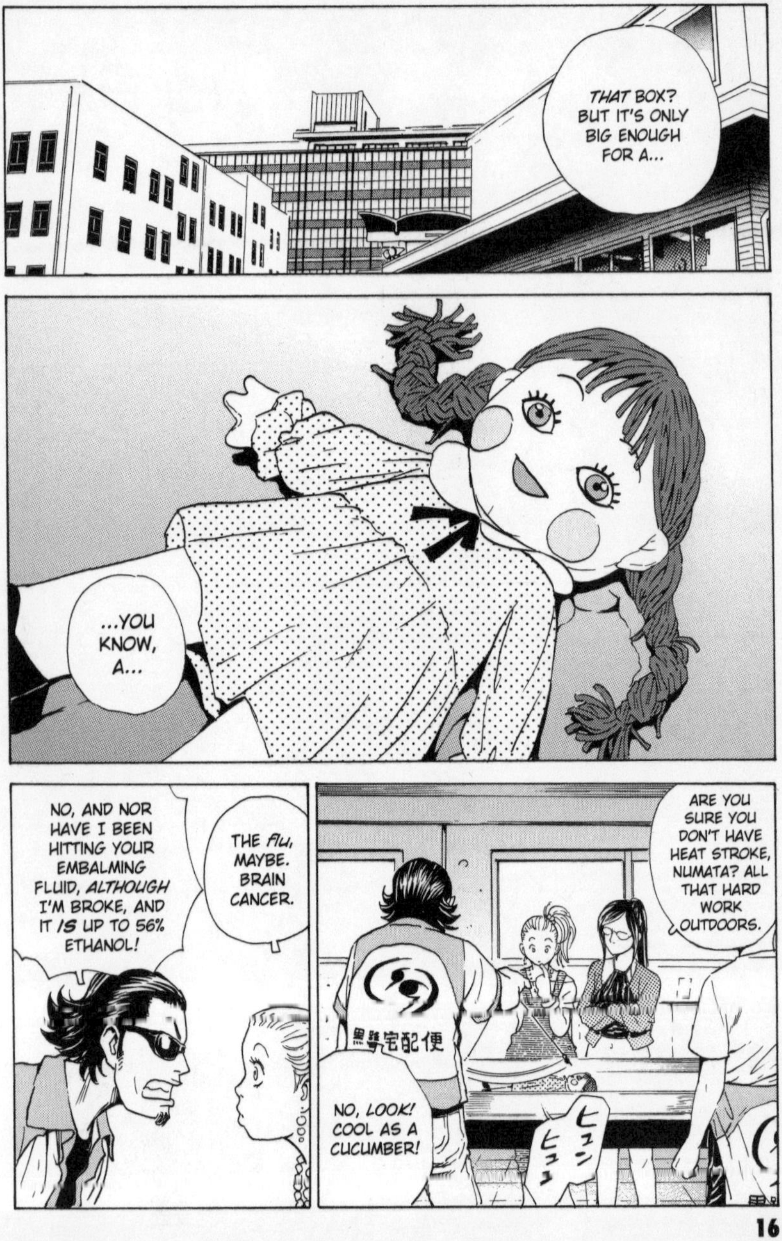
THAT BOX? BUT IT'S ONLY BIG ENOUGH FOR A...
...YOU KNOW, A...
ARE YOU SURE YOU DON'T HAVE HEAT STROKE, NUMATA? ALL THAT HARD WORK OUTDOORS.
NO, LOOK! COOL AS A CUCUMBER!
THE flu, MAYBE. BRAIN CANCER.
NO, AND NOR HAVE I BEEN HITTING YOUR EMBALMING FLUID, ALTHOUGH I'M BROKE, AND IT IS UP TO 56% ETHANOL!

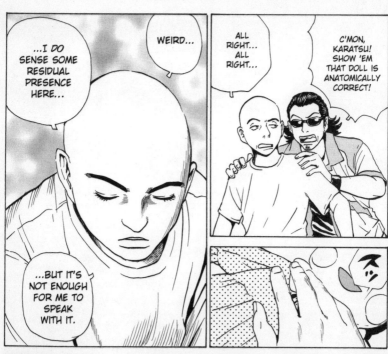

C'MON, KARATSU! SHOW 'EM THAT DOLL IS ANATOMICALLY CORRECT!
ALL RIGHT... ALL RIGHT...
スッ
WEIRD...
...I DO SENSE SOME RESIDUAL PRESENCE HERE...
...BUT IT'S NOT ENOUGH FOR ME TO SPEAK WITH IT.
HMM...I SUPPOSE IT COULD BE SOMETHING INSIDE THE DOLL...
Um, I'LL TAKE A LOOK.
シャキーン
WAAAH! STOP!!

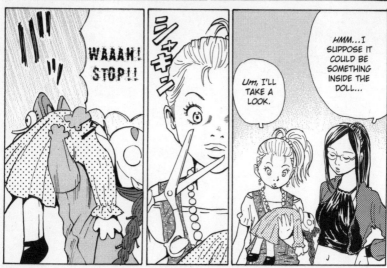

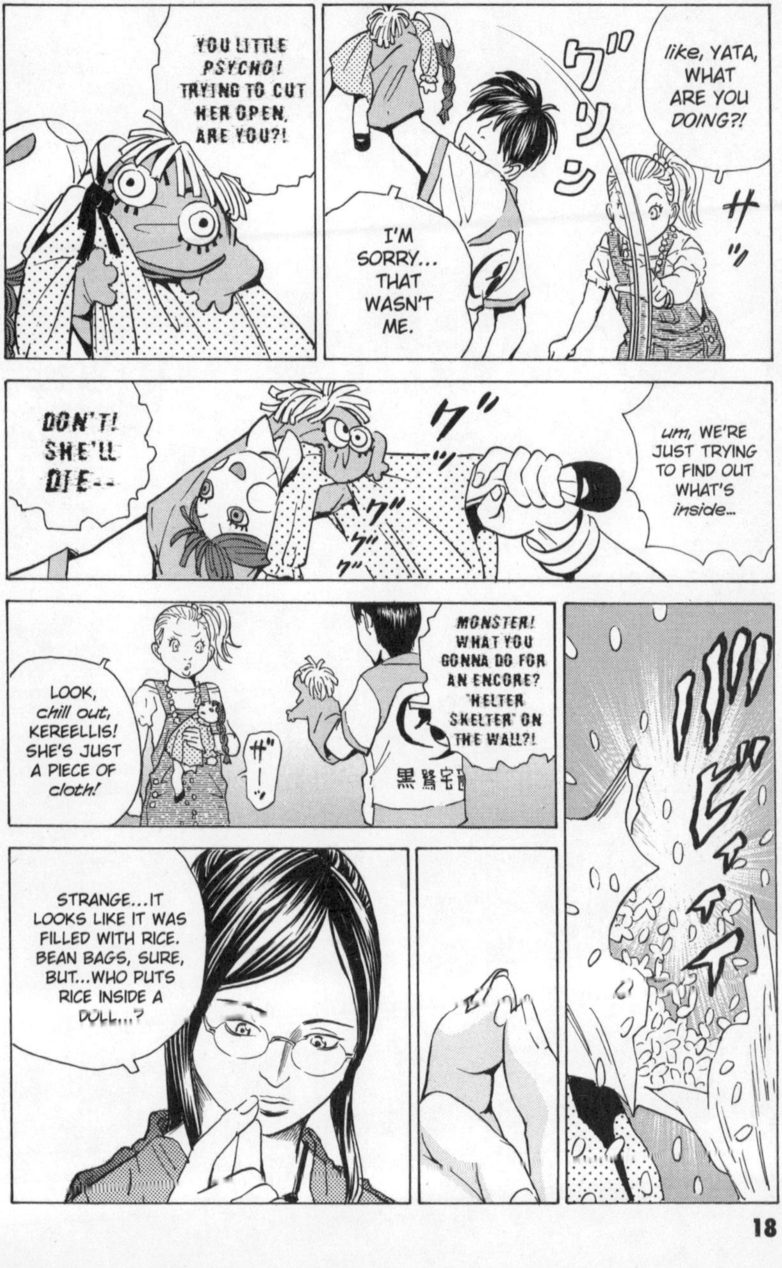
like, YATA, WHAT ARE YOU DOING?!
I'M SORRY... THAT WASN'T ME.
YOU LITTLE PSYCHO! TRYING TO CUT HER OPEN, ARE YOU?!
um, WE'RE JUST TRYING TO FIND OUT WHAT'S inside...
DON'T! SHE'LL DIE--
MONSTER! WHAT YOU GONNA DO FOR AN ENCORE? "HELTER SKELTER" ON THE WALL?!
LOOK, chill out, KEREELLIS! SHE'S JUST A PIECE OF cloth!
STRANGE...IT LOOKS LIKE IT WAS FILLED WITH RICE. BEAN BAGS, SURE, BUT...WHO PUTS RICE INSIDE A DOLL...?

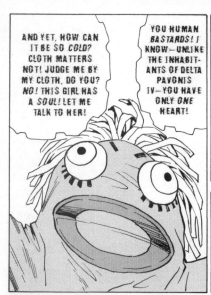

AND *anyway,* KEREELLIS, SOMEONE HAD ALREADY POKED SOME HOLES IN IT.
LOOK. IT'S A THIN TEAR...*box* CUTTER, MAYBE.
SORRY, PAL. KARATSU CAN'T TALK TO IT, AND AS MAKINO POINTS OUT, IT'S JUST...
YOU HUMAN *BASTARDS!* I KNOW—UNLIKE THE INHABIT-ANTS OF DELTA PAVONIS IV—YOU HAVE ONLY *ONE* HEART!
AND YET, HOW CAN IT BE SO *COLD?* CLOTH MATTERS NOT! JUDGE ME BY MY CLOTH, DO YOU? *NO!* THIS GIRL HAS A *SOUL!* LET ME TALK TO HER!
...lolwut?
UH-HUH!
...REALLY ...?
I SEE, I SEE...
駅前集合
...HE *BETTER* NOT BE JOKING.

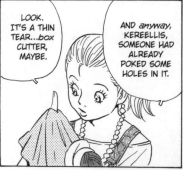

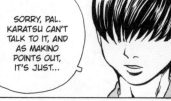

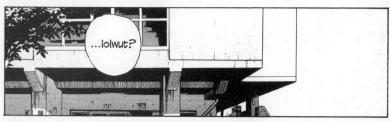

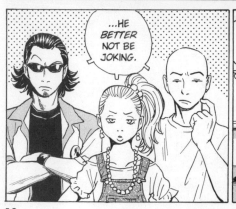

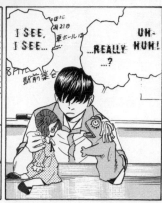

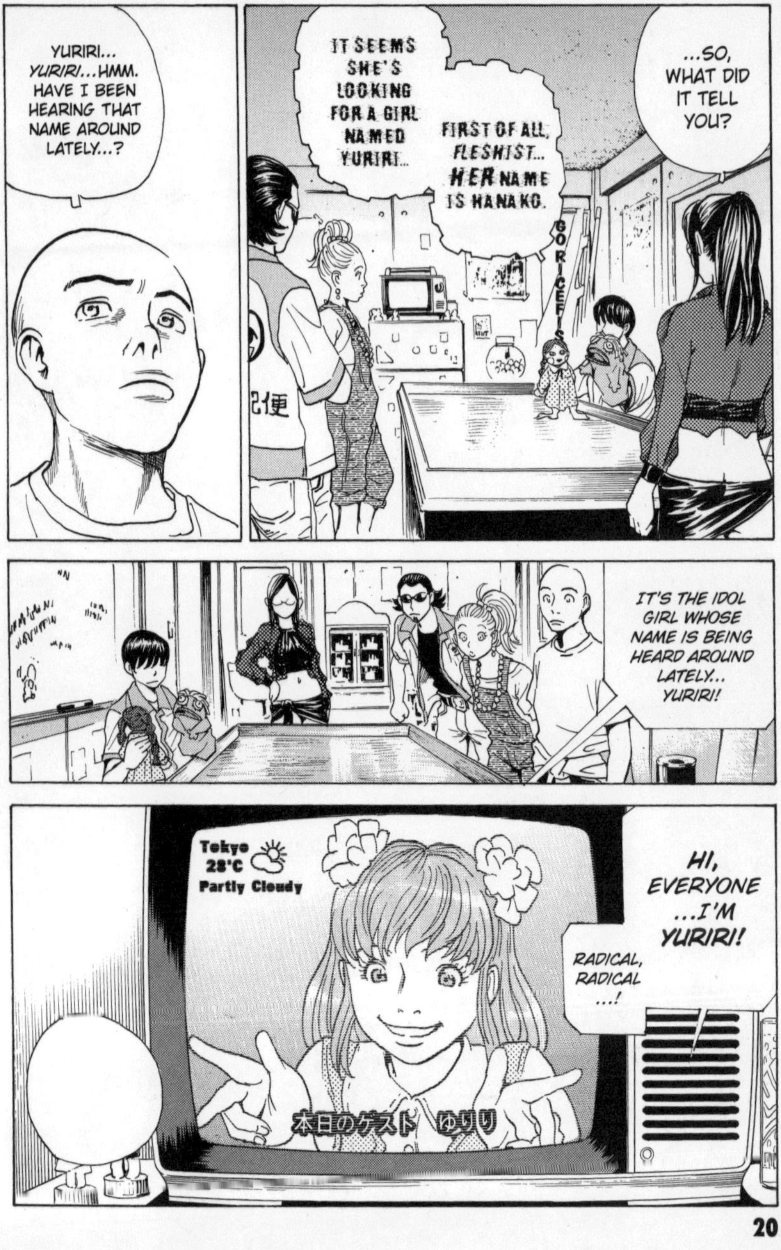
...SO, WHAT DID IT TELL YOU?
FIRST OF ALL, FLESHIST... HER NAME IS HANAKO.
IT SEEMS SHE'S LOOKING FOR A GIRL NAMED YURIRI...
YURIRI... YURIRI...HMM. HAVE I BEEN HEARING THAT NAME AROUND LATELY...?
IT'S THE IDOL GIRL WHOSE NAME IS BEING HEARD AROUND LATELY... YURIRI!
HI, EVERYONE ...I'M YURIRI!
RADICAL, RADICAL ...!
Tokyo 28°C Partly Cloudy
本日のゲスト　ゆりり

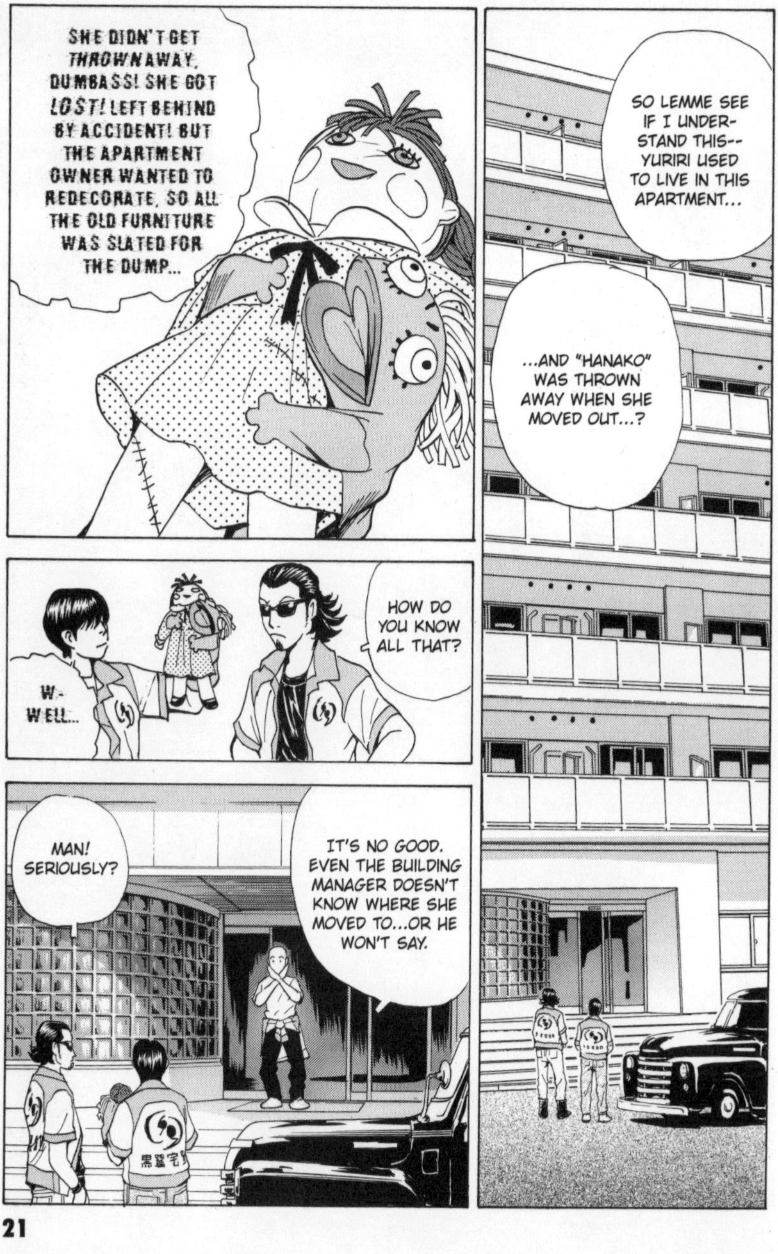
SO LEMME SEE IF I UNDER-STAND THIS--YURIRI USED TO LIVE IN THIS APARTMENT...
...AND "HANAKO" WAS THROWN AWAY WHEN SHE MOVED OUT...?
SHE DIDN'T GET *THROWN* AWAY, DUMBASS! SHE GOT *LOST!* LEFT BEHIND BY ACCIDENT! BUT THE APARTMENT OWNER WANTED TO REDECORATE, SO ALL THE OLD FURNITURE WAS SLATED FOR THE DUMP...
HOW DO YOU KNOW ALL THAT?
W-WELL...
IT'S NO GOOD. EVEN THE BUILDING MANAGER DOESN'T KNOW WHERE SHE MOVED TO...OR HE WON'T SAY.
MAN! SERIOUSLY?

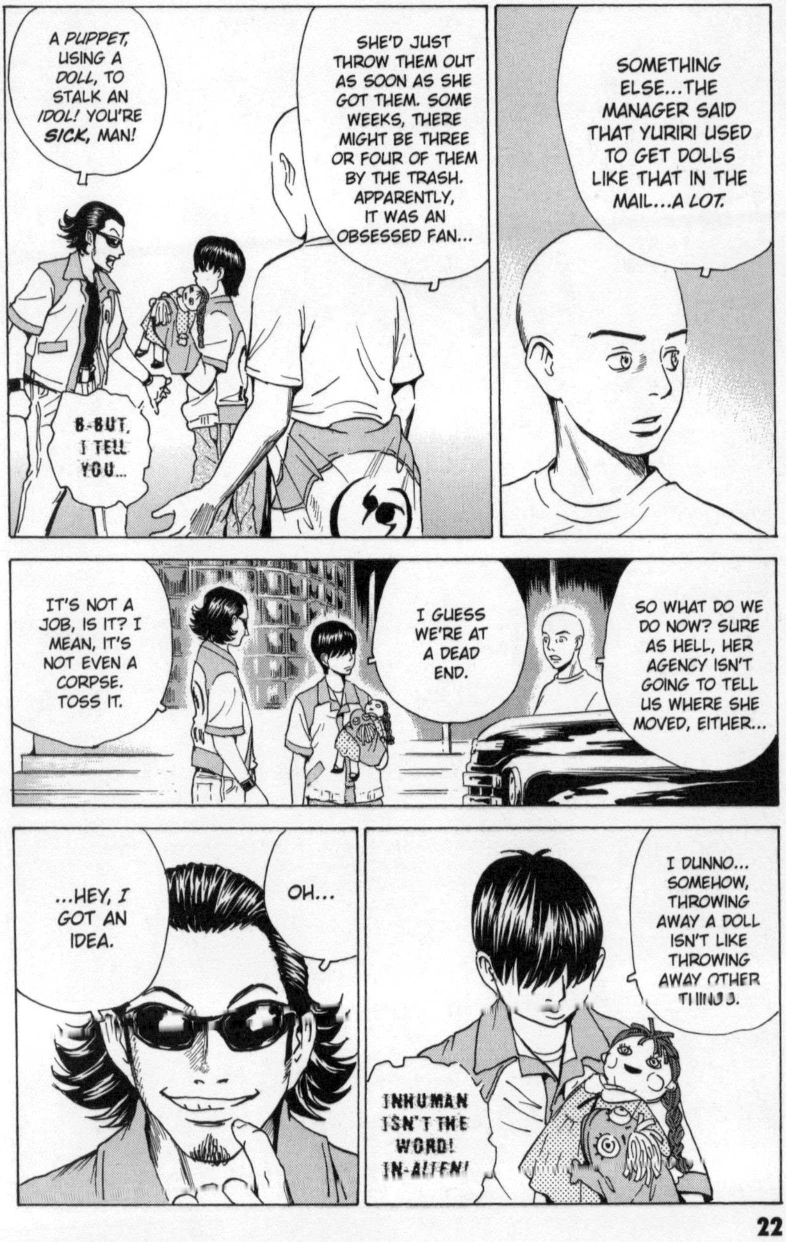
SOMETHING ELSE...THE MANAGER SAID THAT YURIRI USED TO GET DOLLS LIKE THAT IN THE MAIL...A *LOT.*
SHE'D JUST THROW THEM OUT AS SOON AS SHE GOT THEM. SOME WEEKS, THERE MIGHT BE THREE OR FOUR OF THEM BY THE TRASH. APPARENTLY, IT WAS AN OBSESSED FAN...
A *PUPPET,* USING A *DOLL,* TO STALK AN *IDOL!* YOU'RE ***SICK,*** MAN!
B-BUT, I TELL YOU...
SO WHAT DO WE DO NOW? SURE AS HELL, HER AGENCY ISN'T GOING TO TELL US WHERE SHE MOVED, EITHER...
I GUESS WE'RE AT A DEAD END.
IT'S NOT A JOB, IS IT? I MEAN, IT'S NOT EVEN A CORPSE. TOSS IT.
I DUNNO... SOMEHOW, THROWING AWAY A DOLL ISN'T LIKE THROWING AWAY OTHER THINGS.
INHUMAN ISN'T THE WORD! IN-ALIEN!
OH...
...HEY, *I* GOT AN IDEA.

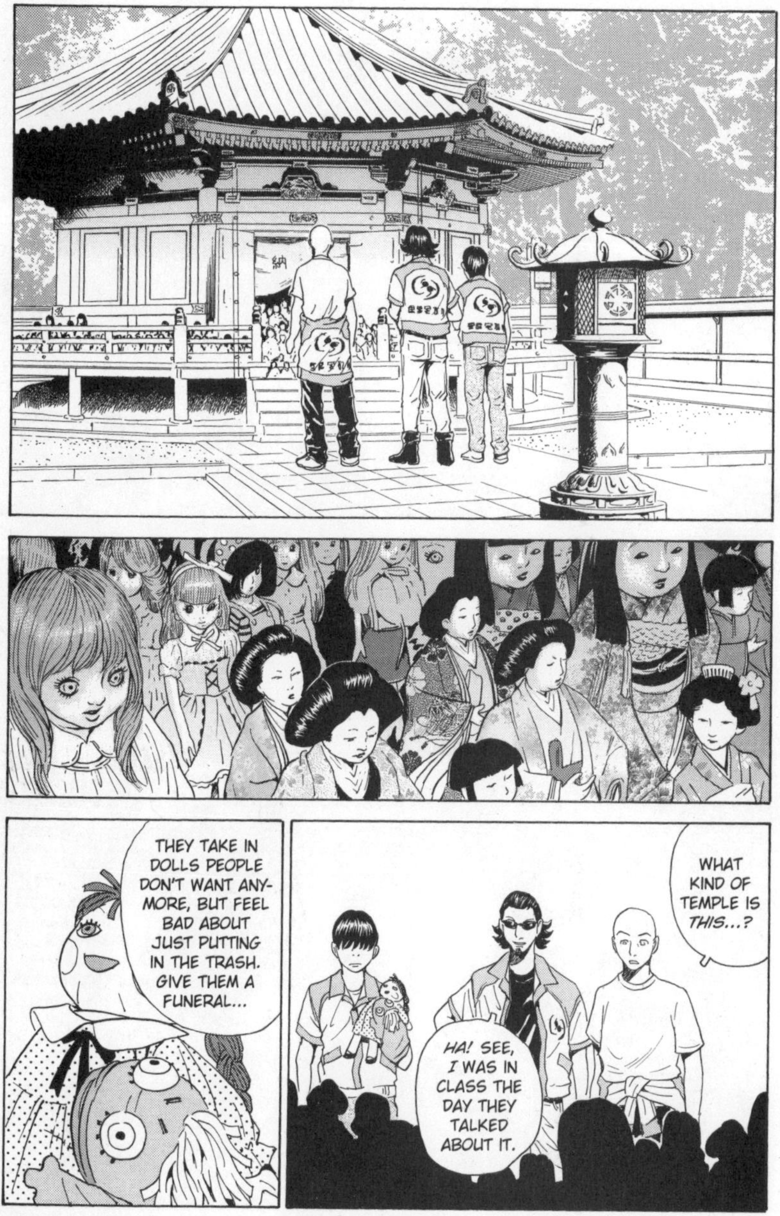
WHAT KIND OF TEMPLE IS *THIS*...?
HA! SEE, *I* WAS IN CLASS THE DAY THEY TALKED ABOUT IT.
THEY TAKE IN DOLLS PEOPLE DON'T WANT ANY-MORE, BUT FEEL BAD ABOUT JUST PUTTING IN THE TRASH. GIVE THEM A FUNERAL...

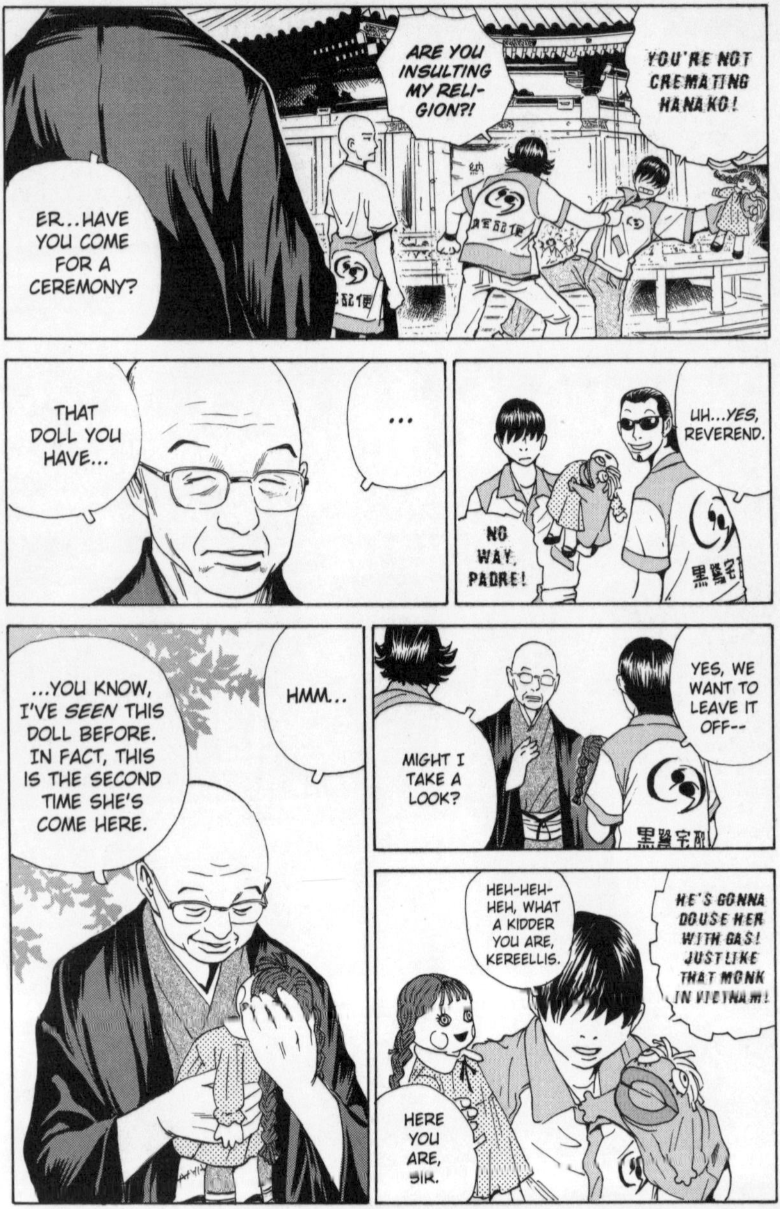
YOU'RE NOT CREMATING HANAKO!
ARE YOU INSULTING MY RELI-GION?!
ER...HAVE YOU COME FOR A CEREMONY?
UH...*YES*, REVEREND.
NO WAY, PADRE!
...
THAT DOLL YOU HAVE...
YES, WE WANT TO LEAVE IT OFF--
MIGHT I TAKE A LOOK?
HE'S GONNA DOUSE HER WITH GAS! JUST LIKE THAT MONK IN VIETNAM!
HEH-HEH-HEH, WHAT A KIDDER YOU ARE, KEREELLIS.
HERE YOU ARE, SIR.
HMM...
...YOU KNOW, I'VE *SEEN* THIS DOLL BEFORE. IN FACT, THIS IS THE SECOND TIME SHE'S COME HERE.

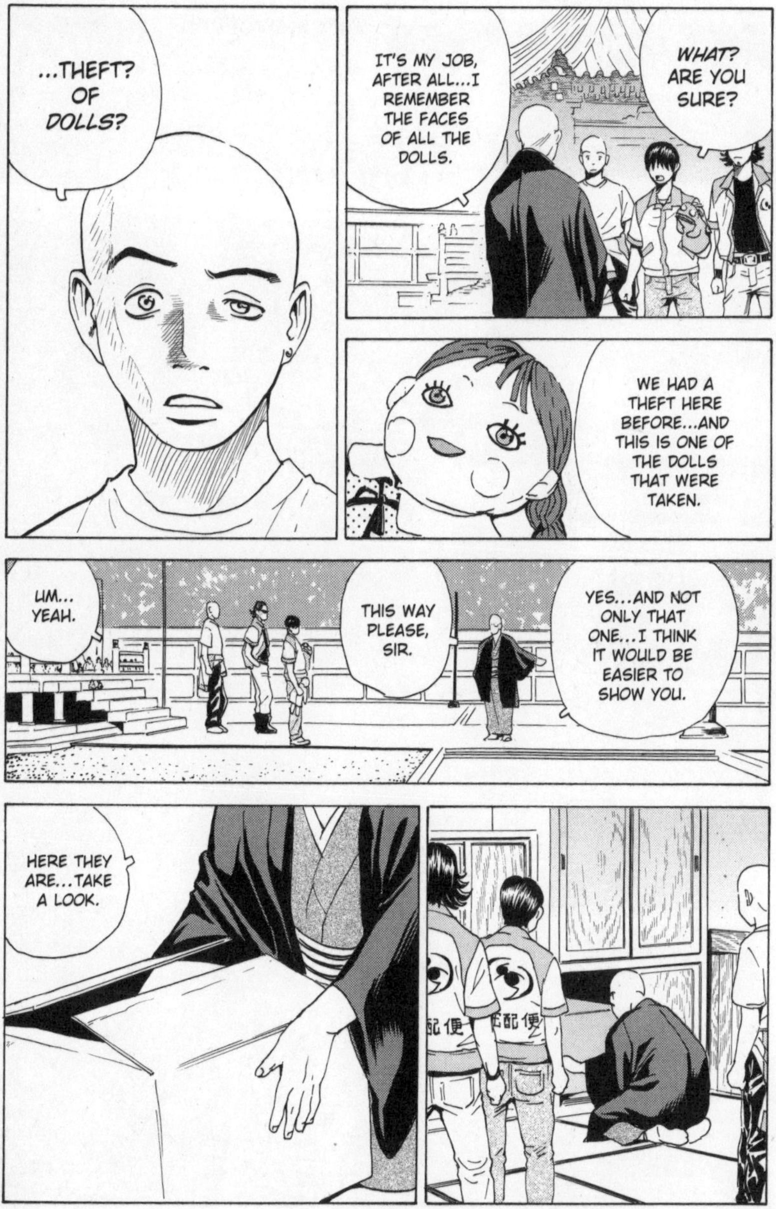
WHAT? ARE YOU SURE?
IT'S MY JOB, AFTER ALL...I REMEMBER THE FACES OF ALL THE DOLLS.
WE HAD A THEFT HERE BEFORE...AND THIS IS ONE OF THE DOLLS THAT WERE TAKEN.
...THEFT? OF DOLLS?
YES...AND NOT ONLY THAT ONE...I THINK IT WOULD BE EASIER TO SHOW YOU.
THIS WAY PLEASE, SIR.
UM... YEAH.
HERE THEY ARE...TAKE A LOOK.

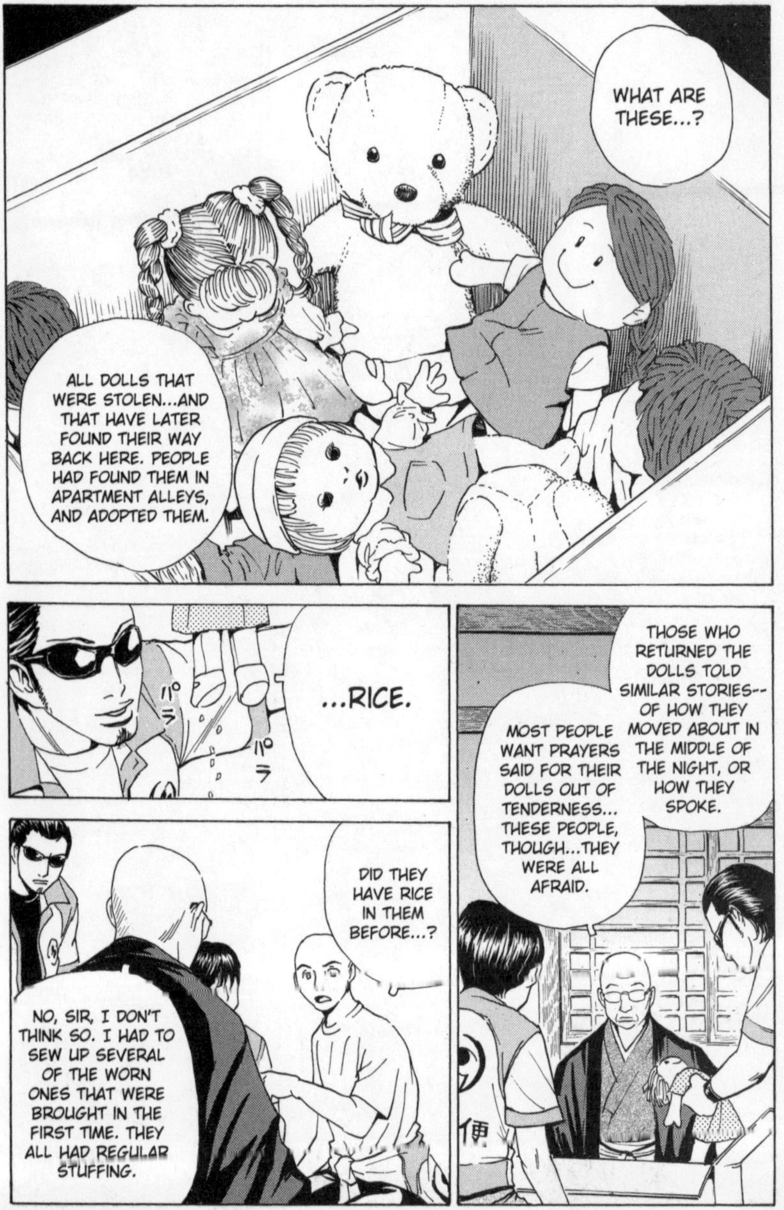
WHAT ARE THESE...?
ALL DOLLS THAT WERE STOLEN...AND THAT HAVE LATER FOUND THEIR WAY BACK HERE. PEOPLE HAD FOUND THEM IN APARTMENT ALLEYS, AND ADOPTED THEM.
THOSE WHO RETURNED THE DOLLS TOLD SIMILAR STORIES--OF HOW THEY MOVED ABOUT IN THE MIDDLE OF THE NIGHT, OR HOW THEY SPOKE.
MOST PEOPLE WANT PRAYERS SAID FOR THEIR DOLLS OUT OF TENDERNESS... THESE PEOPLE, THOUGH...THEY WERE ALL AFRAID.
...RICE.
パラ
パラ
DID THEY HAVE RICE IN THEM BEFORE...?
NO, SIR, I DON'T THINK SO. I HAD TO SEW UP SEVERAL OF THE WORN ONES THAT WERE BROUGHT IN THE FIRST TIME. THEY ALL HAD REGULAR STUFFING.

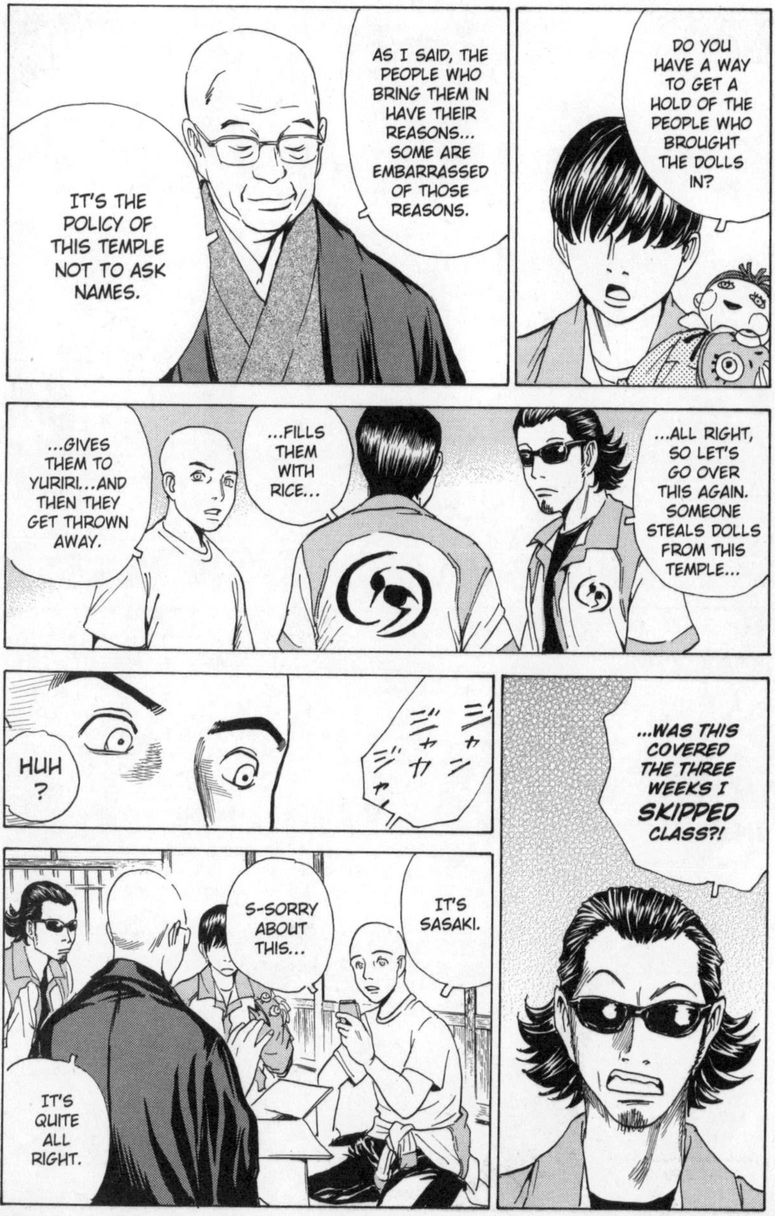
DO YOU HAVE A WAY TO GET A HOLD OF THE PEOPLE WHO BROUGHT THE DOLLS IN?
AS I SAID, THE PEOPLE WHO BRING THEM IN HAVE THEIR REASONS... SOME ARE EMBARRASSED OF THOSE REASONS.
IT'S THE POLICY OF THIS TEMPLE NOT TO ASK NAMES.
...ALL RIGHT, SO LET'S GO OVER THIS AGAIN. SOMEONE STEALS DOLLS FROM THIS TEMPLE...
...FILLS THEM WITH RICE...
...GIVES THEM TO YURIRI...AND THEN THEY GET THROWN AWAY.
...WAS THIS COVERED THE THREE WEEKS I SKIPPED CLASS?!
HUH ?
IT'S SASAKI.
S-SORRY ABOUT THIS...
IT'S QUITE ALL RIGHT.

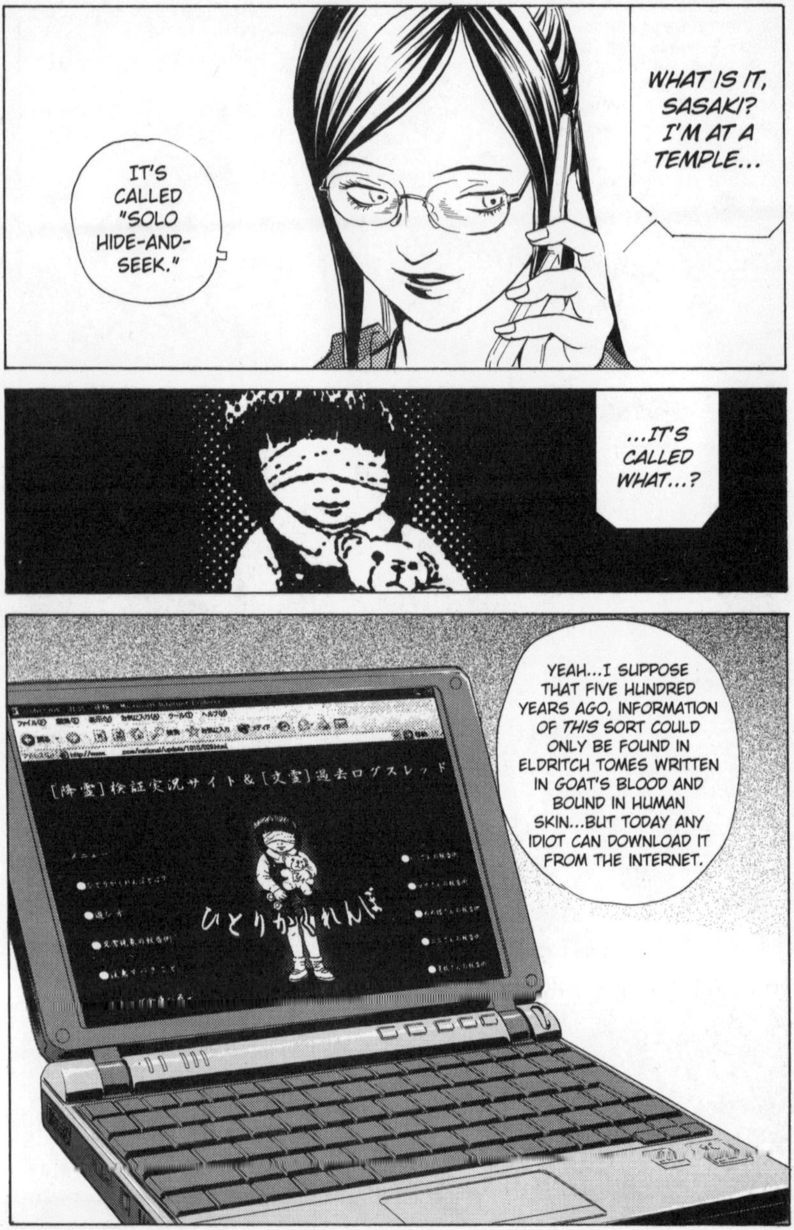
WHAT IS IT, SASAKI? I'M AT A TEMPLE...
IT'S CALLED "SOLO HIDE-AND-SEEK."
...IT'S CALLED WHAT...?
YEAH...I SUPPOSE THAT FIVE HUNDRED YEARS AGO, INFORMATION OF *THIS* SORT COULD ONLY BE FOUND IN ELDRITCH TOMES WRITTEN IN GOAT'S BLOOD AND BOUND IN HUMAN SKIN...BUT TODAY ANY IDIOT CAN DOWNLOAD IT FROM THE INTERNET.

1st delivery: key to an apartment—the end

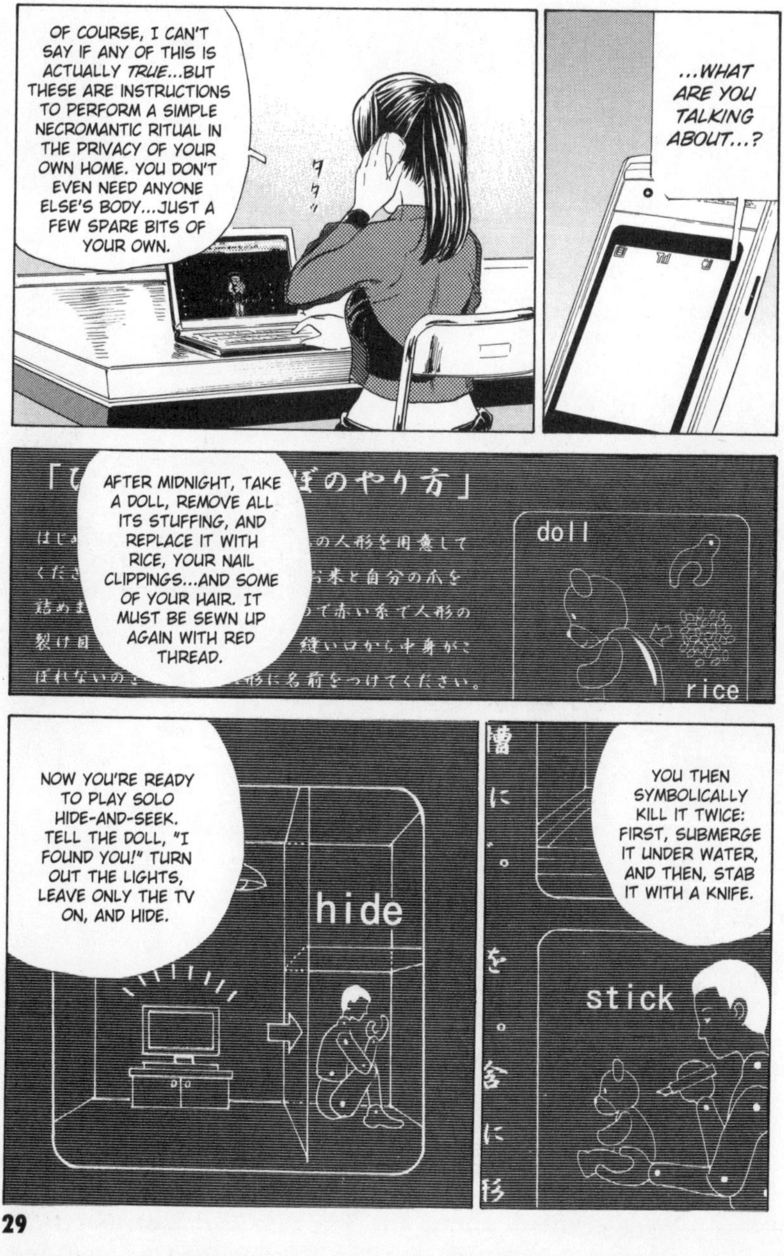
...WHAT ARE YOU TALKING ABOUT...?
OF COURSE, I CAN'T SAY IF ANY OF THIS IS ACTUALLY *TRUE*...BUT THESE ARE INSTRUCTIONS TO PERFORM A SIMPLE NECROMANTIC RITUAL IN THE PRIVACY OF YOUR OWN HOME. YOU DON'T EVEN NEED ANYONE ELSE'S BODY...JUST A FEW SPARE BITS OF YOUR OWN.
AFTER MIDNIGHT, TAKE A DOLL, REMOVE ALL ITS STUFFING, AND REPLACE IT WITH RICE, YOUR NAIL CLIPPINGS...AND SOME OF YOUR HAIR. IT MUST BE SEWN UP AGAIN WITH RED THREAD.
doll
rice
YOU THEN SYMBOLICALLY KILL IT TWICE: FIRST, SUBMERGE IT UNDER WATER, AND THEN, STAB IT WITH A KNIFE.
stick
NOW YOU'RE READY TO PLAY SOLO HIDE-AND-SEEK. TELL THE DOLL, "I FOUND YOU!" TURN OUT THE LIGHTS, LEAVE ONLY THE TV ON, AND HIDE.
hide

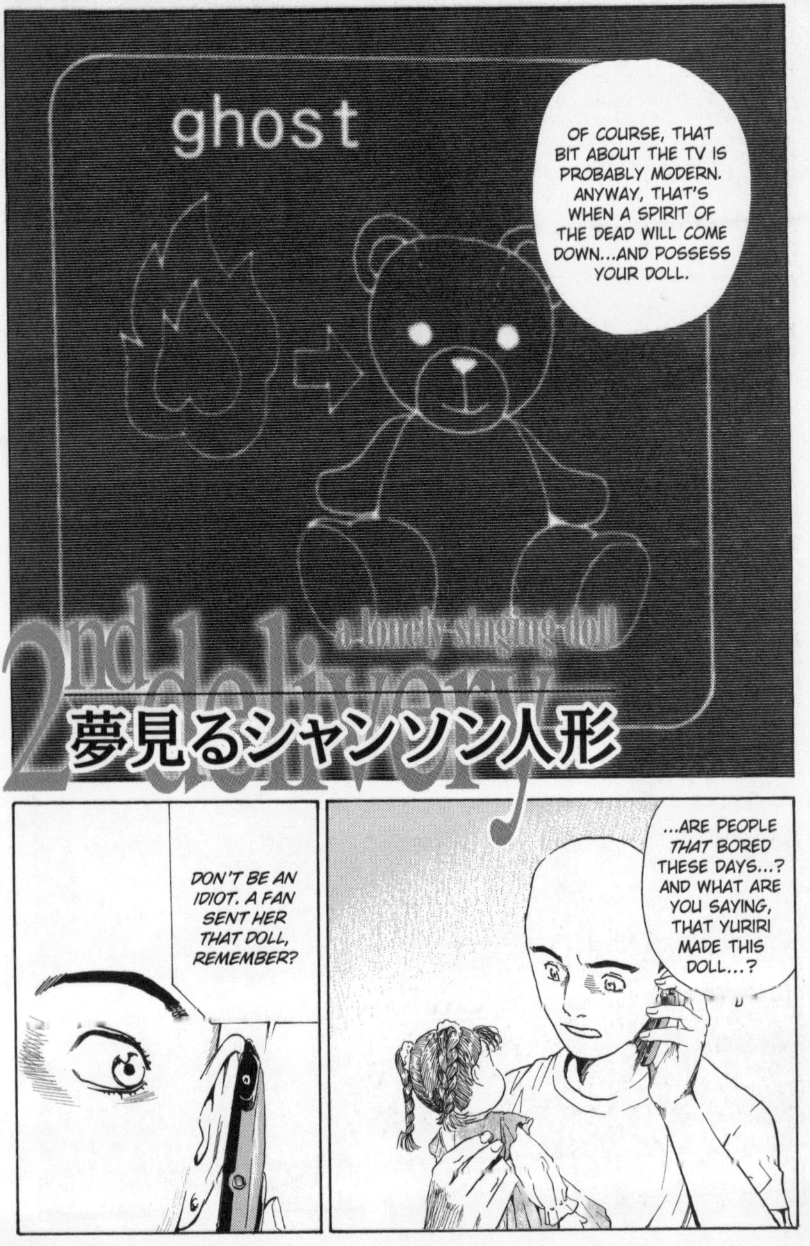
ghost
OF COURSE, THAT BIT ABOUT THE TV IS PROBABLY MODERN. ANYWAY, THAT'S WHEN A SPIRIT OF THE DEAD WILL COME DOWN...AND POSSESS YOUR DOLL.
2nd delivery
a lonely singing doll
夢見るシャンソン人形
...ARE PEOPLE *THAT* BORED THESE DAYS...? AND WHAT ARE YOU SAYING, THAT YURIRI MADE THIS DOLL...?
DON'T BE AN IDIOT. A FAN SENT HER THAT DOLL, REMEMBER?

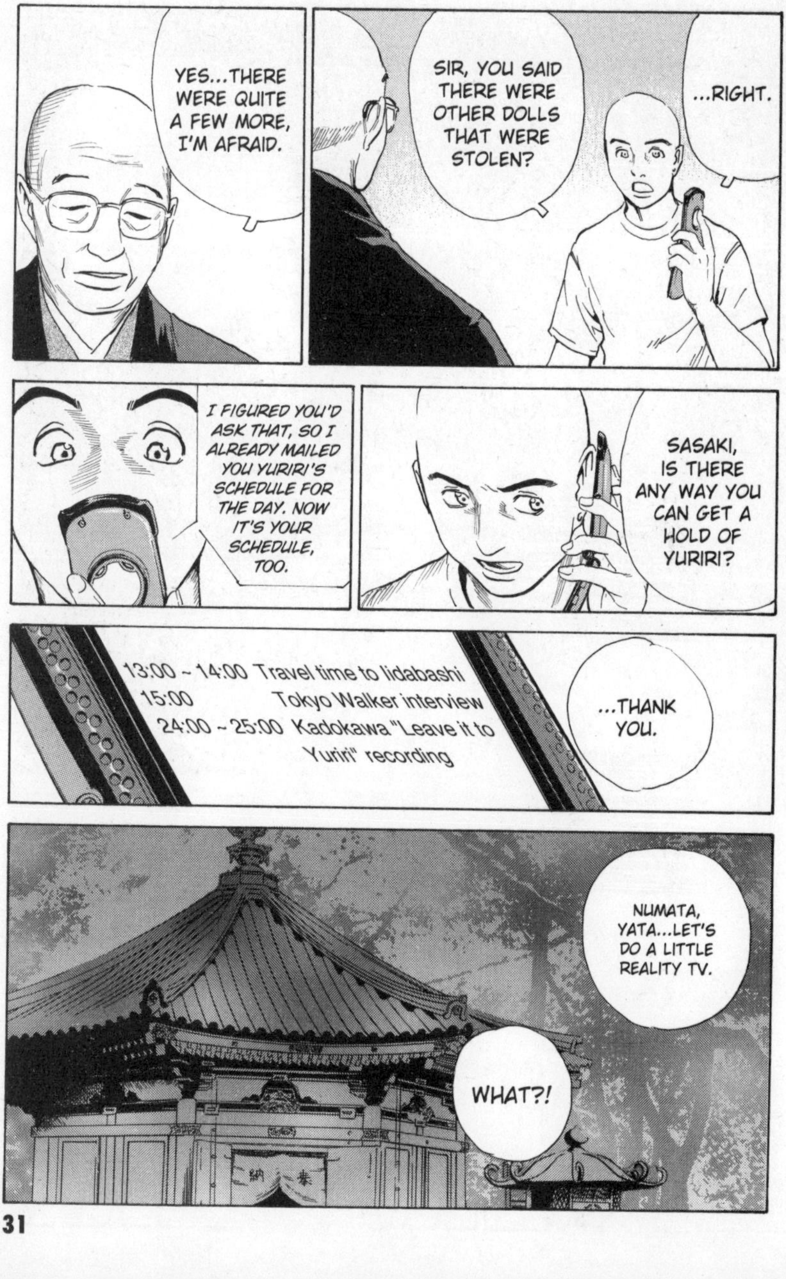
...RIGHT.
SIR, YOU SAID THERE WERE OTHER DOLLS THAT WERE STOLEN?
YES...THERE WERE QUITE A FEW MORE, I'M AFRAID.
SASAKI, IS THERE ANY WAY YOU CAN GET A HOLD OF YURIRI?
I FIGURED YOU'D ASK THAT, SO I ALREADY MAILED YOU YURIRI'S SCHEDULE FOR THE DAY. NOW IT'S YOUR SCHEDULE, TOO.
...THANK YOU.
13:00 ~ 14:00 Travel time to Iidabashi
15:00 Tokyo Walker interview
24:00 ~ 25:00 Kadokawa "Leave it to Yuriri" recording
NUMATA, YATA...LET'S DO A LITTLE REALITY TV.
WHAT?!

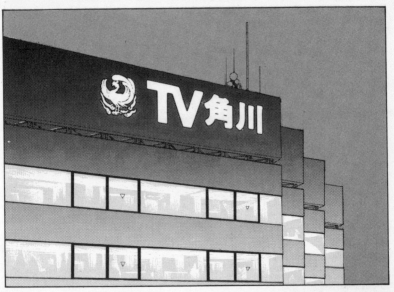

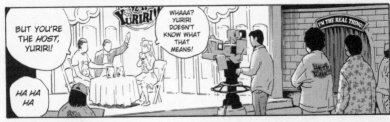

TV角川
I'M THE REAL THING!
WHAAA? YURIRI DOESN'T KNOW WHAT THAT MEANS!
BUT YOU'RE THE *HOST*, YURIRI!
HA HA HA
ヴー… ヴー…
YES... I'M YURIRI'S MANAGER.

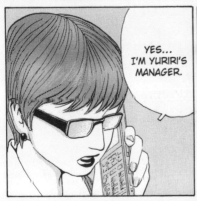

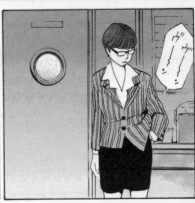

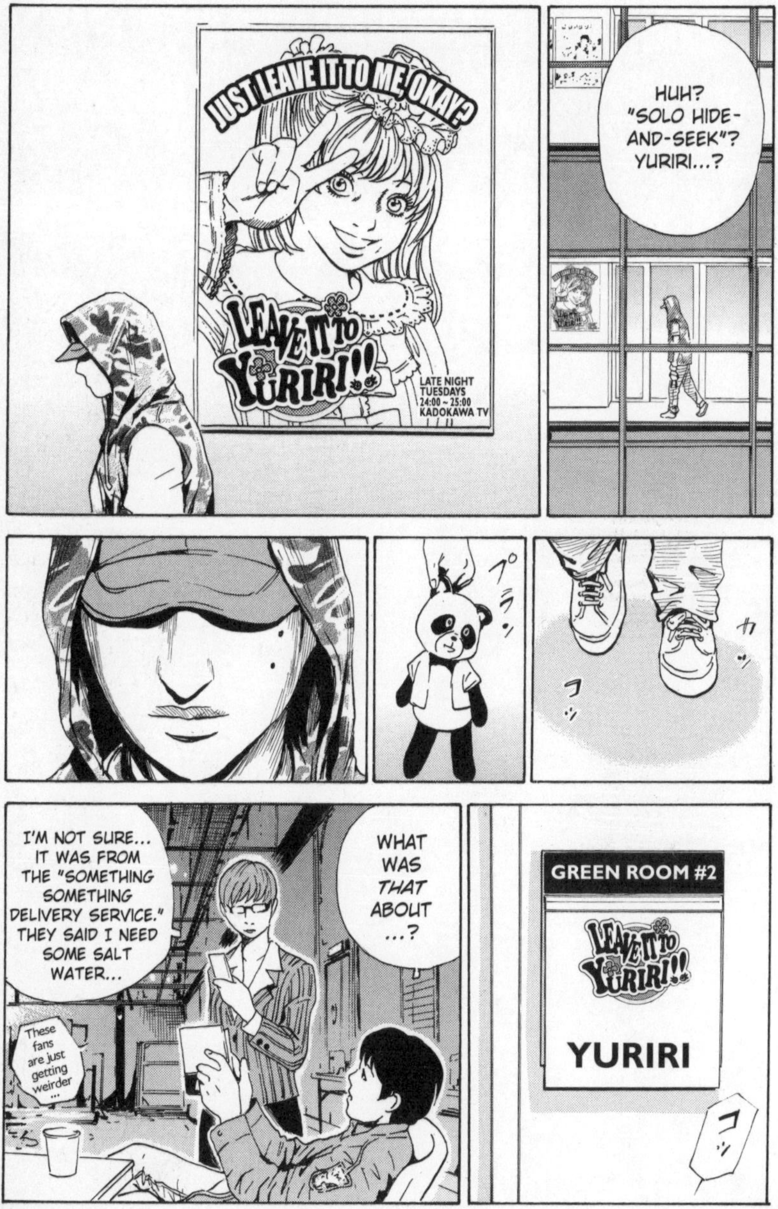
HUH? "SOLO HIDE-AND-SEEK"? YURIRI...?
JUST LEAVE IT TO ME, OKAY?
LEAVE IT TO YURIRI!!
LATE NIGHT TUESDAYS 24:00 ~ 25:00 KADOKAWA TV
カッ
コッ
プラン
GREEN ROOM #2
LEAVE IT TO YURIRI!!
YURIRI
コッ
WHAT WAS THAT ABOUT ...?
I'M NOT SURE... IT WAS FROM THE "SOMETHING SOMETHING DELIVERY SERVICE." THEY SAID I NEED SOME SALT WATER...
These fans are just getting weirder ...

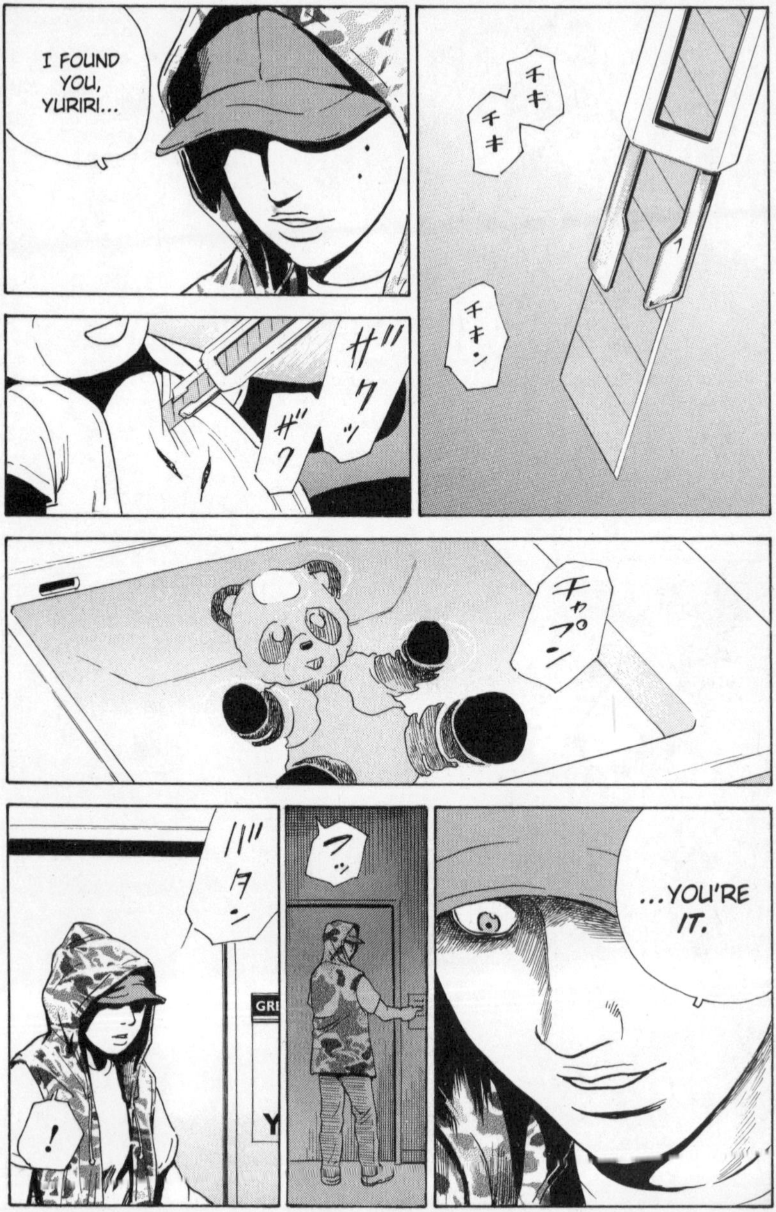
チキ
チキ
チキン
I FOUND YOU, YURIRI...
ザクッ
ザク
チャプン
...YOU'RE IT.
フッ
バタン
!

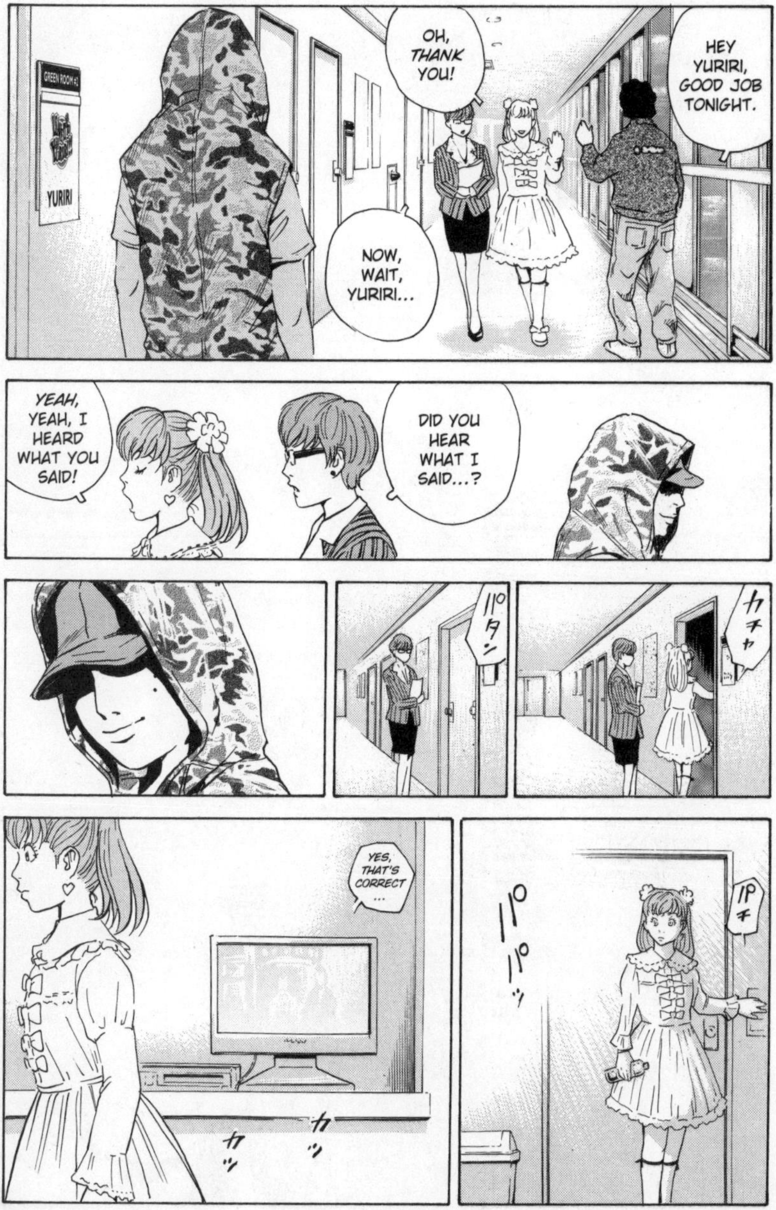
HEY YURIRI, GOOD JOB TONIGHT.
OH, THANK YOU!
YURIRI
NOW, WAIT, YURIRI...
DID YOU HEAR WHAT I SAID...?
YEAH, YEAH, I HEARD WHAT YOU SAID!
カチャ
パタン
パチ
パパーッ
YES, THAT'S CORRECT ...
カッ
カッ

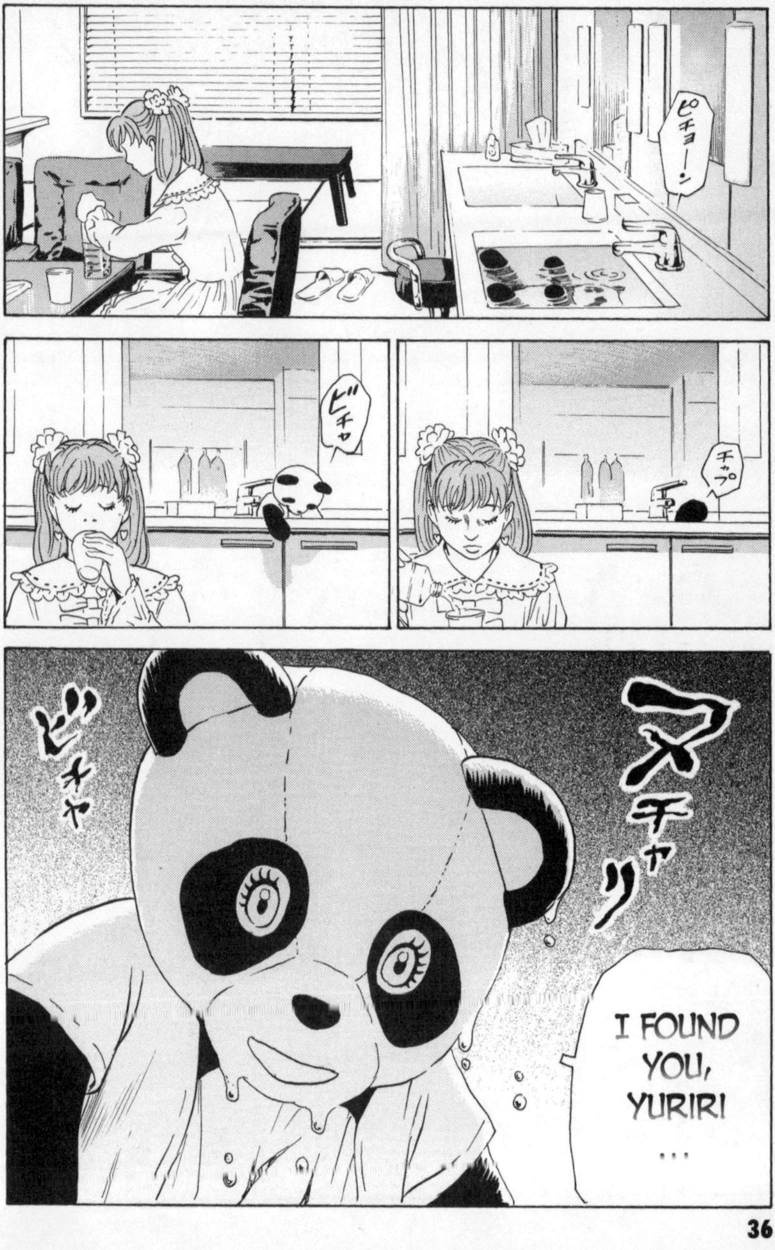
ピチョーン
チャプ
ビチャ
ヌチャリ
ビチャ
I FOUND YOU, YURIRI ...

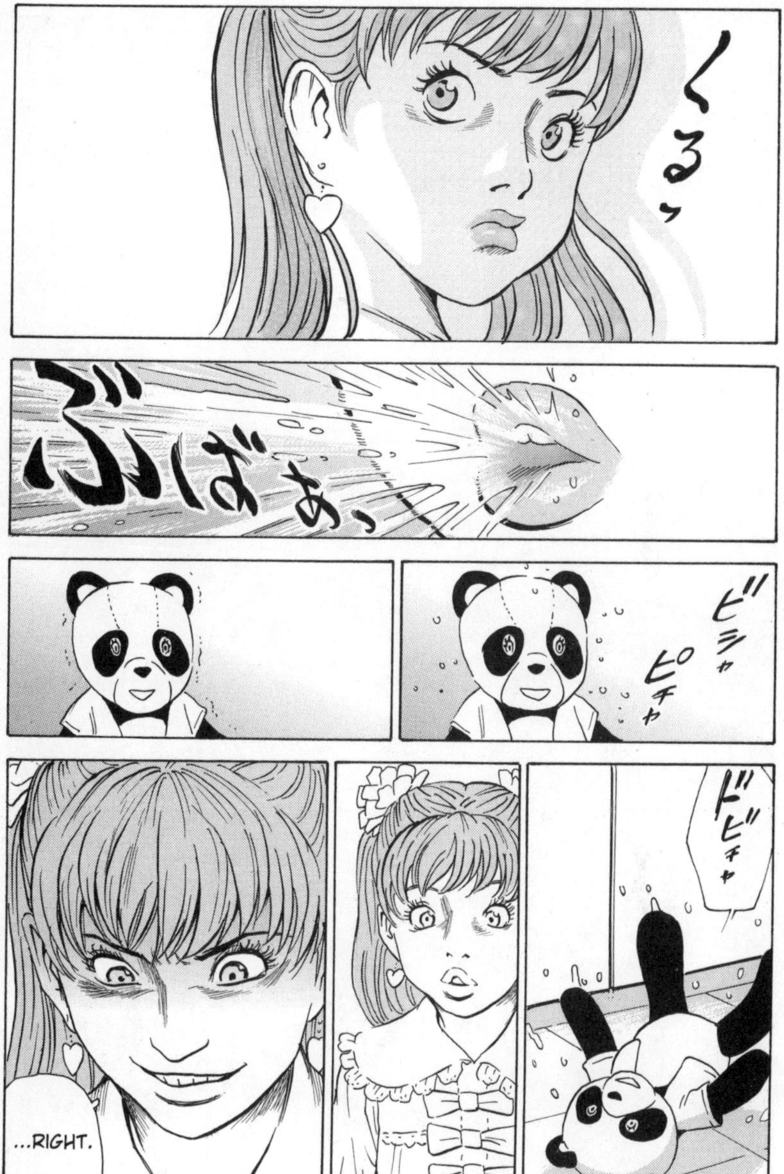
くるっ
ぶばあっ
ビシャ
ピチャ
ドビビチャ
...RIGHT.

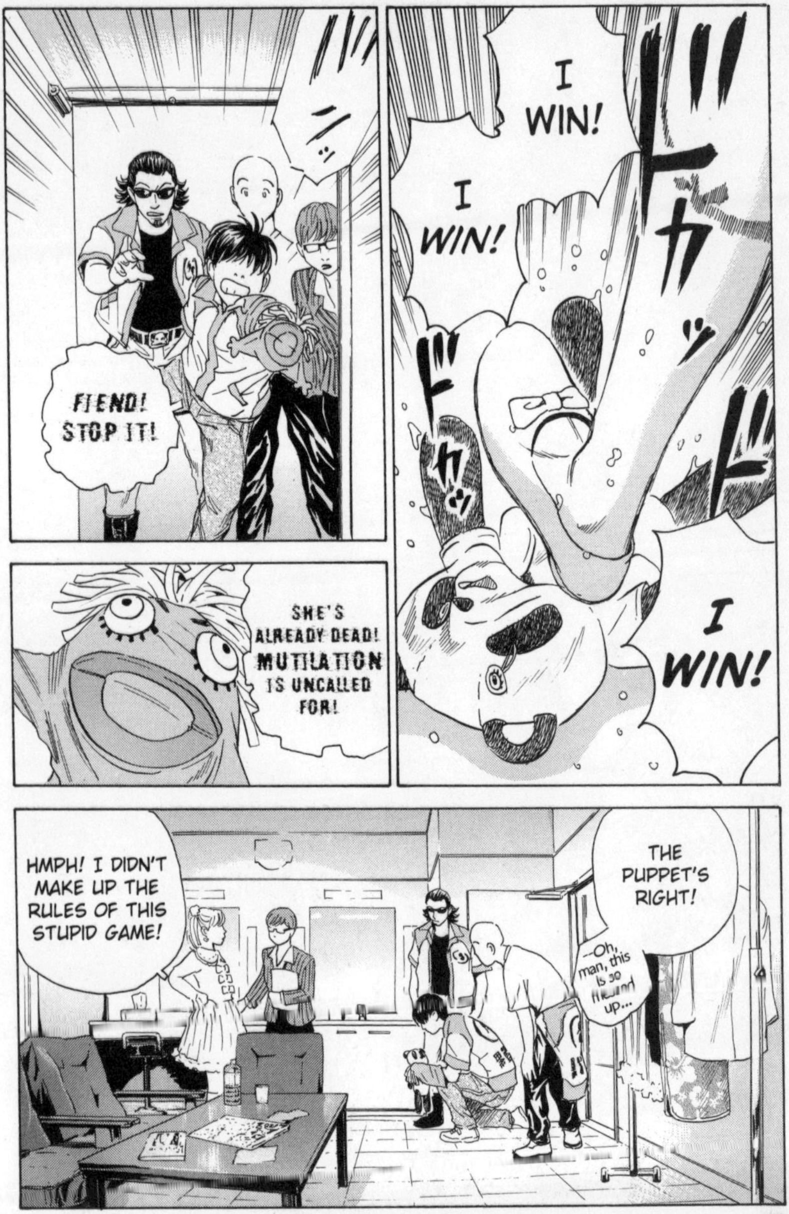
I WIN!
I WIN!
I WIN!
FIEND! STOP IT!
SHE'S ALREADY DEAD! MUTILATION IS UNCALLED FOR!
THE PUPPET'S RIGHT!
--Oh, man, this is so up...
HMPH! I DIDN'T MAKE UP THE RULES OF THIS STUPID GAME!

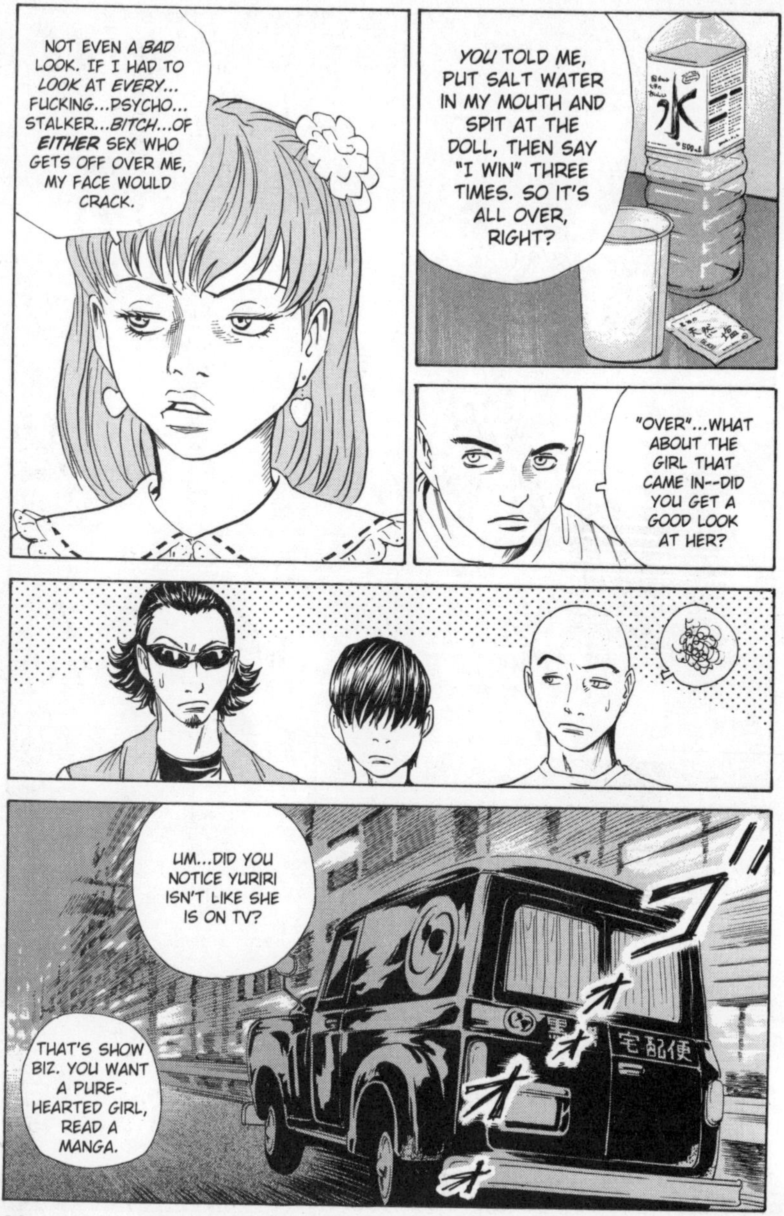
YOU TOLD ME, PUT SALT WATER IN MY MOUTH AND SPIT AT THE DOLL, THEN SAY "I WIN" THREE TIMES. SO IT'S ALL OVER, RIGHT?
"OVER"...WHAT ABOUT THE GIRL THAT CAME IN--DID YOU GET A GOOD LOOK AT HER?
NOT EVEN A BAD LOOK. IF I HAD TO LOOK AT EVERY... FUCKING...PSYCHO... STALKER...BITCH...OF EITHER SEX WHO GETS OFF OVER ME, MY FACE WOULD CRACK.
UM...DID YOU NOTICE YURIRI ISN'T LIKE SHE IS ON TV?
宅配便
THAT'S SHOW BIZ. YOU WANT A PURE-HEARTED GIRL, READ A MANGA.

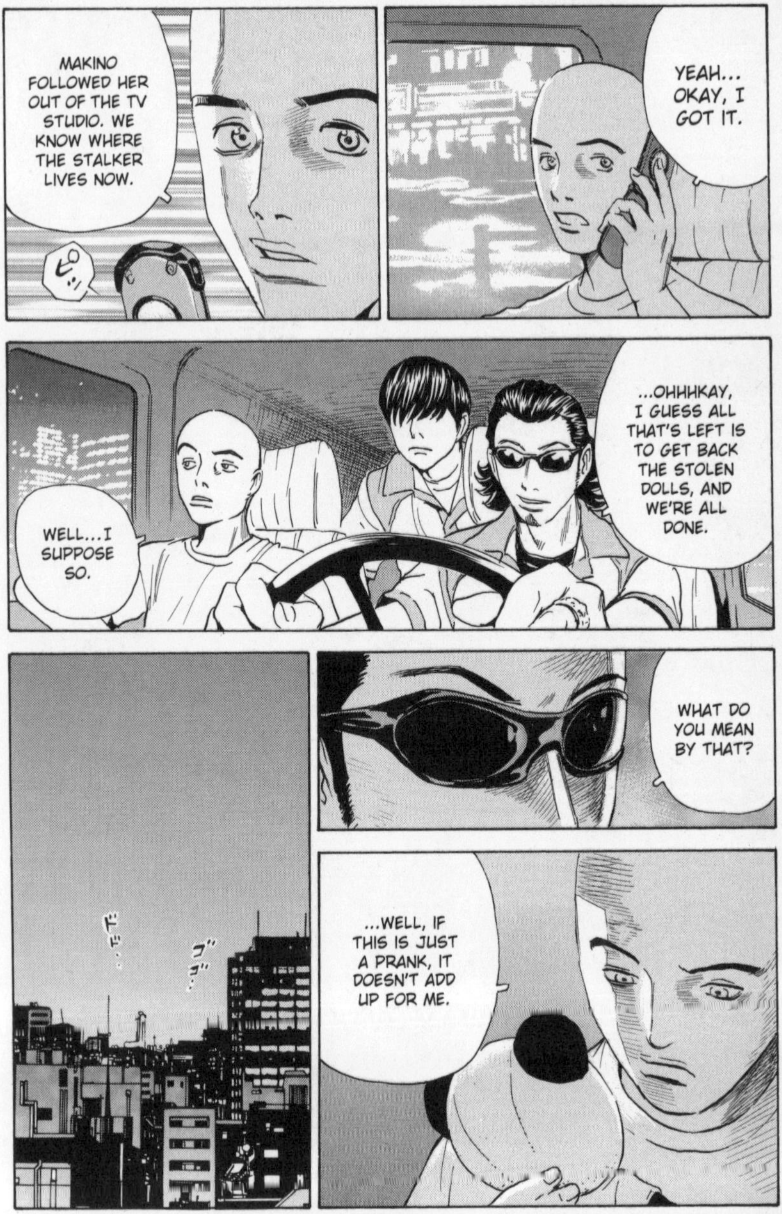
YEAH... OKAY, I GOT IT.
MAKINO FOLLOWED HER OUT OF THE TV STUDIO. WE KNOW WHERE THE STALKER LIVES NOW.
...OHHHKAY, I GUESS ALL THAT'S LEFT IS TO GET BACK THE STOLEN DOLLS, AND WE'RE ALL DONE.
WELL...I SUPPOSE SO.
WHAT DO YOU MEAN BY THAT?
...WELL, IF THIS IS JUST A PRANK, IT DOESN'T ADD UP FOR ME.

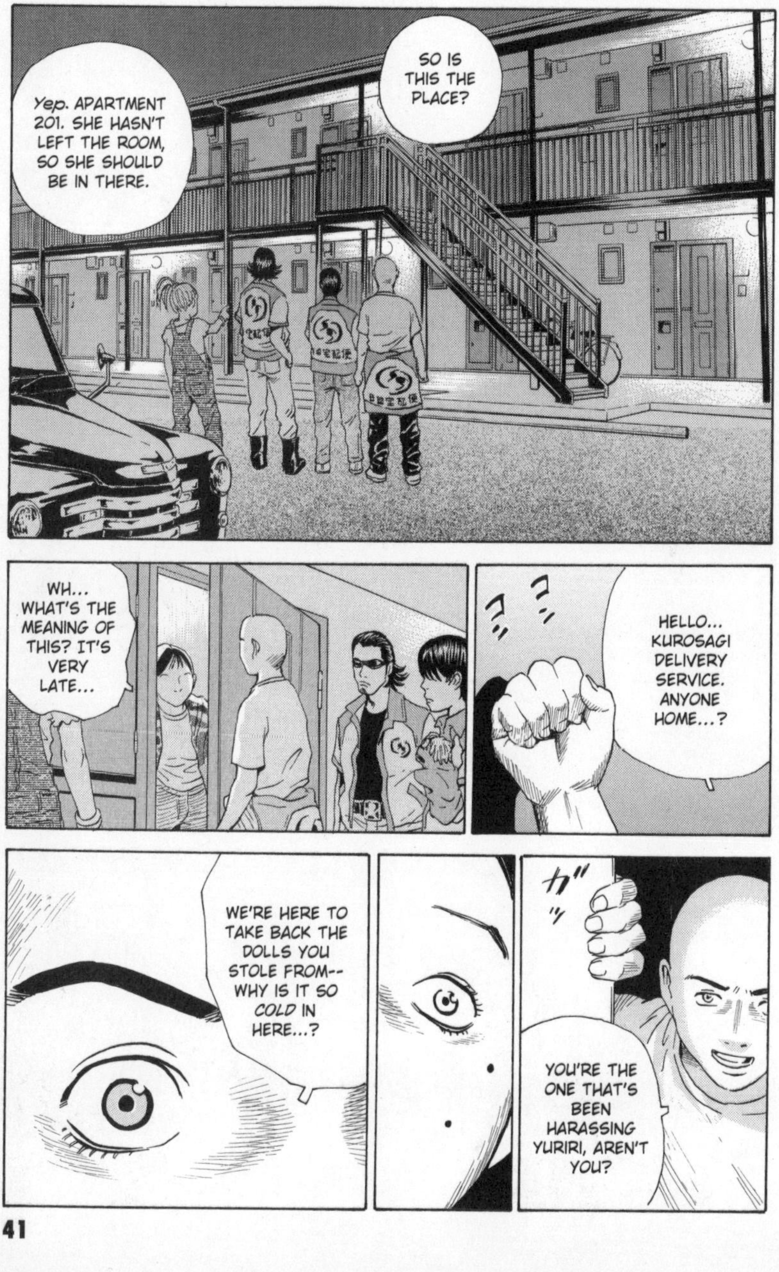
SO IS THIS THE PLACE?
Yep. APARTMENT 201. SHE HASN'T LEFT THE ROOM, SO SHE SHOULD BE IN THERE.
HELLO... KUROSAGI DELIVERY SERVICE. ANYONE HOME...?
WH... WHAT'S THE MEANING OF THIS? IT'S VERY LATE...
ガッ
YOU'RE THE ONE THAT'S BEEN HARASSING YURIRI, AREN'T YOU?
WE'RE HERE TO TAKE BACK THE DOLLS YOU STOLE FROM-- WHY IS IT SO *COLD* IN HERE...?

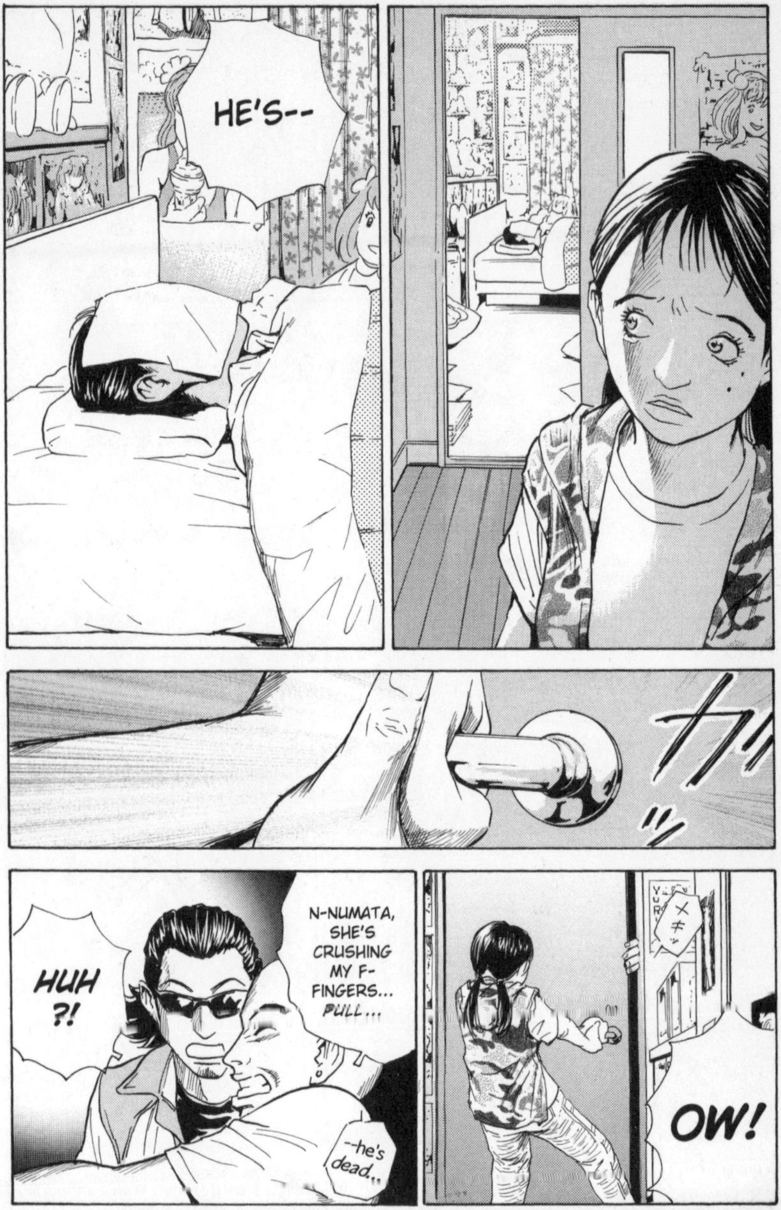
HE'S--
メキッ
OW!
N-NUMATA, SHE'S CRUSHING MY F-FINGERS... PULL...
HUH ?!
--he's dead...

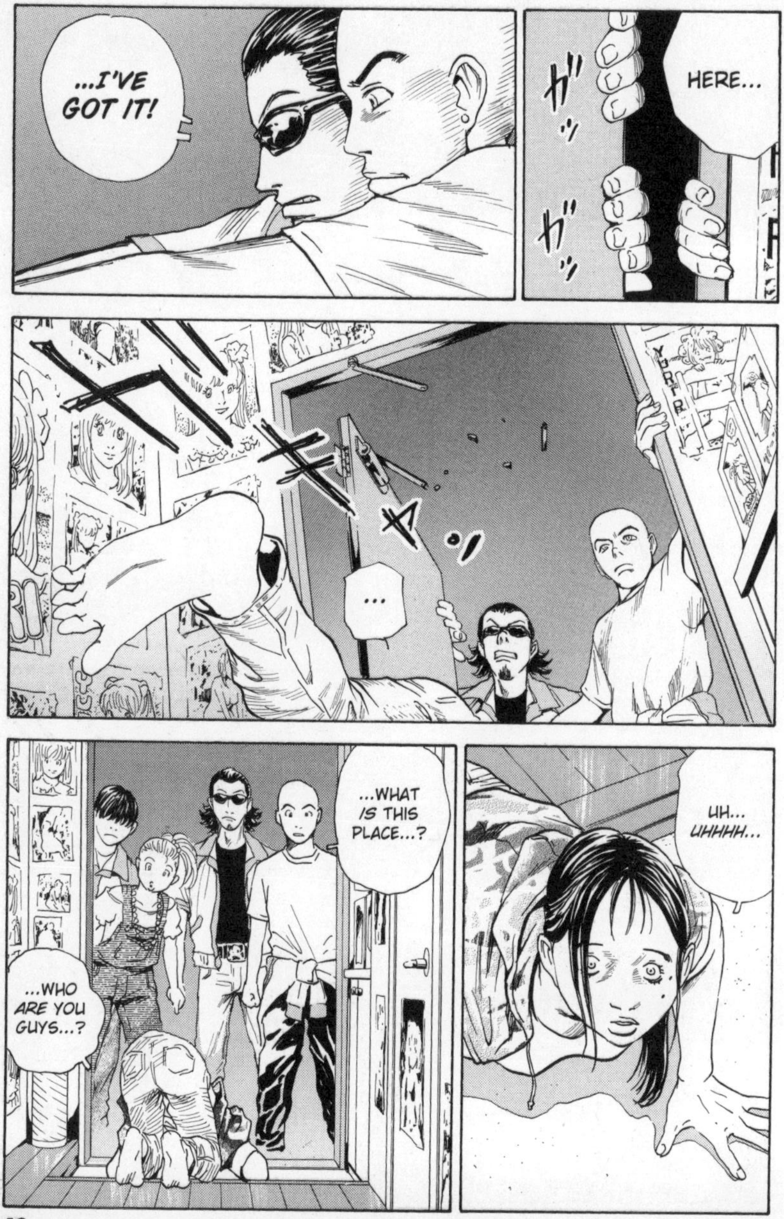
HERE...
ガッ
ガッ
...I'VE GOT IT!
...
UH... UHHHH...
...WHAT IS THIS PLACE...?
...WHO ARE YOU GUYS...?

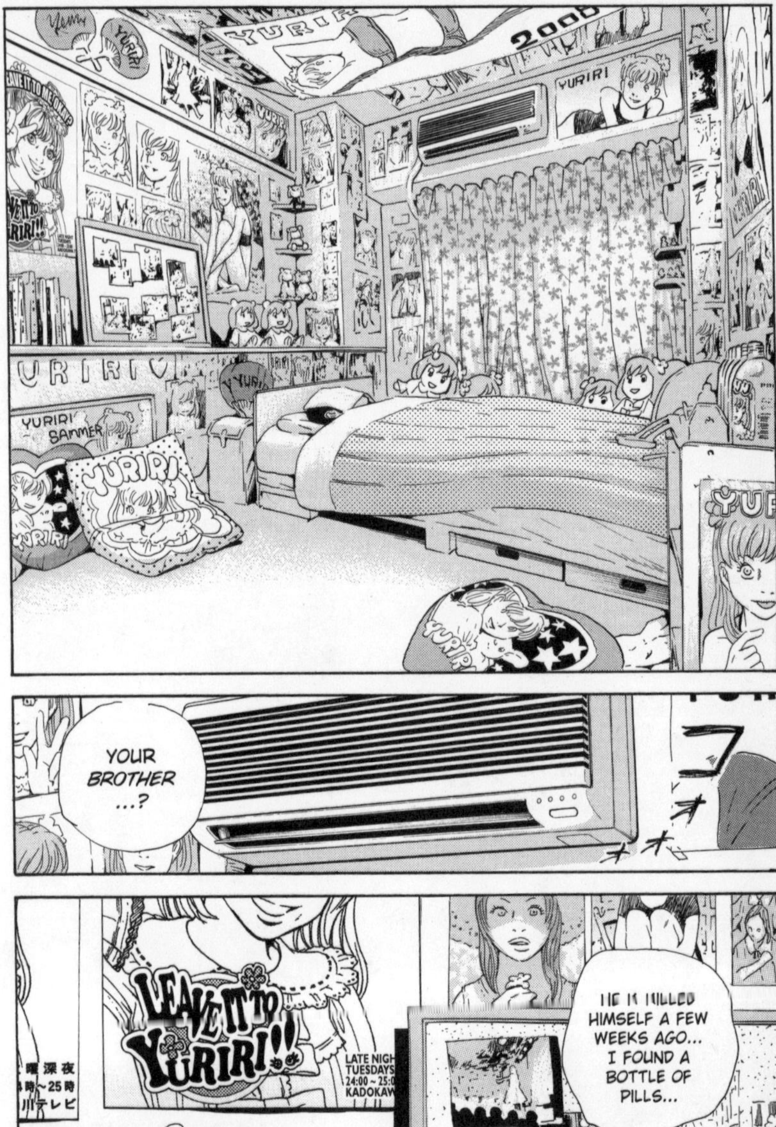
YOUR BROTHER ...?
HE KILLED HIMSELF A FEW WEEKS AGO... I FOUND A BOTTLE OF PILLS...
LEAVE IT TO YURIRI!!

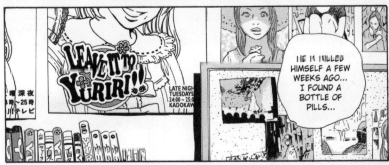

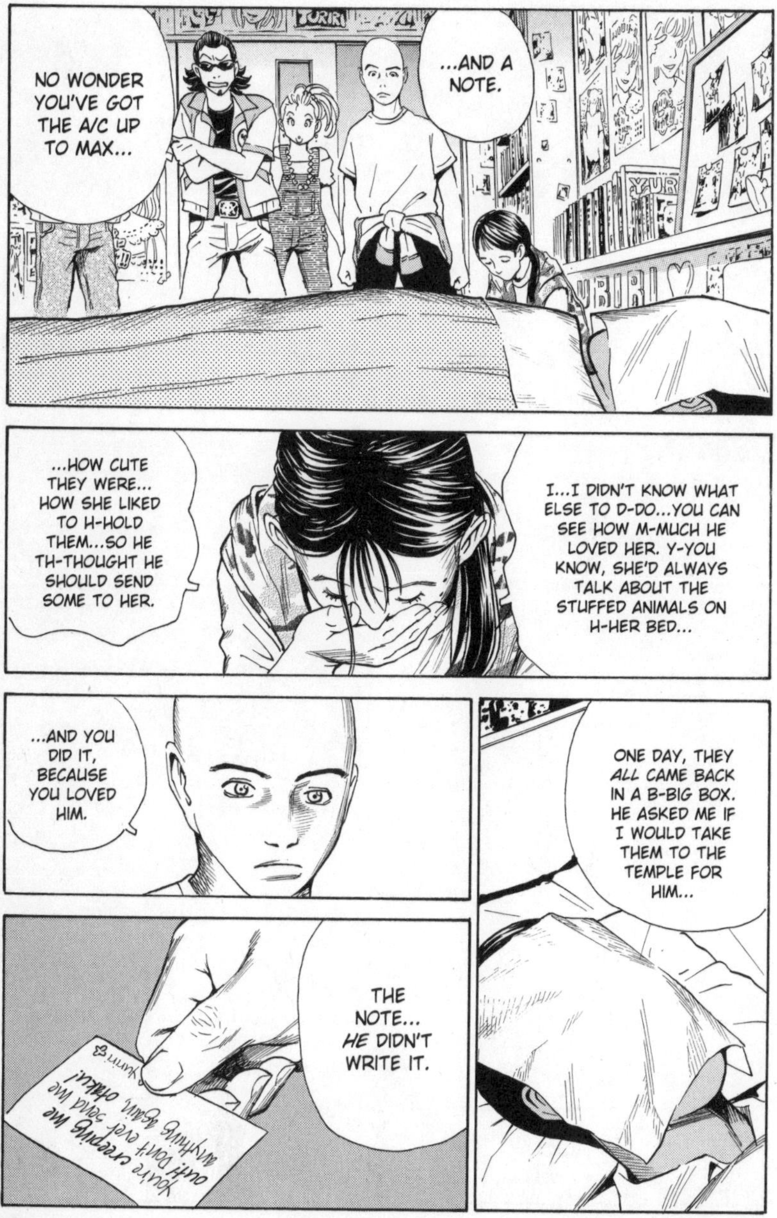

...AND A NOTE.
NO WONDER YOU'VE GOT THE A/C UP TO MAX...
I...I DIDN'T KNOW WHAT ELSE TO D-DO...YOU CAN SEE HOW M-MUCH HE LOVED HER. Y-YOU KNOW, SHE'D ALWAYS TALK ABOUT THE STUFFED ANIMALS ON H-HER BED...
...HOW CUTE THEY WERE... HOW SHE LIKED TO H-HOLD THEM...SO HE TH-THOUGHT HE SHOULD SEND SOME TO HER.
ONE DAY, THEY *ALL* CAME BACK IN A B-BIG BOX. HE ASKED ME IF I WOULD TAKE THEM TO THE TEMPLE FOR HIM...
...AND YOU DID IT, BECAUSE YOU LOVED HIM.
THE NOTE... *HE* DIDN'T WRITE IT.
You're creeping me out! Don't ever send me anything again, otaku!
Yuriri

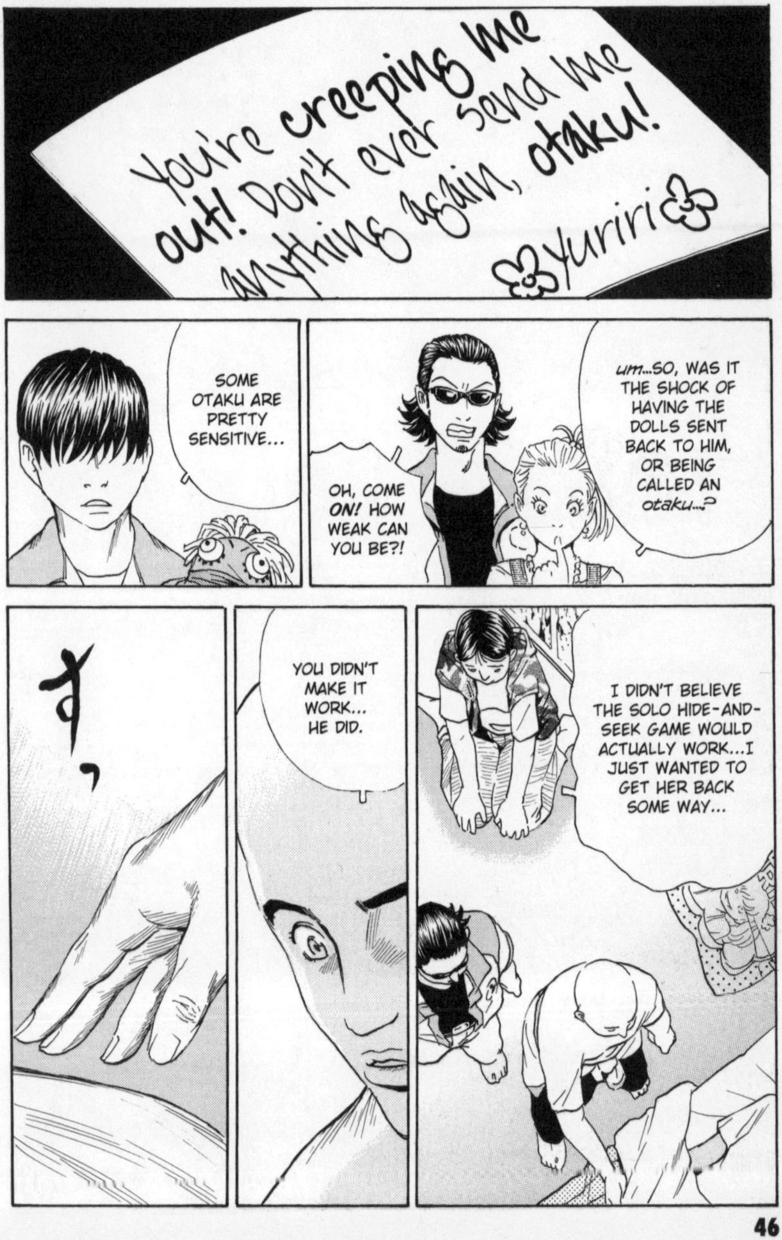
You're creeping me out! Don't ever send me anything again, otaku!
Yuriri
um...SO, WAS IT THE SHOCK OF HAVING THE DOLLS SENT BACK TO HIM, OR BEING CALLED AN otaku...?
OH, COME ON! HOW WEAK CAN YOU BE?!
SOME OTAKU ARE PRETTY SENSITIVE...
I DIDN'T BELIEVE THE SOLO HIDE-AND-SEEK GAME WOULD ACTUALLY WORK...I JUST WANTED TO GET HER BACK SOME WAY...
YOU DIDN'T MAKE IT WORK... HE DID.
す、

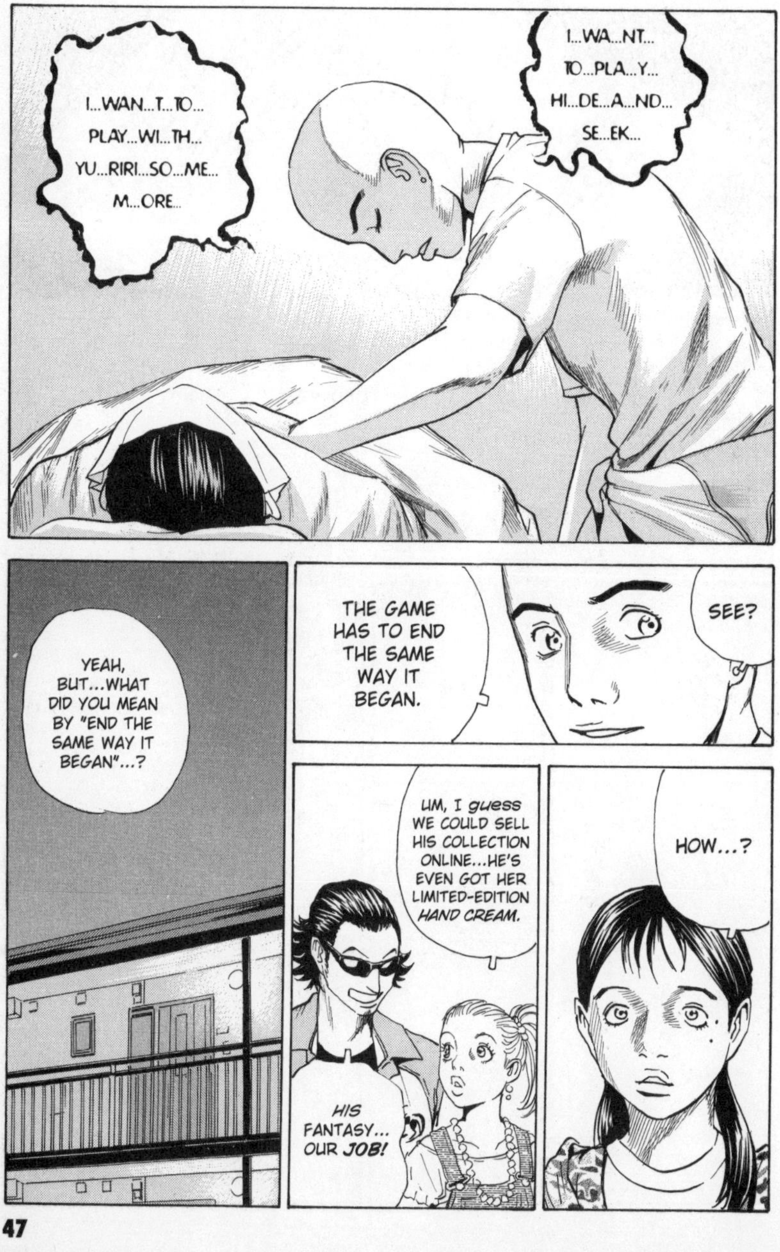
I...WA...NT... TO...PLA...Y... HI...DE...A...ND... SE...EK...
I...WAN...T...TO... PLAY...WI...TH... YU...RIRI...SO...ME... M...ORE...
SEE?
THE GAME HAS TO END THE SAME WAY IT BEGAN.
HOW...?
UM, I *guess* WE COULD SELL HIS COLLECTION ONLINE...HE'S EVEN GOT HER LIMITED-EDITION *HAND CREAM.*
HIS FANTASY... OUR *JOB!*
YEAH, BUT...WHAT DID YOU MEAN BY "END THE SAME WAY IT BEGAN"...?

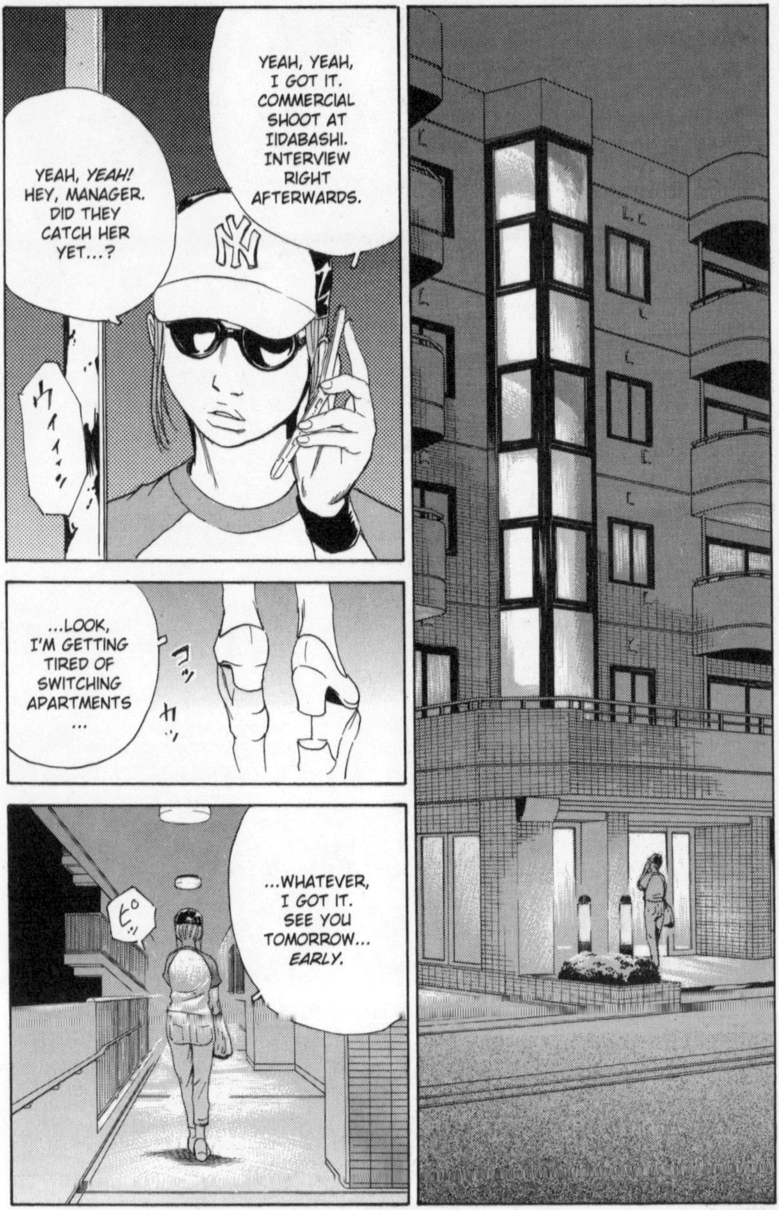
YEAH, YEAH, I GOT IT. COMMERCIAL SHOOT AT IIDABASHI. INTERVIEW RIGHT AFTERWARDS.
YEAH, *YEAH!* HEY, MANAGER. DID THEY CATCH HER YET...?
ウィィィッ
カッ
カッ
...LOOK, I'M GETTING TIRED OF SWITCHING APARTMENTS ...
...WHATEVER, I GOT IT. SEE YOU TOMORROW... *EARLY.*
ピッ

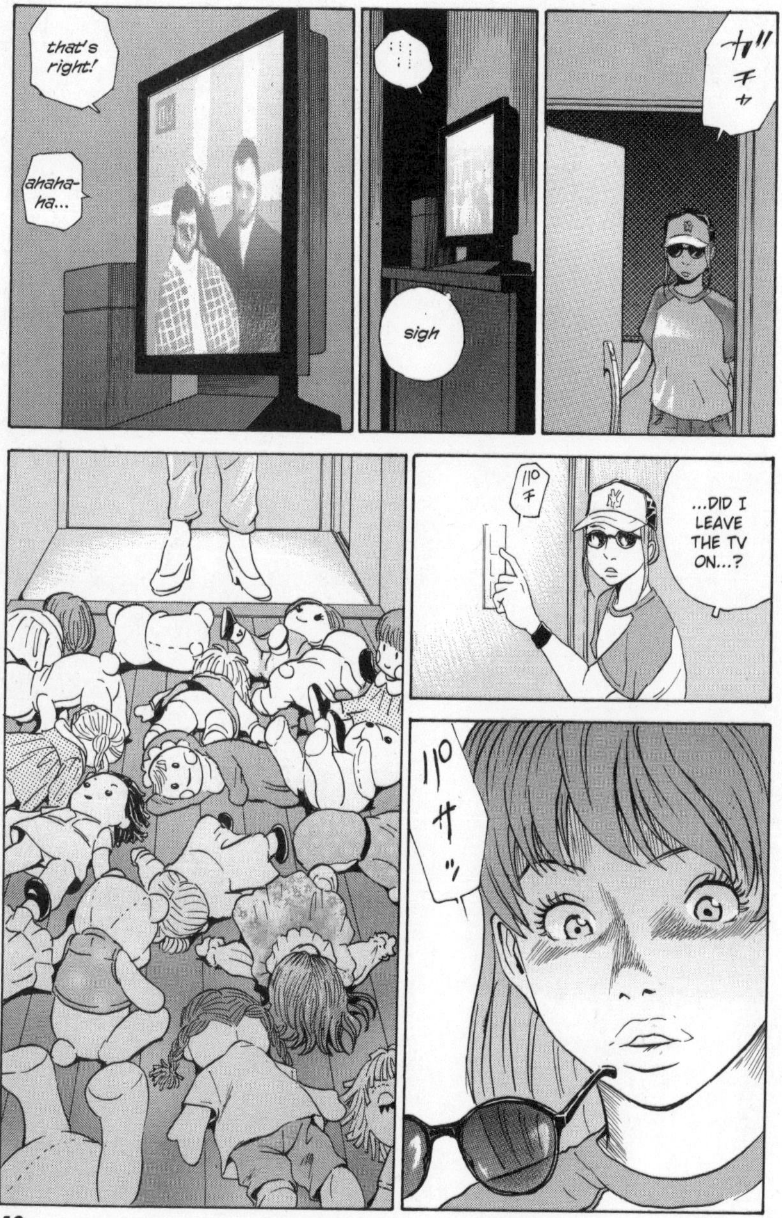
ガチャ
sigh
that's right!
ahaha-ha...
パチ
...DID I LEAVE THE TV ON...?
パサッ

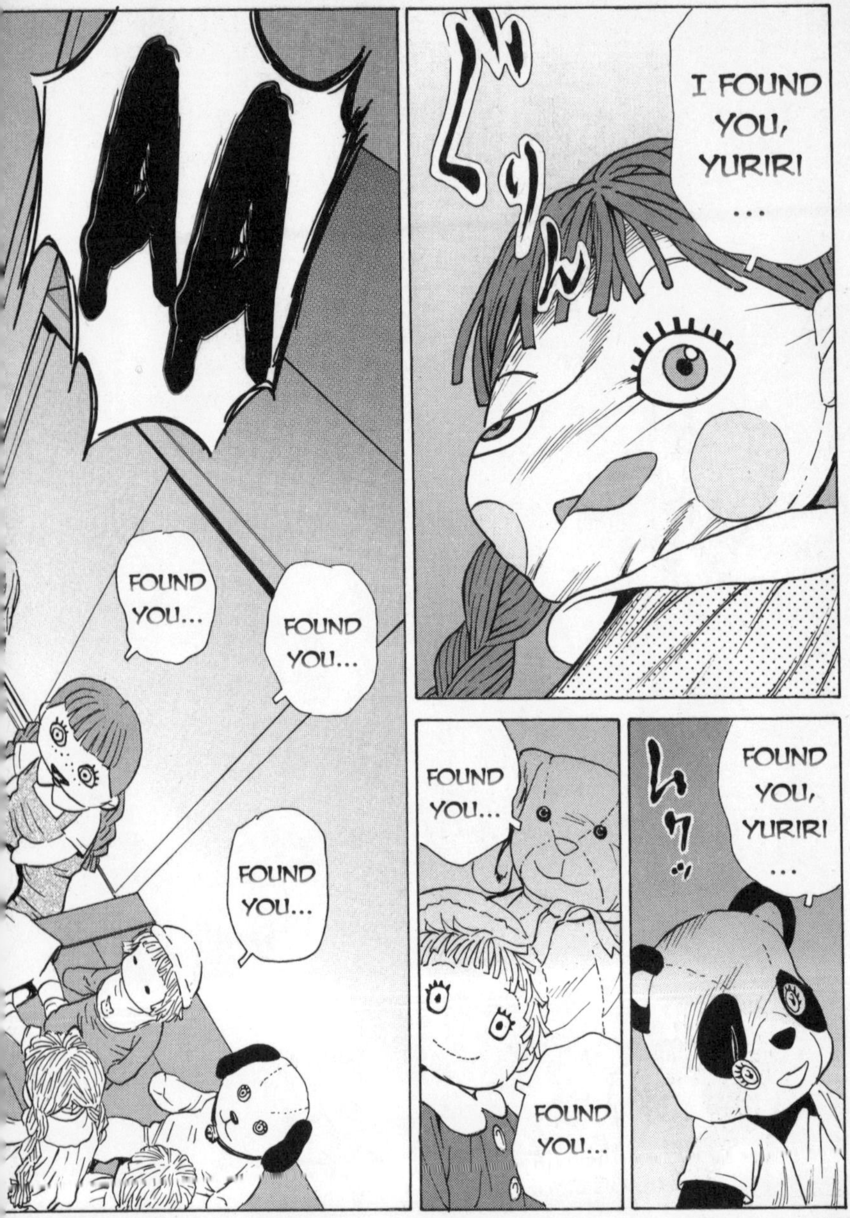
I FOUND YOU, YURIRI ...
FOUND YOU, YURIRI ...
FOUND YOU...
FOUND YOU...
FOUND YOU...
FOUND YOU...
FOUND YOU...

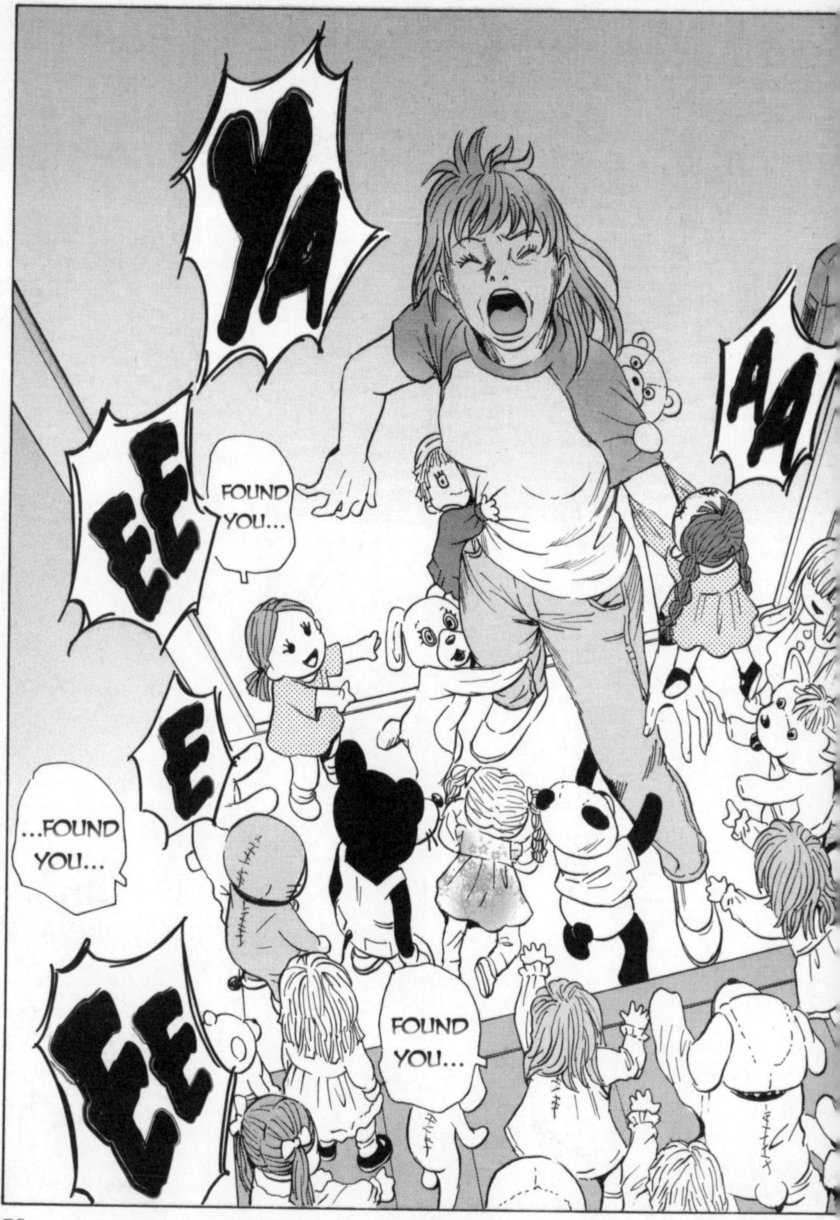
YA
AA
FOUND YOU...
EE
E
...FOUND YOU...
FOUND YOU...
EE

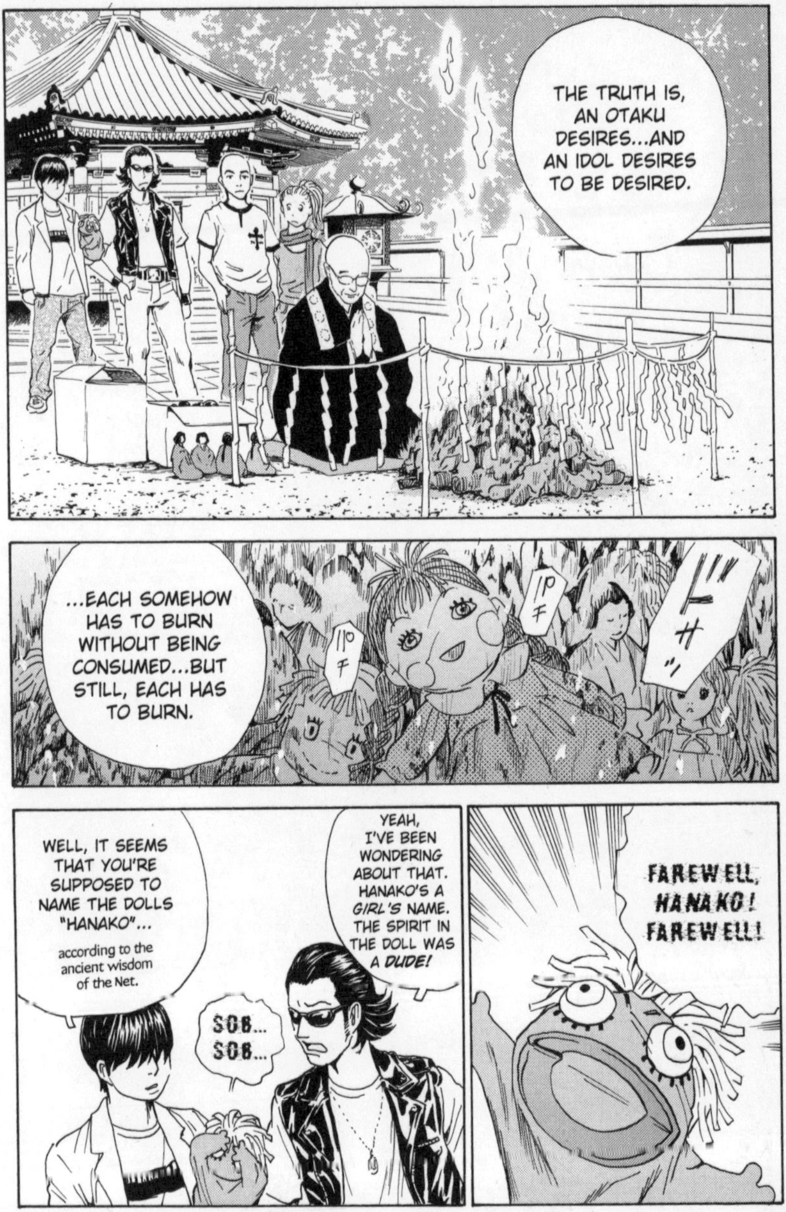
THE TRUTH IS, AN OTAKU DESIRES...AND AN IDOL DESIRES TO BE DESIRED.
...EACH SOMEHOW HAS TO BURN WITHOUT BEING CONSUMED...BUT STILL, EACH HAS TO BURN.
FAREWELL, HANAKO! FAREWELL!
WELL, IT SEEMS THAT YOU'RE SUPPOSED TO NAME THE DOLLS "HANAKO"... according to the ancient wisdom of the Net.
YEAH, I'VE BEEN WONDERING ABOUT THAT. HANAKO'S A *GIRL'S* NAME. THE SPIRIT IN THE DOLL WAS A *DUDE!*
SOB... SOB...

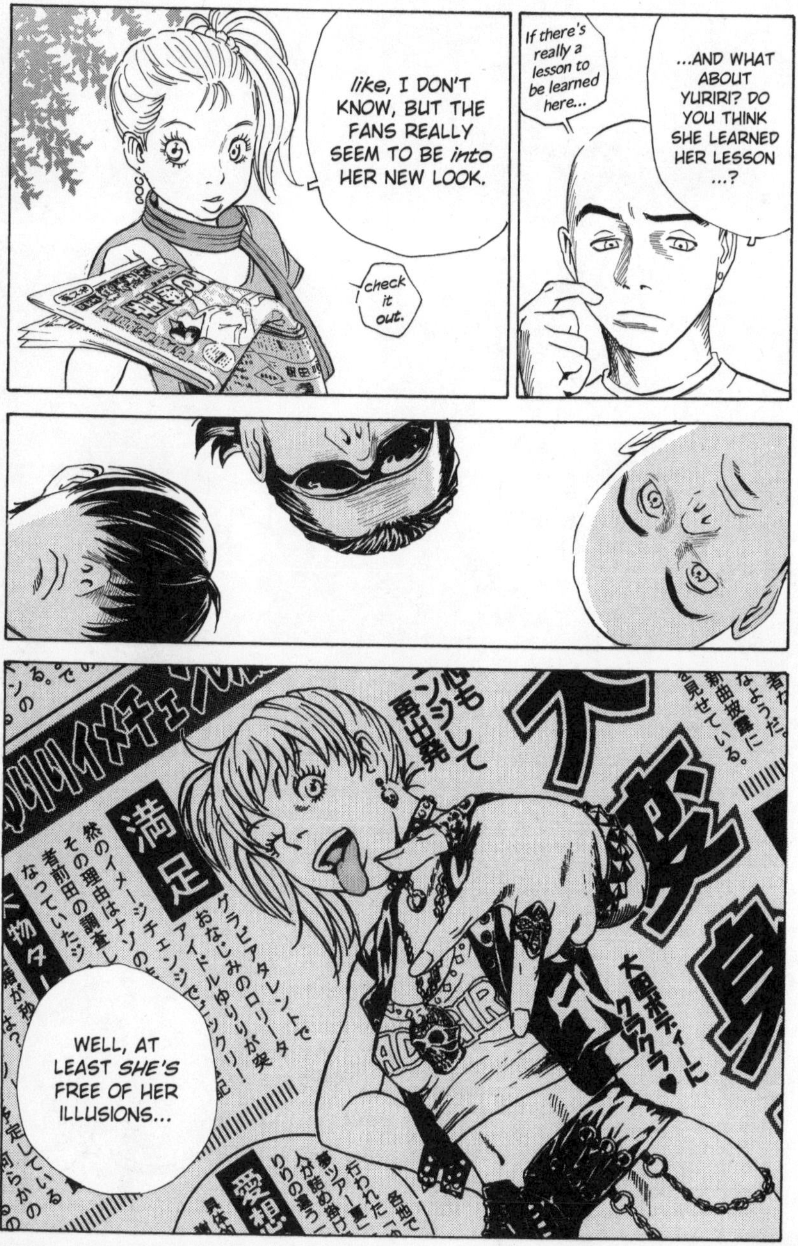
...AND WHAT ABOUT YURIRI? DO YOU THINK SHE LEARNED HER LESSON ...?
If there's really a lesson to be learned here...
like, I DON'T KNOW, BUT THE FANS REALLY SEEM TO BE *into* HER NEW LOOK.
check it out.
WELL, AT LEAST *SHE'S* FREE OF HER ILLUSIONS...

2nd delivery: a lonely singing doll—the end

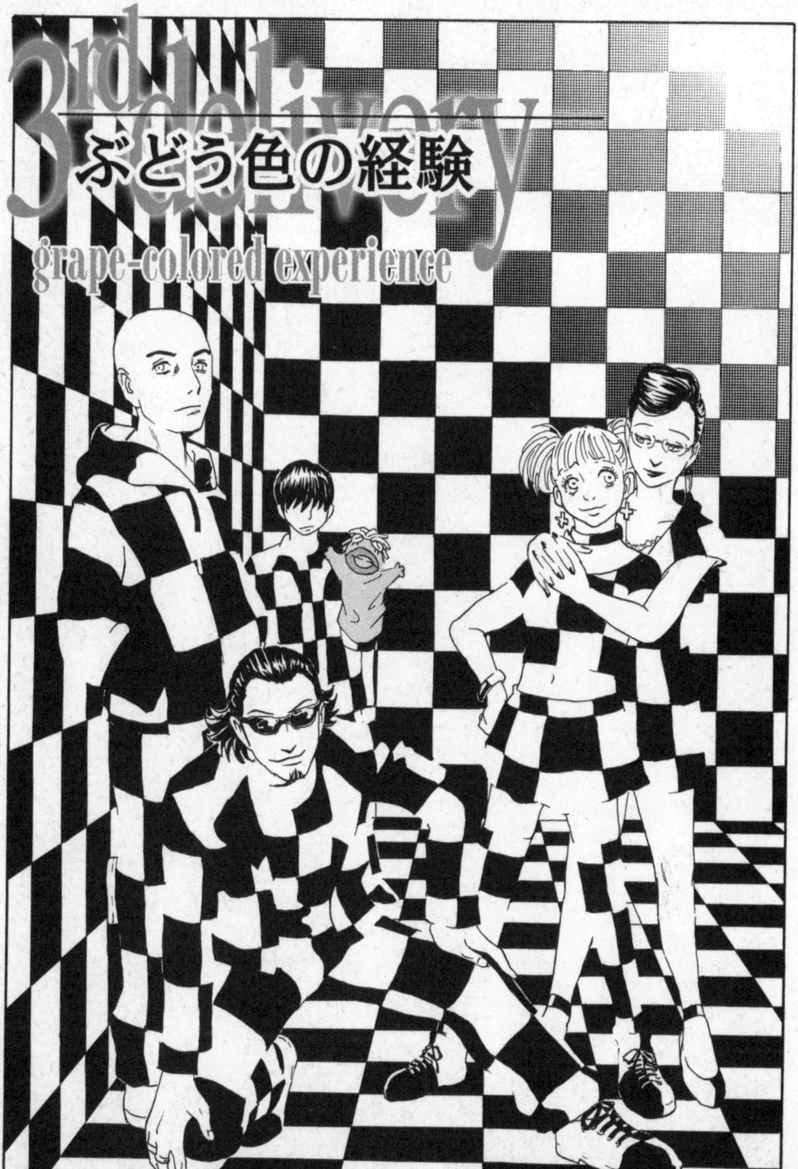
3rd delivery
ぶどう色の経験
grape-colored experience

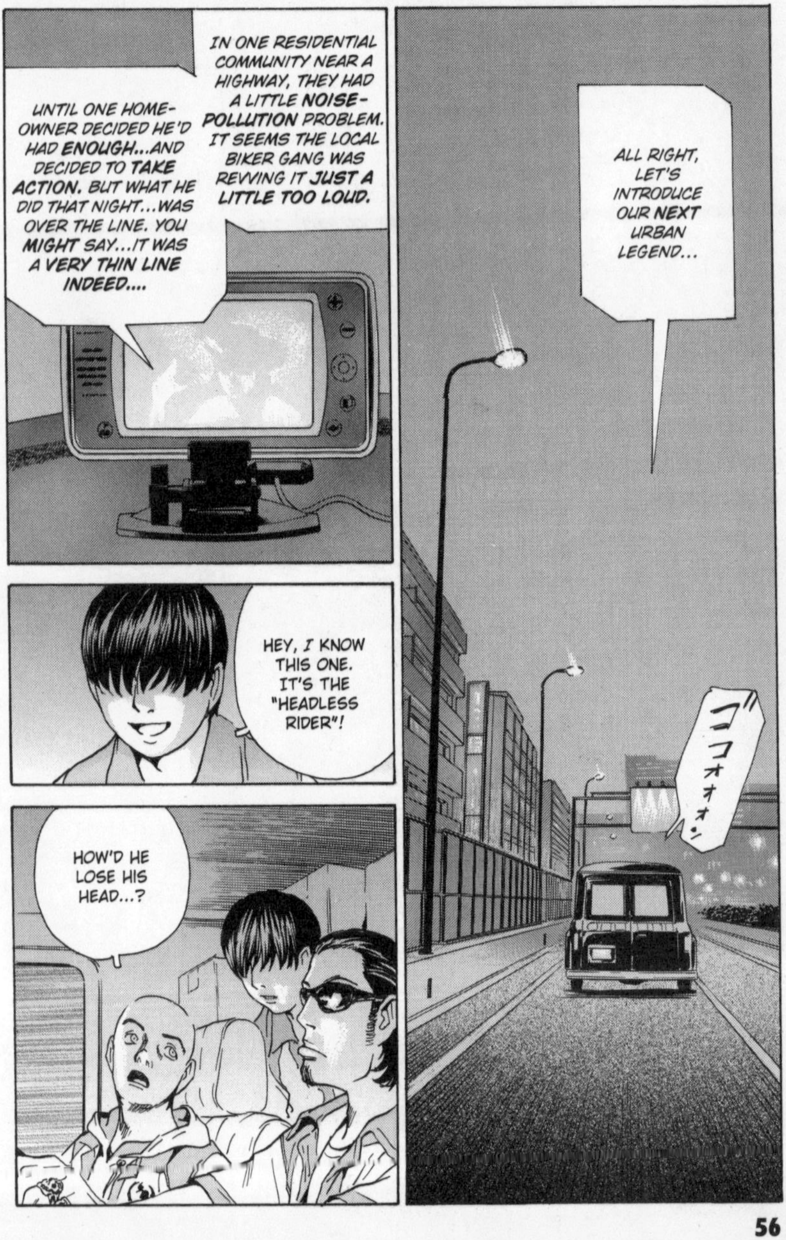
ALL RIGHT, LET'S INTRODUCE OUR NEXT URBAN LEGEND...
ゴゴオオオン
IN ONE RESIDENTIAL COMMUNITY NEAR A HIGHWAY, THEY HAD A LITTLE NOISE-POLLUTION PROBLEM. IT SEEMS THE LOCAL BIKER GANG WAS REVVING IT JUST A LITTLE TOO LOUD.
UNTIL ONE HOME-OWNER DECIDED HE'D HAD ENOUGH...AND DECIDED TO TAKE ACTION. BUT WHAT HE DID THAT NIGHT...WAS OVER THE LINE. YOU MIGHT SAY...IT WAS A VERY THIN LINE INDEED....
HEY, I KNOW THIS ONE. IT'S THE "HEADLESS RIDER"!
HOW'D HE LOSE HIS HEAD...?

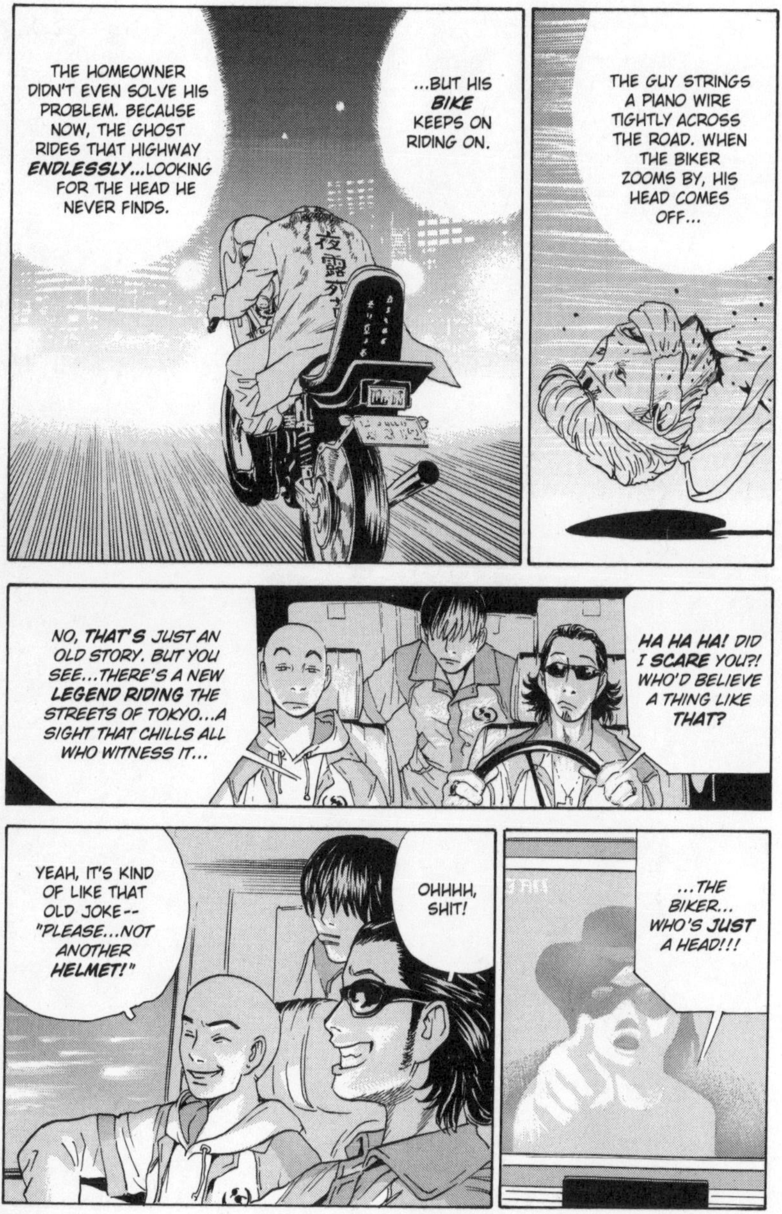
THE GUY STRINGS A PIANO WIRE TIGHTLY ACROSS THE ROAD. WHEN THE BIKER ZOOMS BY, HIS HEAD COMES OFF...
THE HOMEOWNER DIDN'T EVEN SOLVE HIS PROBLEM. BECAUSE NOW, THE GHOST RIDES THAT HIGHWAY ENDLESSLY...LOOKING FOR THE HEAD HE NEVER FINDS.
...BUT HIS BIKE KEEPS ON RIDING ON.
HA HA HA! DID I SCARE YOU?! WHO'D BELIEVE A THING LIKE THAT?
NO, THAT'S JUST AN OLD STORY. BUT YOU SEE...THERE'S A NEW LEGEND RIDING THE STREETS OF TOKYO...A SIGHT THAT CHILLS ALL WHO WITNESS IT...
...THE BIKER... WHO'S JUST A HEAD!!!
OHHHH, SHIT!
YEAH, IT'S KIND OF LIKE THAT OLD JOKE-- "PLEASE...NOT ANOTHER HELMET!"

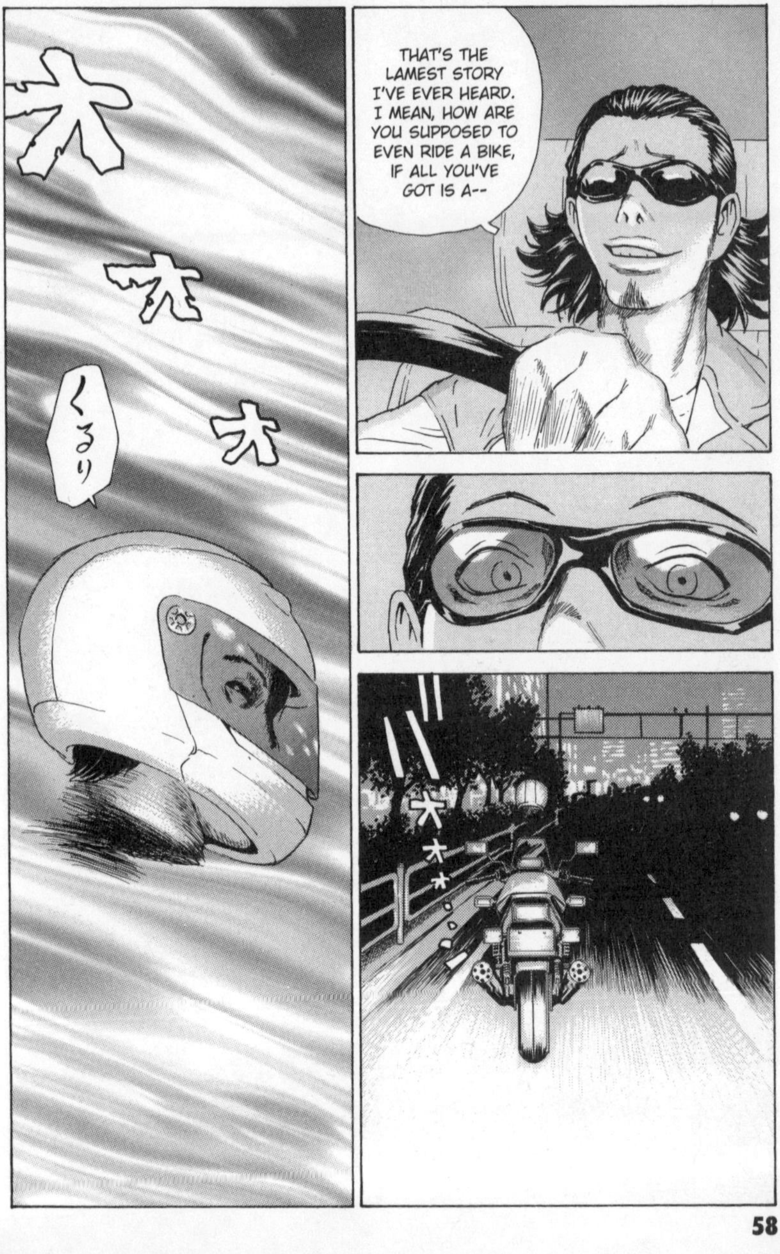
THAT'S THE LAMEST STORY I'VE EVER HEARD. I MEAN, HOW ARE YOU SUPPOSED TO EVEN RIDE A BIKE, IF ALL YOU'VE GOT IS A--
くるり

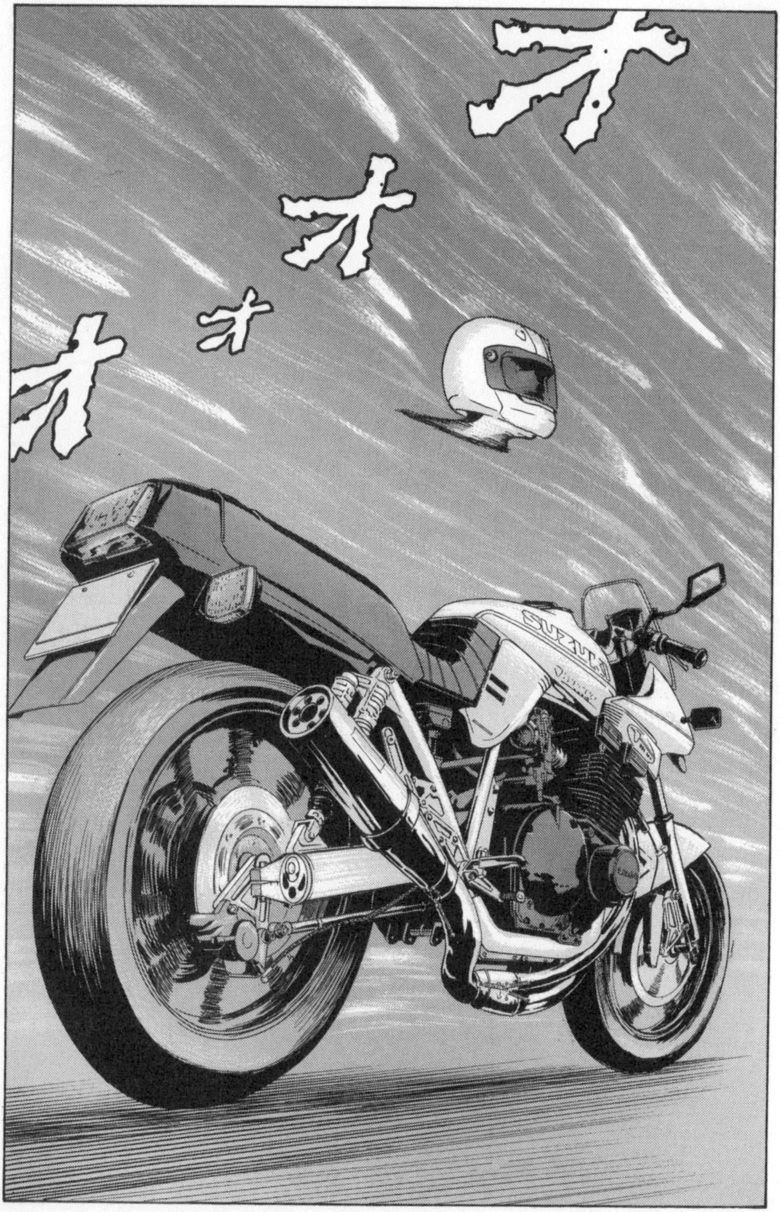
オオォオ
SUZUKI

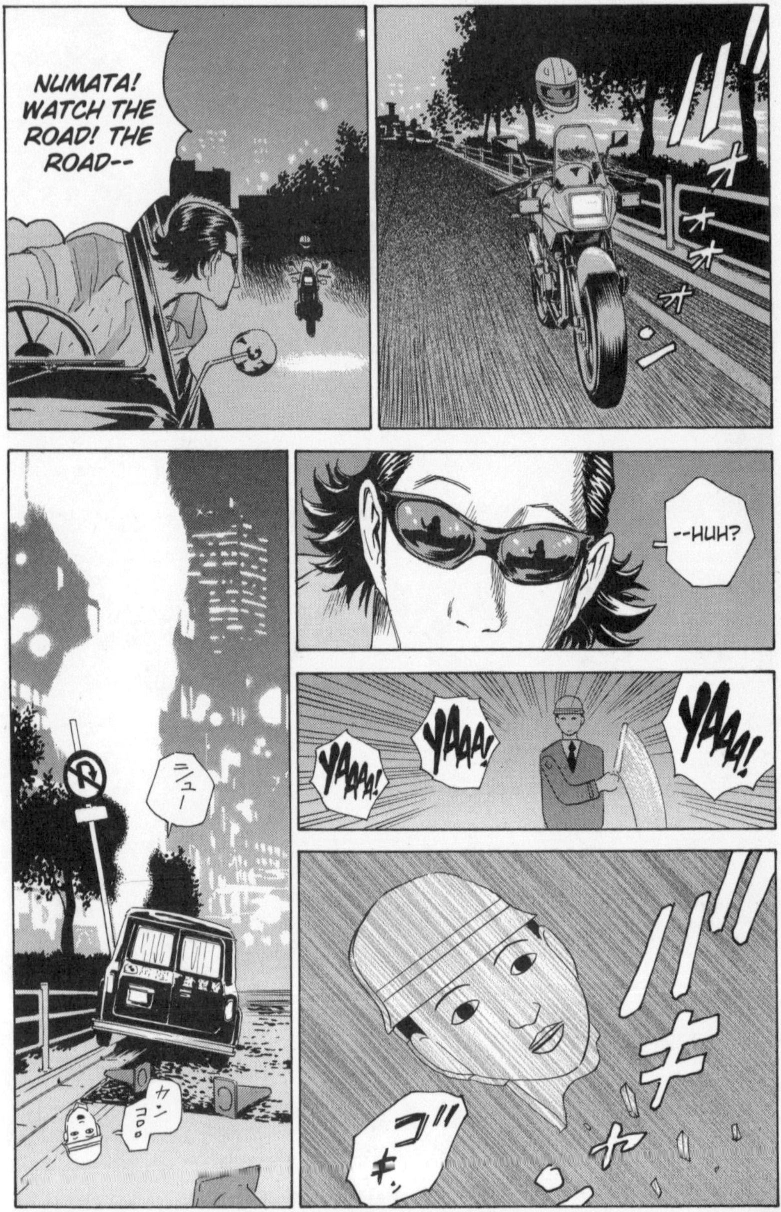
NUMATA! WATCH THE ROAD! THE ROAD--
--HUH?
YAAAA!
YAAA!
YAAAA!
シュー
カンコロ。

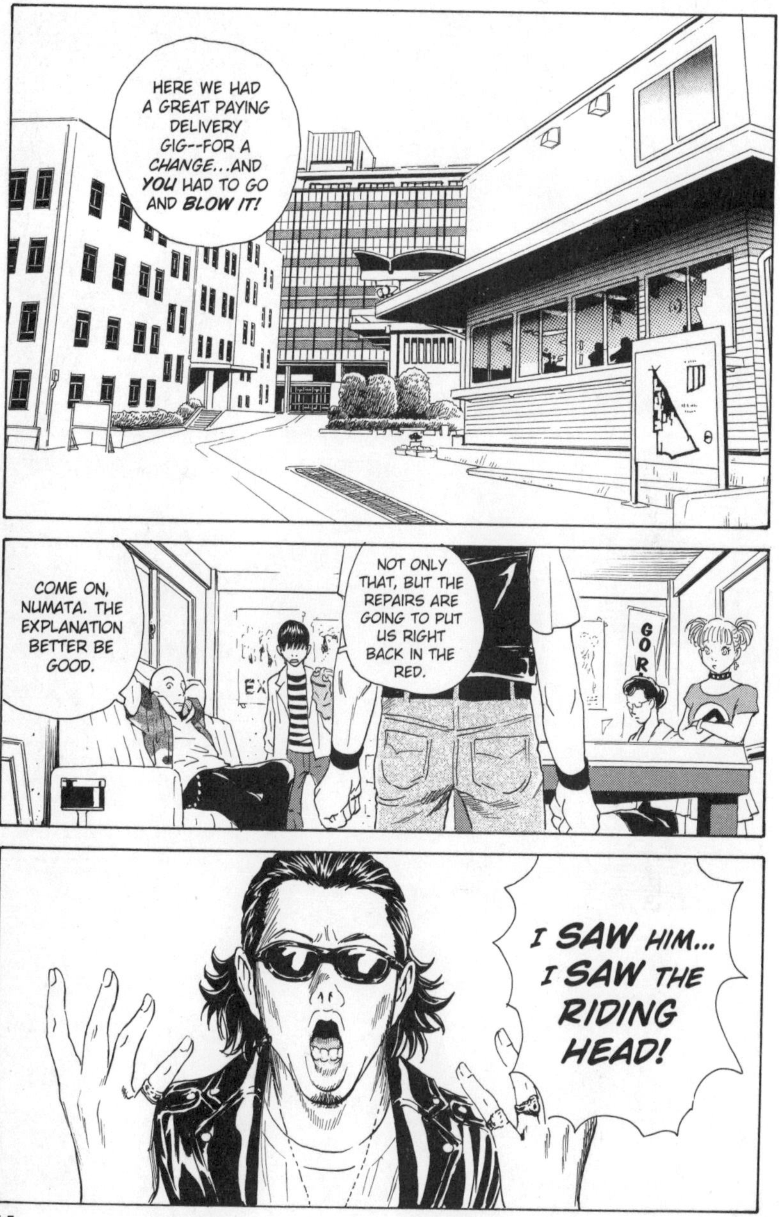
HERE WE HAD A GREAT PAYING DELIVERY GIG--FOR A CHANGE...AND YOU HAD TO GO AND BLOW IT!
NOT ONLY THAT, BUT THE REPAIRS ARE GOING TO PUT US RIGHT BACK IN THE RED.
COME ON, NUMATA. THE EXPLANATION BETTER BE GOOD.
I SAW HIM... I SAW THE RIDING HEAD!

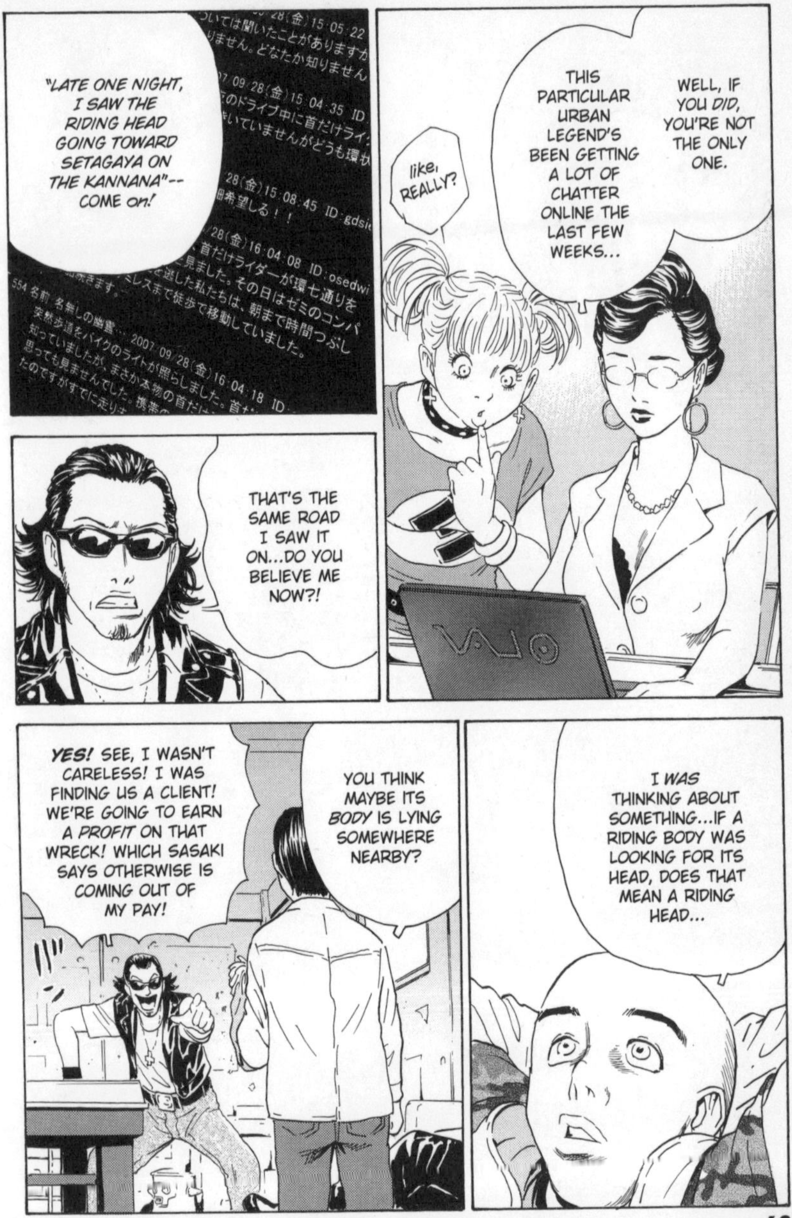
WELL, IF YOU *DID*, YOU'RE NOT THE ONLY ONE.
THIS PARTICULAR URBAN LEGEND'S BEEN GETTING A LOT OF CHATTER ONLINE THE LAST FEW WEEKS...
like, REALLY?
"LATE ONE NIGHT, I SAW THE RIDING HEAD GOING TOWARD SETAGAYA ON THE KANNANA"-- COME *on!*
THAT'S THE SAME ROAD I SAW IT ON...DO YOU BELIEVE ME NOW?!
I *WAS* THINKING ABOUT SOMETHING...IF A RIDING BODY WAS LOOKING FOR ITS HEAD, DOES THAT MEAN A RIDING HEAD...
YOU THINK MAYBE ITS *BODY* IS LYING SOMEWHERE NEARBY?
YES! SEE, I WASN'T CARELESS! I WAS FINDING US A CLIENT! WE'RE GOING TO EARN A *PROFIT* ON THAT WRECK! WHICH SASAKI SAYS OTHERWISE IS COMING OUT OF MY PAY!

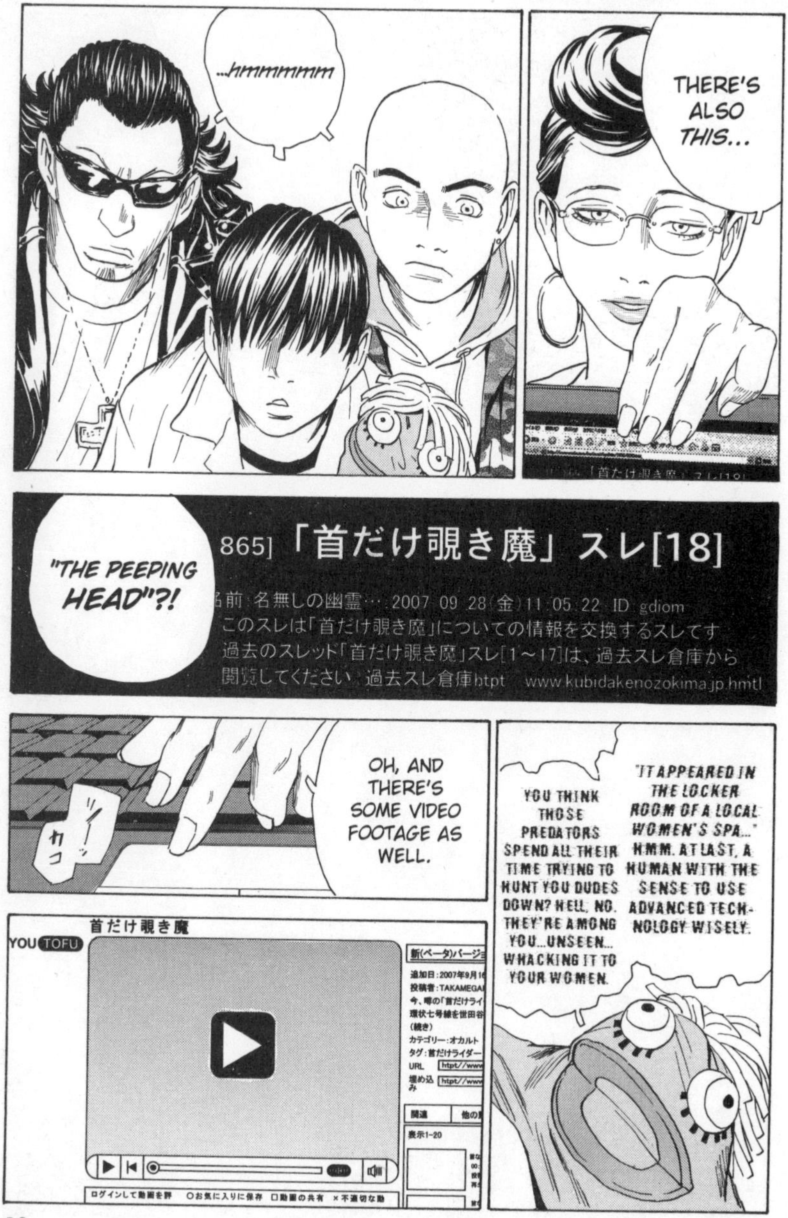

THERE'S ALSO THIS...
...hmmmmmm
"THE PEEPING HEAD"?!
865]「首だけ覗き魔」スレ[18]
名前:名無しの幽霊…:2007 09 28(金)11:05:22 ID:gdiom
このスレは「首だけ覗き魔」についての情報を交換するスレてす
過去のスレッド「首だけ覗き魔」スレ[1〜17]は、過去スレ倉庫から
閲覧してください:過去スレ倉庫htpt www.kubidakenozokima.jp.hmtl
"IT APPEARED IN THE LOCKER ROOM OF A LOCAL WOMEN'S SPA..." HMM. AT LAST, A HUMAN WITH THE SENSE TO USE ADVANCED TECHNOLOGY WISELY.
YOU THINK THOSE PREDATORS SPEND ALL THEIR TIME TRYING TO HUNT YOU DUDES DOWN? HELL, NO. THEY'RE AMONG YOU...UNSEEN... WHACKING IT TO YOUR WOMEN.
OH, AND THERE'S SOME VIDEO FOOTAGE AS WELL.
ツーーッ
カコ
首だけ覗き魔
YOU TOFU
新(ベータ)バージョ
追加日:2007年9月16
投稿者:TAKAMEGAI
今、噂の「首だけライ
環状七号線を世田谷
(続き)
カテゴリー:オカルト
タグ:首だけライダー
URL http://www
埋め込み http://www
関連 他の
表示1-20
ログインして動画を評 ○お気に入りに保存 □動画の共有 ×不適切な動

UMM... THIS WAS SOMEONE'S HIDDEN CAMERA, RIGHT...?

YEAH. PRESUMABLY HE JUST WANTED TO CATCH THE GIRLS...BUT THEN HE CAUGHT SOMETHING ELSE AS WELL.

HOW 'BOUT THERE?

IS IT THERE?

SOMETHING ELSE? WHERE?

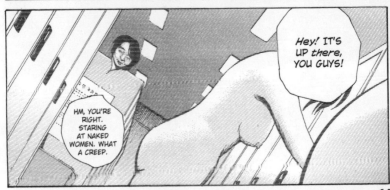

Hey! IT'S UP *there,* YOU GUYS!

HM, YOU'RE RIGHT. STARING AT NAKED WOMEN. WHAT A CREEP.

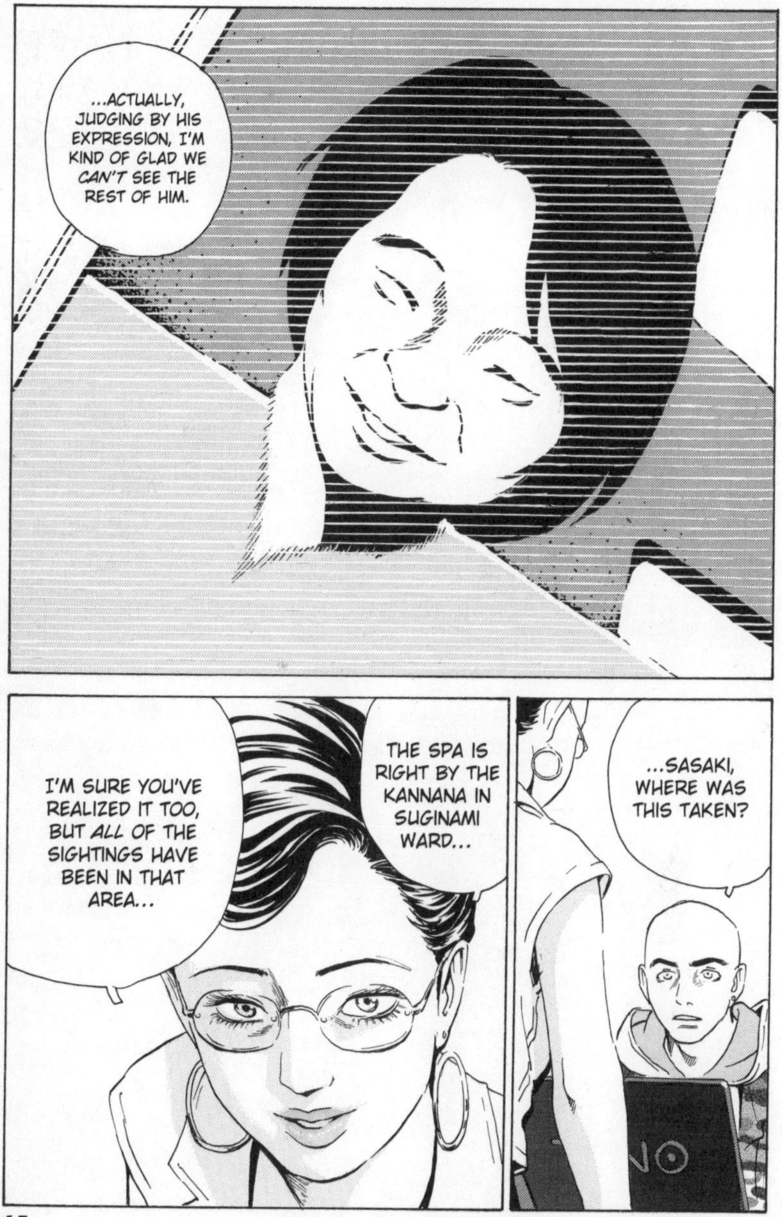
...ACTUALLY, JUDGING BY HIS EXPRESSION, I'M KIND OF GLAD WE *CAN'T* SEE THE REST OF HIM.
...SASAKI, WHERE WAS THIS TAKEN?
THE SPA IS RIGHT BY THE KANNANA IN SUGINAMI WARD...
I'M SURE YOU'VE REALIZED IT TOO, BUT *ALL* OF THE SIGHTINGS HAVE BEEN IN THAT AREA...

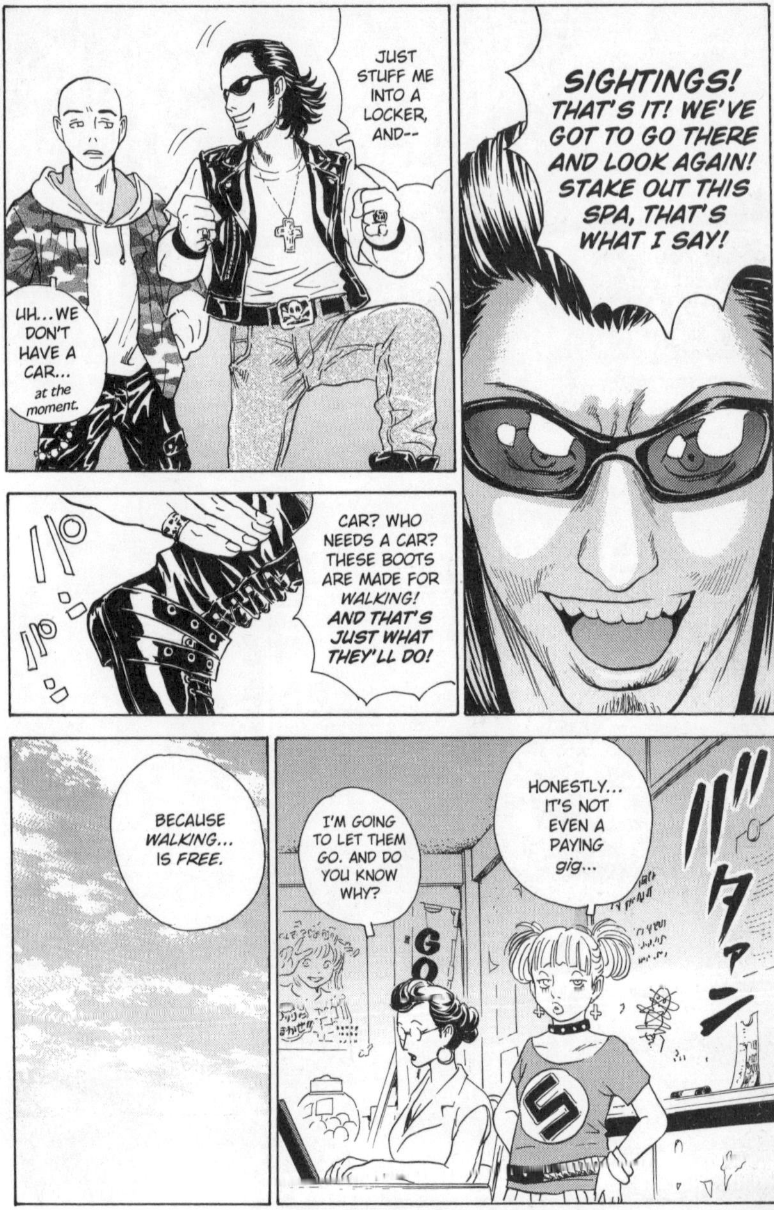
SIGHTINGS! THAT'S IT! WE'VE GOT TO GO THERE AND LOOK AGAIN! STAKE OUT THIS SPA, THAT'S WHAT I SAY!
JUST STUFF ME INTO A LOCKER, AND--
UH... WE DON'T HAVE A CAR... at the moment.
CAR? WHO NEEDS A CAR? THESE BOOTS ARE MADE FOR *WALKING!* ***AND THAT'S JUST WHAT THEY'LL DO!***
HONESTLY... IT'S NOT EVEN A PAYING *gig*...
I'M GOING TO LET THEM GO. AND DO YOU KNOW WHY?
BECAUSE *WALKING*... IS *FREE*.

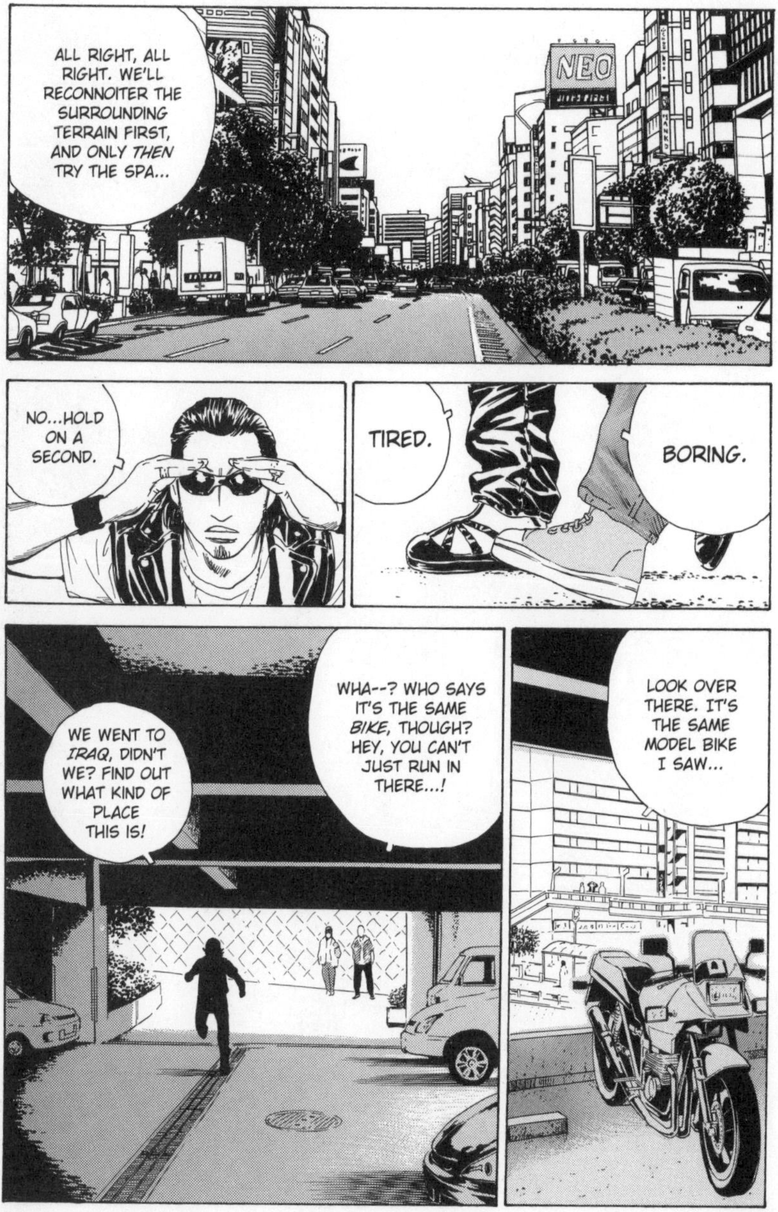
ALL RIGHT, ALL RIGHT. WE'LL RECONNOITER THE SURROUNDING TERRAIN FIRST, AND ONLY *THEN* TRY THE SPA...
NEO
BORING.
TIRED.
NO...HOLD ON A SECOND.
LOOK OVER THERE. IT'S THE SAME MODEL BIKE I SAW...
WHA--? WHO SAYS IT'S THE SAME *BIKE*, THOUGH? HEY, YOU CAN'T JUST RUN IN THERE...!
WE WENT TO *IRAQ*, DIDN'T WE? FIND OUT WHAT KIND OF PLACE THIS IS!

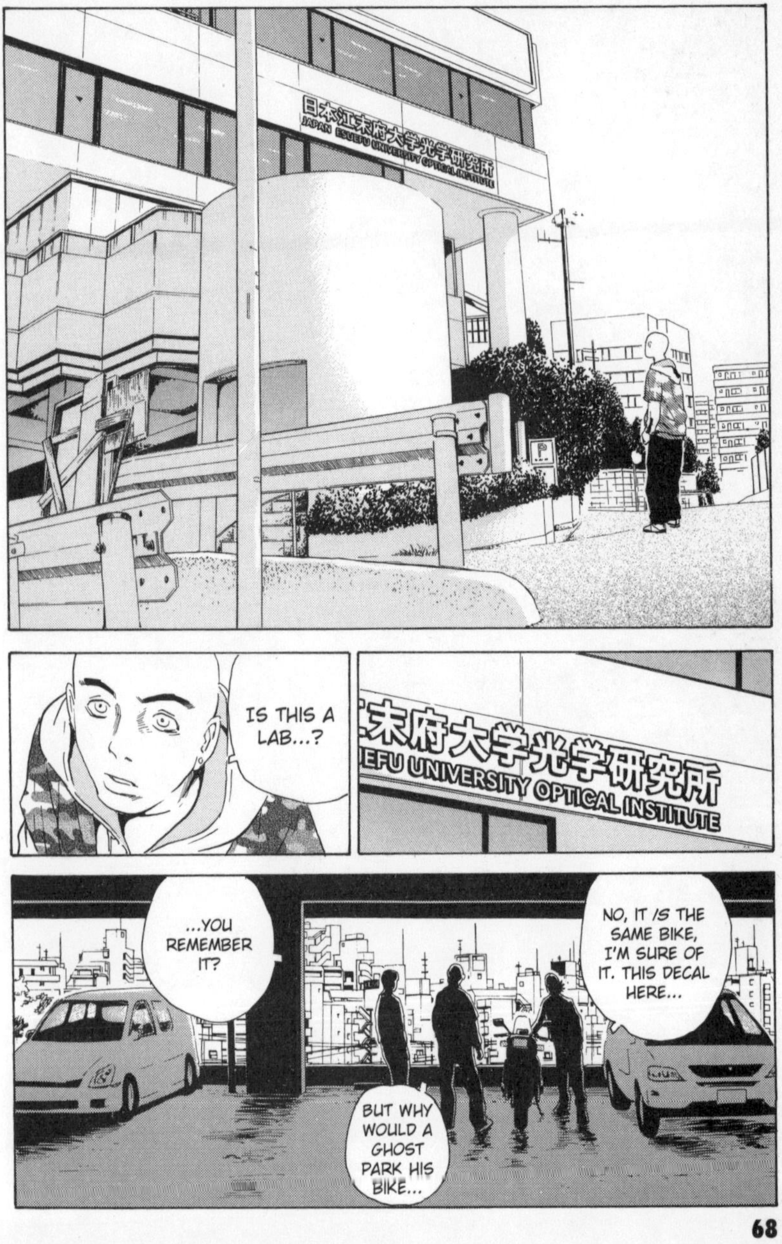
日本江末府大学光学研究所
JAPAN ESUEFU UNIVERSITY OPTICAL INSTITUTE
末府大学光学研究所
EFU UNIVERSITY OPTICAL INSTITUTE
IS THIS A LAB...?
NO, IT *IS* THE SAME BIKE, I'M SURE OF IT. THIS DECAL HERE...
...YOU REMEMBER IT?
BUT WHY WOULD A GHOST PARK HIS BIKE...

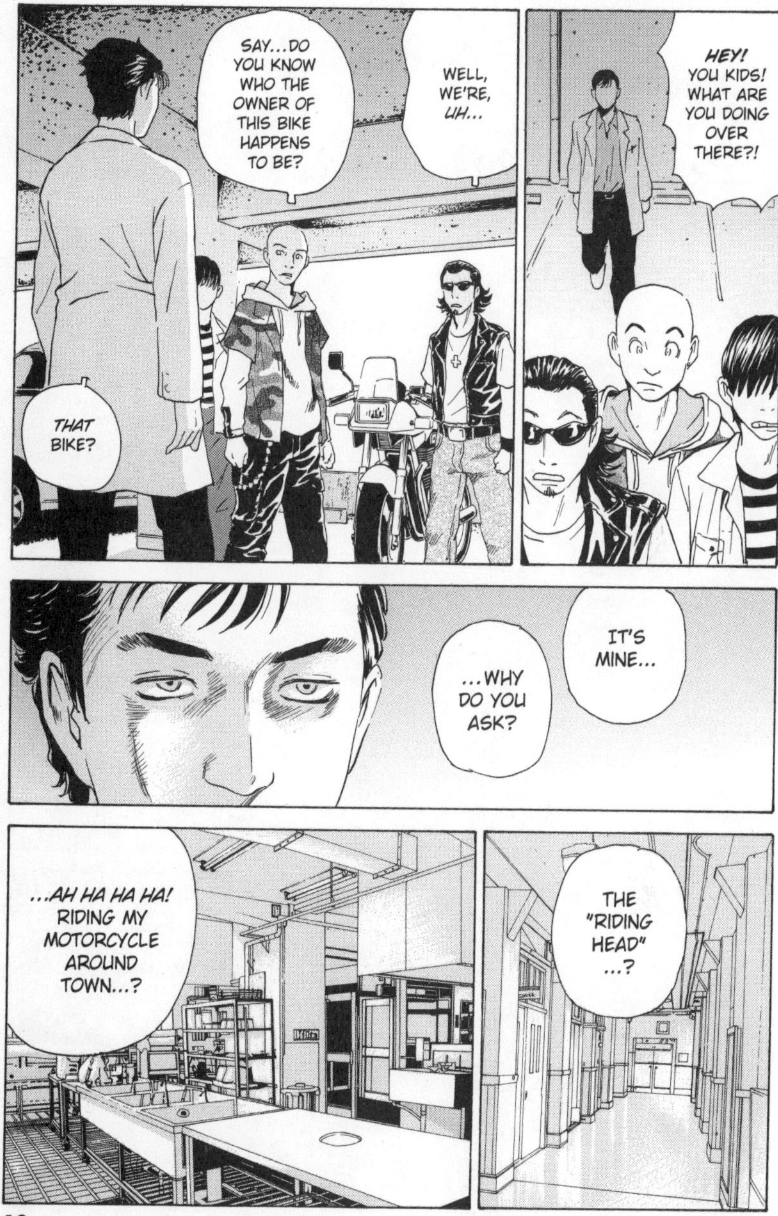
HEY! YOU KIDS! WHAT ARE YOU DOING OVER THERE?!
WELL, WE'RE, UH...
SAY...DO YOU KNOW WHO THE OWNER OF THIS BIKE HAPPENS TO BE?
THAT BIKE?
IT'S MINE...
...WHY DO YOU ASK?
THE "RIDING HEAD" ...?
...AH HA HA HA! RIDING MY MOTORCYCLE AROUND TOWN...?

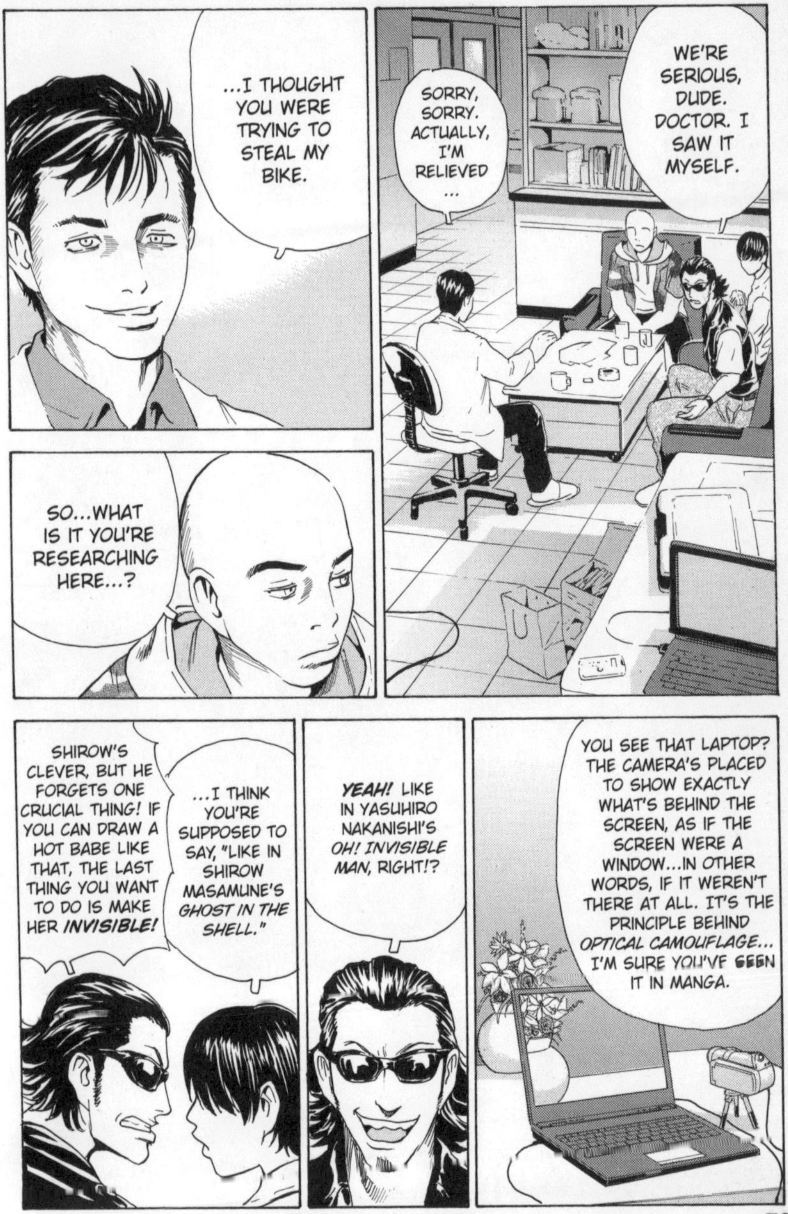
WE'RE SERIOUS, DUDE. DOCTOR. I SAW IT MYSELF.
SORRY, SORRY. ACTUALLY, I'M RELIEVED ...
...I THOUGHT YOU WERE TRYING TO STEAL MY BIKE.
SO...WHAT IS IT YOU'RE RESEARCHING HERE...?
YOU SEE THAT LAPTOP? THE CAMERA'S PLACED TO SHOW EXACTLY WHAT'S BEHIND THE SCREEN, AS IF THE SCREEN WERE A WINDOW...IN OTHER WORDS, IF IT WEREN'T THERE AT ALL. IT'S THE PRINCIPLE BEHIND *OPTICAL CAMOUFLAGE*... I'M SURE YOU'VE SEEN IT IN MANGA.
YEAH! LIKE IN YASUHIRO NAKANISHI'S *OH! INVISIBLE MAN*, RIGHT!?
...I THINK YOU'RE SUPPOSED TO SAY, "LIKE IN SHIROW MASAMUNE'S *GHOST IN THE SHELL*."
SHIROW'S CLEVER, BUT HE FORGETS ONE CRUCIAL THING! IF YOU CAN DRAW A HOT BABE LIKE THAT, THE LAST THING YOU WANT TO DO IS MAKE HER ***INVISIBLE!***

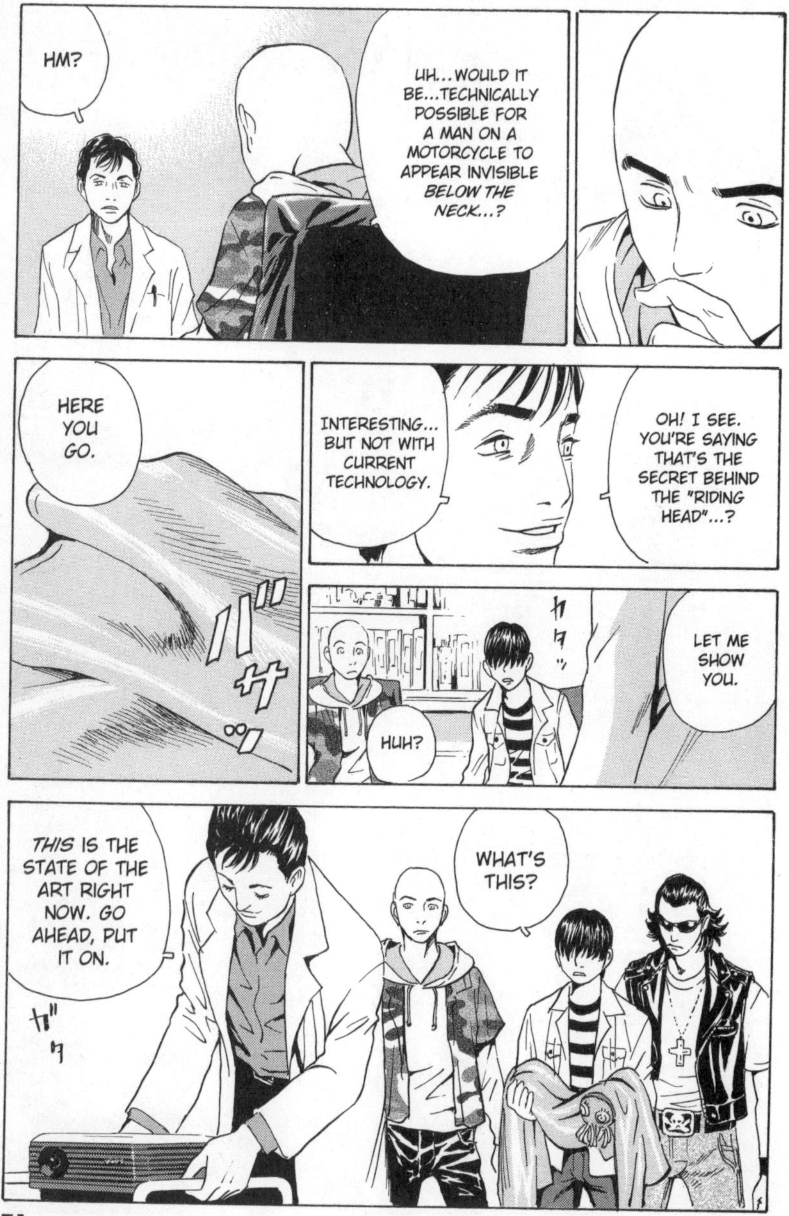
UH...WOULD IT BE...TECHNICALLY POSSIBLE FOR A MAN ON A MOTORCYCLE TO APPEAR INVISIBLE *BELOW THE NECK*...?
HM?
OH! I SEE. YOU'RE SAYING THAT'S THE SECRET BEHIND THE "RIDING HEAD"...?
INTERESTING... BUT NOT WITH CURRENT TECHNOLOGY.
LET ME SHOW YOU.
カタッ
HUH?
HERE YOU GO.
バサッ
WHAT'S THIS?
THIS IS THE STATE OF THE ART RIGHT NOW. GO AHEAD, PUT IT ON.

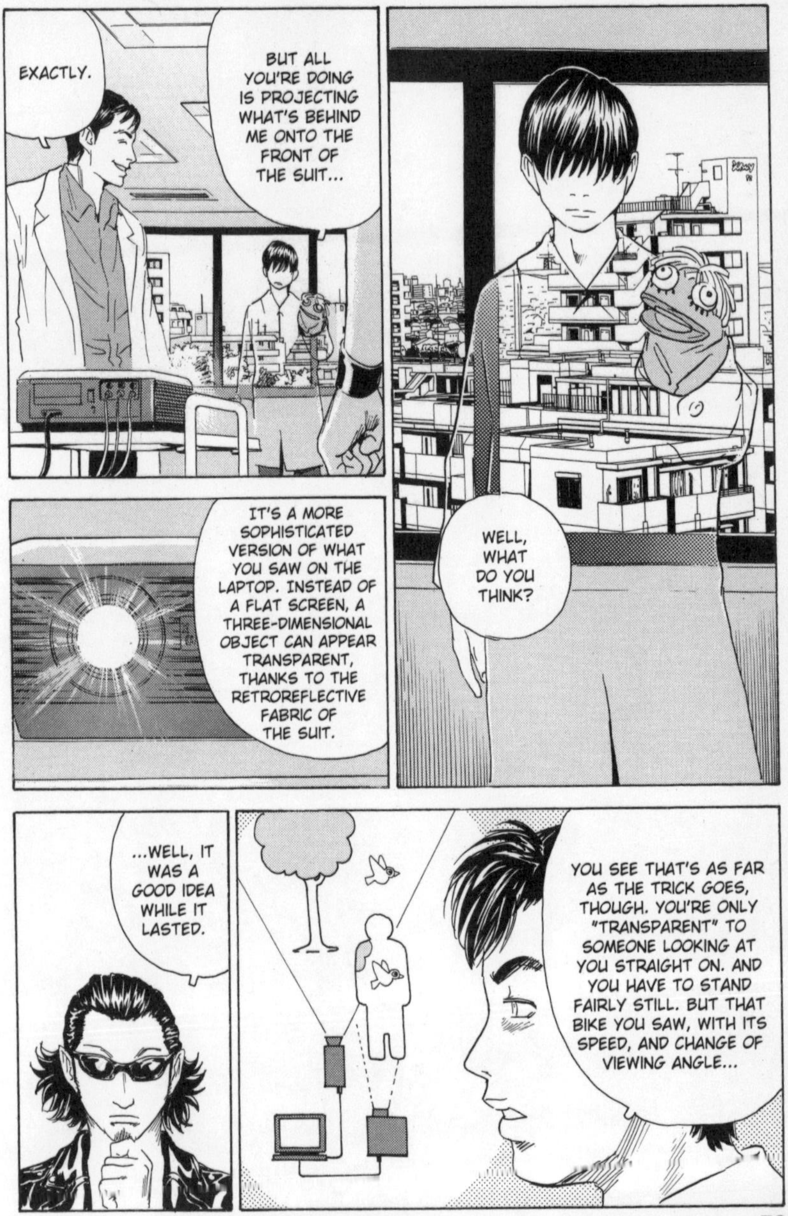
WELL, WHAT DO YOU THINK?
BUT ALL YOU'RE DOING IS PROJECTING WHAT'S BEHIND ME ONTO THE FRONT OF THE SUIT...
EXACTLY.
IT'S A MORE SOPHISTICATED VERSION OF WHAT YOU SAW ON THE LAPTOP. INSTEAD OF A FLAT SCREEN, A THREE-DIMENSIONAL OBJECT CAN APPEAR TRANSPARENT, THANKS TO THE RETROREFLECTIVE FABRIC OF THE SUIT.
YOU SEE THAT'S AS FAR AS THE TRICK GOES, THOUGH. YOU'RE ONLY "TRANSPARENT" TO SOMEONE LOOKING AT YOU STRAIGHT ON. AND YOU HAVE TO STAND FAIRLY STILL. BUT THAT BIKE YOU SAW, WITH ITS SPEED, AND CHANGE OF VIEWING ANGLE...
...WELL, IT WAS A GOOD IDEA WHILE IT LASTED.

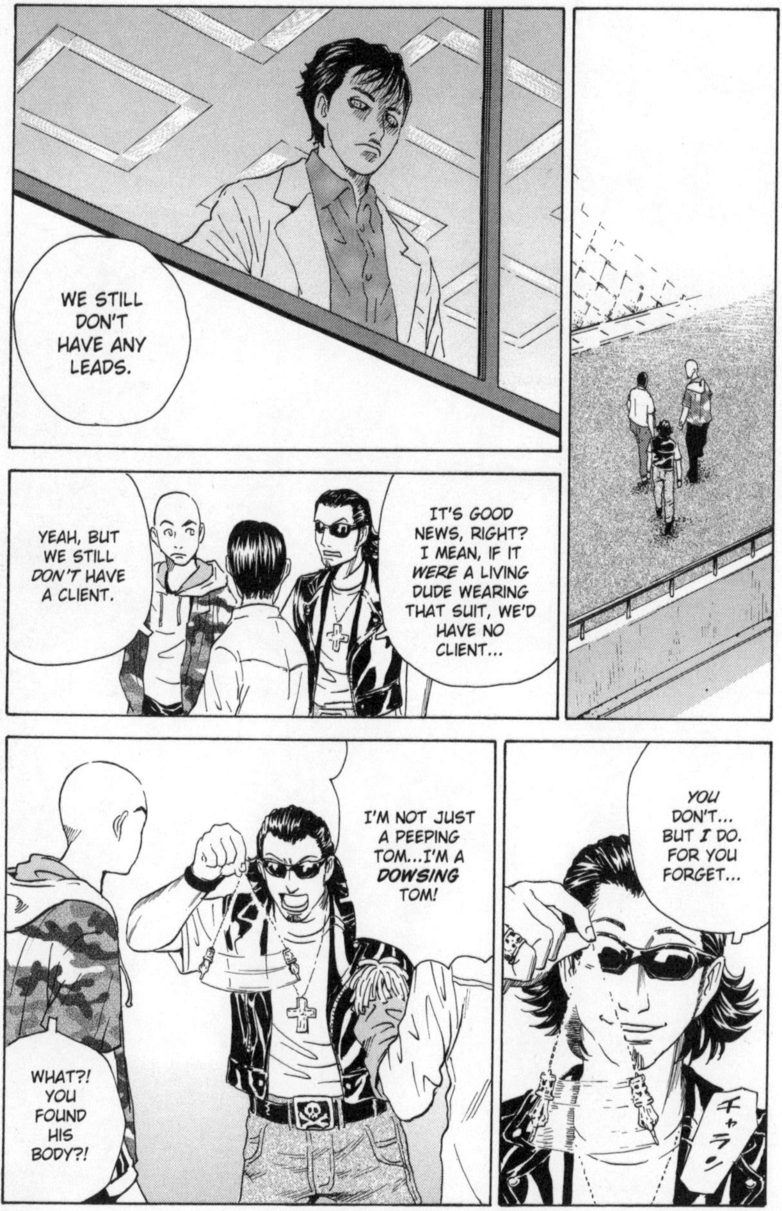
WE STILL DON'T HAVE ANY LEADS.
IT'S GOOD NEWS, RIGHT? I MEAN, IF IT *WERE* A LIVING DUDE WEARING THAT SUIT, WE'D HAVE NO CLIENT...
YEAH, BUT WE STILL *DON'T* HAVE A CLIENT.
YOU DON'T... BUT *I* DO. FOR YOU FORGET...
チャラン
I'M NOT JUST A PEEPING TOM...I'M A ***DOWSING*** TOM!
WHAT?! YOU FOUND HIS BODY?!

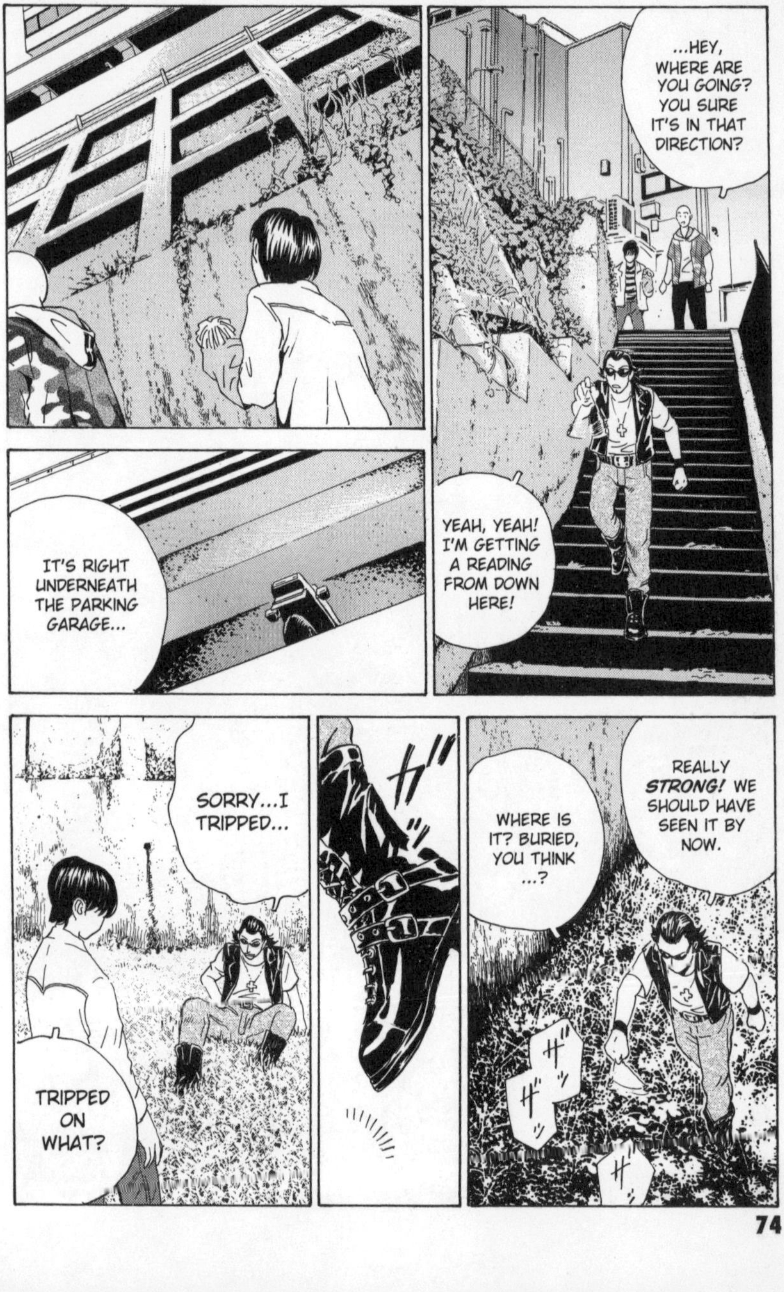
...HEY, WHERE ARE YOU GOING? YOU SURE IT'S IN THAT DIRECTION?
YEAH, YEAH! I'M GETTING A READING FROM DOWN HERE!
IT'S RIGHT UNDERNEATH THE PARKING GARAGE...
REALLY **STRONG!** WE SHOULD HAVE SEEN IT BY NOW.
WHERE IS IT? BURIED, YOU THINK ...?
ザッ
ザッ
ザ
ガ
SORRY...I TRIPPED...
TRIPPED ON WHAT?

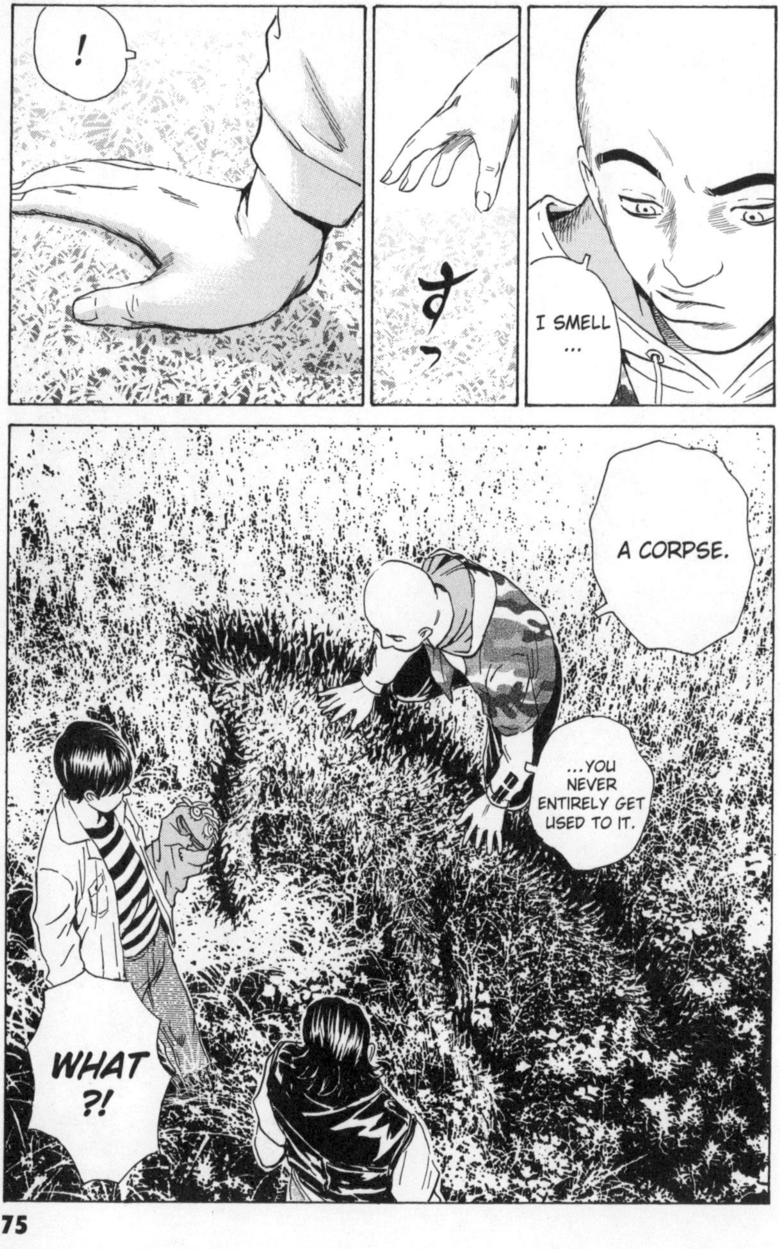
I SMELL ...
すっ
!
A CORPSE.
...YOU NEVER ENTIRELY GET USED TO IT.
WHAT ?!

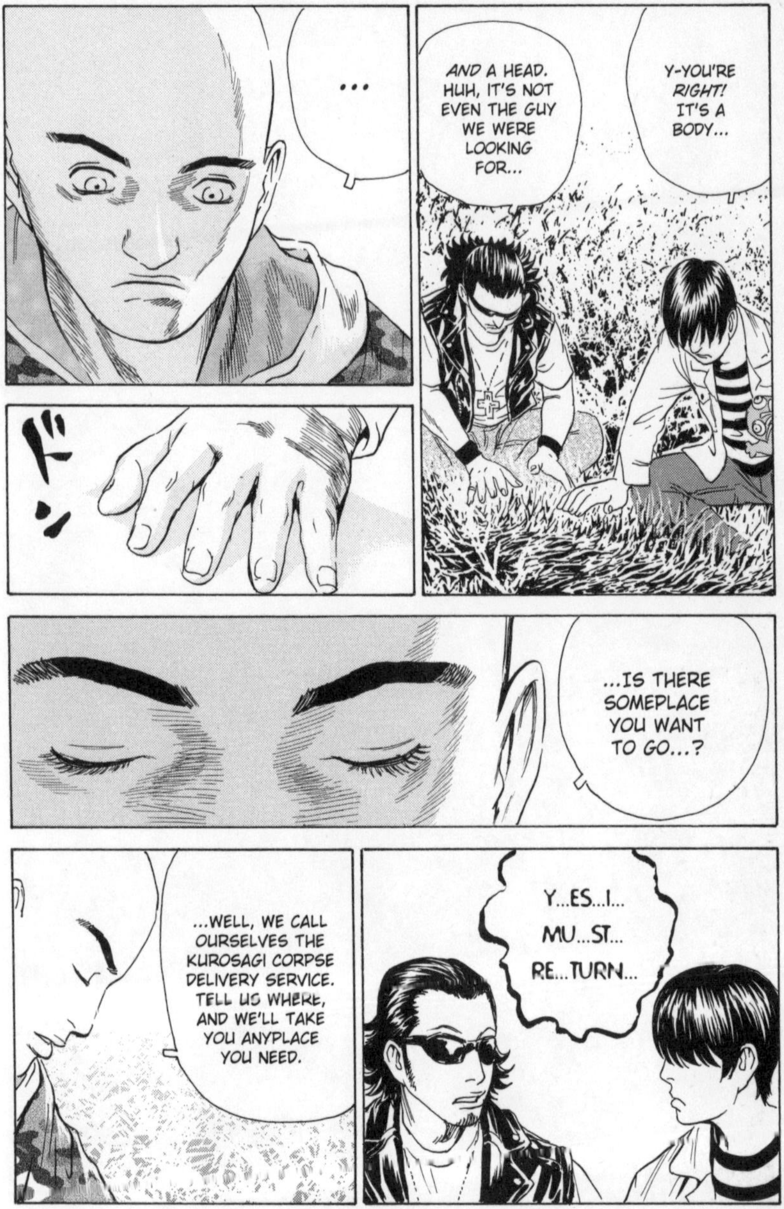
Y-YOU'RE *RIGHT!* IT'S A BODY...
AND A HEAD. HUH, IT'S NOT EVEN THE GUY WE WERE LOOKING FOR...
...
ドン
...IS THERE SOMEPLACE YOU WANT TO GO...?
Y...ES...I... MU...ST... RE...TURN...
...WELL, WE CALL OURSELVES THE KUROSAGI CORPSE DELIVERY SERVICE. TELL US WHERE, AND WE'LL TAKE YOU ANYPLACE YOU NEED.

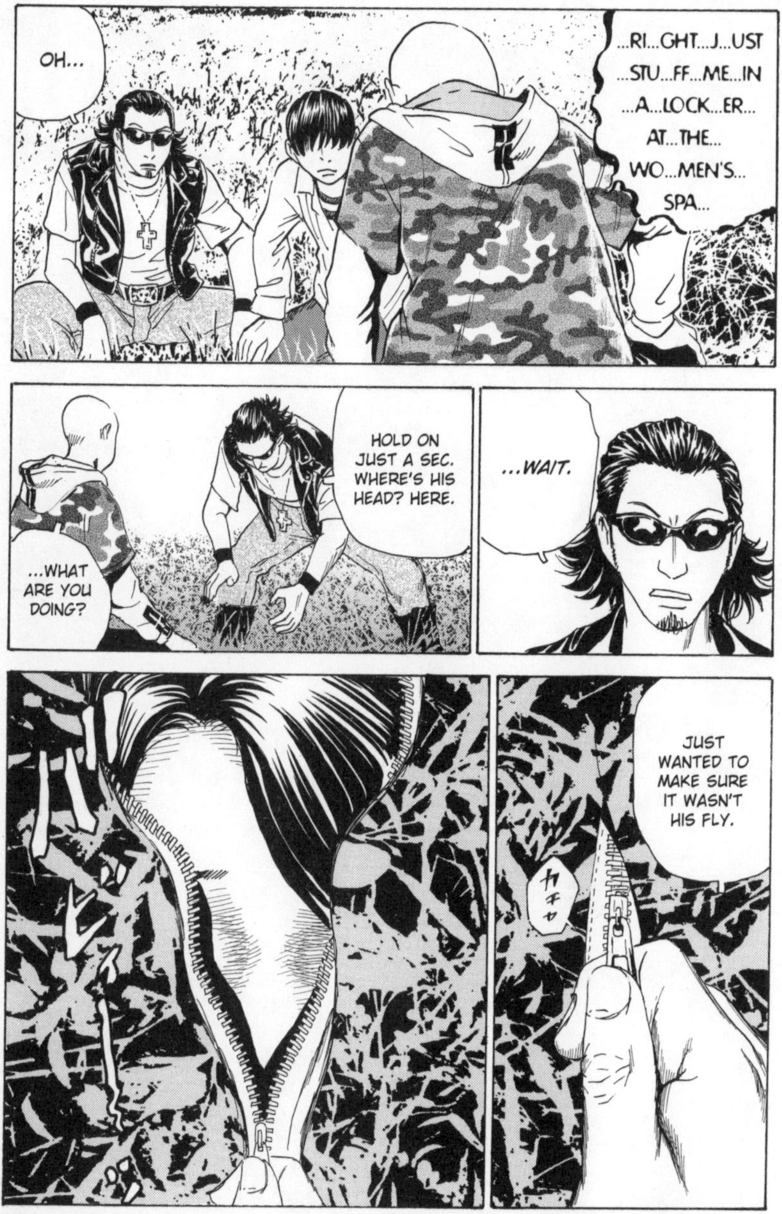
...RI...GHT...J...UST ...STU...FF...ME...IN ...A...LOCK...ER... AT...THE... WO...MEN'S... SPA...
OH...
...WAIT.
HOLD ON JUST A SEC. WHERE'S HIS HEAD? HERE.
...WHAT ARE YOU DOING?
JUST WANTED TO MAKE SURE IT WASN'T HIS FLY.
カチャ

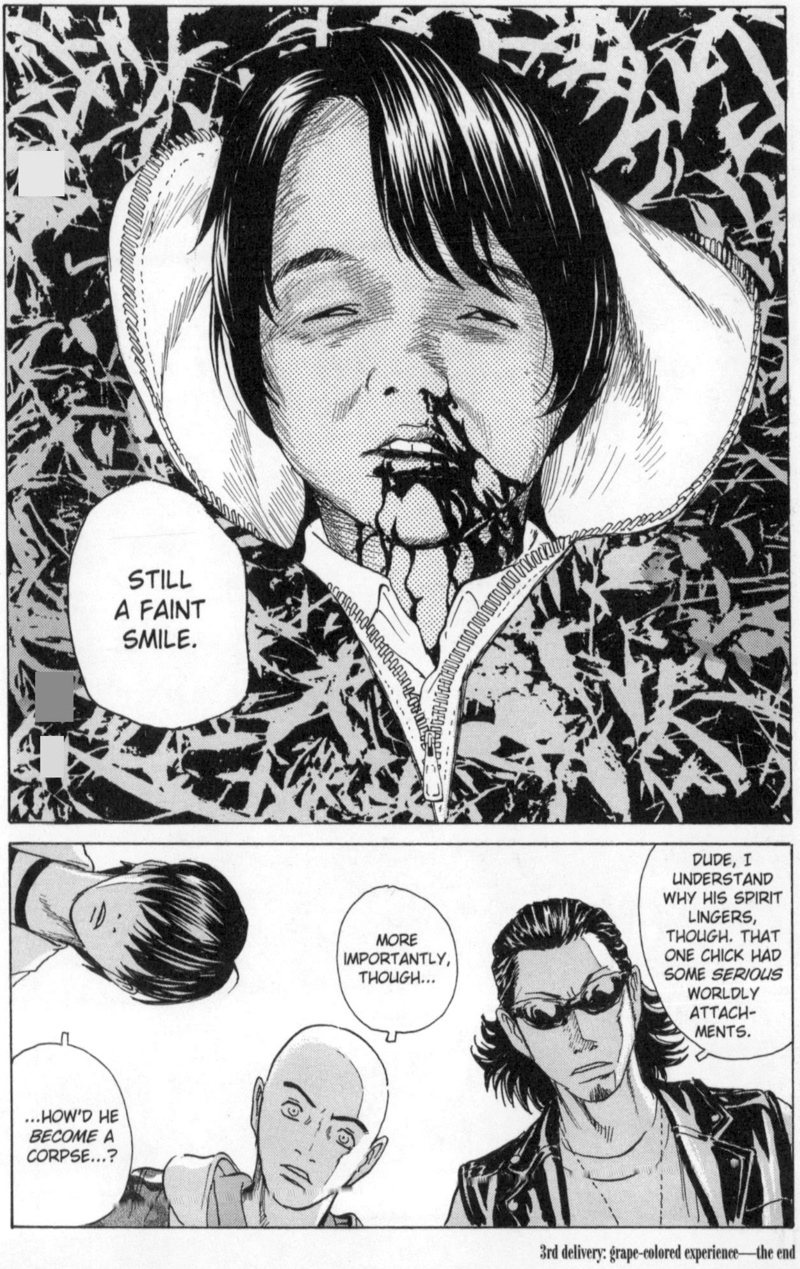
STILL A FAINT SMILE.
DUDE, I UNDERSTAND WHY HIS SPIRIT LINGERS, THOUGH. THAT ONE CHICK HAD SOME *SERIOUS* WORLDLY ATTACH-MENTS.
MORE IMPORTANTLY, THOUGH...
...HOW'D HE *BECOME A* CORPSE...?

3rd delivery: grape-colored experience—the end

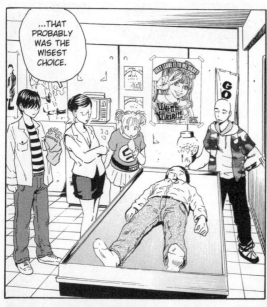

SO THEN YOU DECIDED TO BRING THE BODY HERE INSTEAD OF THE WOMEN'S SPA...
...THAT PROBABLY WAS THE WISEST CHOICE.
JUST LEAVE IT TO ME OKAY?
LEAVE IT to YURIRI!!
ESUEFU UNIVERSITY OPTICAL INSTITUTE...
スッ
JEU
jef
JAPAN ESUEFU UNIVERSITY OPTICAL INSTITUTE
日本江末府大学光学研究所
SO THEN THIS OSHII IS THE SOURCE OF THE RECENT URBAN LEGEND...?
BUT... *hmm?*
HMM?
ムニュ

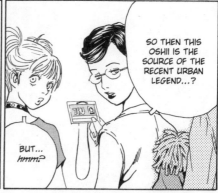

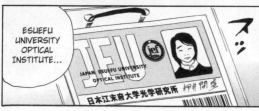

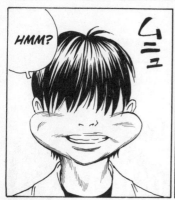

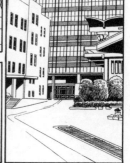

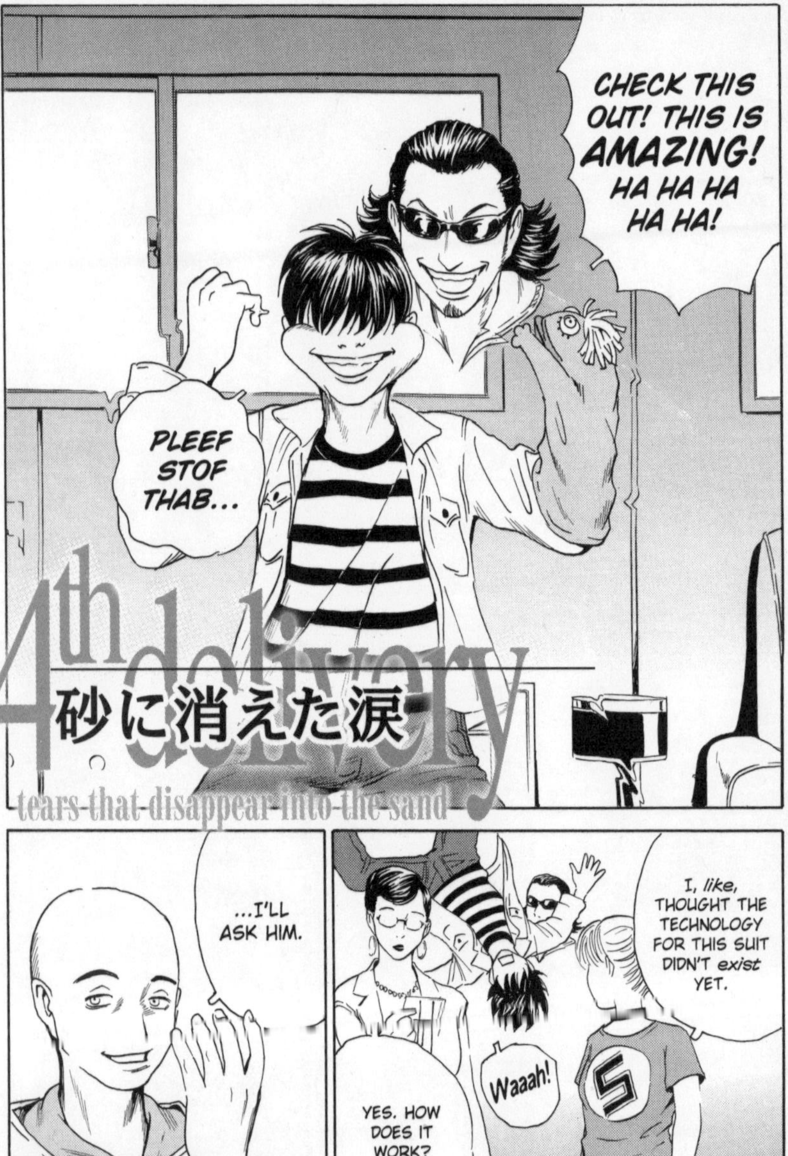
CHECK THIS OUT! THIS IS AMAZING! HA HA HA HA HA!
PLEEF STOF THAB...
4th delivery
砂に消えた涙
tears that disappear into the sand
I, *like*, THOUGHT THE TECHNOLOGY FOR THIS SUIT DIDN'T *exist* YET.
Waaah!
YES. HOW DOES IT WORK?
...I'LL ASK HIM.

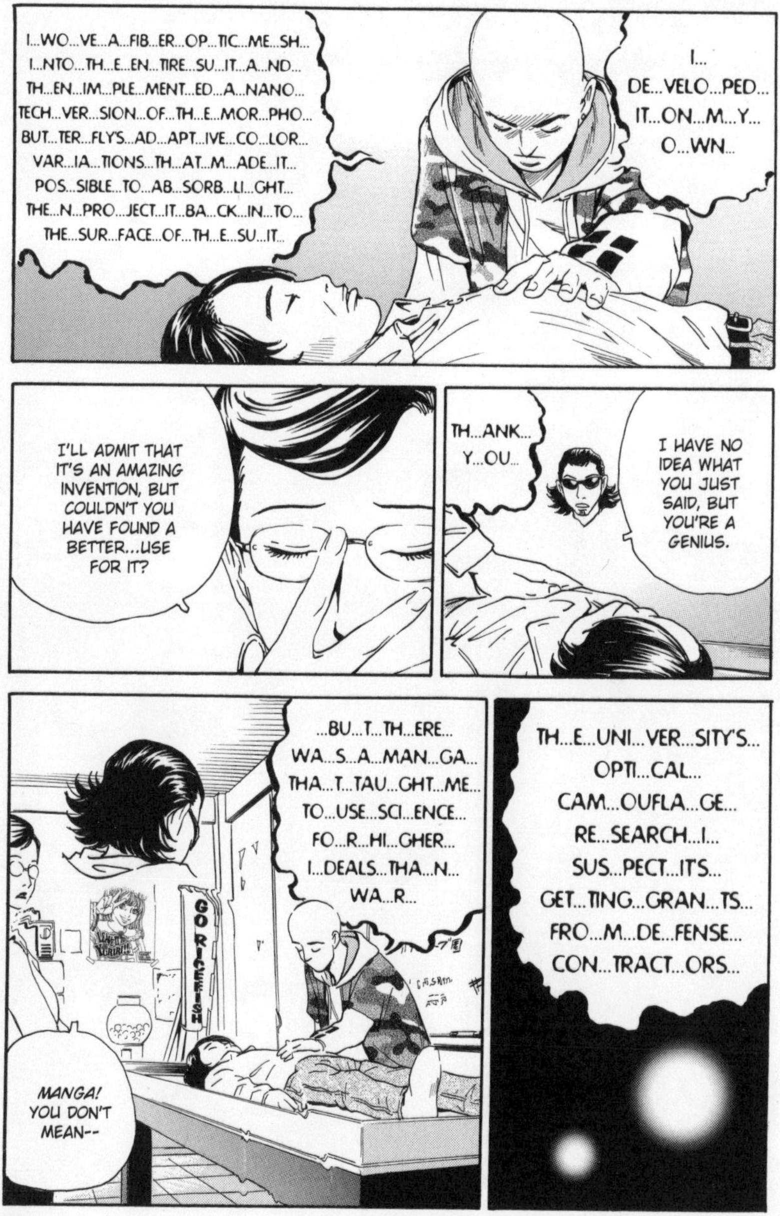
I... DE...VELO...PED... IT...ON...M...Y... O...WN...
I...WO...VE...A...FIB...ER...OP...TIC...ME...SH... I...NTO...TH...E...EN...TIRE...SU...IT...A...ND... TH...EN...IM...PLE...MENT...ED...A...NANO... TECH...VER...SION...OF...TH...E...MOR...PHO... BUT...TER...FLY'S...AD...APT...IVE...CO...LOR... VAR...IA...TIONS...TH...AT...M...ADE...IT... POS...SIBLE...TO...AB...SORB...LI...GHT... THE...N...PRO...JECT...IT...BA...CK...IN...TO... THE...SUR...FACE...OF...TH...E...SU...IT...
I HAVE NO IDEA WHAT YOU JUST SAID, BUT YOU'RE A GENIUS.
TH...ANK... Y...OU...
I'LL ADMIT THAT IT'S AN AMAZING INVENTION, BUT COULDN'T YOU HAVE FOUND A BETTER...USE FOR IT?
TH...E...UNI...VER...SITY'S... OPTI...CAL... CAM...OUFLA...GE... RE...SEARCH...I... SUS...PECT...IT'S... GET...TING...GRAN...TS... FRO...M...DE...FENSE... CON...TRACT...ORS...
...BU...T...TH...ERE... WA...S...A...MAN...GA... THA...T...TAU...GHT...ME... TO...USE...SCI...ENCE... FO...R...HI...GHER... I...DEALS...THA...N... WA...R...
GO RICEFISH
MANGA! YOU DON'T MEAN--

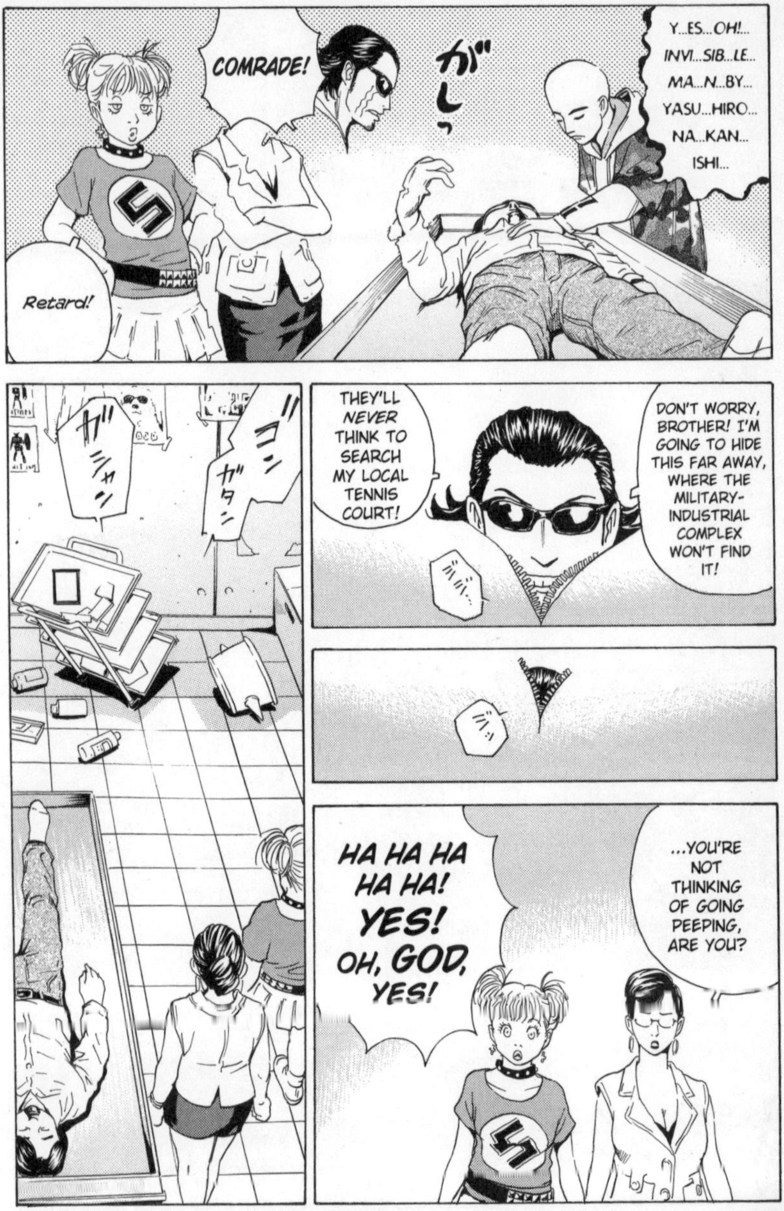
Y...ES...OH!... INVI...SIB...LE... MA...N...BY... YASU...HIRO... NA...KAN... ISHI...
がしっ
COMRADE!
Retard!
DON'T WORRY, BROTHER! I'M GOING TO HIDE THIS FAR AWAY, WHERE THE MILITARY-INDUSTRIAL COMPLEX WON'T FIND IT!
THEY'LL NEVER THINK TO SEARCH MY LOCAL TENNIS COURT!
ジジジ…
ジッ
...YOU'RE NOT THINKING OF GOING PEEPING, ARE YOU?
HA HA HA HA HA! YES! OH, GOD, YES!
ゴン
ガタン
ガシャン

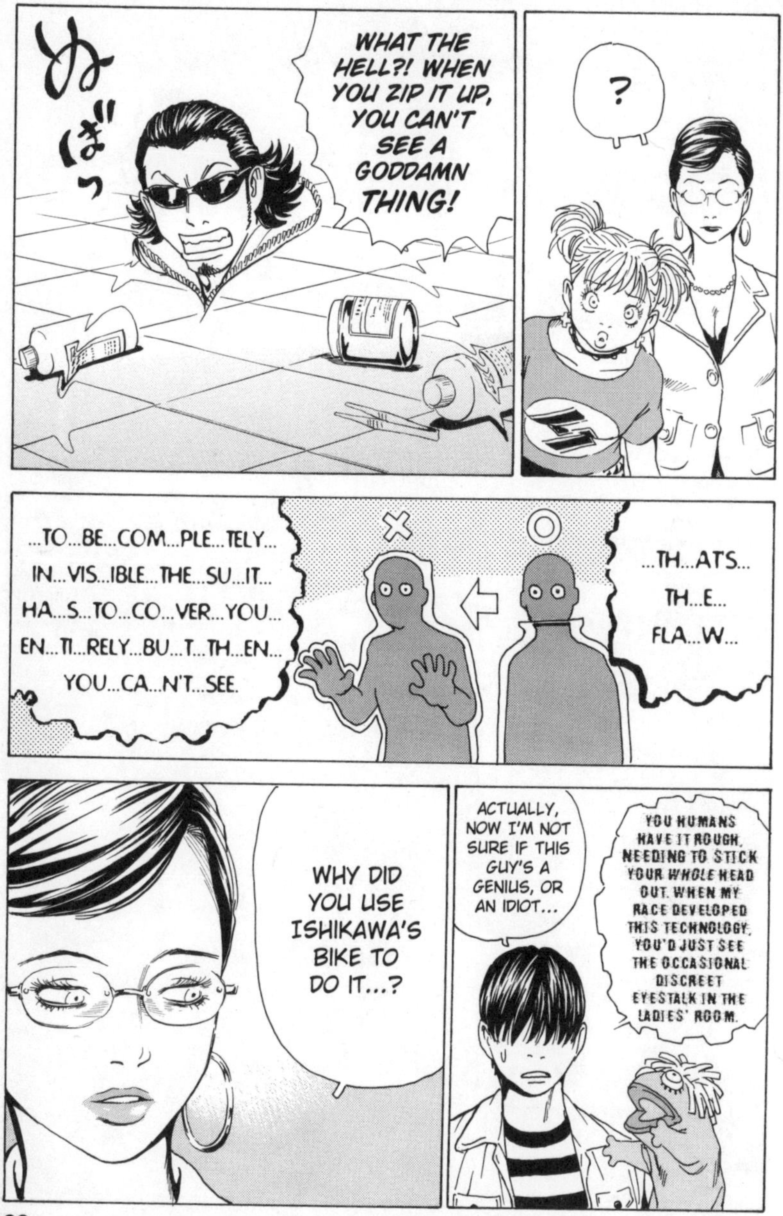
?
ぬぼっ
WHAT THE HELL?! WHEN YOU ZIP IT UP, YOU CAN'T SEE A GODDAMN THING!
...TH...ATS... TH...E... FLA...W...
...TO...BE...COM...PLE...TELY... IN...VIS...IBLE...THE...SU...IT... HA...S...TO...CO...VER...YOU... EN...TI...RELY...BU...T...TH...EN... YOU...CA...N'T...SEE.
YOU HUMANS HAVE IT ROUGH, NEEDING TO STICK YOUR *WHOLE* HEAD OUT. WHEN MY RACE DEVELOPED THIS TECHNOLOGY, YOU'D JUST SEE THE OCCASIONAL DISCREET EYESTALK IN THE LADIES' ROOM.
ACTUALLY, NOW I'M NOT SURE IF THIS GUY'S A GENIUS, OR AN IDIOT...
WHY DID YOU USE ISHIKAWA'S BIKE TO DO IT...?

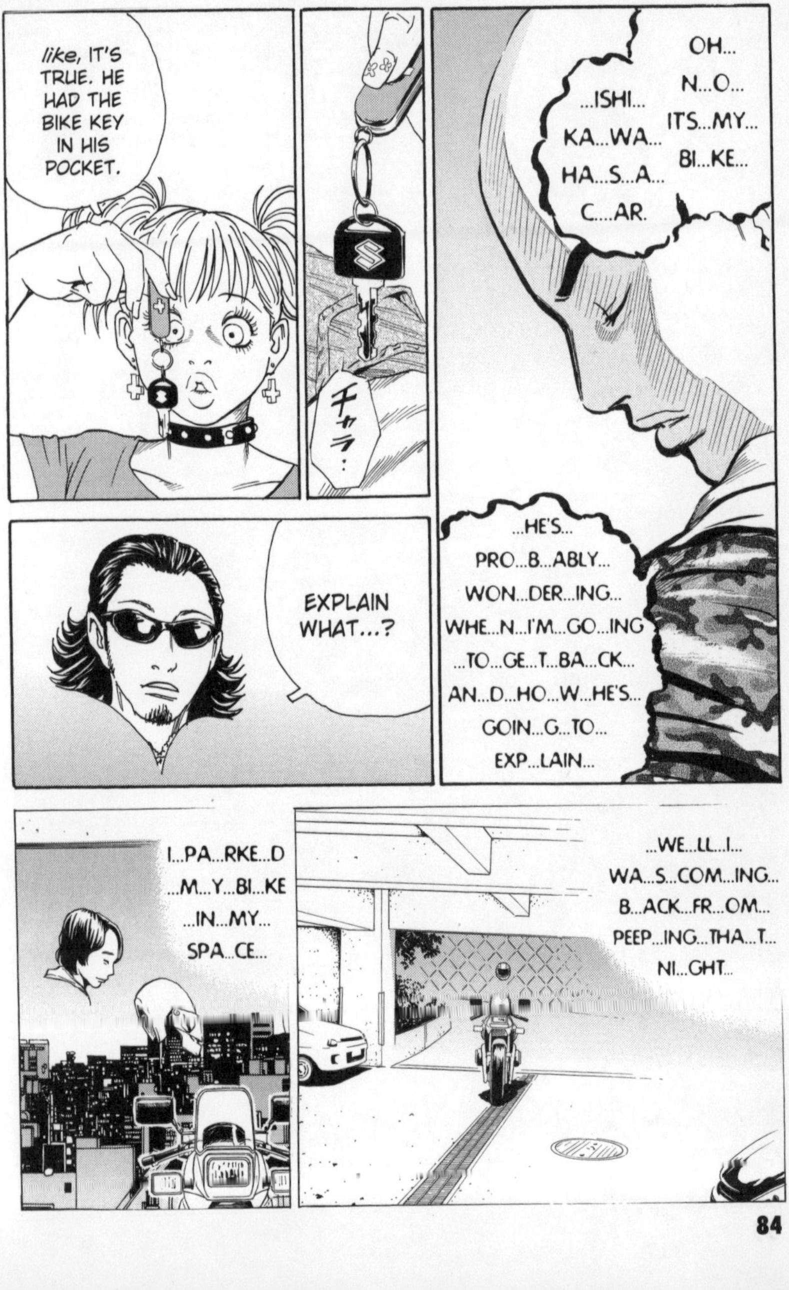

OH... N...O... IT'S...MY... BI...KE...
...ISHI... KA...WA... HA...S...A... C...AR.
...HE'S... PRO...B...ABLY... WON...DER...ING... WHE...N...I'M...GO...ING ...TO...GE...T...BA...CK... AN...D...HO...W...HE'S... GOIN...G...TO... EXP...LAIN...
チャラ…
like, IT'S TRUE. HE HAD THE BIKE KEY IN HIS POCKET.
EXPLAIN WHAT...?
...WE...LL...I... WA...S...COM...ING... B...ACK...FR...OM... PEEP...ING...THA...T... NI...GHT...
I...PA...RKE...D ...M...Y...BI...KE ...IN...MY... SPA...CE...

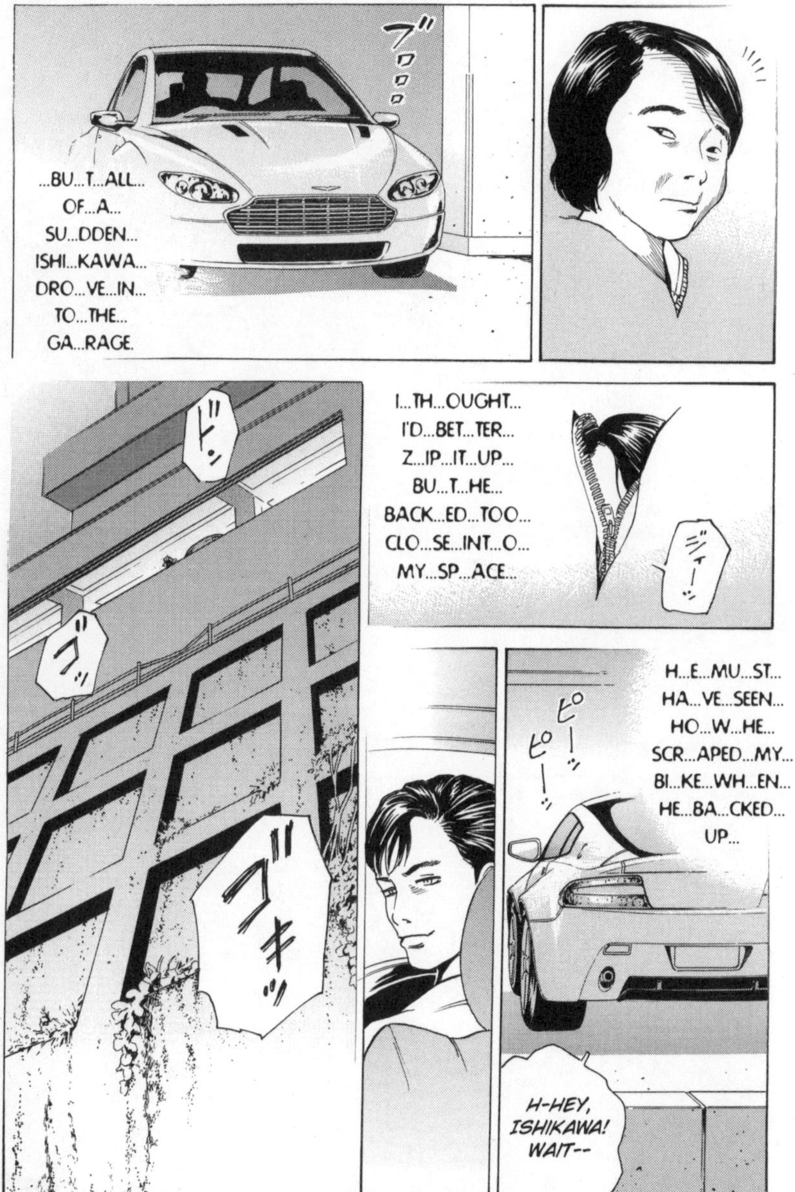
ブロロロ
...BU...T...ALL... OF...A... SU...DDEN... ISHI...KAWA... DRO...VE...IN... TO...THE... GA...RAGE.
I...TH...OUGHT... I'D...BET...TER... Z...IP...IT...UP... BU...T...HE... BACK...ED...TOO... CLO...SE...INT...O... MY...SP...ACE...
ジィーッ
H...E...MU...ST... HA...VE...SEEN... HO...W...HE... SCR...APED...MY... BI...KE...WH...EN... HE...BA...CKED... UP...
ピーッ
ピーッ
H-HEY, ISHIKAWA! WAIT--
ドンッ
グッ
ゴキッ

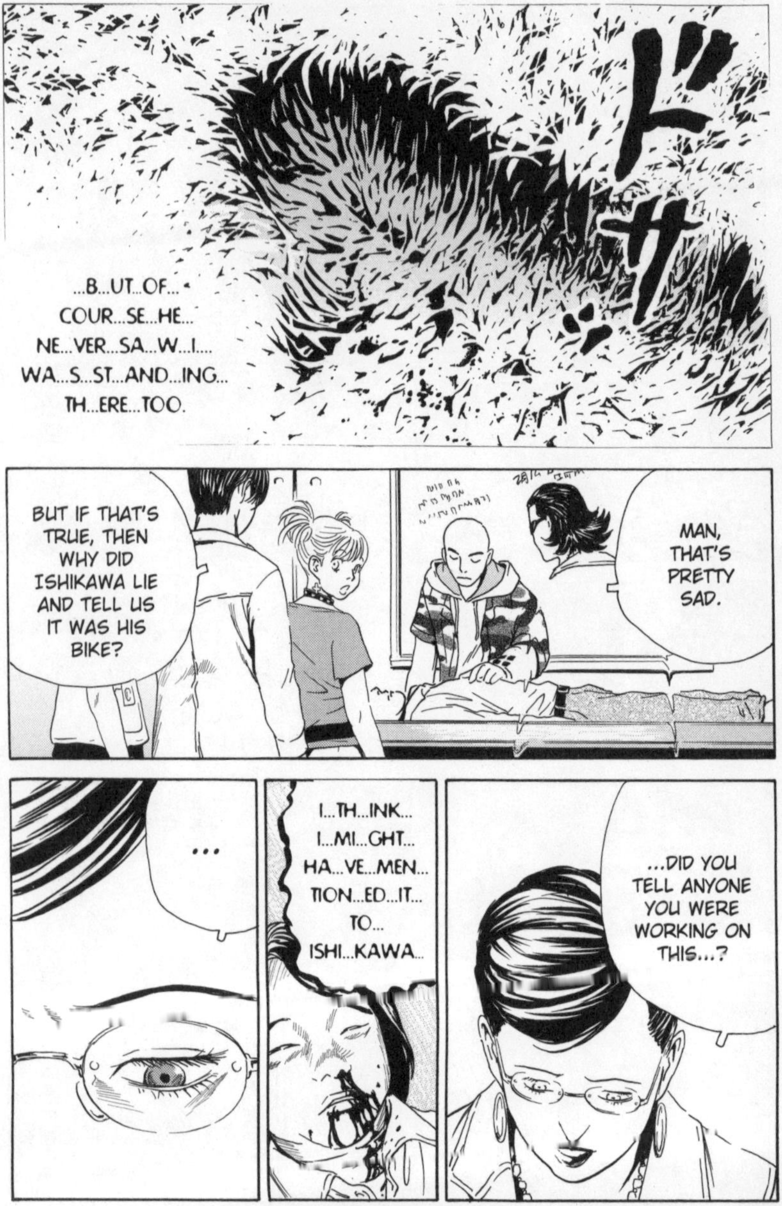
ドサッ
...B...UT...OF... COUR...SE...HE... NE...VER...SA...W...I... WA...S...ST...AND...ING... TH...ERE...TOO.
MAN, THAT'S PRETTY SAD.
BUT IF THAT'S TRUE, THEN WHY DID ISHIKAWA LIE AND TELL US IT WAS HIS BIKE?
...DID YOU TELL ANYONE YOU WERE WORKING ON THIS...?
I...TH...INK... I...MI...GHT... HA...VE...MEN... TION...ED...IT... TO... ISHI...KAWA...
...

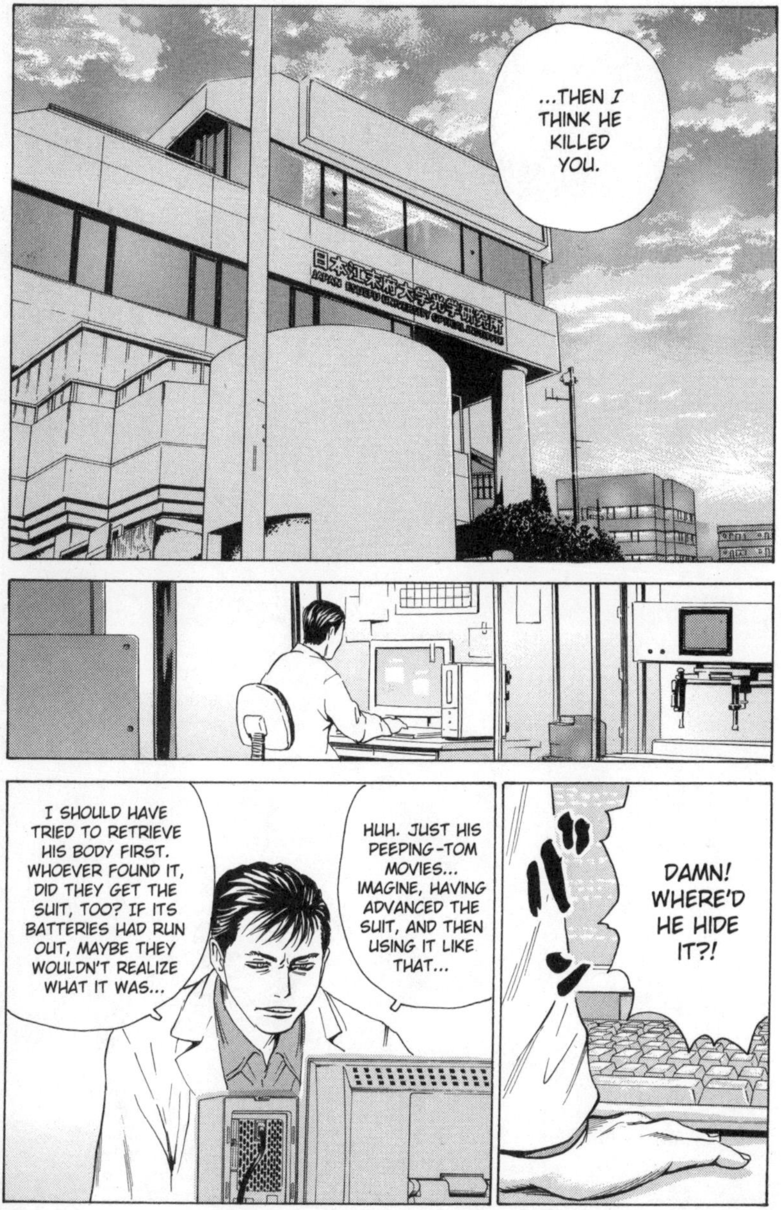
...THEN *I* THINK HE KILLED YOU.
DAMN! WHERE'D HE HIDE IT?!
HUH. JUST HIS PEEPING-TOM MOVIES... IMAGINE, HAVING ADVANCED THE SUIT, AND THEN USING IT LIKE THAT...
I SHOULD HAVE TRIED TO RETRIEVE HIS BODY FIRST. WHOEVER FOUND IT, DID THEY GET THE SUIT, TOO? IF ITS BATTERIES HAD RUN OUT, MAYBE THEY WOULDN'T REALIZE WHAT IT WAS...

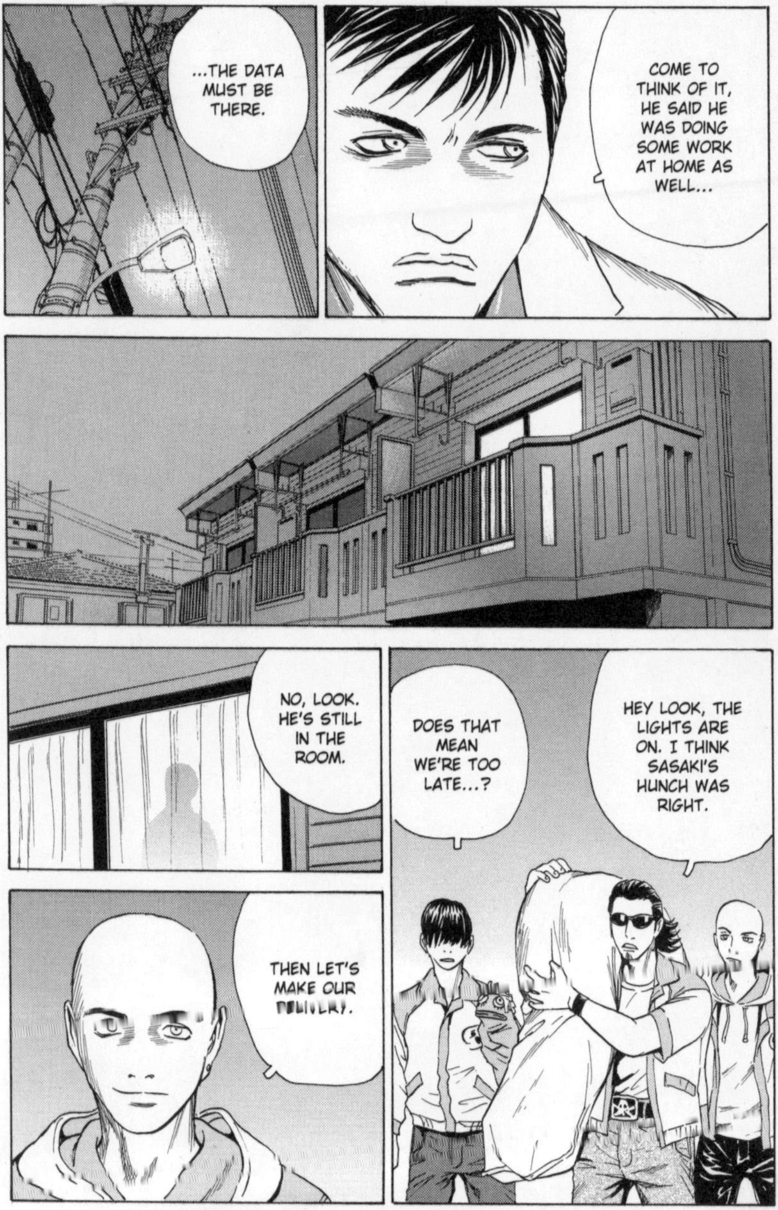
COME TO THINK OF IT, HE SAID HE WAS DOING SOME WORK AT HOME AS WELL...
...THE DATA MUST BE THERE.
HEY LOOK, THE LIGHTS ARE ON. I THINK SASAKI'S HUNCH WAS RIGHT.
DOES THAT MEAN WE'RE TOO LATE...?
NO, LOOK. HE'S STILL IN THE ROOM.
THEN LET'S MAKE OUR DELIVERY.

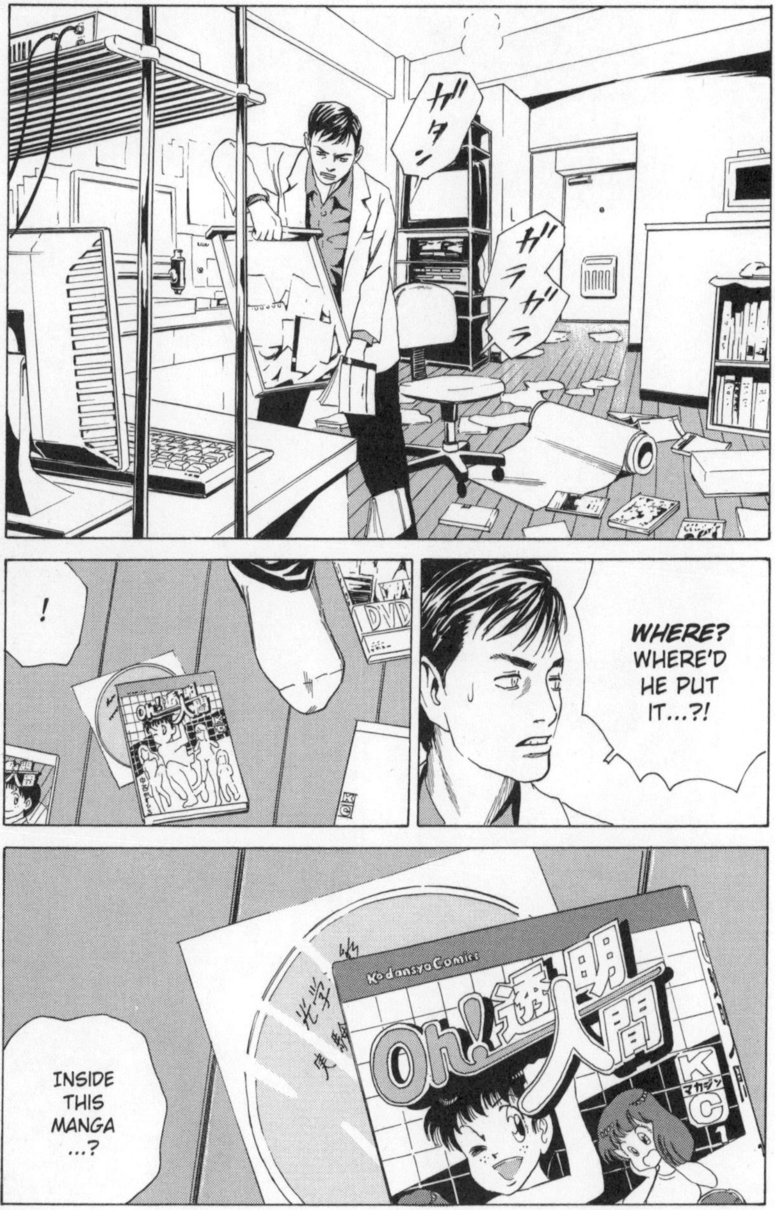
ガタン
ガラガラ
WHERE? WHERE'D HE PUT IT...?!
DVD
!
Kodansya Comics
Oh!透明人間
マガジン
KC
1
INSIDE THIS MANGA ...?

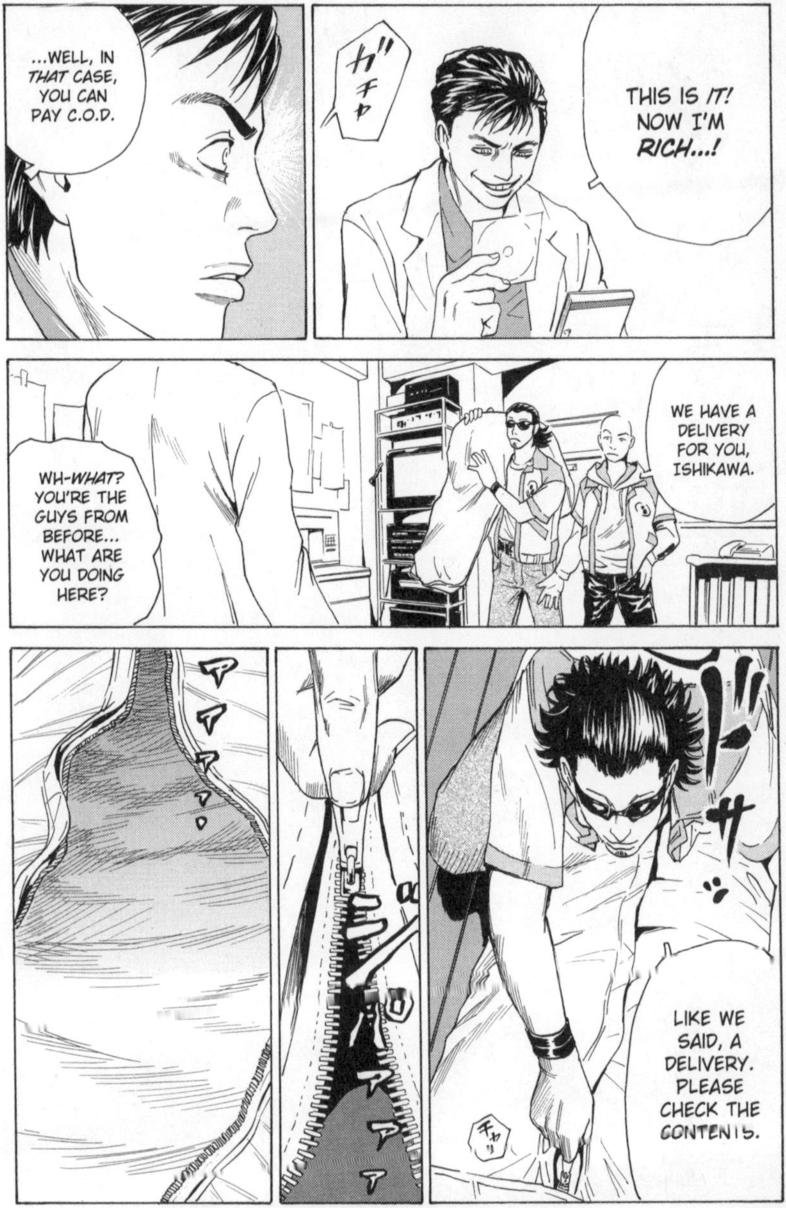
ガチャ
THIS IS *IT!* NOW I'M *RICH...!*
...WELL, IN *THAT* CASE, YOU CAN PAY C.O.D.
WE HAVE A DELIVERY FOR YOU, ISHIKAWA.
WH-*WHAT?* YOU'RE THE GUYS FROM BEFORE... WHAT ARE YOU DOING HERE?
LIKE WE SAID, A DELIVERY. PLEASE CHECK THE CONTENTS.
チャリ

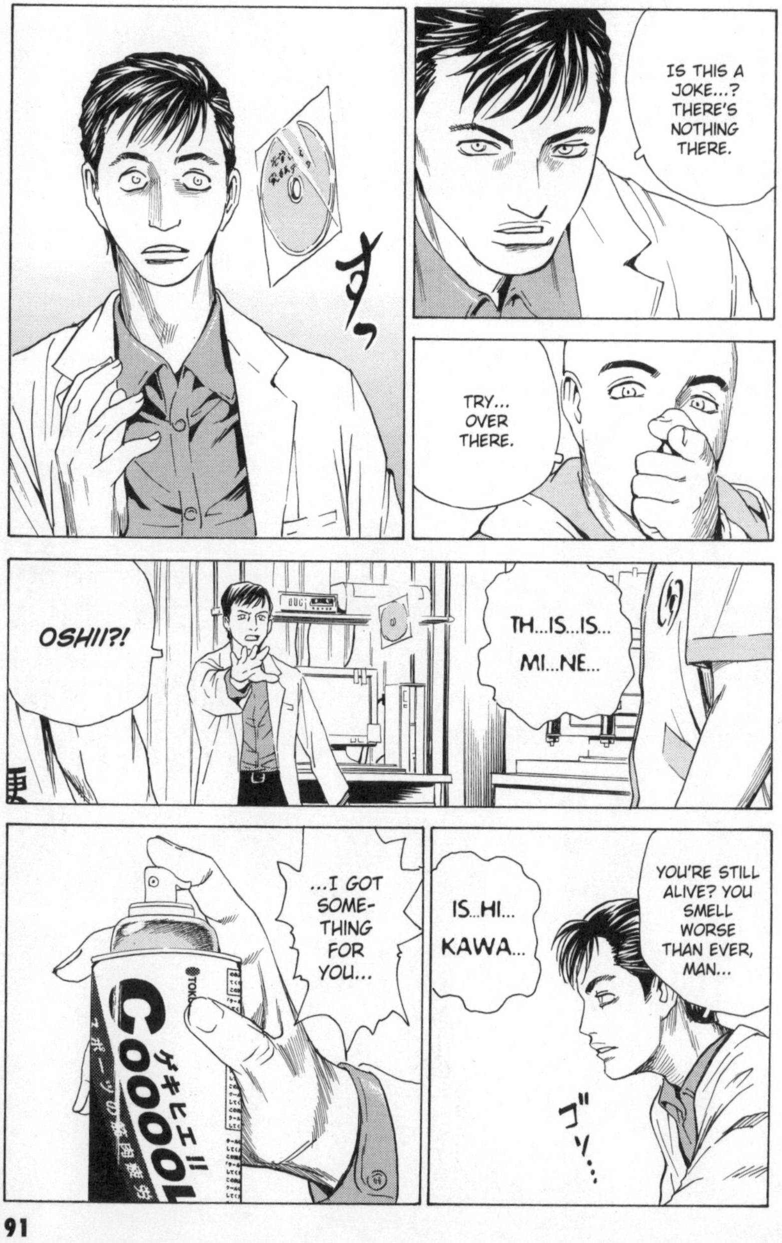
IS THIS A JOKE...? THERE'S NOTHING THERE.
TRY... OVER THERE.
すっ
TH...IS...IS... MI...NE...
OSHII?!
YOU'RE STILL ALIVE? YOU SMELL WORSE THAN EVER, MAN...
IS...HI... KAWA...
ゴソ...
...I GOT SOME-THING FOR YOU...

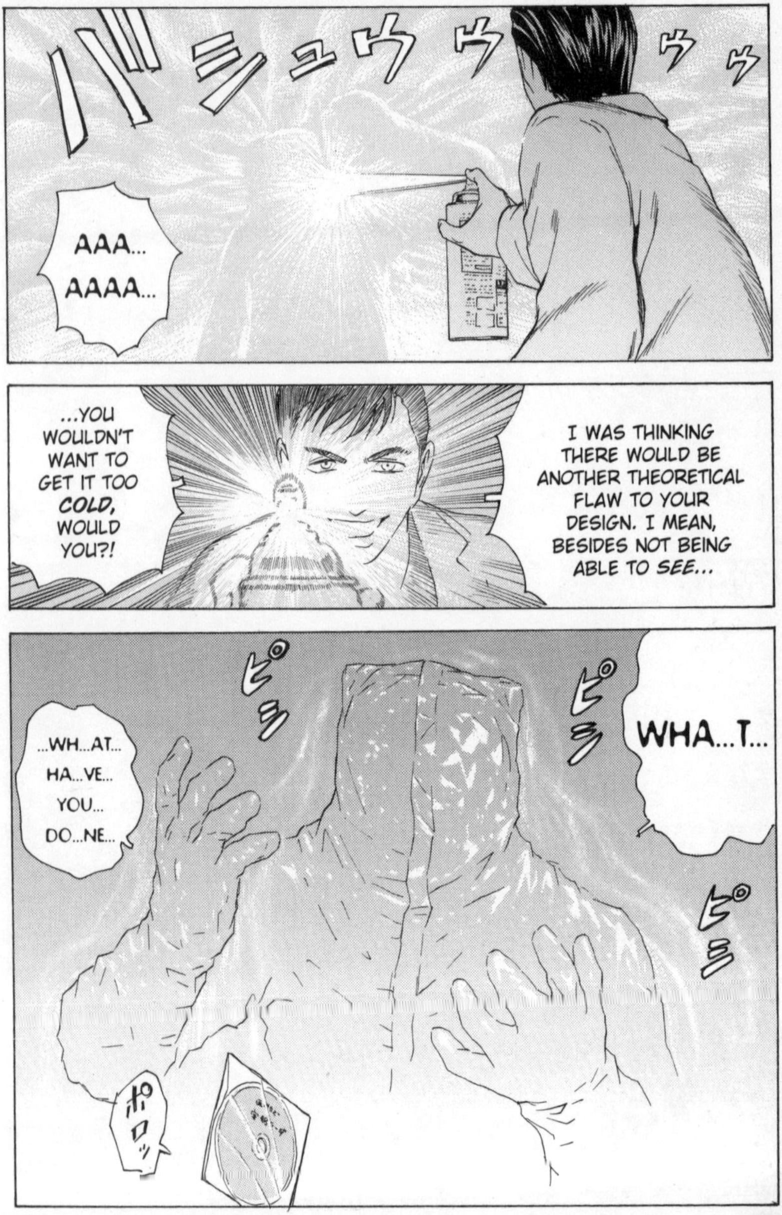

バシュウウゥゥ
AAA... AAAA...
I WAS THINKING THERE WOULD BE ANOTHER THEORETICAL FLAW TO YOUR DESIGN. I MEAN, BESIDES NOT BEING ABLE TO *SEE*...
...YOU WOULDN'T WANT TO GET IT TOO ***COLD,*** WOULD YOU?!
WHA...T...
ピシ
ピシ
ピシ
...WH...AT... HA...VE... YOU... DO...NE...
ポロッ

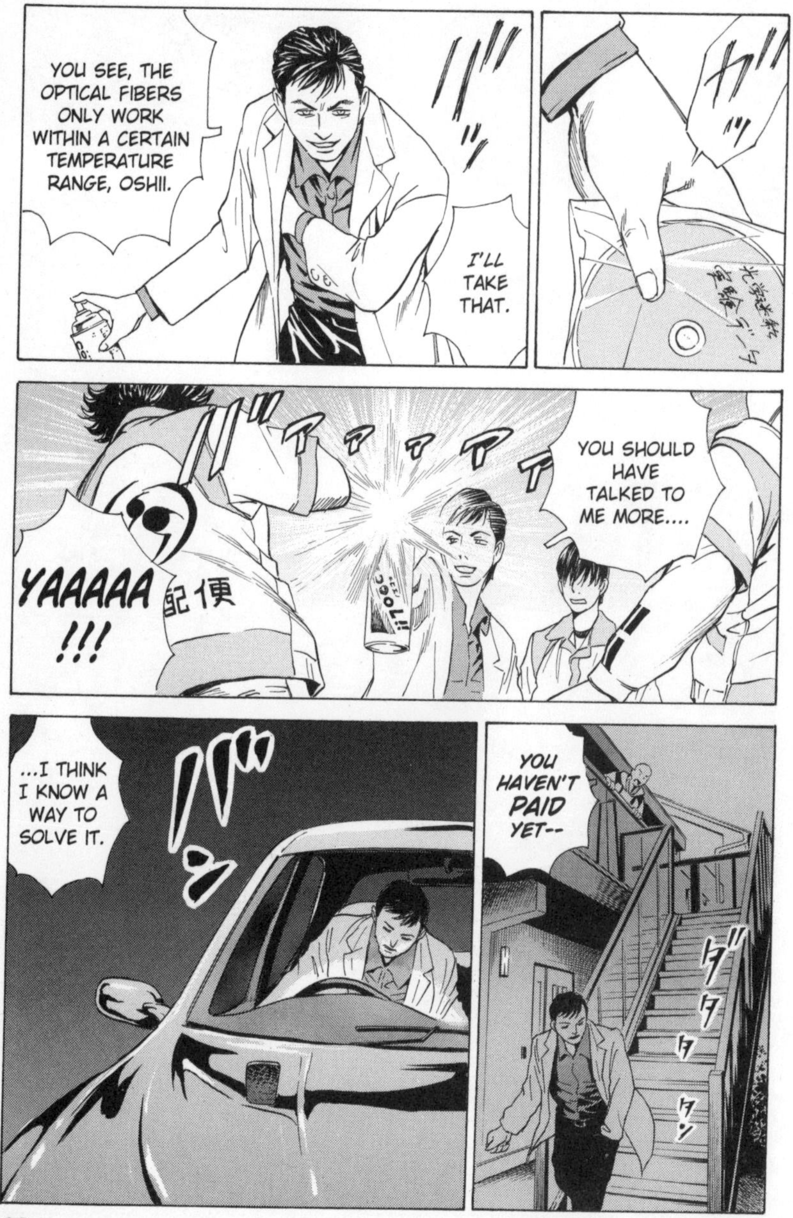
YOU SEE, THE OPTICAL FIBERS ONLY WORK WITHIN A CERTAIN TEMPERATURE RANGE, OSHII.
I'LL TAKE THAT.
YOU SHOULD HAVE TALKED TO ME MORE....
YAAAAA!!!
配便
YOU HAVEN'T PAID YET--
...I THINK I KNOW A WAY TO SOLVE IT.

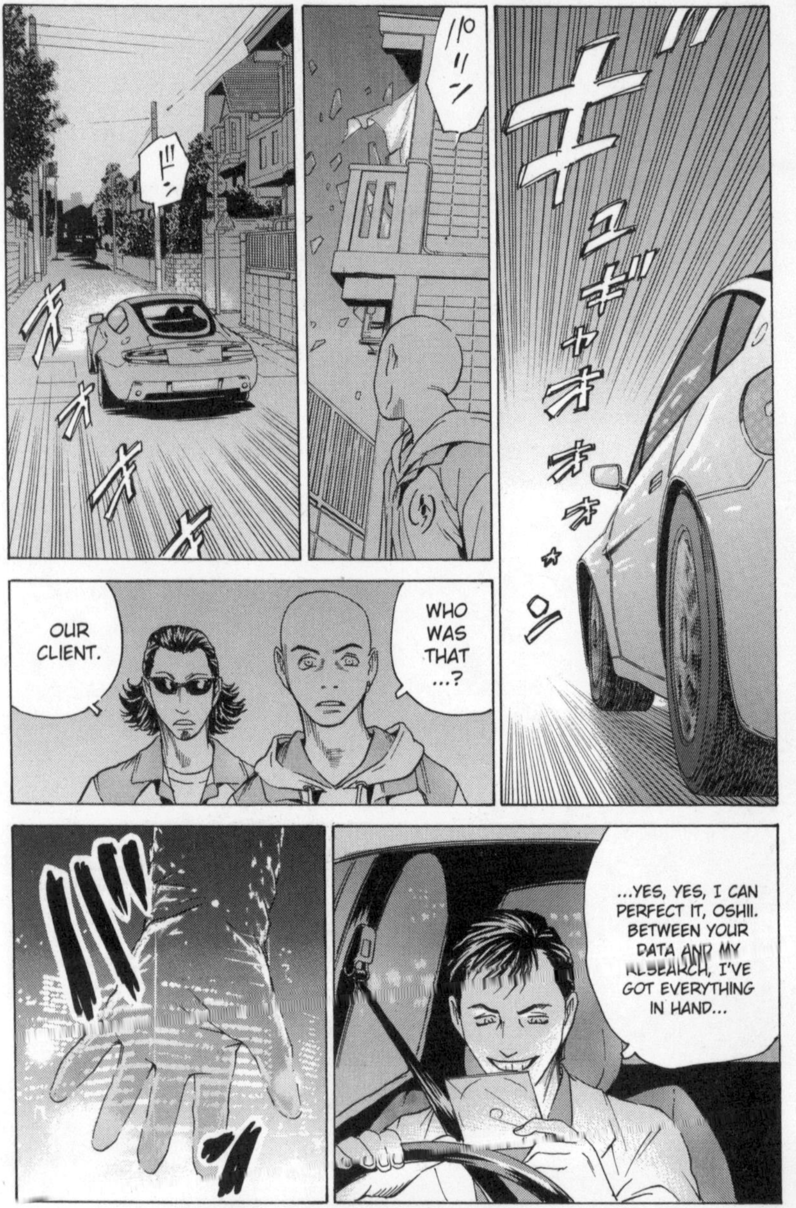
WHO WAS THAT ...?
OUR CLIENT.
...YES, YES, I CAN PERFECT IT, OSHII. BETWEEN YOUR DATA AND MY RESEARCH, I'VE GOT EVERYTHING IN HAND...

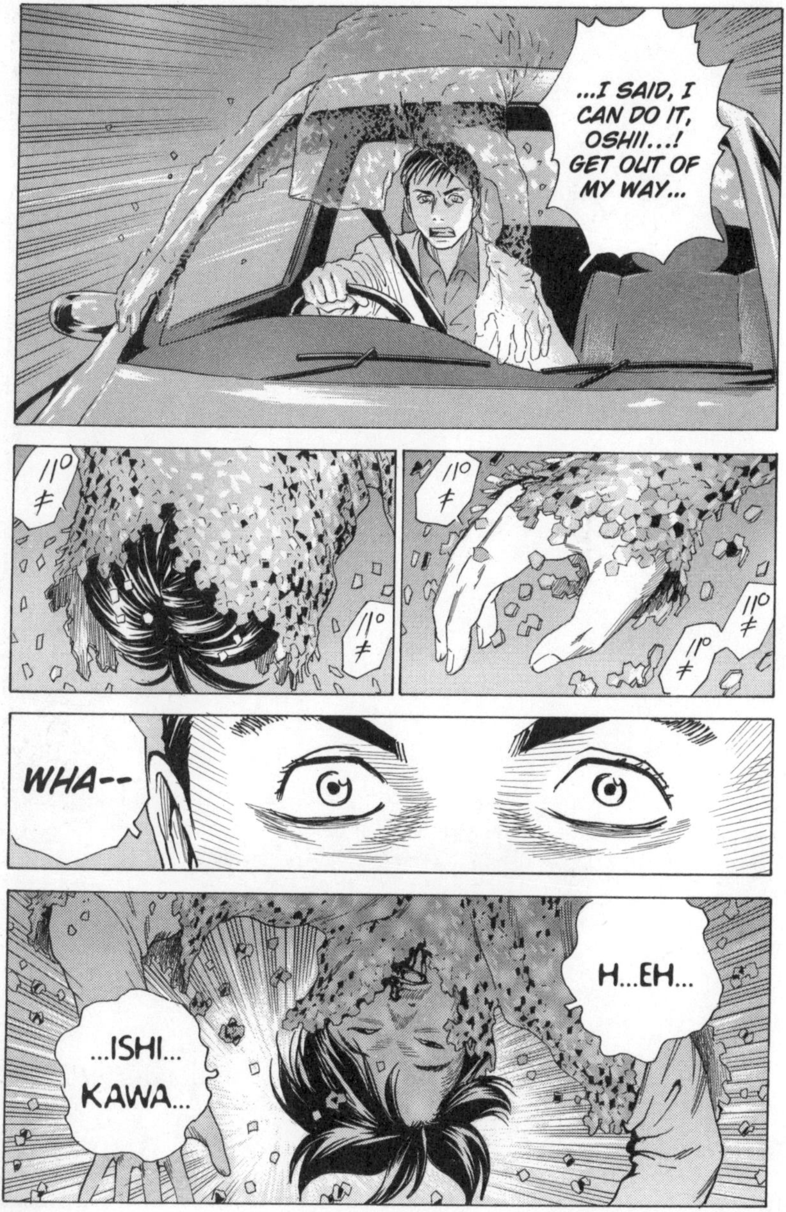
...I SAID, I CAN DO IT, OSHII...! GET OUT OF MY WAY...
パキ
パキ
パキ
パキ
パキ
WHA--
H...EH...
...ISHI... KAWA...

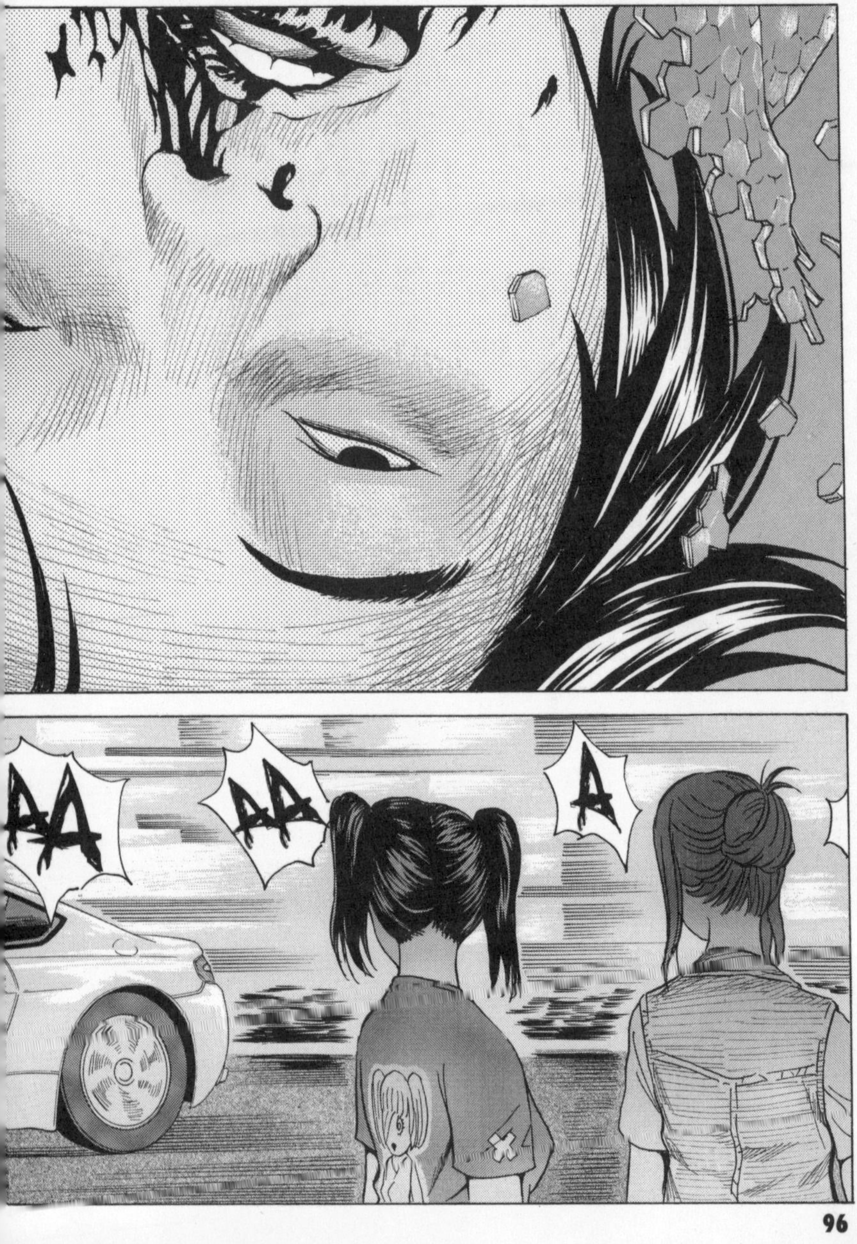
A
AA
AA

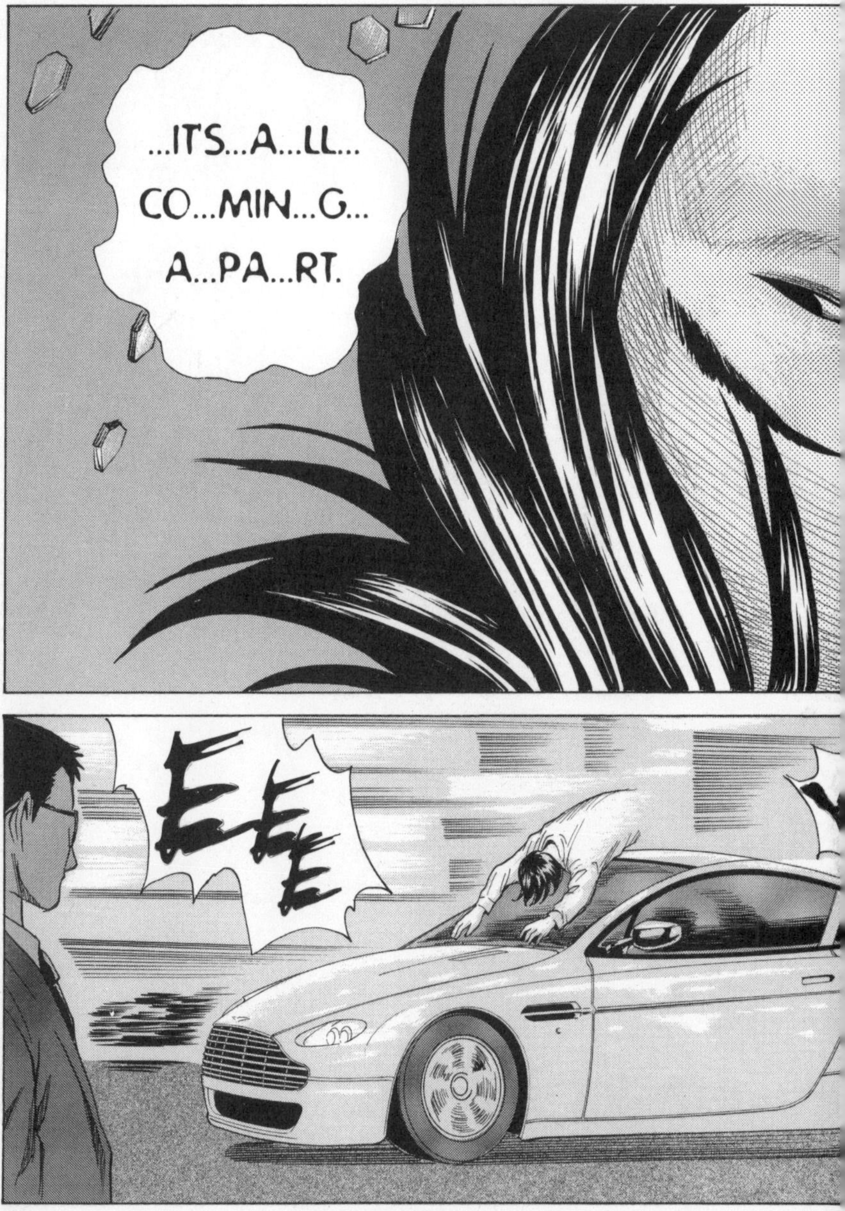
...ITS...A...LL... CO...MIN...G... A...PA...RT.
EEE

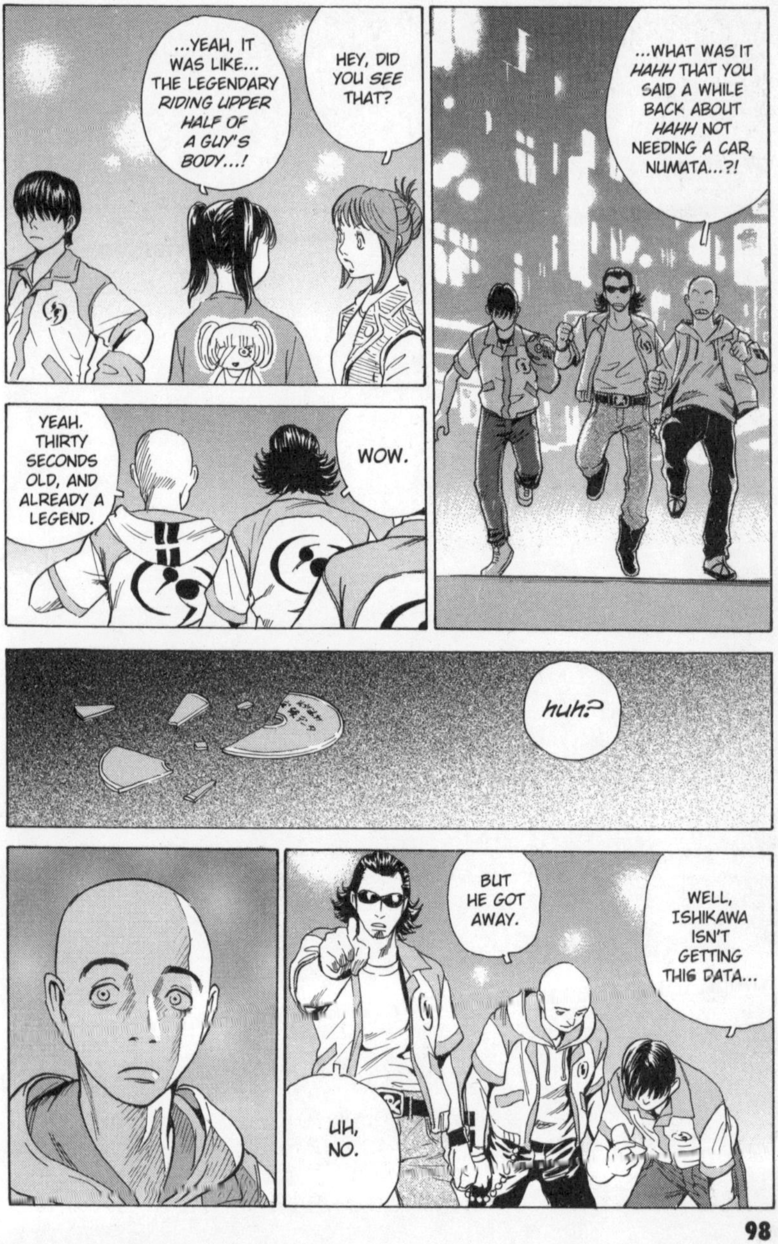
...WHAT WAS IT HAHH THAT YOU SAID A WHILE BACK ABOUT HAHH NOT NEEDING A CAR, NUMATA...?!
HEY, DID YOU SEE THAT?
...YEAH, IT WAS LIKE... THE LEGENDARY RIDING UPPER HALF OF A GUY'S BODY...!
WOW.
YEAH. THIRTY SECONDS OLD, AND ALREADY A LEGEND.
huh?
WELL, ISHIKAWA ISN'T GETTING THIS DATA...
BUT HE GOT AWAY.
UH, NO.

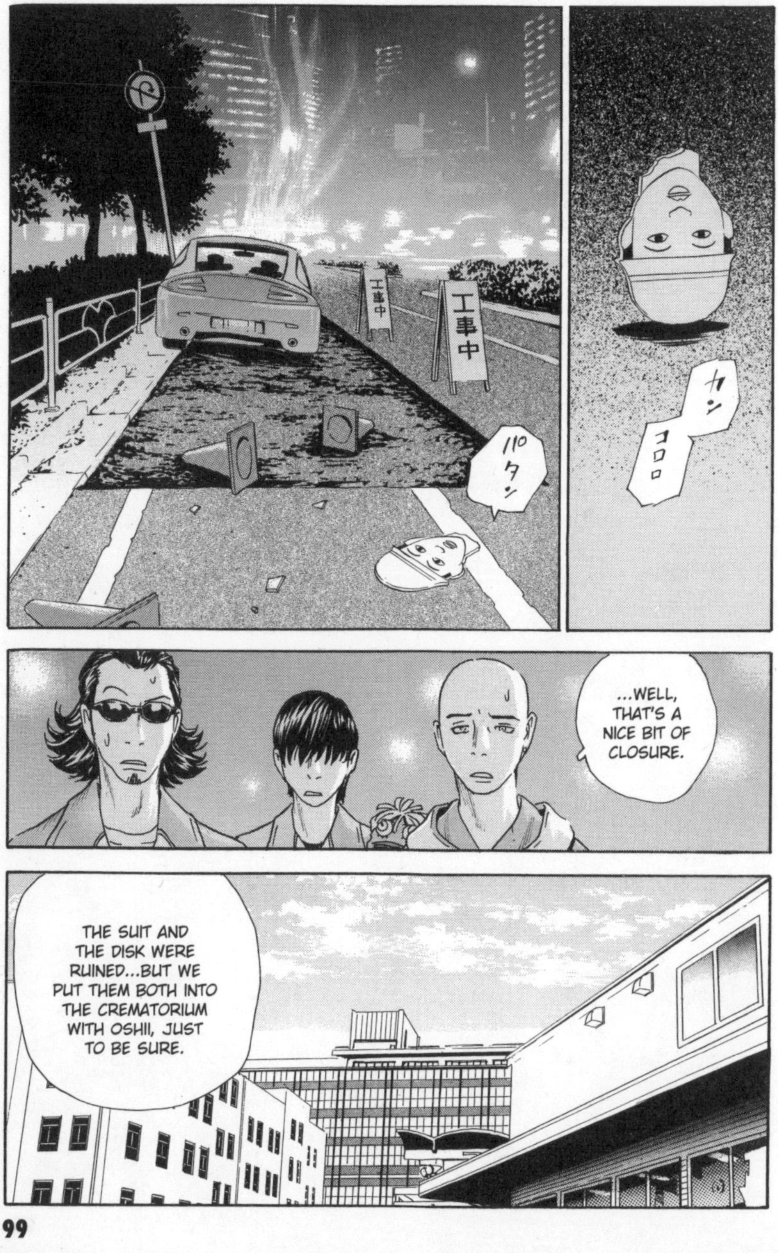

カン
コロロ
パタン
...WELL, THAT'S A NICE BIT OF CLOSURE.
THE SUIT AND THE DISK WERE RUINED...BUT WE PUT THEM BOTH INTO THE CREMATORIUM WITH OSHII, JUST TO BE SURE.

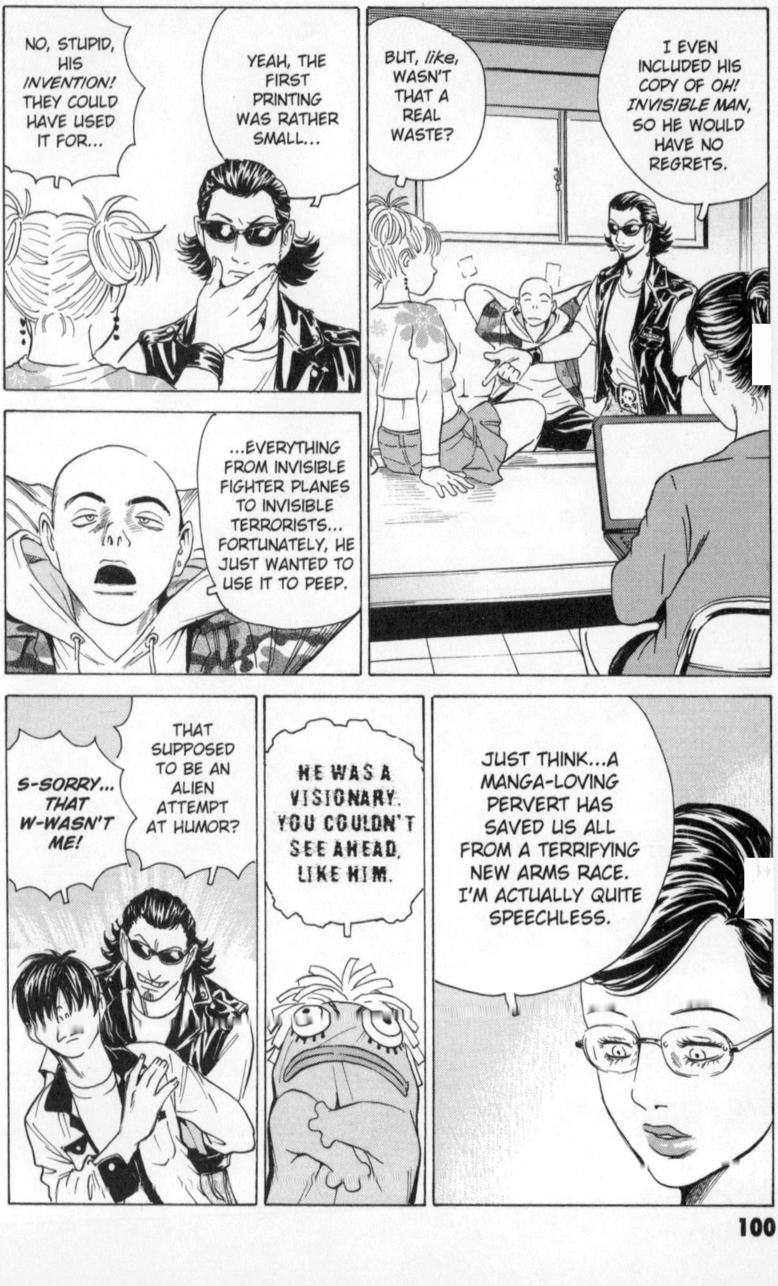
I EVEN INCLUDED HIS COPY OF OH! INVISIBLE MAN, SO HE WOULD HAVE NO REGRETS.
BUT, like, WASN'T THAT A REAL WASTE?
YEAH, THE FIRST PRINTING WAS RATHER SMALL...
NO, STUPID, HIS INVENTION! THEY COULD HAVE USED IT FOR...
...EVERYTHING FROM INVISIBLE FIGHTER PLANES TO INVISIBLE TERRORISTS... FORTUNATELY, HE JUST WANTED TO USE IT TO PEEP.
JUST THINK...A MANGA-LOVING PERVERT HAS SAVED US ALL FROM A TERRIFYING NEW ARMS RACE. I'M ACTUALLY QUITE SPEECHLESS.
HE WAS A VISIONARY. YOU COULDN'T SEE AHEAD, LIKE HIM.
THAT SUPPOSED TO BE AN ALIEN ATTEMPT AT HUMOR?
S-SORRY... THAT W-WASN'T ME!

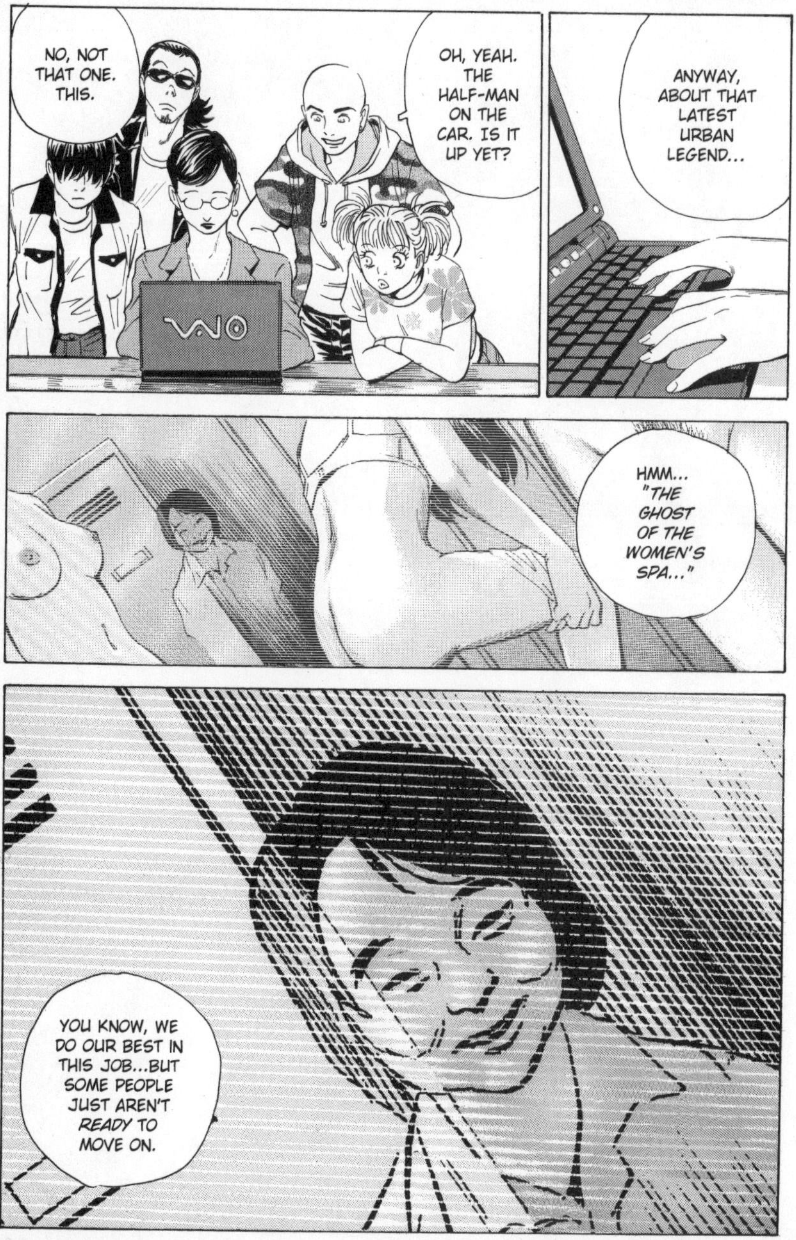
ANYWAY, ABOUT THAT LATEST URBAN LEGEND...
OH, YEAH. THE HALF-MAN ON THE CAR. IS IT UP YET?
NO, NOT THAT ONE. THIS.
HMM... "THE GHOST OF THE WOMEN'S SPA..."
YOU KNOW, WE DO OUR BEST IN THIS JOB...BUT SOME PEOPLE JUST AREN'T *READY* TO MOVE ON.

4th delivery: tears that disappear into the sand—the end

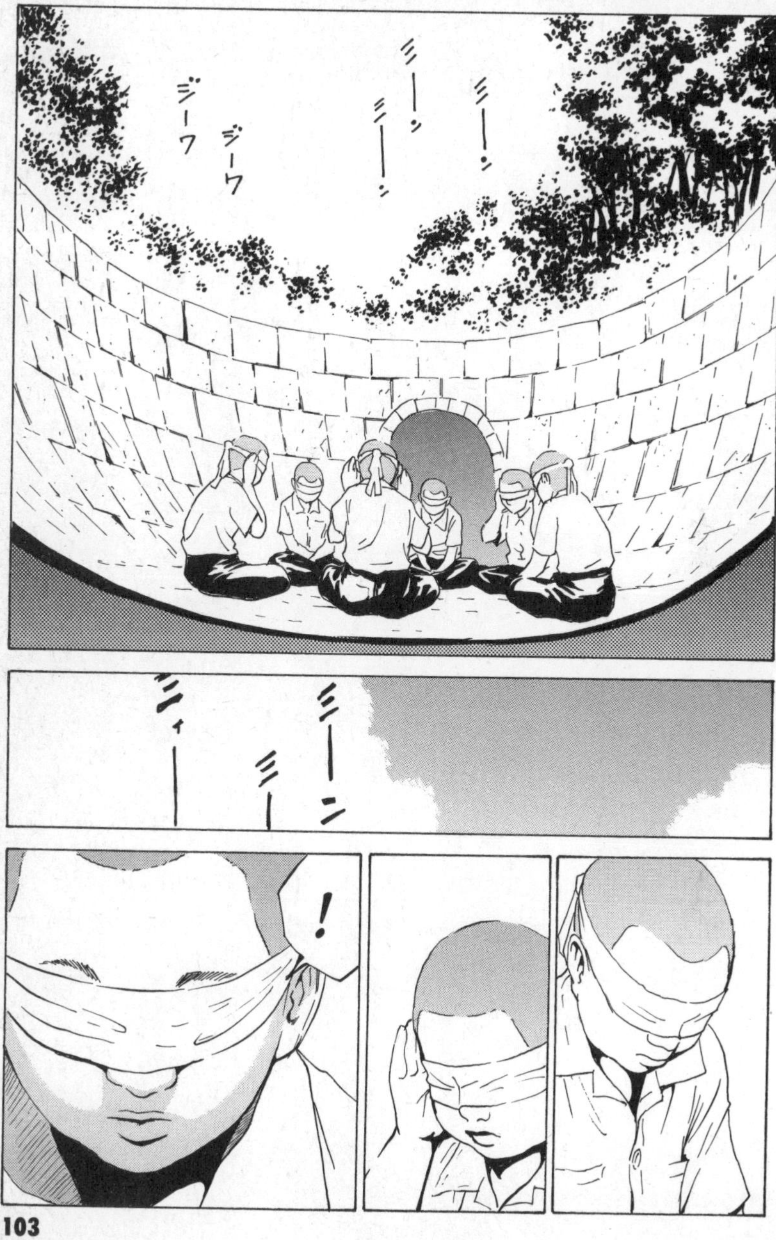
ミーン
ミーーン
ジーワ
ジーワ
ミーン
ミー
ミィー
!

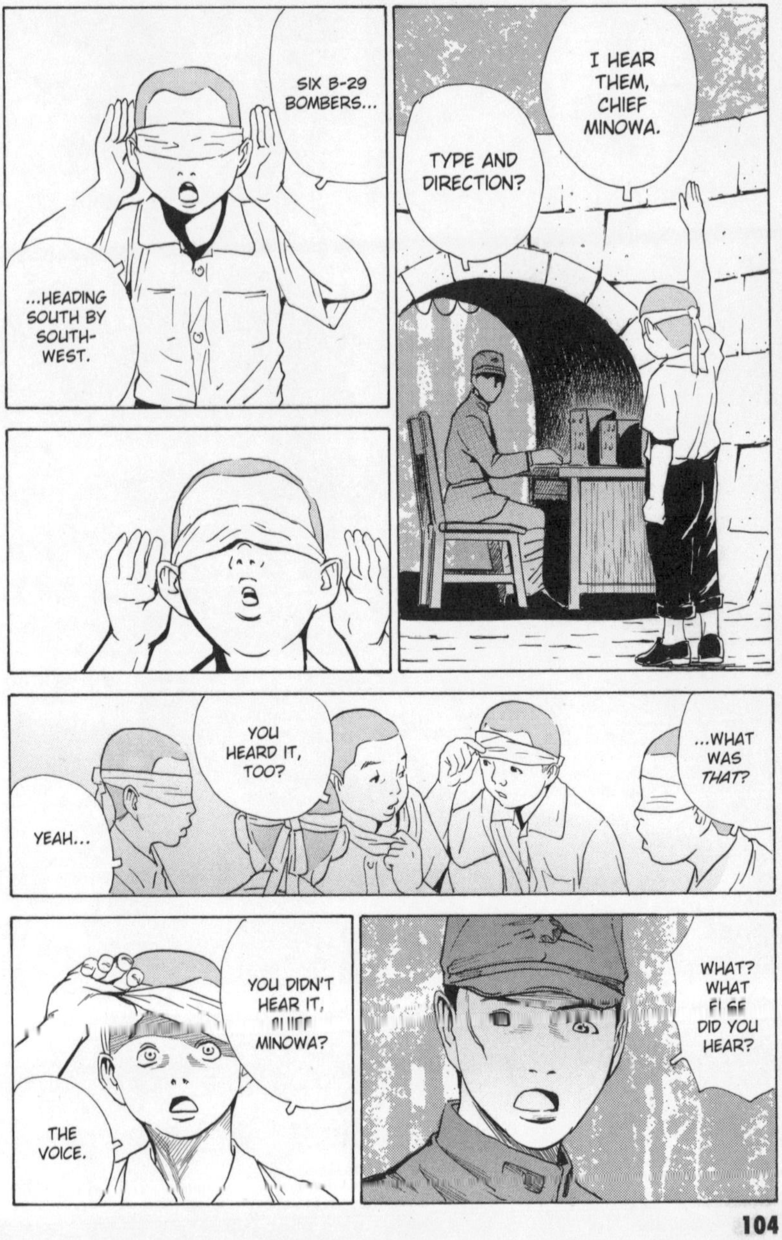
I HEAR THEM, CHIEF MINOWA.
TYPE AND DIRECTION?
SIX B-29 BOMBERS...
...HEADING SOUTH BY SOUTH-WEST.
...WHAT WAS *THAT*?
YOU HEARD IT, TOO?
YEAH...
WHAT? WHAT ELSE DID YOU HEAR?
YOU DIDN'T HEAR IT, CHIEF MINOWA?
THE VOICE.

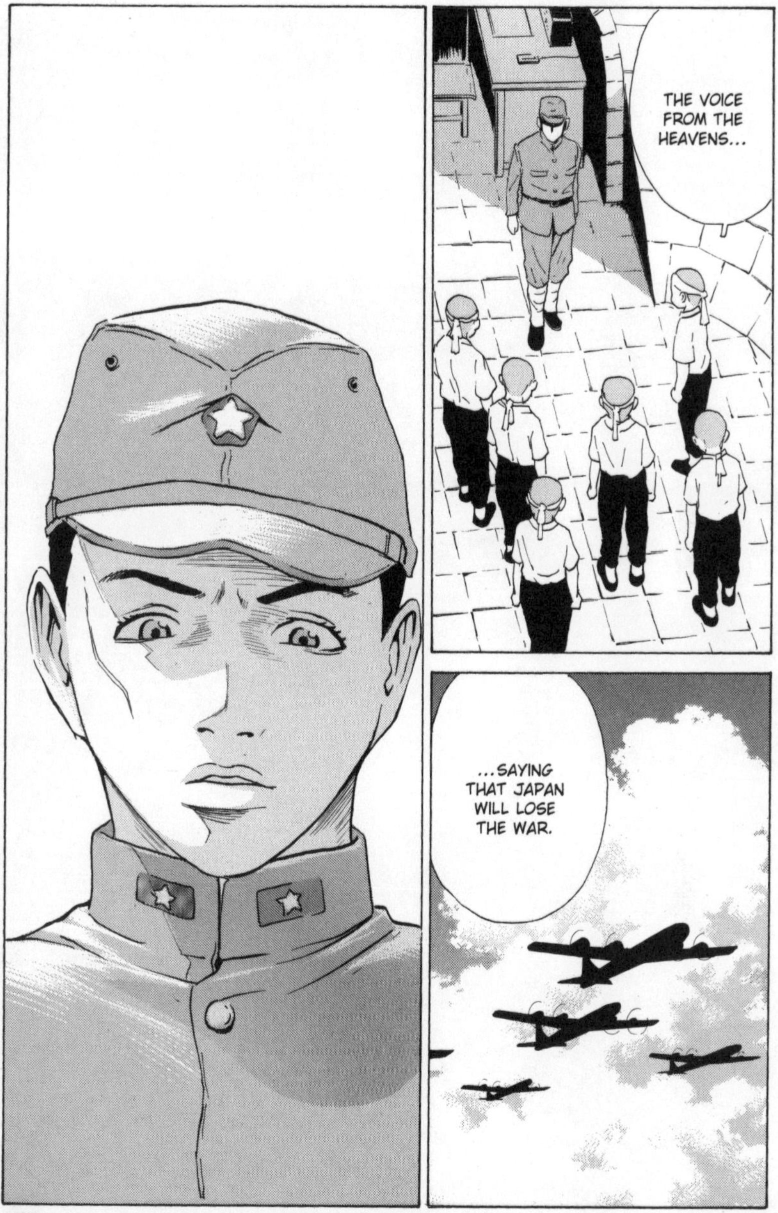
THE VOICE FROM THE HEAVENS...
...SAYING THAT JAPAN WILL LOSE THE WAR.

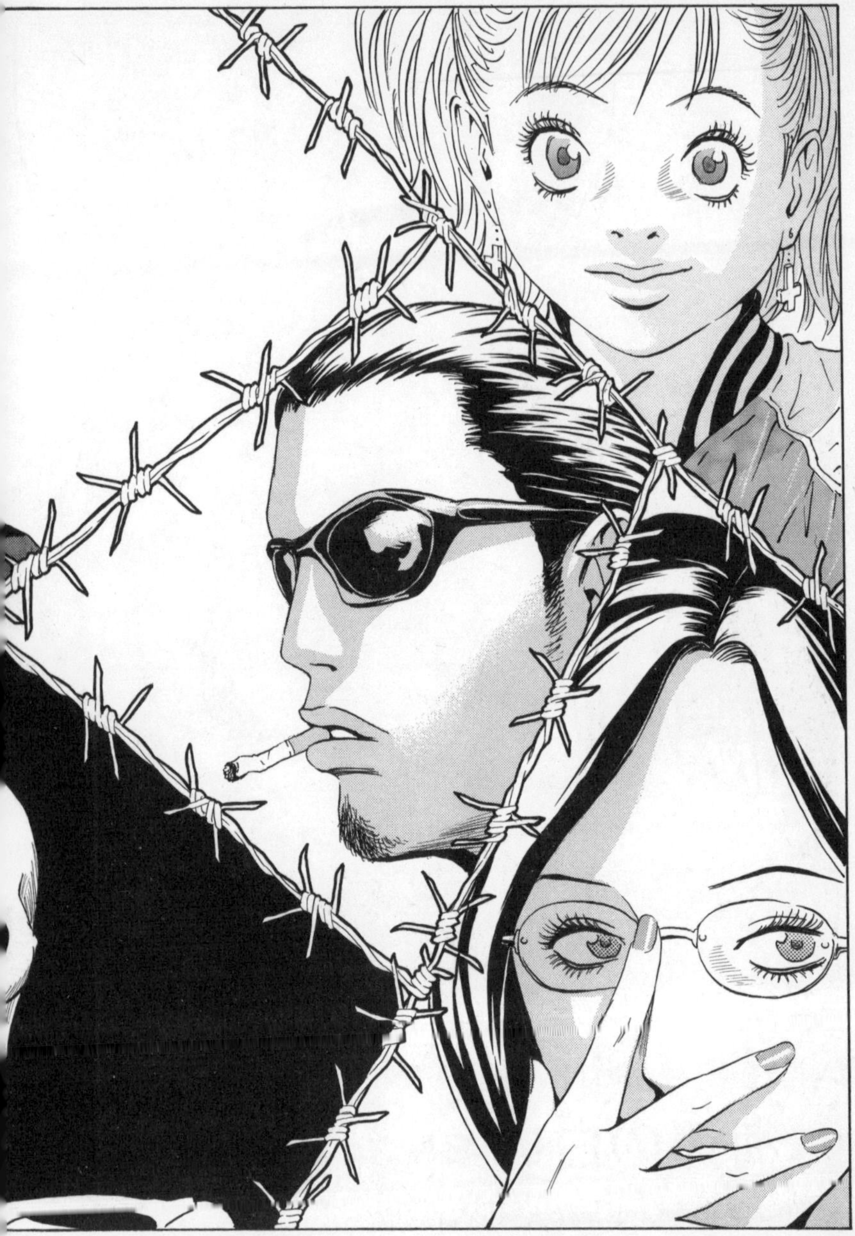

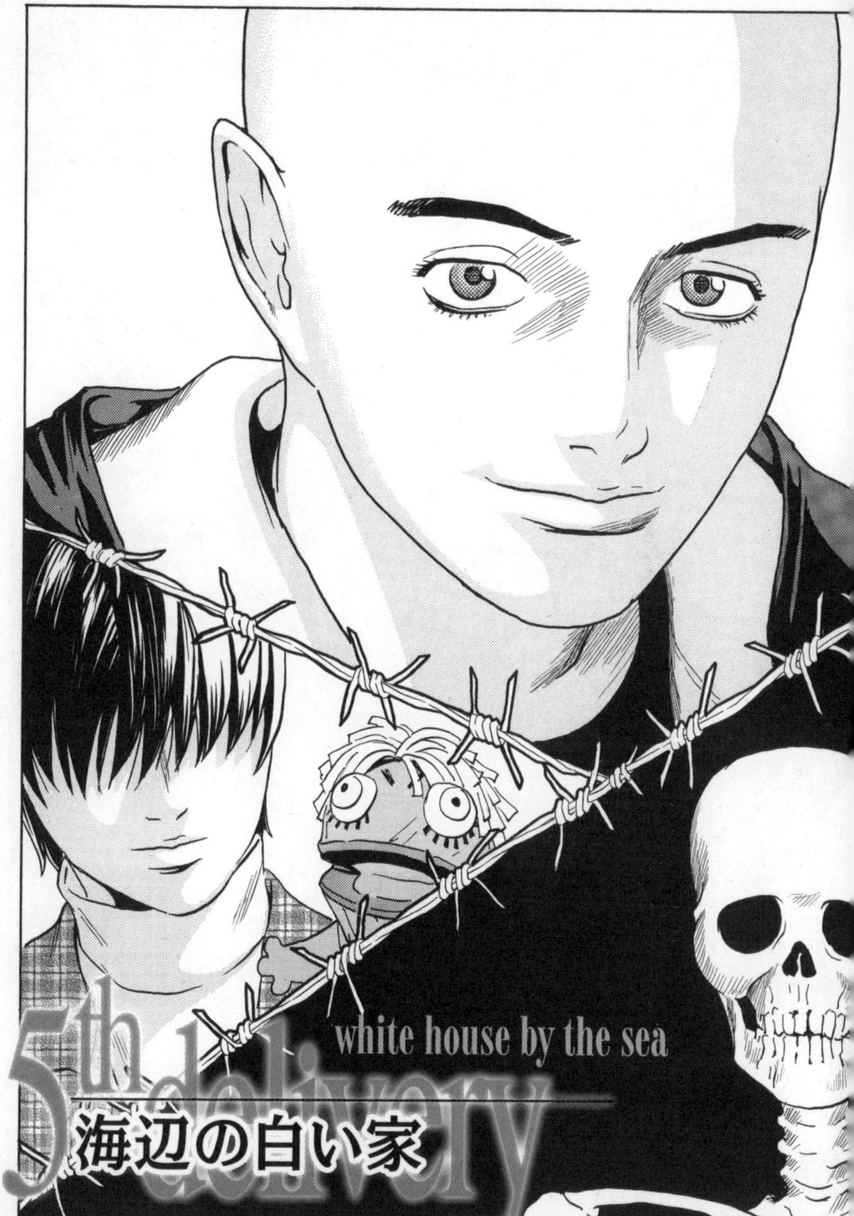
5th delivery
white house by the sea
海辺の白い家

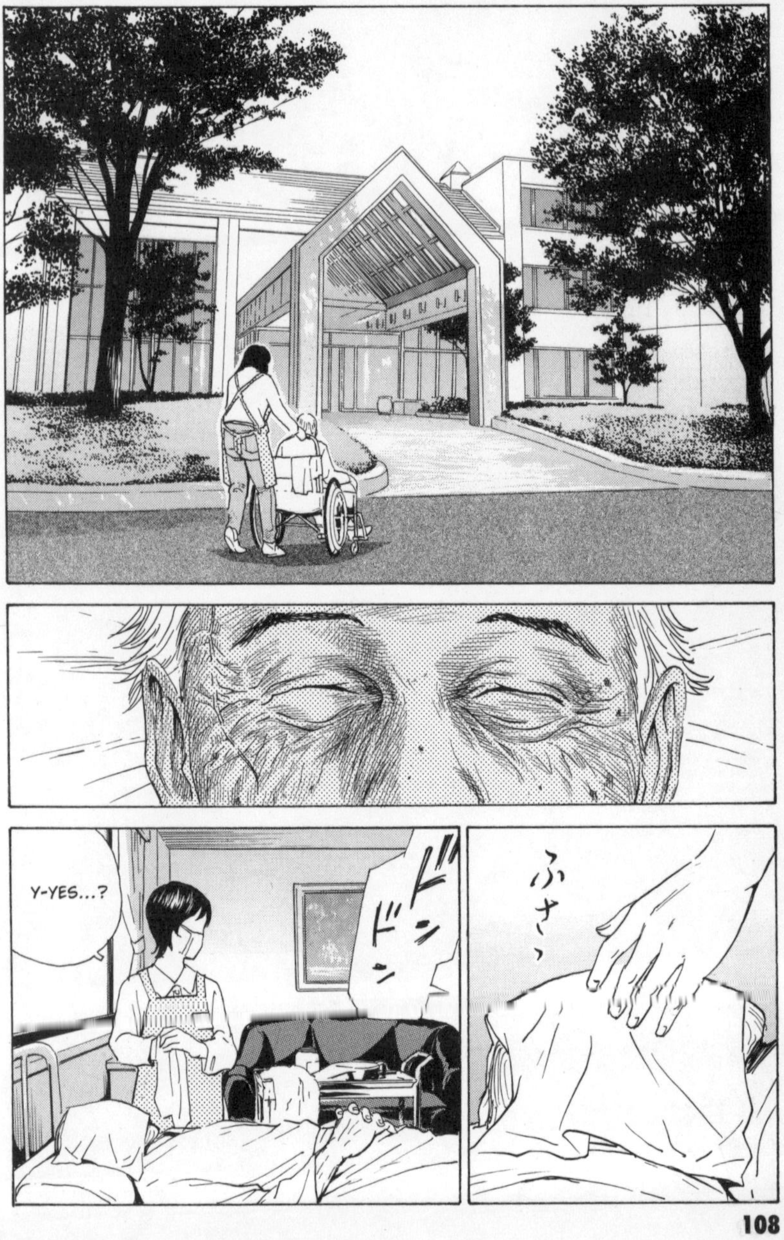
ふさっ
ドンドン
Y-YES...?

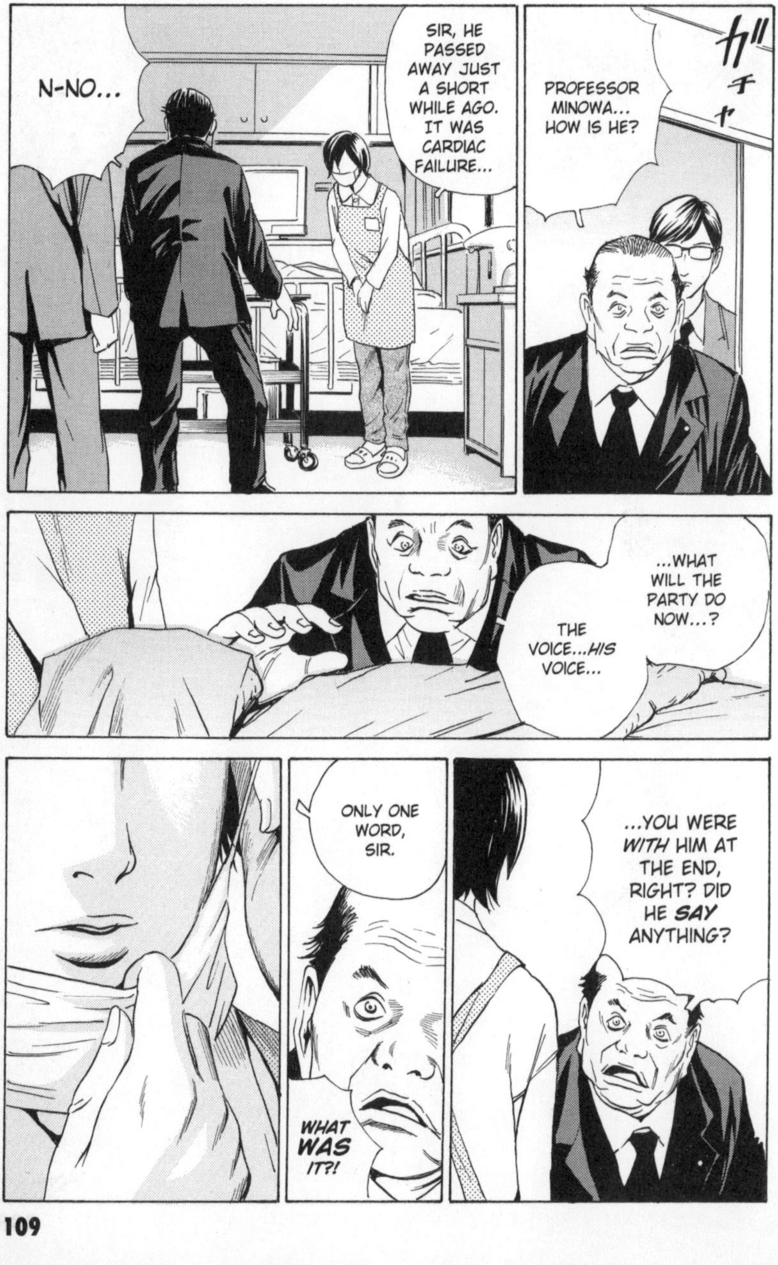
ガチャ
PROFESSOR MINOWA... HOW IS HE?
SIR, HE PASSED AWAY JUST A SHORT WHILE AGO. IT WAS CARDIAC FAILURE...
N-NO...
...WHAT WILL THE PARTY DO NOW...?
THE VOICE...*HIS* VOICE...
...YOU WERE *WITH* HIM AT THE END, RIGHT? DID HE **SAY** ANYTHING?
ONLY ONE WORD, SIR.
WHAT **WAS** *IT?!*

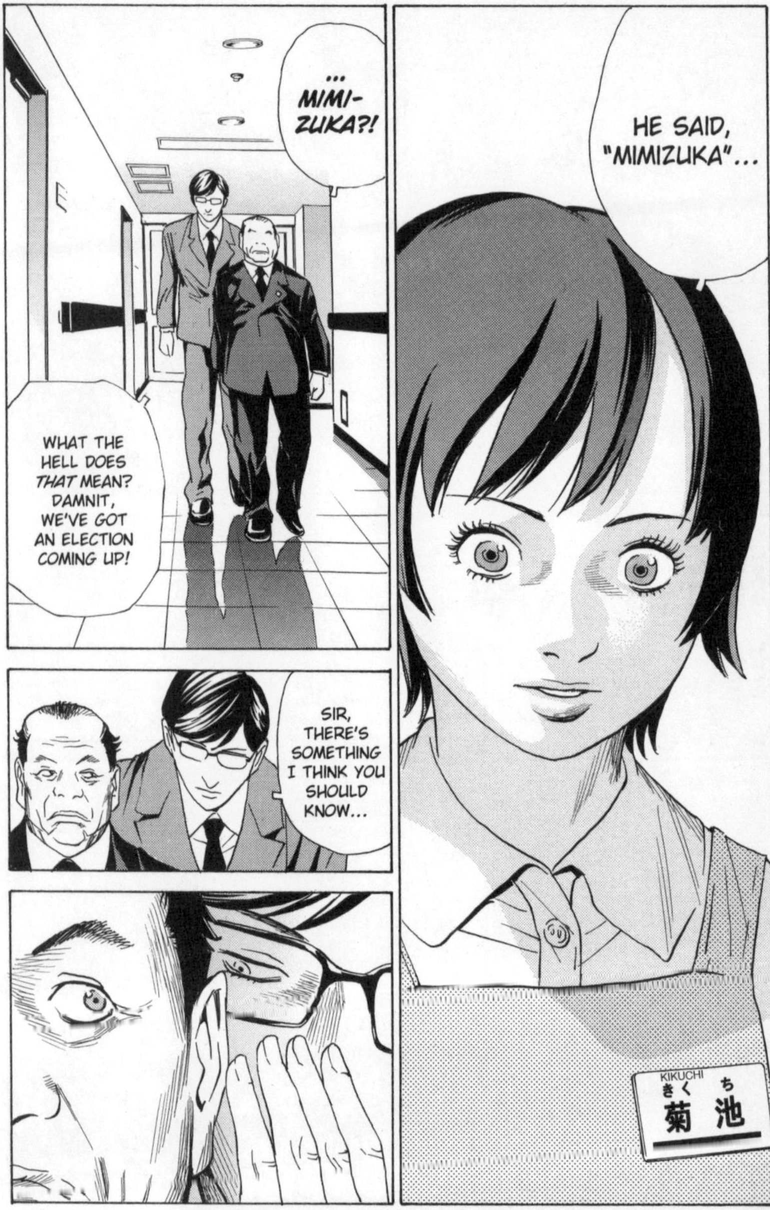
HE SAID, "MIMIZUKA"...
KIKUCHI
きくち
菊池
...MIMI-ZUKA?!
WHAT THE HELL DOES THAT MEAN? DAMNIT, WE'VE GOT AN ELECTION COMING UP!
SIR, THERE'S SOMETHING I THINK YOU SHOULD KNOW...

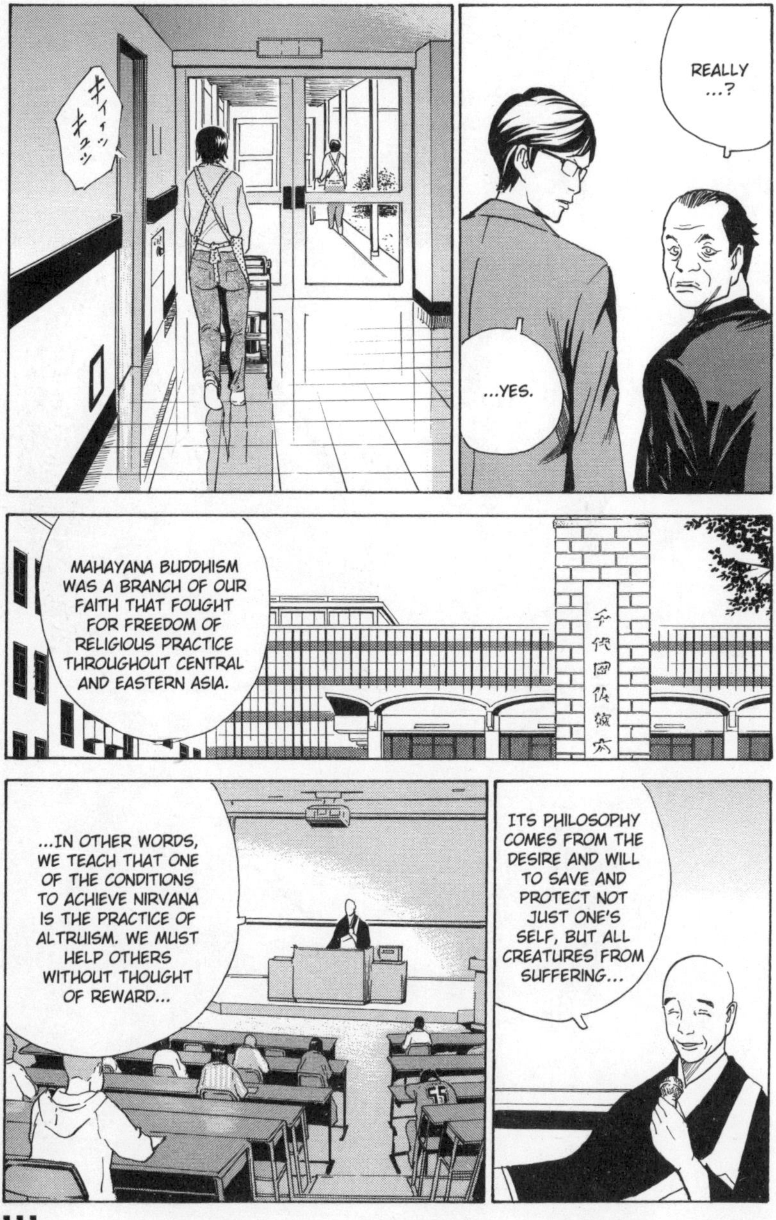
REALLY ...?
...YES.
キイィッ
キュッ
MAHAYANA BUDDHISM WAS A BRANCH OF OUR FAITH THAT FOUGHT FOR FREEDOM OF RELIGIOUS PRACTICE THROUGHOUT CENTRAL AND EASTERN ASIA.
ITS PHILOSOPHY COMES FROM THE DESIRE AND WILL TO SAVE AND PROTECT NOT JUST ONE'S SELF, BUT ALL CREATURES FROM SUFFERING...
...IN OTHER WORDS, WE TEACH THAT ONE OF THE CONDITIONS TO ACHIEVE NIRVANA IS THE PRACTICE OF ALTRUISM. WE MUST HELP OTHERS WITHOUT THOUGHT OF REWARD...

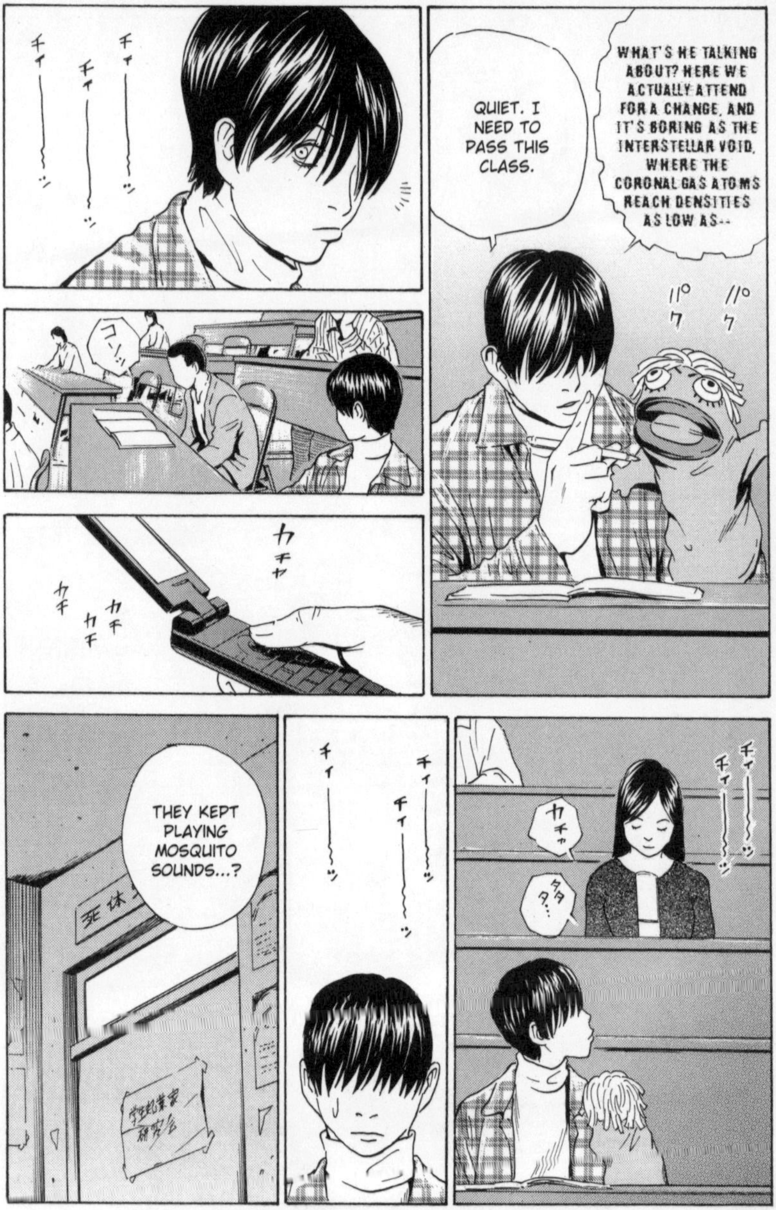
WHAT'S HE TALKING ABOUT? HERE WE ACTUALLY ATTEND FOR A CHANGE, AND IT'S BORING AS THE INTERSTELLAR VOID, WHERE THE CORONAL GAS ATOMS REACH DENSITIES AS LOW AS--
QUIET. I NEED TO PASS THIS CLASS.
パク パク
カチャ
カチ カチ カチ
カチャ
タタタ…
THEY KEPT PLAYING MOSQUITO SOUNDS...?

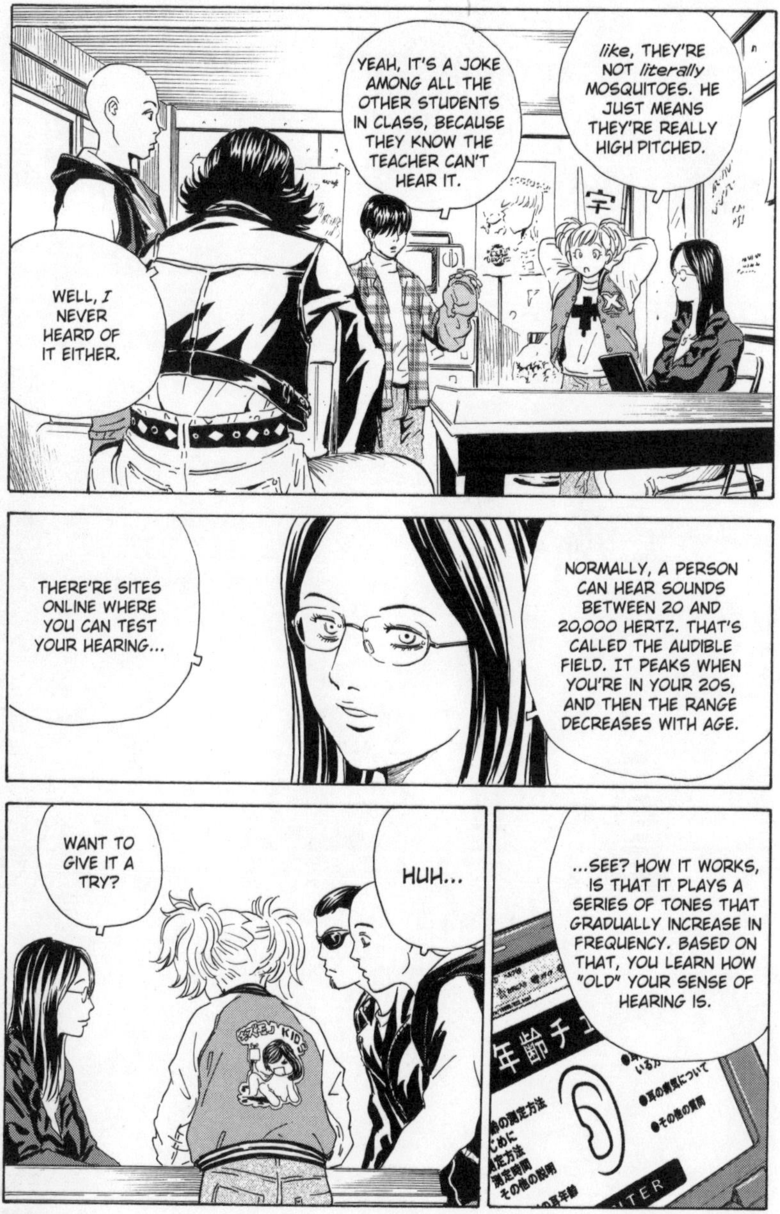

like, THEY'RE NOT *literally* MOSQUITOES. HE JUST MEANS THEY'RE REALLY HIGH PITCHED.
YEAH, IT'S A JOKE AMONG ALL THE OTHER STUDENTS IN CLASS, BECAUSE THEY KNOW THE TEACHER CAN'T HEAR IT.
WELL, *I* NEVER HEARD OF IT EITHER.
NORMALLY, A PERSON CAN HEAR SOUNDS BETWEEN 20 AND 20,000 HERTZ. THAT'S CALLED THE AUDIBLE FIELD. IT PEAKS WHEN YOU'RE IN YOUR 20S, AND THEN THE RANGE DECREASES WITH AGE.
THERE'RE SITES ONLINE WHERE YOU CAN TEST YOUR HEARING...
...SEE? HOW IT WORKS, IS THAT IT PLAYS A SERIES OF TONES THAT GRADUALLY INCREASE IN FREQUENCY. BASED ON THAT, YOU LEARN HOW "OLD" YOUR SENSE OF HEARING IS.
●耳の病気について
●その他の質問
HUH...
WANT TO GIVE IT A TRY?

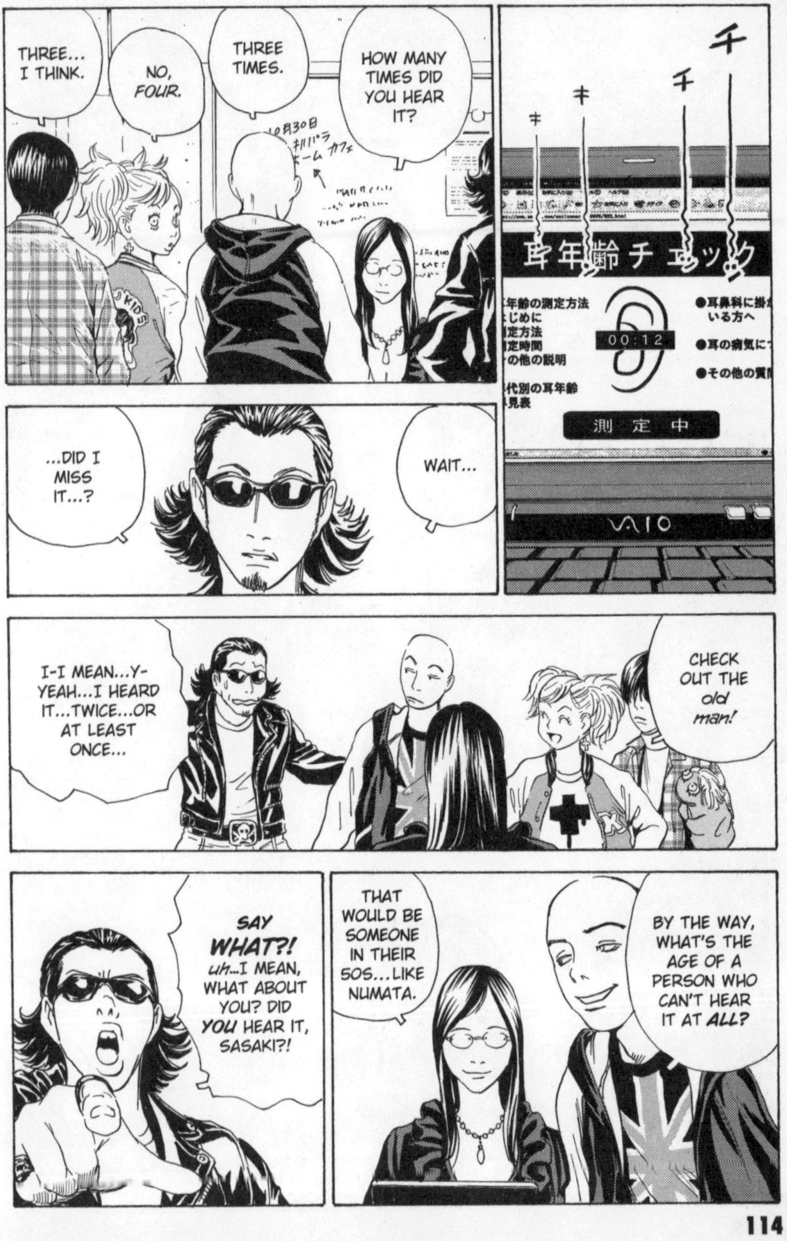
キ
キ
チ
チ
耳年齢チェック
00:12
測定中
VAIO
HOW MANY TIMES DID YOU HEAR IT?
THREE TIMES.
NO, FOUR.
THREE... I THINK.
WAIT...
...DID I MISS IT...?
CHECK OUT THE old man!
I-I MEAN...Y-YEAH...I HEARD IT...TWICE...OR AT LEAST ONCE...
BY THE WAY, WHAT'S THE AGE OF A PERSON WHO CAN'T HEAR IT AT ALL?
THAT WOULD BE SOMEONE IN THEIR 50S...LIKE NUMATA.
SAY WHAT?! uh...I MEAN, WHAT ABOUT YOU? DID YOU HEAR IT, SASAKI?!

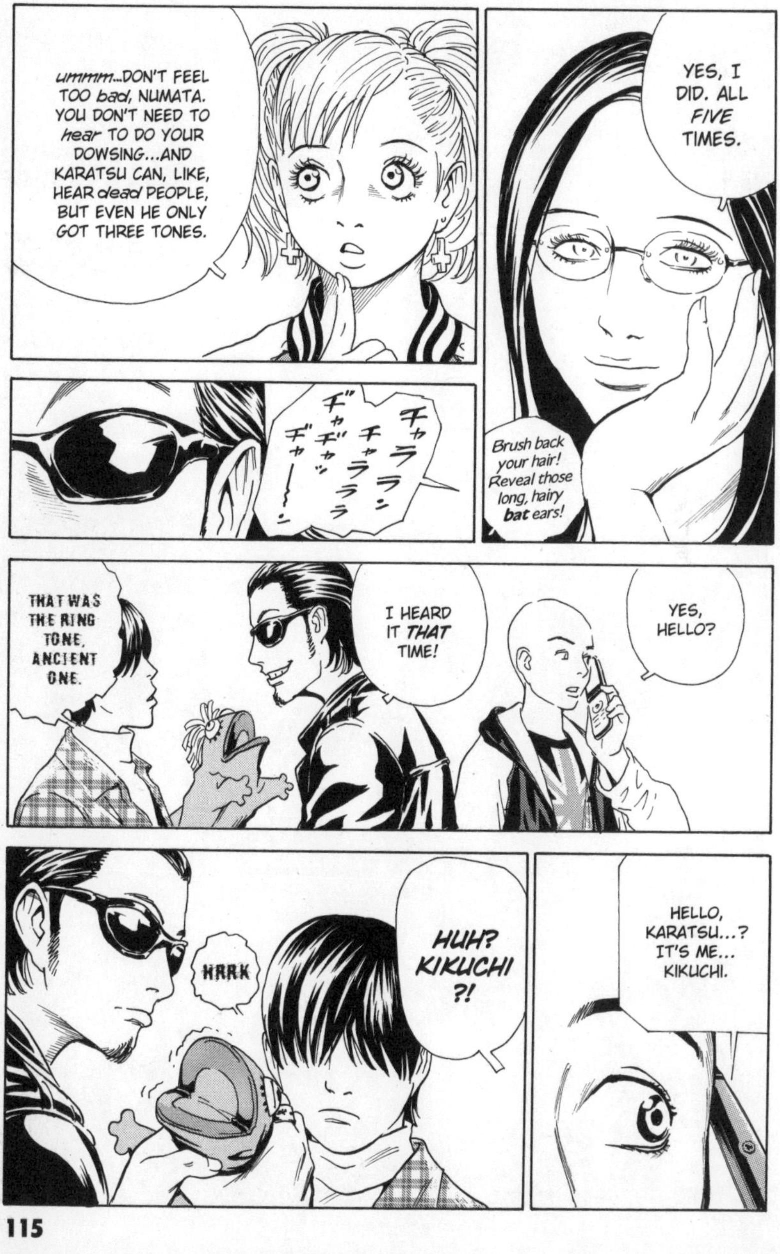
YES, I DID. ALL FIVE TIMES.
Brush back your hair! Reveal those long, hairy **bat** ears!
ummm...DON'T FEEL TOO *bad*, NUMATA. YOU DON'T NEED TO *hear* TO DO YOUR DOWSING...AND KARATSU CAN, LIKE, HEAR *dead* PEOPLE, BUT EVEN HE ONLY GOT THREE TONES.
チャララン チャラララ ヂャヂャッ ヂャー~~ン
YES, HELLO?
I HEARD IT *THAT* TIME!
THAT WAS THE RING TONE, ANCIENT ONE.
HELLO, KARATSU...? IT'S ME... KIKUCHI.
HUH? KIKUCHI?!
HRRK

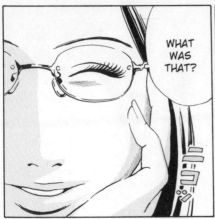

KIKUCHI... ISN'T SHE THE ONE FROM THAT BABY-DROP CASE...?
THAT NURSE THAT SEEMED TO HIT IT OFF WITH KARATSU...?
チラッ
WHAT WAS THAT?
ニコッ
W-WELL, WE DIDN'T MEAN TO INFER ANYTHING... OR IS THAT "IMPLY"...
I WAS *ASKING* WHAT THE CALL WAS ABOUT.
WELL... NOTHING REALLY... SHE WANTS TO SEE ME... I GUESS.
ピッ
She's never smiled like that before, Numata...
OH, HOW VERY NICE FOR YOU.
Don't look back. It could mean death.

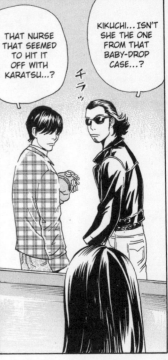

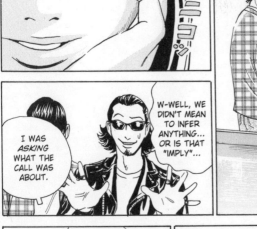

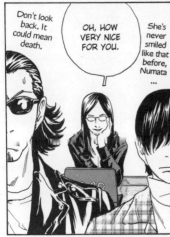

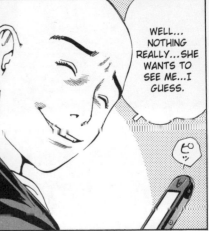

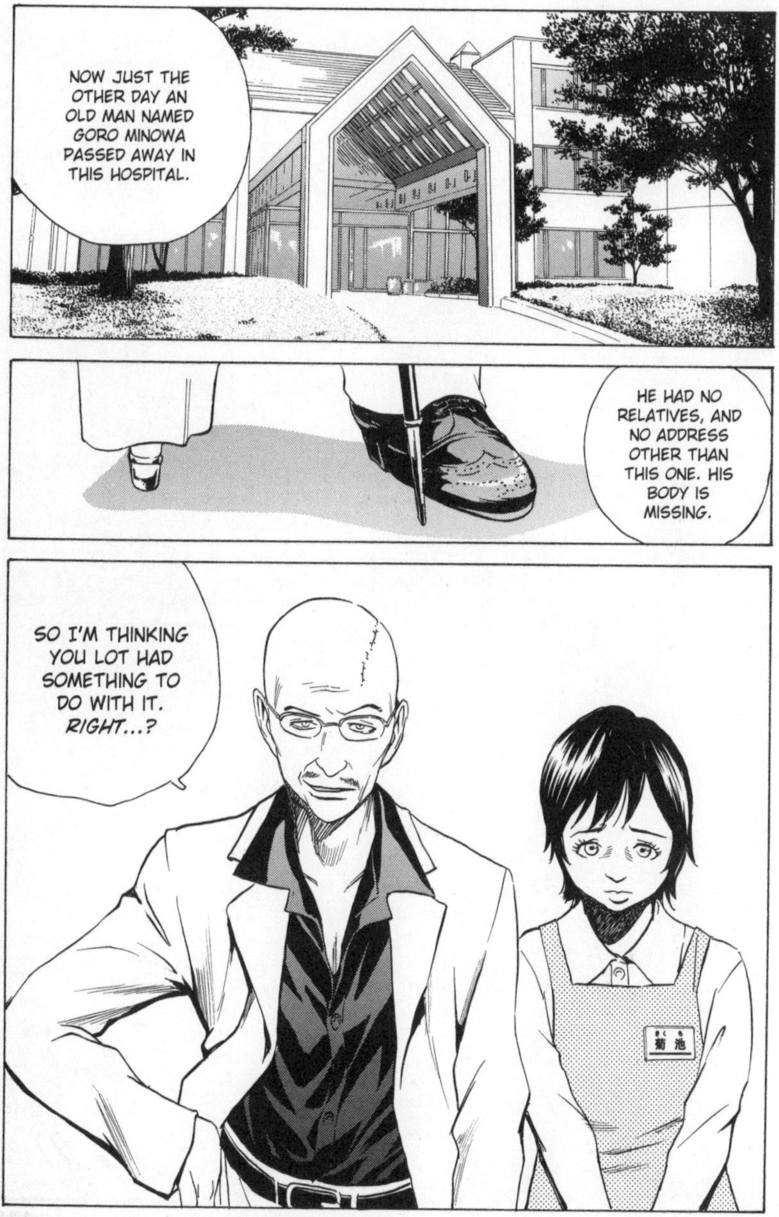
NOW JUST THE OTHER DAY AN OLD MAN NAMED GORO MINOWA PASSED AWAY IN THIS HOSPITAL.
HE HAD NO RELATIVES, AND NO ADDRESS OTHER THAN THIS ONE. HIS BODY IS MISSING.
SO I'M THINKING YOU LOT HAD SOMETHING TO DO WITH IT. *RIGHT...?*
菊池

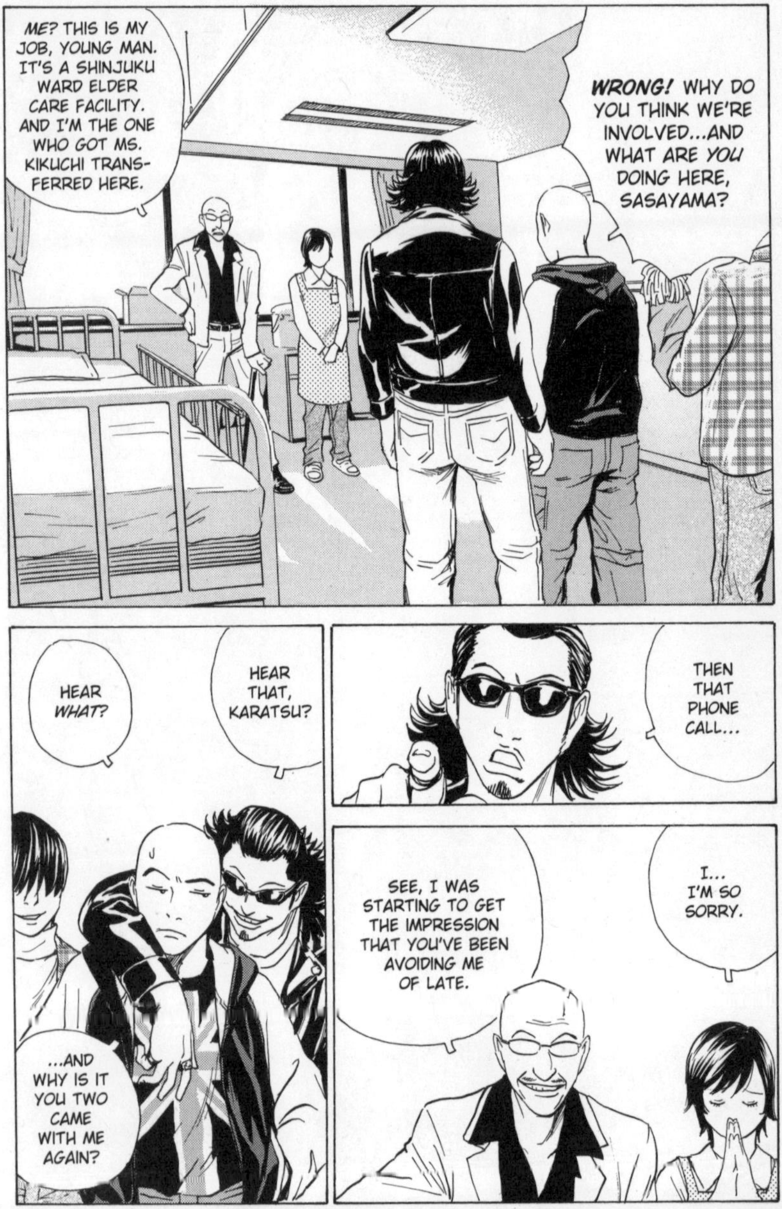
WRONG! WHY DO YOU THINK WE'RE INVOLVED...AND WHAT ARE YOU DOING HERE, SASAYAMA?
ME? THIS IS MY JOB, YOUNG MAN. IT'S A SHINJUKU WARD ELDER CARE FACILITY. AND I'M THE ONE WHO GOT MS. KIKUCHI TRANS-FERRED HERE.
THEN THAT PHONE CALL...
HEAR THAT, KARATSU?
HEAR WHAT?
I... I'M SO SORRY.
SEE, I WAS STARTING TO GET THE IMPRESSION THAT YOU'VE BEEN AVOIDING ME OF LATE.
...AND WHY IS IT YOU TWO CAME WITH ME AGAIN?

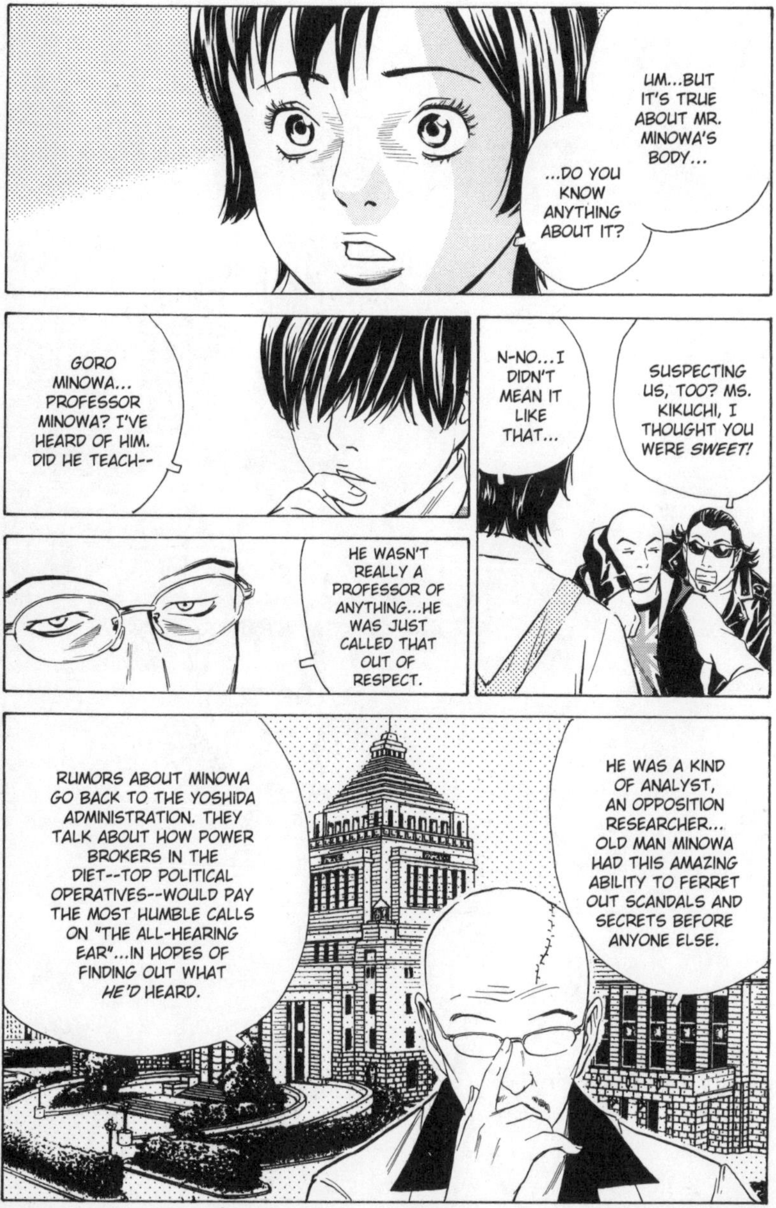
UM...BUT IT'S TRUE ABOUT MR. MINOWA'S BODY...
...DO YOU KNOW ANYTHING ABOUT IT?
SUSPECTING US, TOO? MS. KIKUCHI, I THOUGHT YOU WERE *SWEET!*
N-NO...I DIDN'T MEAN IT LIKE THAT...
GORO MINOWA... PROFESSOR MINOWA? I'VE HEARD OF HIM. DID HE TEACH--
HE WASN'T REALLY A PROFESSOR OF ANYTHING...HE WAS JUST CALLED THAT OUT OF RESPECT.
HE WAS A KIND OF ANALYST, AN OPPOSITION RESEARCHER... OLD MAN MINOWA HAD THIS AMAZING ABILITY TO FERRET OUT SCANDALS AND SECRETS BEFORE ANYONE ELSE.
RUMORS ABOUT MINOWA GO BACK TO THE YOSHIDA ADMINISTRATION. THEY TALK ABOUT HOW POWER BROKERS IN THE DIET--TOP POLITICAL OPERATIVES--WOULD PAY THE MOST HUMBLE CALLS ON "THE ALL-HEARING EAR"...IN HOPES OF FINDING OUT WHAT *HE'D* HEARD.

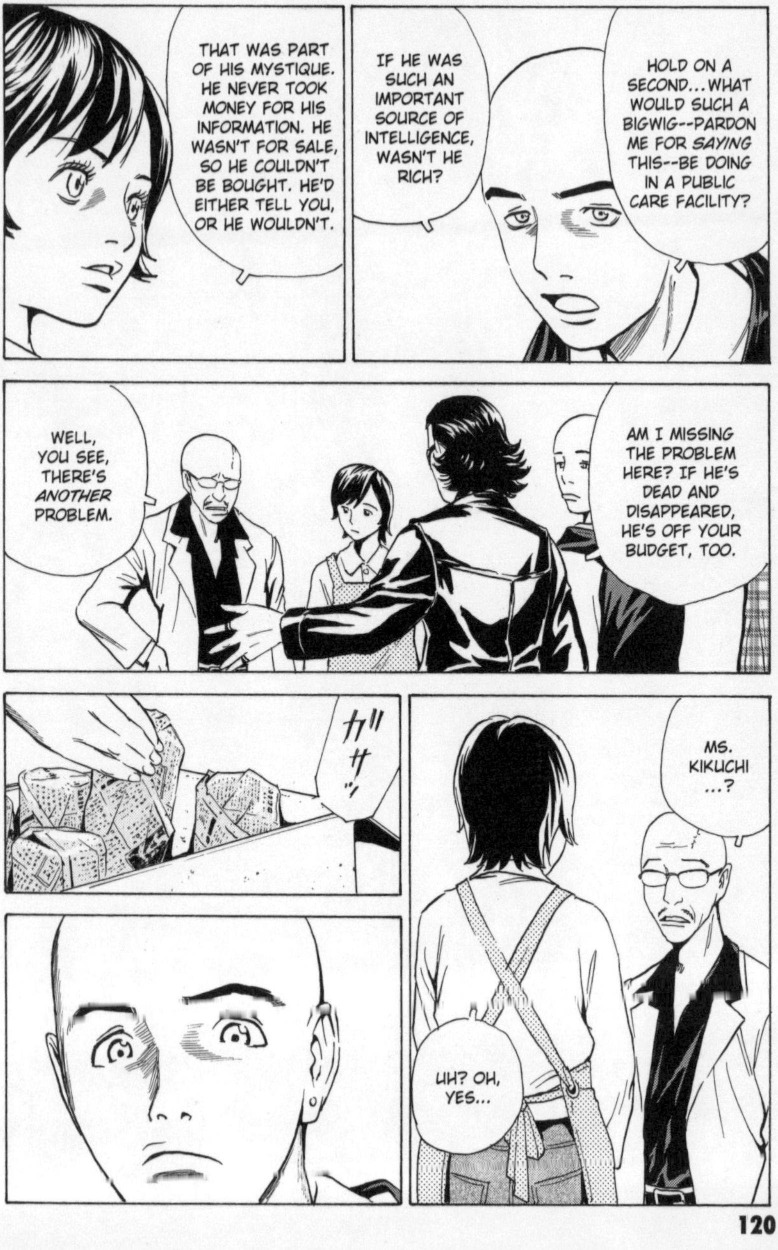
HOLD ON A SECOND... WHAT WOULD SUCH A BIGWIG--PARDON ME FOR *SAYING* THIS--BE DOING IN A PUBLIC CARE FACILITY?
IF HE WAS SUCH AN IMPORTANT SOURCE OF INTELLIGENCE, WASN'T HE RICH?
THAT WAS PART OF HIS MYSTIQUE. HE NEVER TOOK MONEY FOR HIS INFORMATION. HE WASN'T FOR SALE, SO HE COULDN'T BE BOUGHT. HE'D EITHER TELL YOU, OR HE WOULDN'T.
AM I MISSING THE PROBLEM HERE? IF HE'S DEAD AND DISAPPEARED, HE'S OFF YOUR BUDGET, TOO.
WELL, YOU SEE, THERE'S *ANOTHER* PROBLEM.
MS. KIKUCHI ...?
UH? OH, YES...
ガサッ

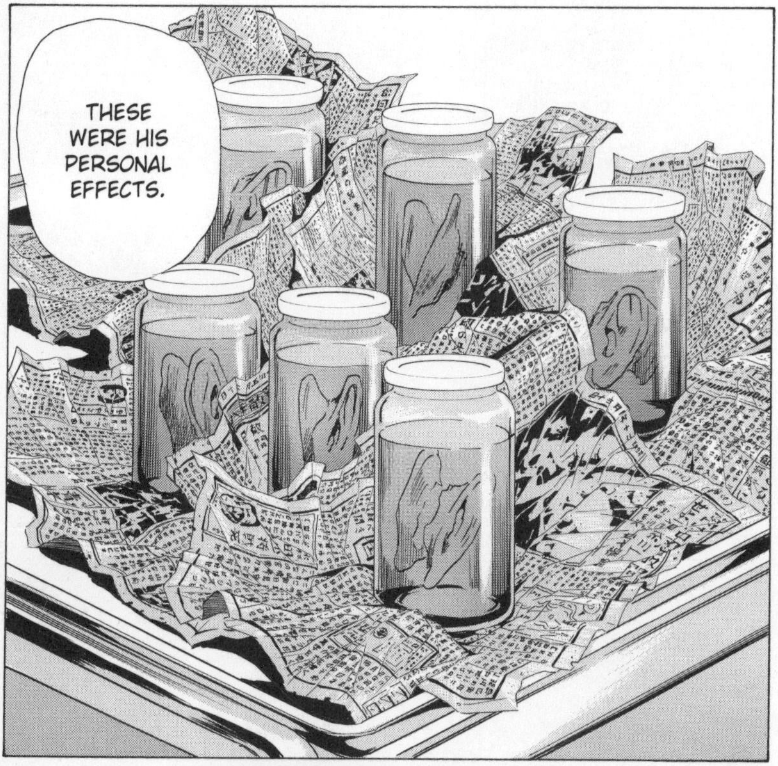
THESE WERE HIS PERSONAL EFFECTS.

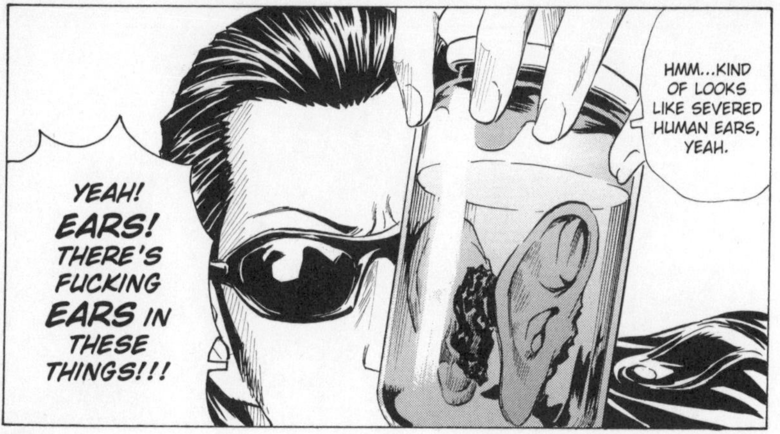
HMM...KIND OF LOOKS LIKE SEVERED HUMAN EARS, YEAH.
YEAH! EARS! THERE'S FUCKING EARS IN THESE THINGS!!!

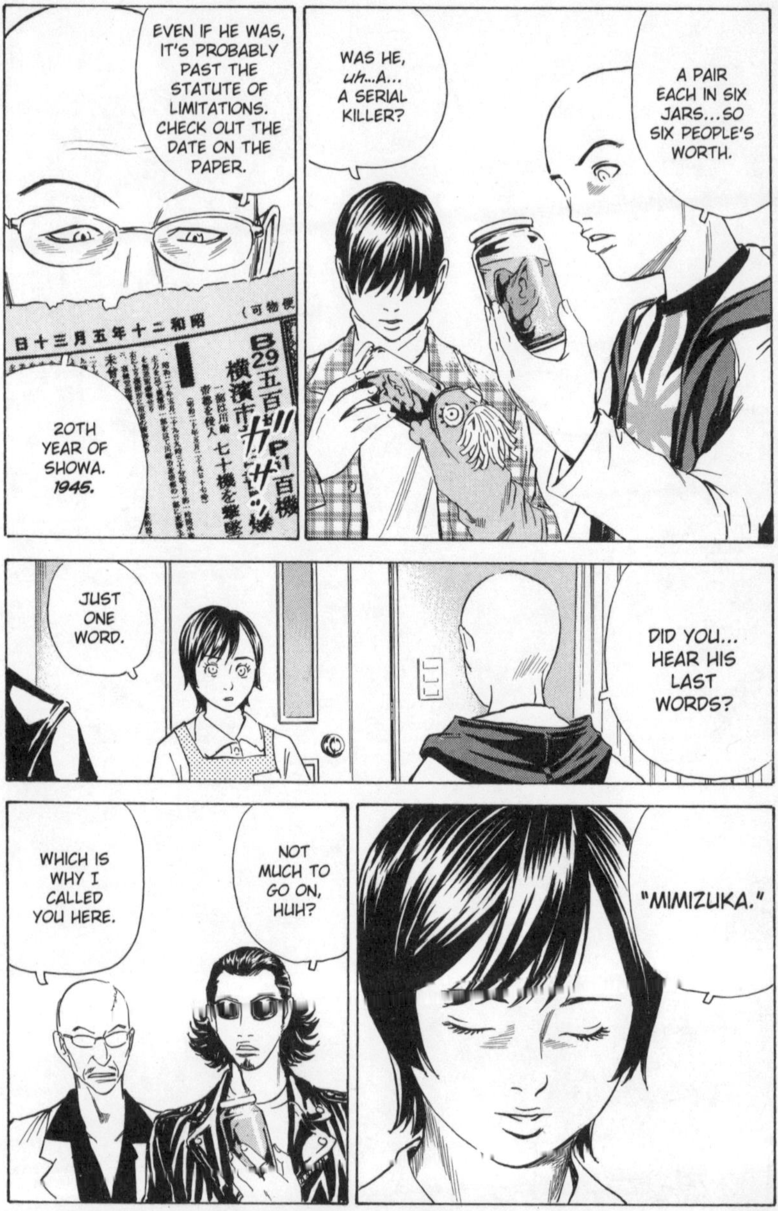
A PAIR EACH IN SIX JARS...SO SIX PEOPLE'S WORTH.
WAS HE, uh...A... A SERIAL KILLER?
EVEN IF HE WAS, IT'S PROBABLY PAST THE STATUTE OF LIMITATIONS. CHECK OUT THE DATE ON THE PAPER.
20TH YEAR OF SHOWA. 1945.
DID YOU... HEAR HIS LAST WORDS?
JUST ONE WORD.
"MIMIZUKA."
NOT MUCH TO GO ON, HUH?
WHICH IS WHY I CALLED YOU HERE.

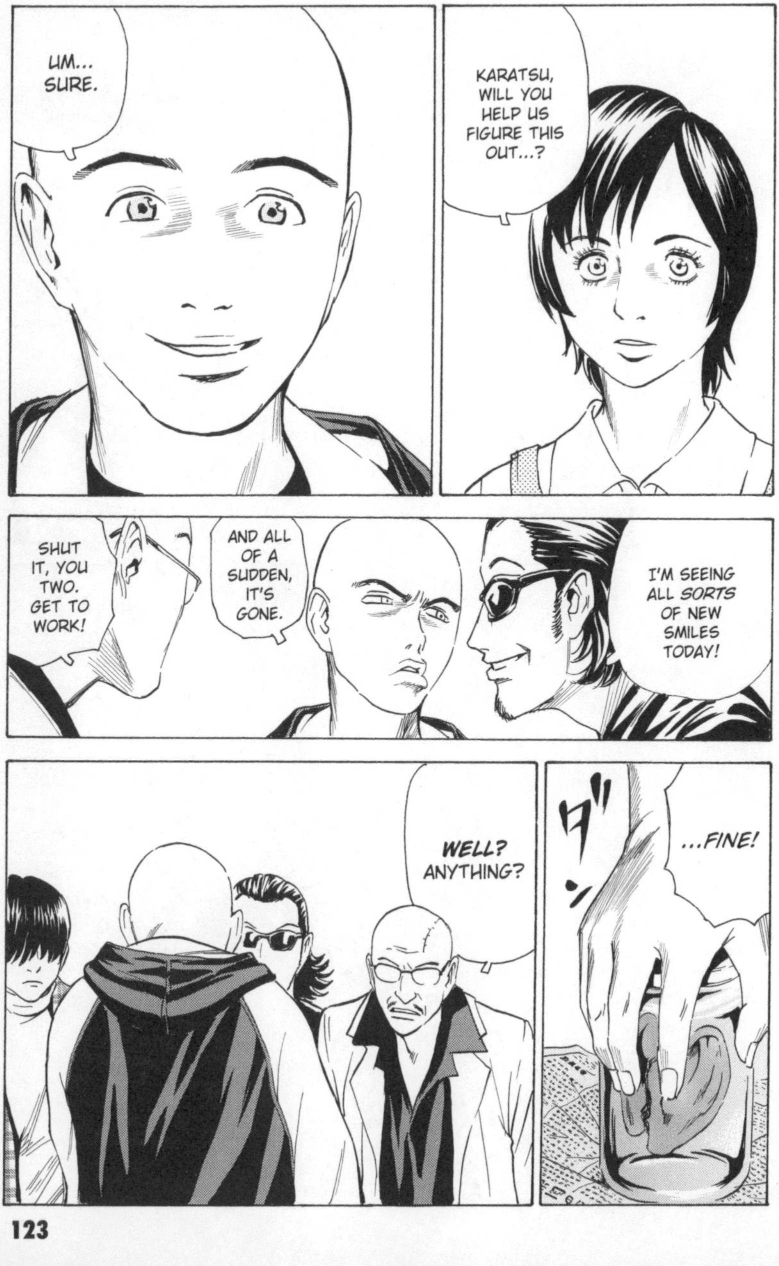
KARATSU, WILL YOU HELP US FIGURE THIS OUT...?
UM... SURE.
I'M SEEING ALL *SORTS* OF NEW SMILES TODAY!
AND ALL OF A SUDDEN, IT'S GONE.
SHUT IT, YOU TWO. GET TO WORK!
ダッ
...FINE!
WELL? ANYTHING?

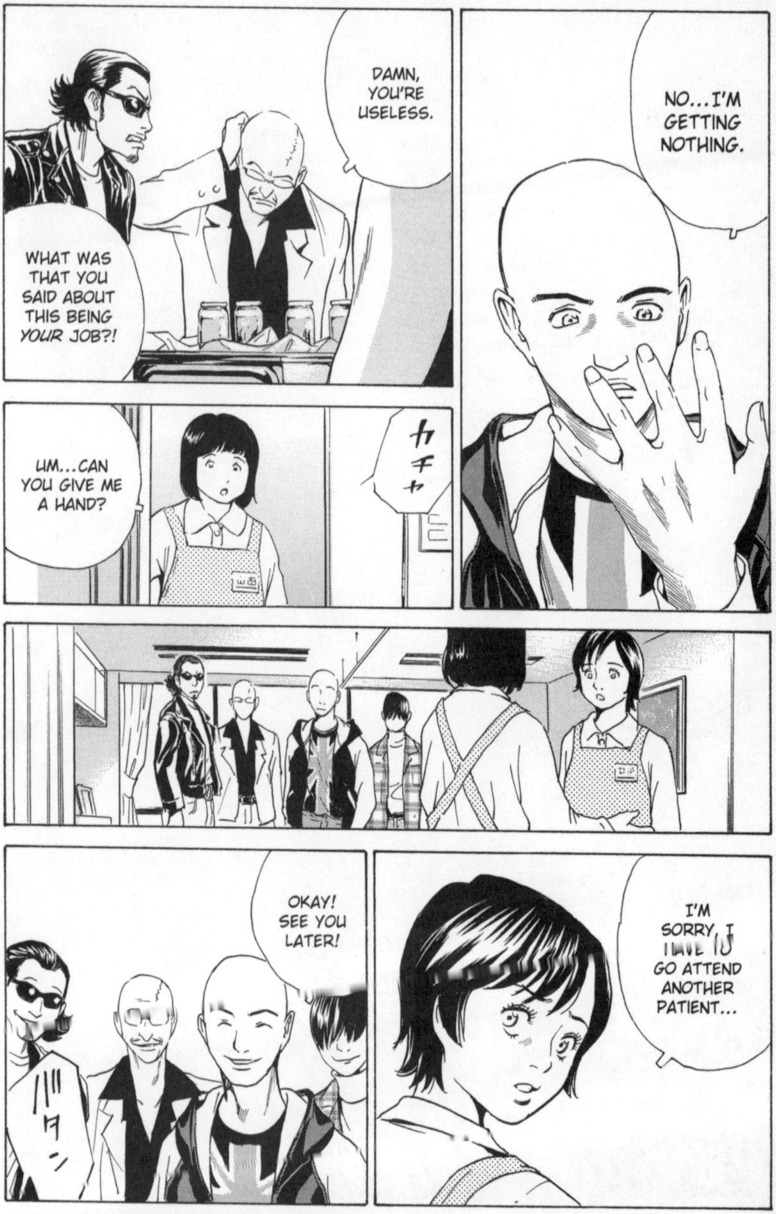
NO...I'M GETTING NOTHING.
DAMN, YOU'RE USELESS.
WHAT WAS THAT YOU SAID ABOUT THIS BEING *YOUR* JOB?!
カチャ
UM...CAN YOU GIVE ME A HAND?
I'M SORRY, I HAVE TO GO ATTEND ANOTHER PATIENT...
OKAY! SEE YOU LATER!
バタン

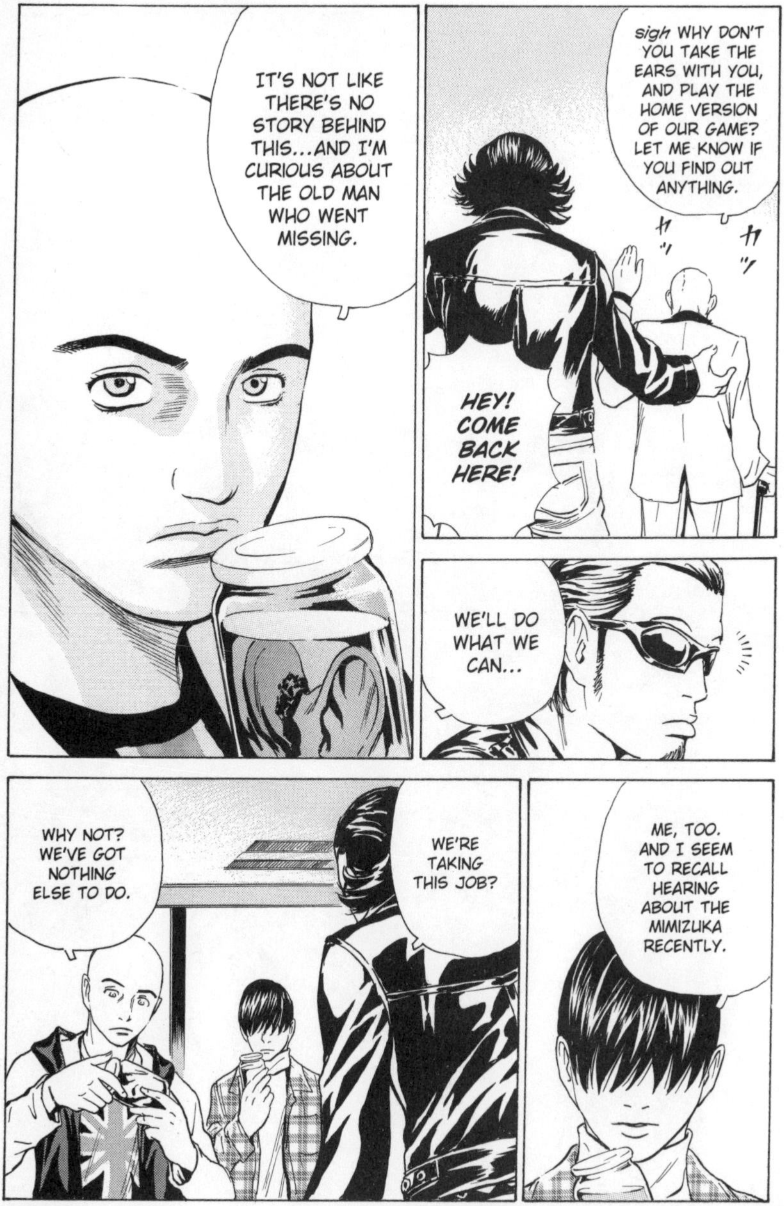

sigh WHY DON'T YOU TAKE THE EARS WITH YOU, AND PLAY THE HOME VERSION OF OUR GAME? LET ME KNOW IF YOU FIND OUT ANYTHING.
カツ
カツ
HEY! COME BACK HERE!
WE'LL DO WHAT WE CAN...
IT'S NOT LIKE THERE'S NO STORY BEHIND THIS...AND I'M CURIOUS ABOUT THE OLD MAN WHO WENT MISSING.
ME, TOO. AND I SEEM TO RECALL HEARING ABOUT THE MIMIZUKA RECENTLY.
WE'RE TAKING THIS JOB?
WHY NOT? WE'VE GOT NOTHING ELSE TO DO.

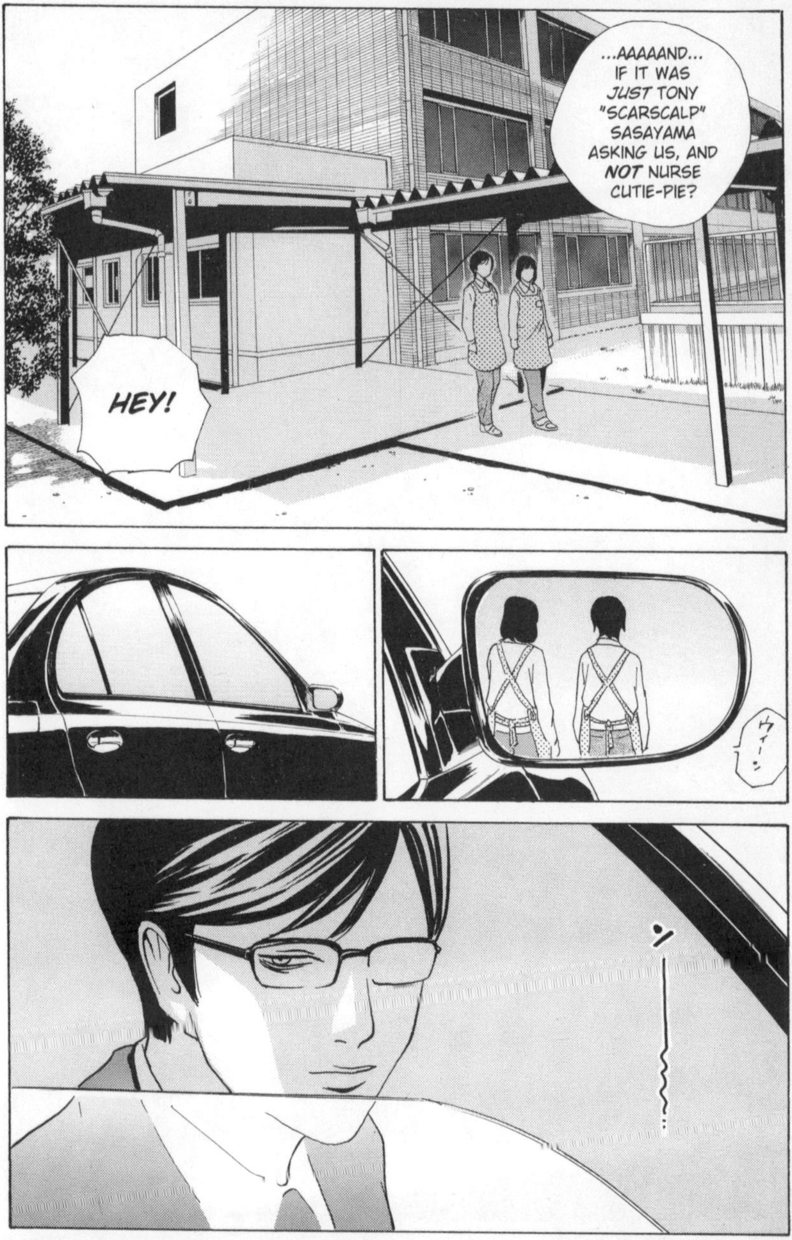
...AAAAAND... IF IT WAS *JUST* TONY "SCARSCALP" SASAYAMA ASKING US, AND *NOT* NURSE CUTIE-PIE?
HEY!
ウィーン

5th delivery: white house by the sea—the end

6th delivery

ある事情

a certain situation

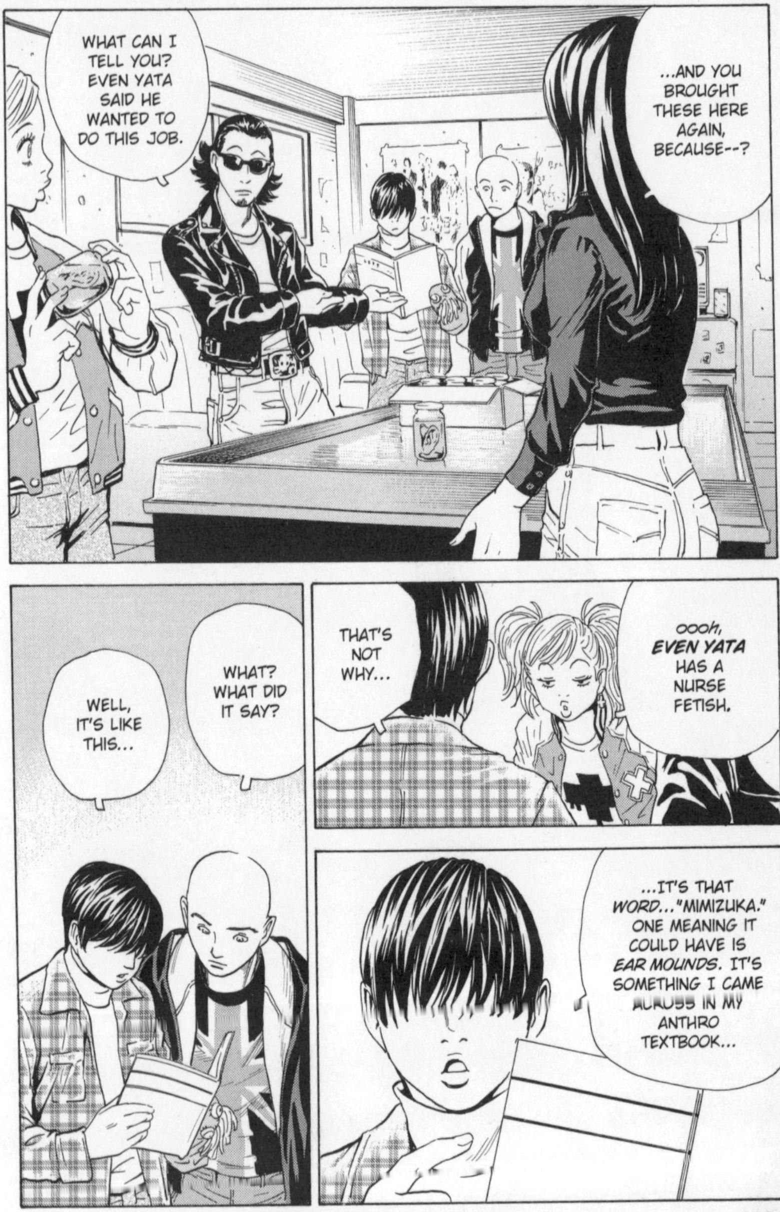
...AND YOU BROUGHT THESE HERE AGAIN, BECAUSE--?
WHAT CAN I TELL YOU? EVEN YATA SAID HE WANTED TO DO THIS JOB.
oooh, EVEN YATA HAS A NURSE FETISH.
THAT'S NOT WHY...
WHAT? WHAT DID IT SAY?
WELL, IT'S LIKE THIS...
...IT'S THAT WORD..."MIMIZUKA." ONE MEANING IT COULD HAVE IS EAR MOUNDS. IT'S SOMETHING I CAME ACROSS IN MY ANTHRO TEXTBOOK...

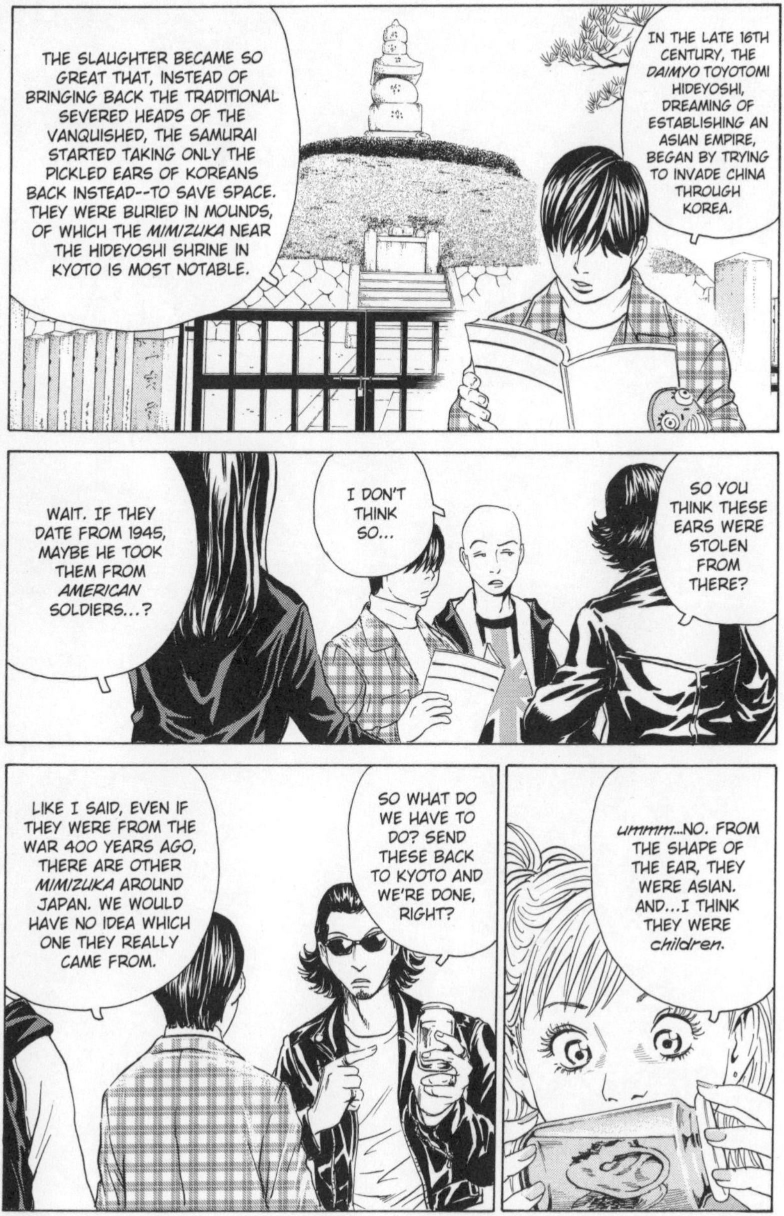
IN THE LATE 16TH CENTURY, THE DAIMYO TOYOTOMI HIDEYOSHI, DREAMING OF ESTABLISHING AN ASIAN EMPIRE, BEGAN BY TRYING TO INVADE CHINA THROUGH KOREA.
THE SLAUGHTER BECAME SO GREAT THAT, INSTEAD OF BRINGING BACK THE TRADITIONAL SEVERED HEADS OF THE VANQUISHED, THE SAMURAI STARTED TAKING ONLY THE PICKLED EARS OF KOREANS BACK INSTEAD--TO SAVE SPACE. THEY WERE BURIED IN MOUNDS, OF WHICH THE MIMIZUKA NEAR THE HIDEYOSHI SHRINE IN KYOTO IS MOST NOTABLE.
SO YOU THINK THESE EARS WERE STOLEN FROM THERE?
I DON'T THINK SO...
WAIT. IF THEY DATE FROM 1945, MAYBE HE TOOK THEM FROM AMERICAN SOLDIERS...?
ummm...NO. FROM THE SHAPE OF THE EAR, THEY WERE ASIAN. AND...I THINK THEY WERE children.
SO WHAT DO WE HAVE TO DO? SEND THESE BACK TO KYOTO AND WE'RE DONE, RIGHT?
LIKE I SAID, EVEN IF THEY WERE FROM THE WAR 400 YEARS AGO, THERE ARE OTHER MIMIZUKA AROUND JAPAN. WE WOULD HAVE NO IDEA WHICH ONE THEY REALLY CAME FROM.

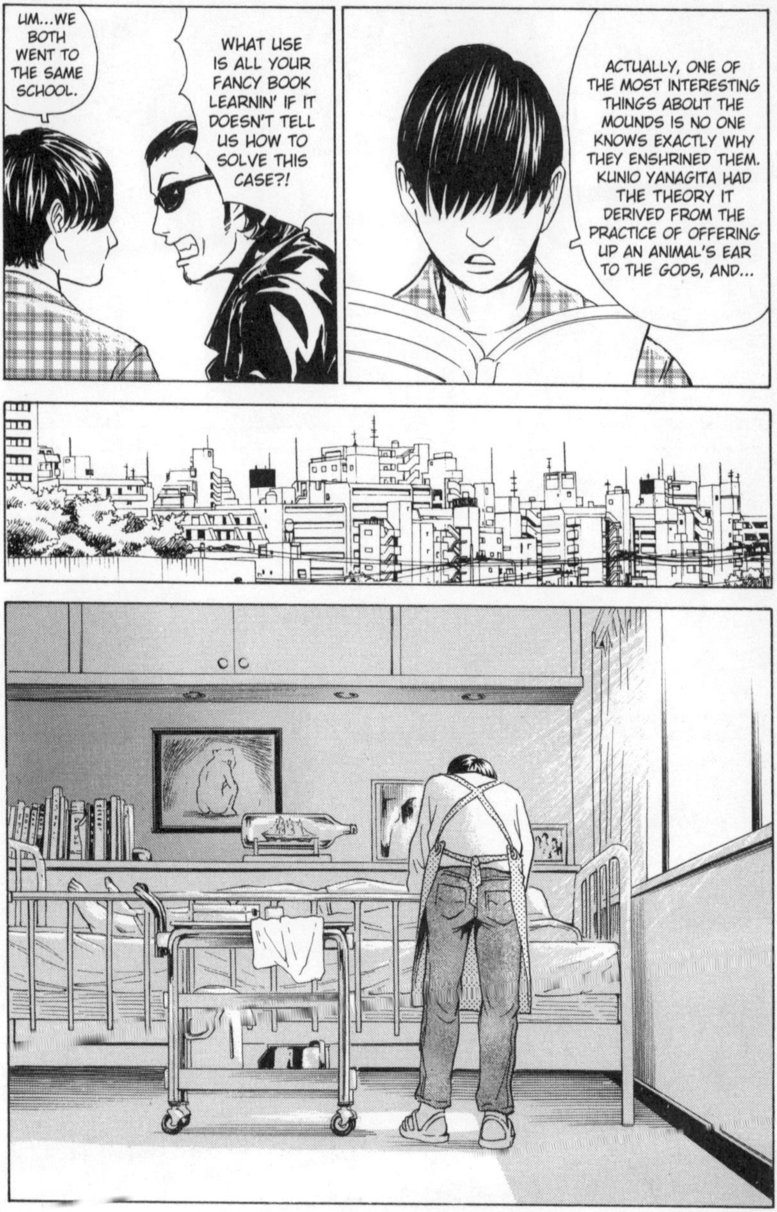
ACTUALLY, ONE OF THE MOST INTERESTING THINGS ABOUT THE MOUNDS IS NO ONE KNOWS EXACTLY WHY THEY ENSHRINED THEM. KUNIO YANAGITA HAD THE THEORY IT DERIVED FROM THE PRACTICE OF OFFERING UP AN ANIMAL'S EAR TO THE GODS, AND...
WHAT USE IS ALL YOUR FANCY BOOK LEARNIN' IF IT DOESN'T TELL US HOW TO SOLVE THIS CASE?!
UM...WE BOTH WENT TO THE SAME SCHOOL.

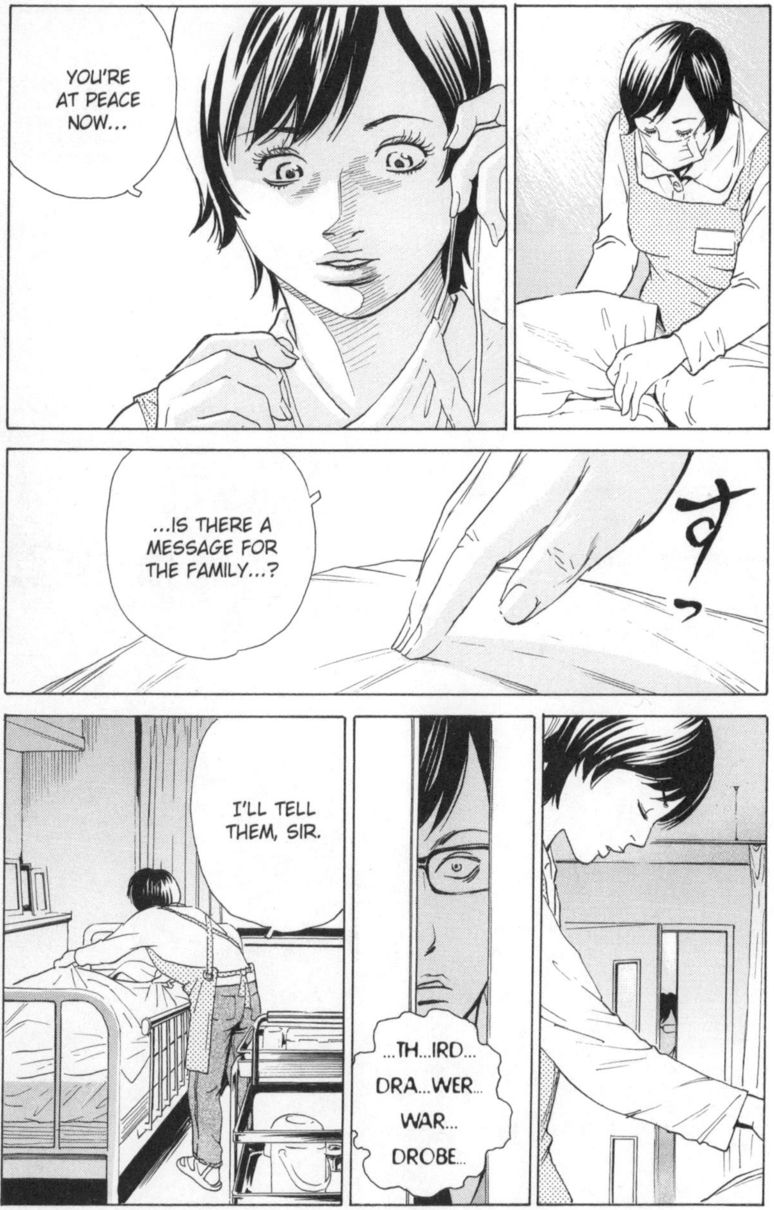
YOU'RE AT PEACE NOW...
...IS THERE A MESSAGE FOR THE FAMILY...?
すっ
...TH...IRD... DRA...WER... WAR... DROBE...
I'LL TELL THEM, SIR.

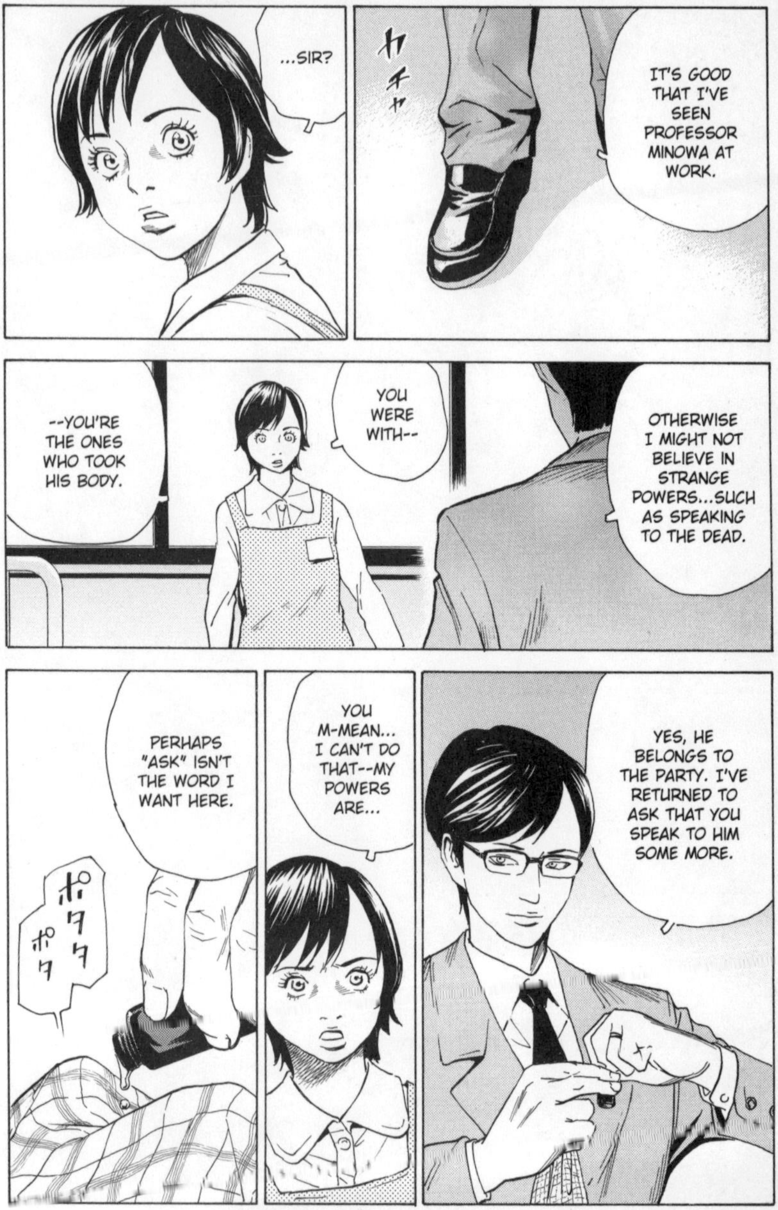
IT'S GOOD THAT I'VE SEEN PROFESSOR MINOWA AT WORK.
カチャ
...SIR?
OTHERWISE I MIGHT NOT BELIEVE IN STRANGE POWERS...SUCH AS SPEAKING TO THE DEAD.
YOU WERE WITH--
--YOU'RE THE ONES WHO TOOK HIS BODY.
YES, HE BELONGS TO THE PARTY. I'VE RETURNED TO ASK THAT YOU SPEAK TO HIM SOME MORE.
YOU M-MEAN... I CAN'T DO THAT--MY POWERS ARE...
PERHAPS "ASK" ISN'T THE WORD I WANT HERE.
ポタタ
ポタ

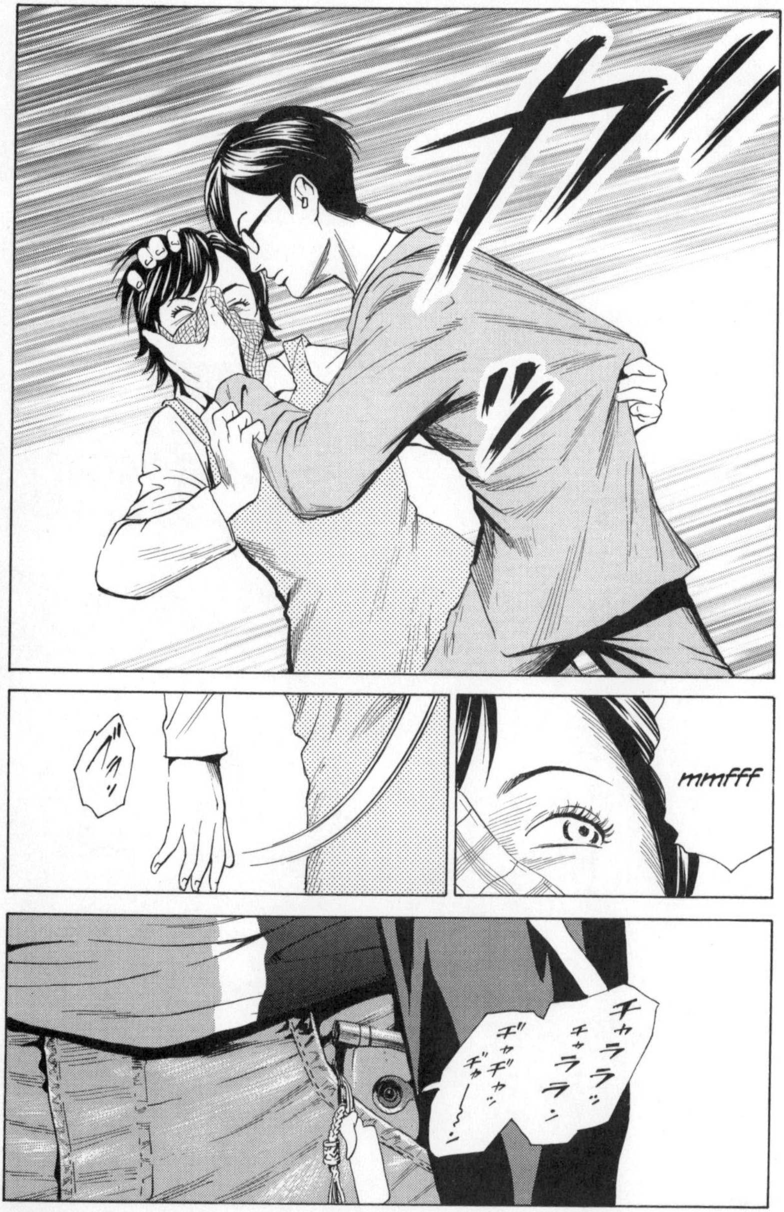
mmfff
ブラッ
チャラララッ
チャラララ…
ヂャヂャッ
ヂャー…

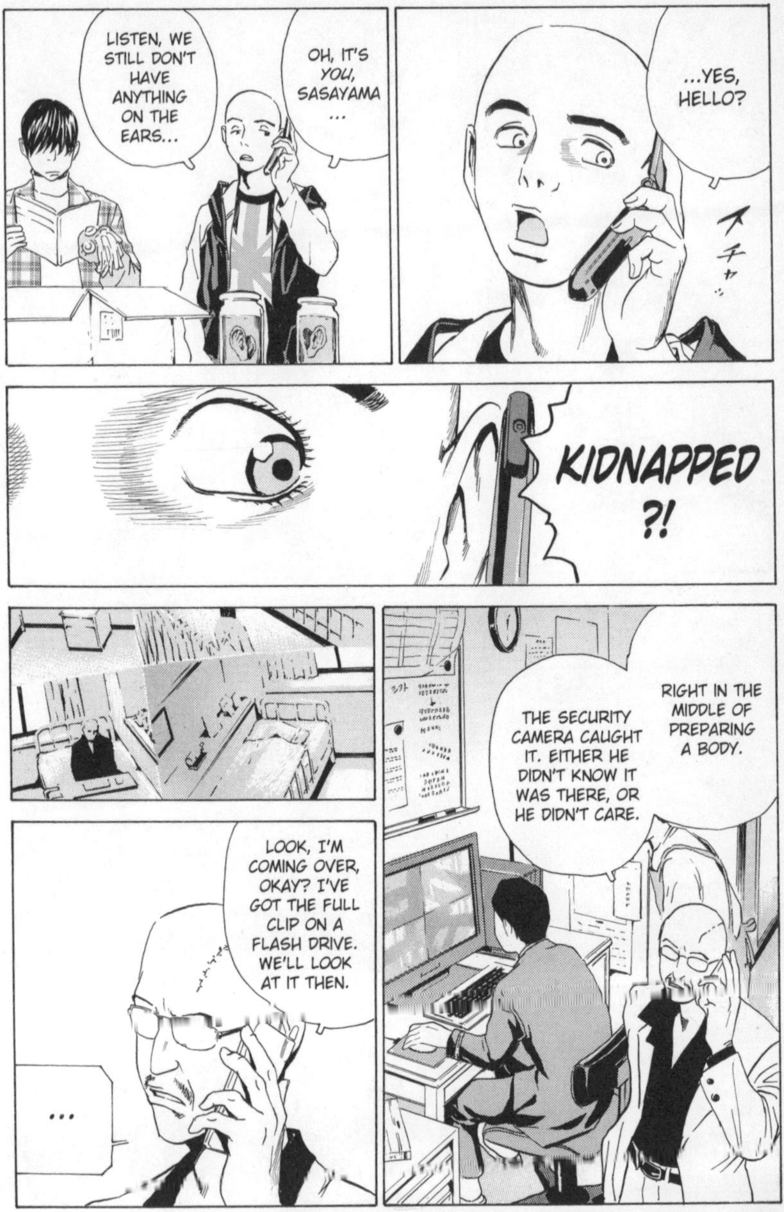
...YES, HELLO?
スチャッ
OH, IT'S YOU, SASAYAMA...
LISTEN, WE STILL DON'T HAVE ANYTHING ON THE EARS...
KIDNAPPED?!
RIGHT IN THE MIDDLE OF PREPARING A BODY.
THE SECURITY CAMERA CAUGHT IT. EITHER HE DIDN'T KNOW IT WAS THERE, OR HE DIDN'T CARE.
LOOK, I'M COMING OVER, OKAY? I'VE GOT THE FULL CLIP ON A FLASH DRIVE. WE'LL LOOK AT IT THEN.
...

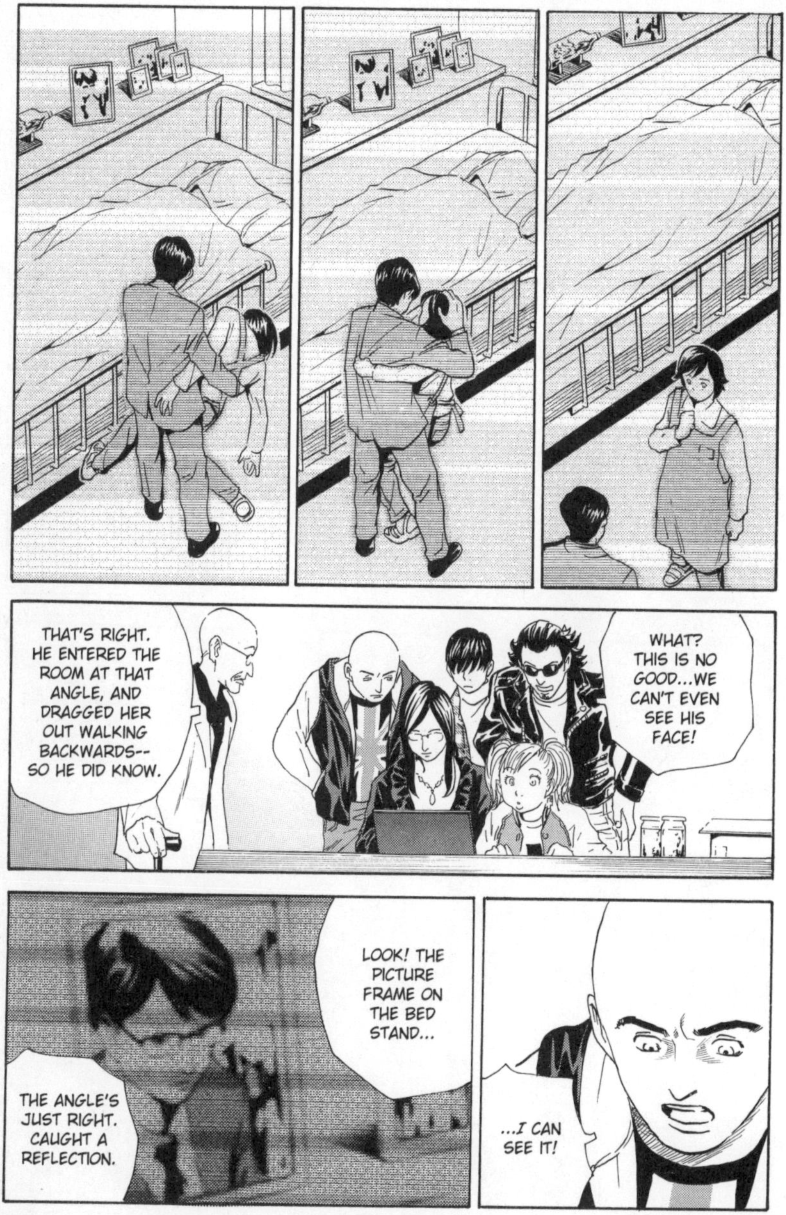
WHAT? THIS IS NO GOOD...WE CAN'T EVEN SEE HIS FACE!
THAT'S RIGHT. HE ENTERED THE ROOM AT THAT ANGLE, AND DRAGGED HER OUT WALKING BACKWARDS--SO HE DID KNOW.
...I CAN SEE IT!
LOOK! THE PICTURE FRAME ON THE BED STAND...
THE ANGLE'S JUST RIGHT. CAUGHT A REFLECTION.

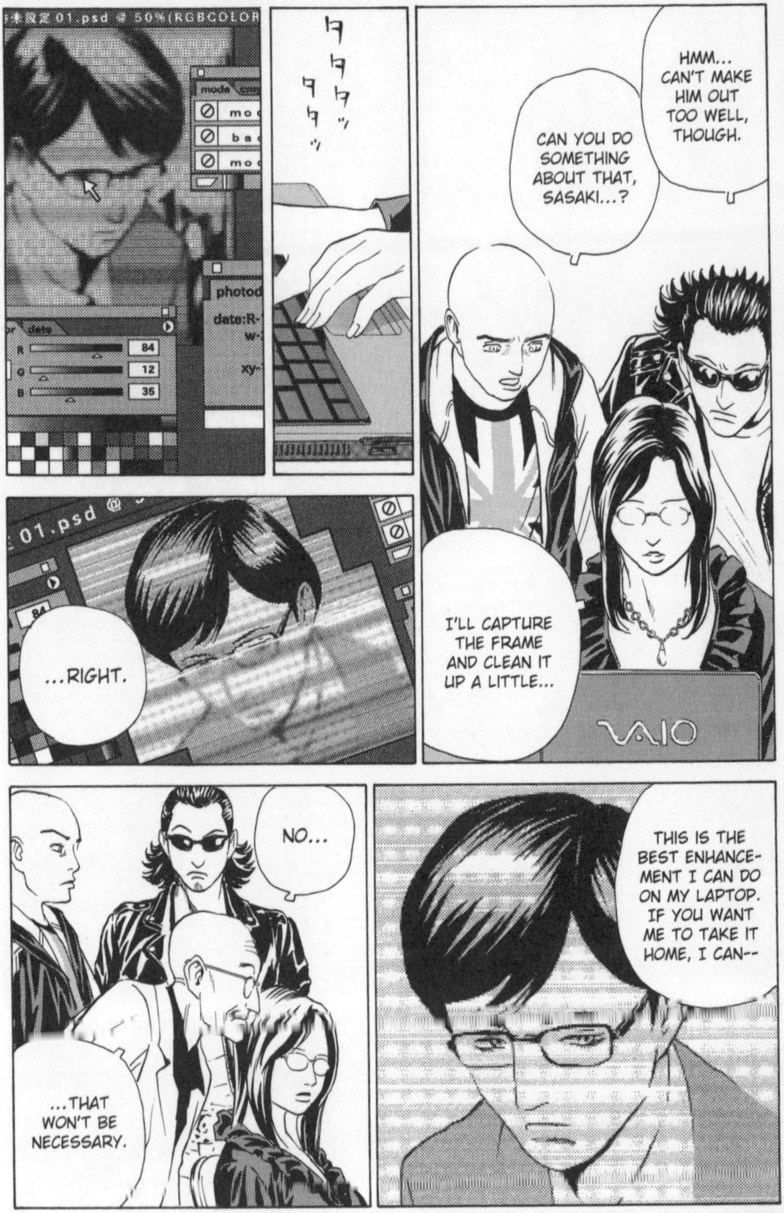

HMM... CAN'T MAKE HIM OUT TOO WELL, THOUGH.
CAN YOU DO SOMETHING ABOUT THAT, SASAKI...?
I'LL CAPTURE THE FRAME AND CLEAN IT UP A LITTLE...
タタタッ
タタッ
...RIGHT.
THIS IS THE BEST ENHANCEMENT I CAN DO ON MY LAPTOP. IF YOU WANT ME TO TAKE IT HOME, I CAN--
NO...
...THAT WON'T BE NECESSARY.

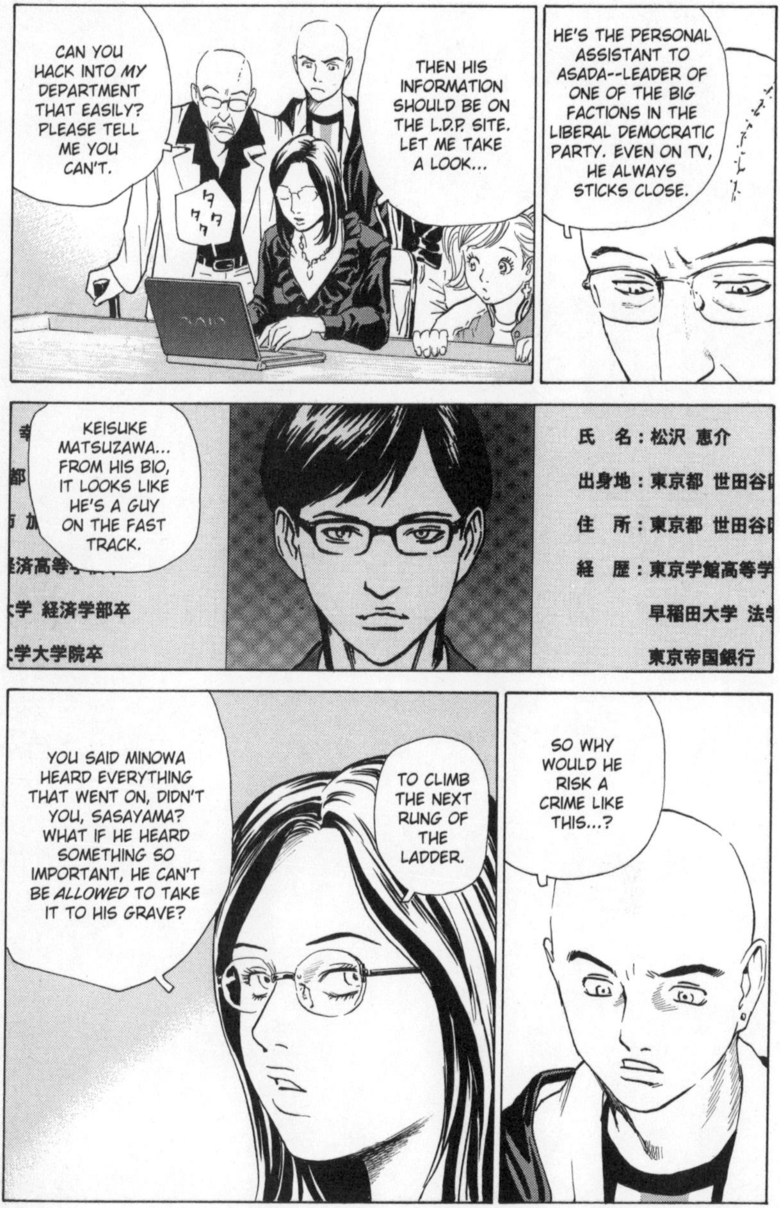
HE'S THE PERSONAL ASSISTANT TO ASADA--LEADER OF ONE OF THE BIG FACTIONS IN THE LIBERAL DEMOCRATIC PARTY. EVEN ON TV, HE ALWAYS STICKS CLOSE.
THEN HIS INFORMATION SHOULD BE ON THE L.D.P. SITE. LET ME TAKE A LOOK...
CAN YOU HACK INTO *MY* DEPARTMENT THAT EASILY? PLEASE TELL ME YOU CAN'T.
タタタタ
氏　名：松沢 恵介
出身地：東京都 世田谷
住　所：東京都 世田谷
経　歴：東京学館高等学
早稲田大学 法
東京帝国銀行
KEISUKE MATSUZAWA... FROM HIS BIO, IT LOOKS LIKE HE'S A GUY ON THE FAST TRACK.
SO WHY WOULD HE RISK A CRIME LIKE THIS...?
TO CLIMB THE NEXT RUNG OF THE LADDER.
YOU SAID MINOWA HEARD EVERYTHING THAT WENT ON, DIDN'T YOU, SASAYAMA? WHAT IF HE HEARD SOMETHING SO IMPORTANT, HE CAN'T BE *ALLOWED* TO TAKE IT TO HIS GRAVE?

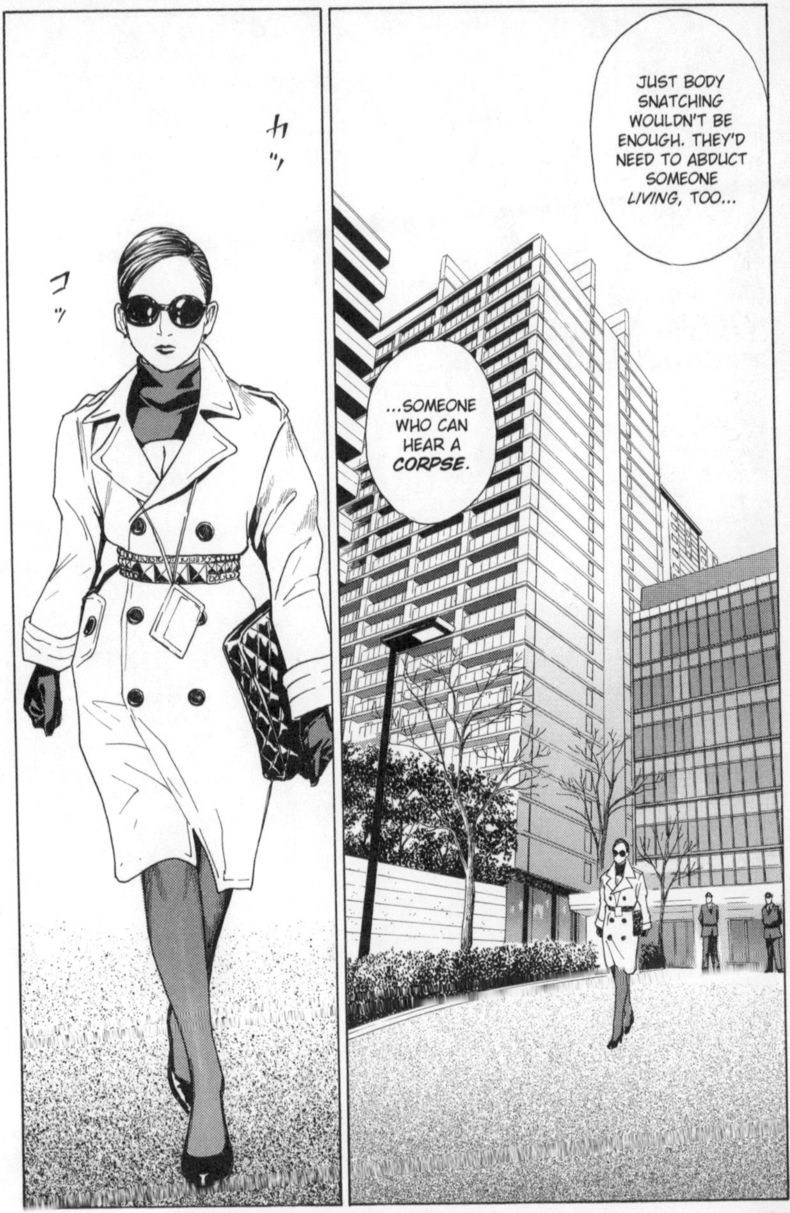
JUST BODY SNATCHING WOULDN'T BE ENOUGH. THEY'D NEED TO ABDUCT SOMEONE *LIVING*, TOO...
...SOMEONE WHO CAN HEAR A ***CORPSE***.
カッ
コッ

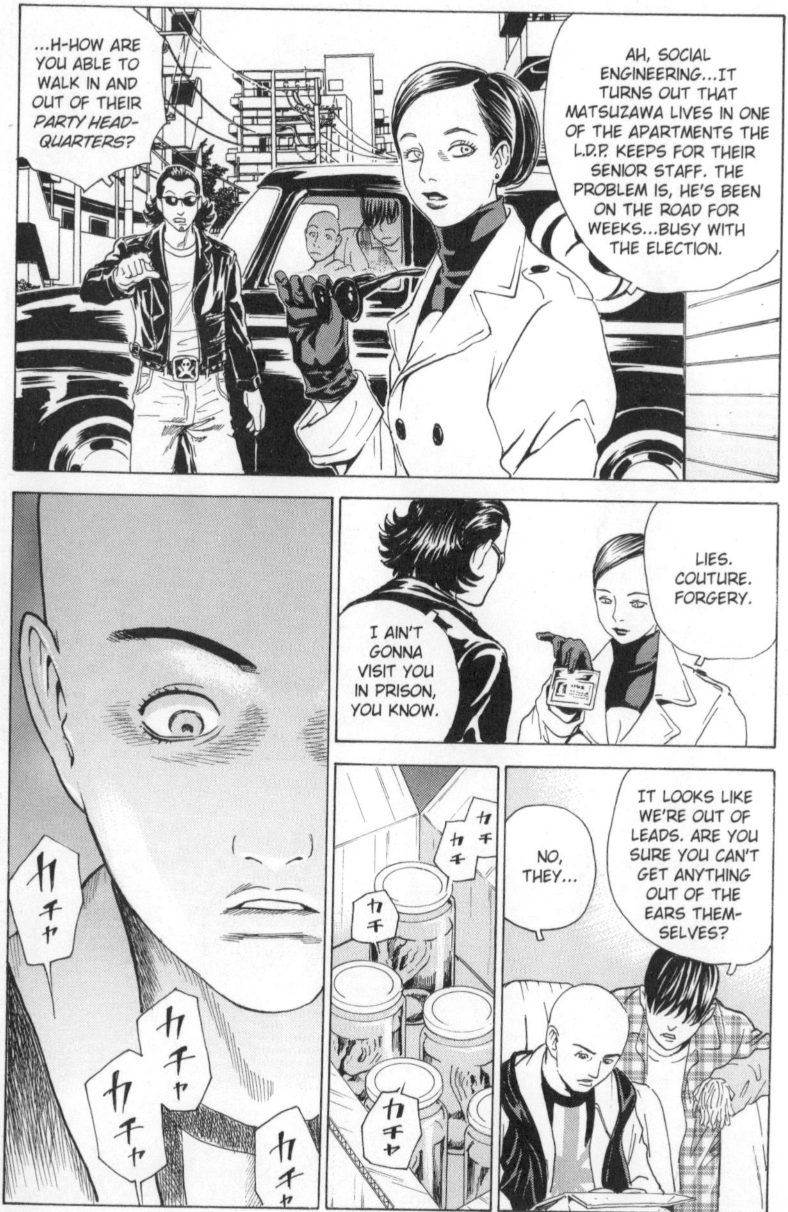
AH, SOCIAL ENGINEERING...IT TURNS OUT THAT MATSUZAWA LIVES IN ONE OF THE APARTMENTS THE L.D.P. KEEPS FOR THEIR SENIOR STAFF. THE PROBLEM IS, HE'S BEEN ON THE ROAD FOR WEEKS...BUSY WITH THE ELECTION.
...H-HOW ARE YOU ABLE TO WALK IN AND OUT OF THEIR *PARTY HEAD-QUARTERS?*
LIES. COUTURE. FORGERY.
I AIN'T GONNA VISIT YOU IN PRISON, YOU KNOW.
IT LOOKS LIKE WE'RE OUT OF LEADS. ARE YOU SURE YOU CAN'T GET ANYTHING OUT OF THE EARS THEM-SELVES?
NO, THEY...
カチ
カチ
カチ
カチャ
カチャ
カチャ
カチャ
カチャ

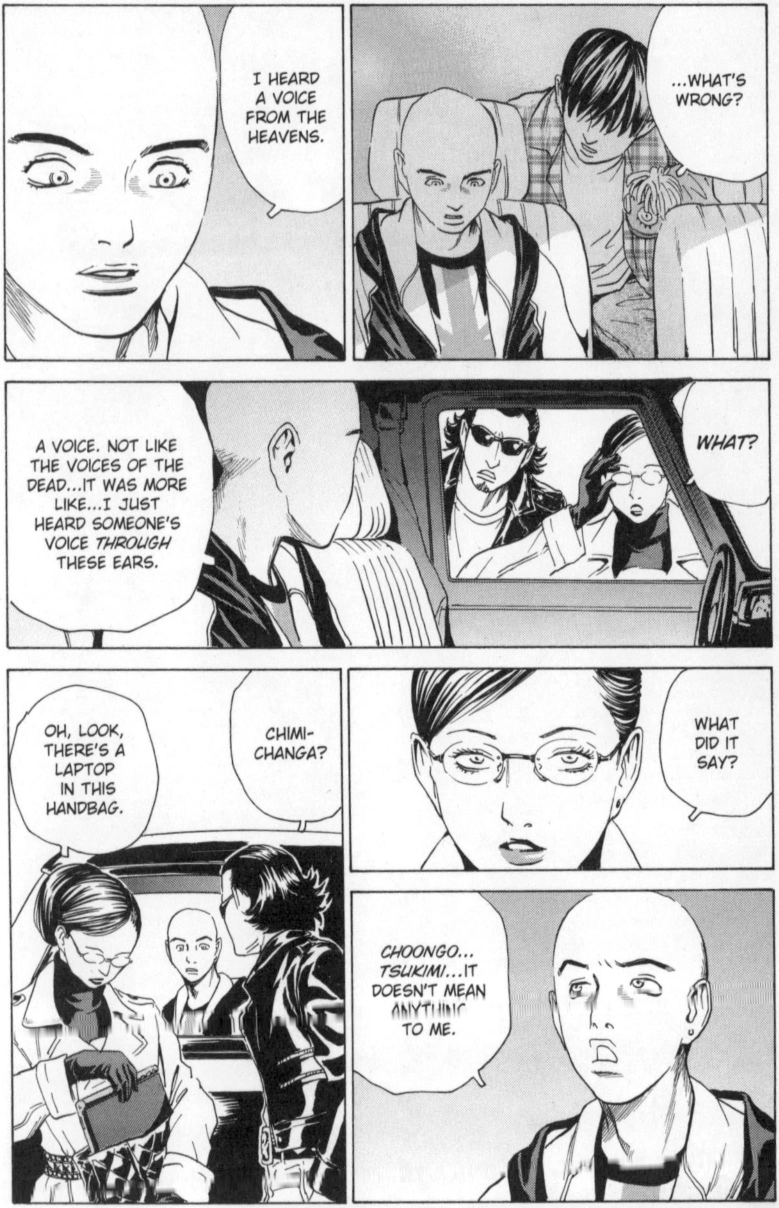
...WHAT'S WRONG?
I HEARD A VOICE FROM THE HEAVENS.
WHAT?
A VOICE. NOT LIKE THE VOICES OF THE DEAD...IT WAS MORE LIKE...I JUST HEARD SOMEONE'S VOICE *THROUGH* THESE EARS.
WHAT DID IT SAY?
CHOONGO... *TSUKIMI*...IT DOESN'T MEAN ANYTHING TO ME.
CHIMI-CHANGA?
OH, LOOK, THERE'S A LAPTOP IN THIS HANDBAG.

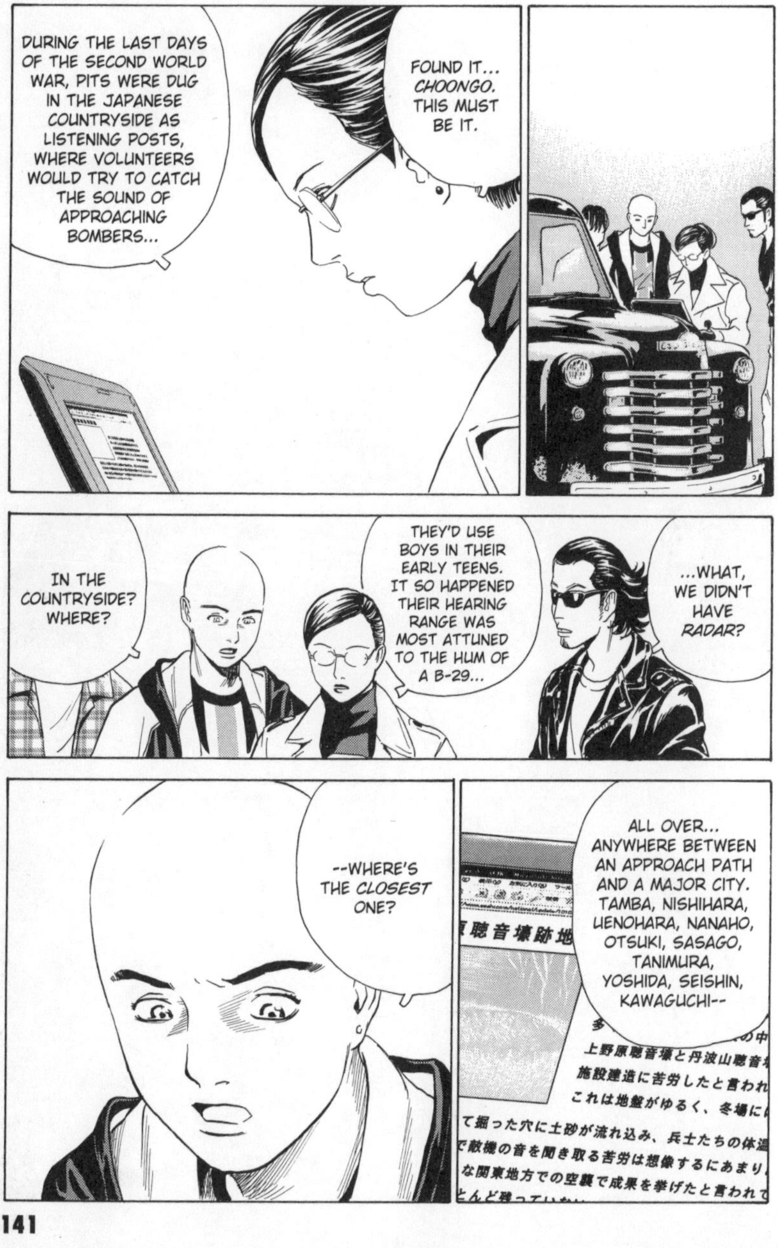
FOUND IT... *CHOONGO.* THIS MUST BE IT.
DURING THE LAST DAYS OF THE SECOND WORLD WAR, PITS WERE DUG IN THE JAPANESE COUNTRYSIDE AS LISTENING POSTS, WHERE VOLUNTEERS WOULD TRY TO CATCH THE SOUND OF APPROACHING BOMBERS...
...WHAT, WE DIDN'T HAVE *RADAR?*
THEY'D USE BOYS IN THEIR EARLY TEENS. IT SO HAPPENED THEIR HEARING RANGE WAS MOST ATTUNED TO THE HUM OF A B-29...
IN THE COUNTRYSIDE? WHERE?
ALL OVER... ANYWHERE BETWEEN AN APPROACH PATH AND A MAJOR CITY. TAMBA, NISHIHARA, UENOHARA, NANAHO, OTSUKI, SASAGO, TANIMURA, YOSHIDA, SEISHIN, KAWAGUCHI--
原聴音壕跡地
上野原聴音壕と丹波山聴音
施設建造に苦労したと言われ
これは地盤がゆるく、冬場に
て掘った穴に土砂が流れ込み、兵士たちの体
で敵機の音を聞き取る苦労は想像するにあまり
な関東地方での空襲で成果を挙げたと言われて
--WHERE'S THE *CLOSEST* ONE?

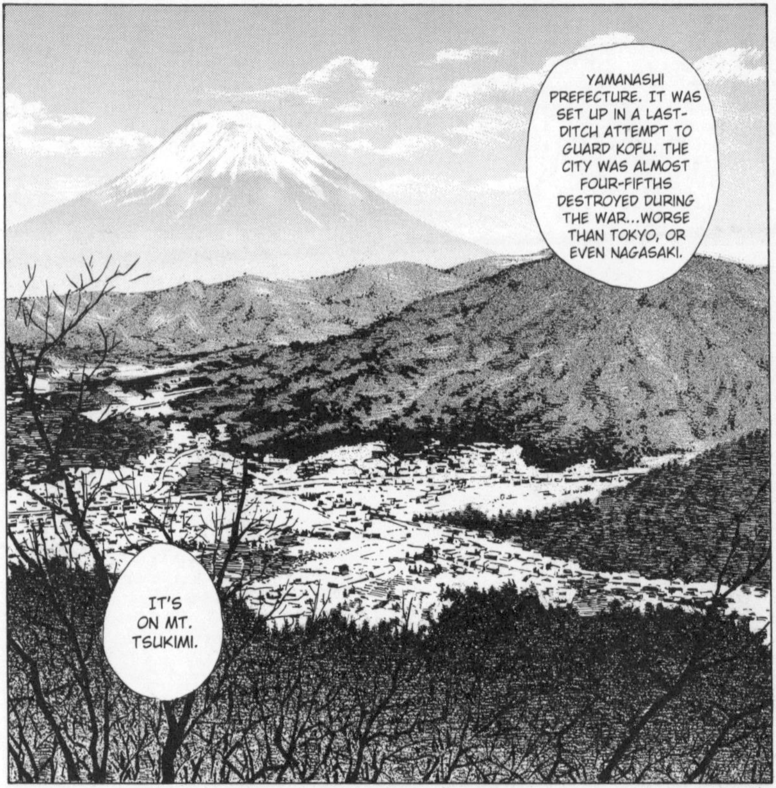
YAMANASHI PREFECTURE. IT WAS SET UP IN A LAST-DITCH ATTEMPT TO GUARD KOFU. THE CITY WAS ALMOST FOUR-FIFTHS DESTROYED DURING THE WAR...WORSE THAN TOKYO, OR EVEN NAGASAKI.
IT'S ON MT. TSUKIMI.
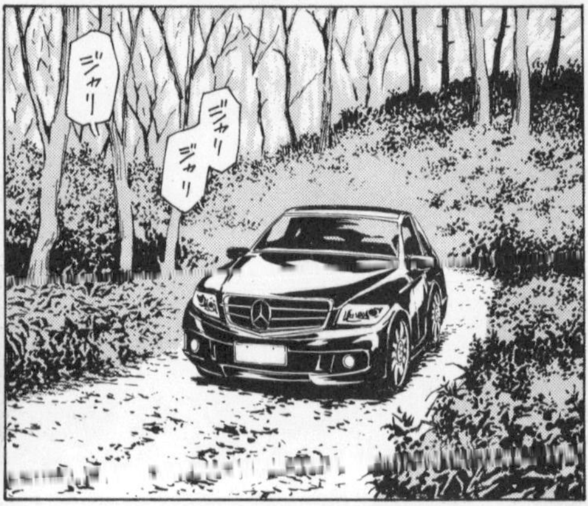
ジャリ
ジャリ
ジャリ
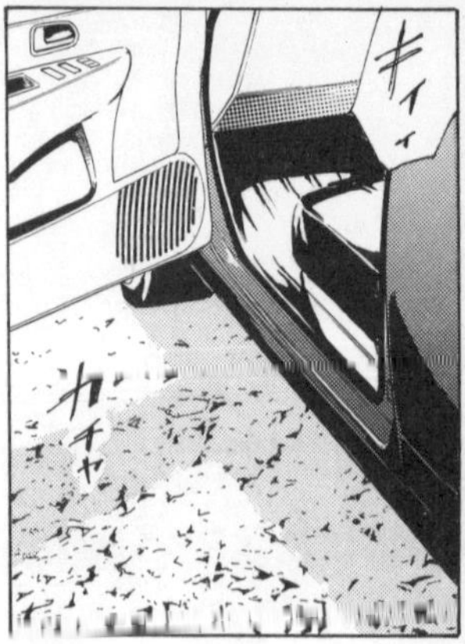
キイィ
カチャ

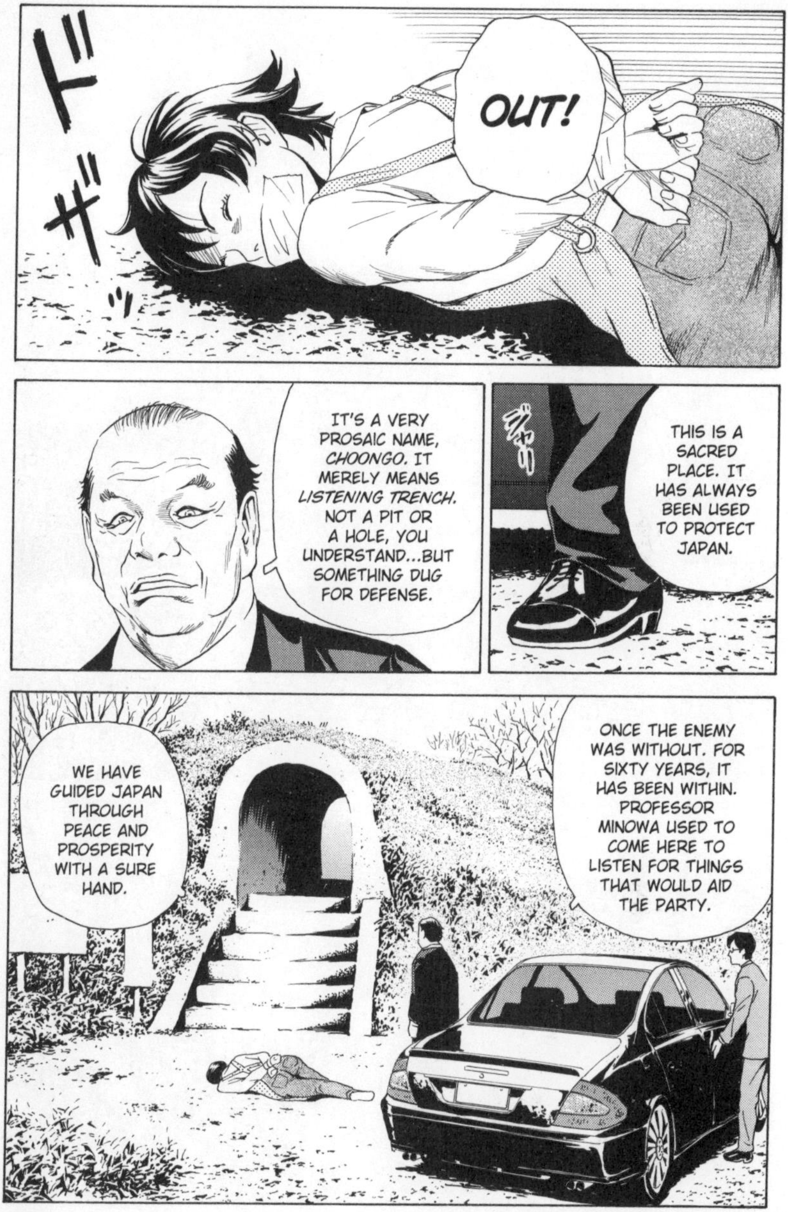
ドザッ
OUT!
ジャリ
THIS IS A SACRED PLACE. IT HAS ALWAYS BEEN USED TO PROTECT JAPAN.
IT'S A VERY PROSAIC NAME, *CHOONGO*. IT MERELY MEANS *LISTENING TRENCH*. NOT A PIT OR A HOLE, YOU UNDERSTAND...BUT SOMETHING DUG FOR DEFENSE.
ONCE THE ENEMY WAS WITHOUT. FOR SIXTY YEARS, IT HAS BEEN WITHIN. PROFESSOR MINOWA USED TO COME HERE TO LISTEN FOR THINGS THAT WOULD AID THE PARTY.
WE HAVE GUIDED JAPAN THROUGH PEACE AND PROSPERITY WITH A SURE HAND.

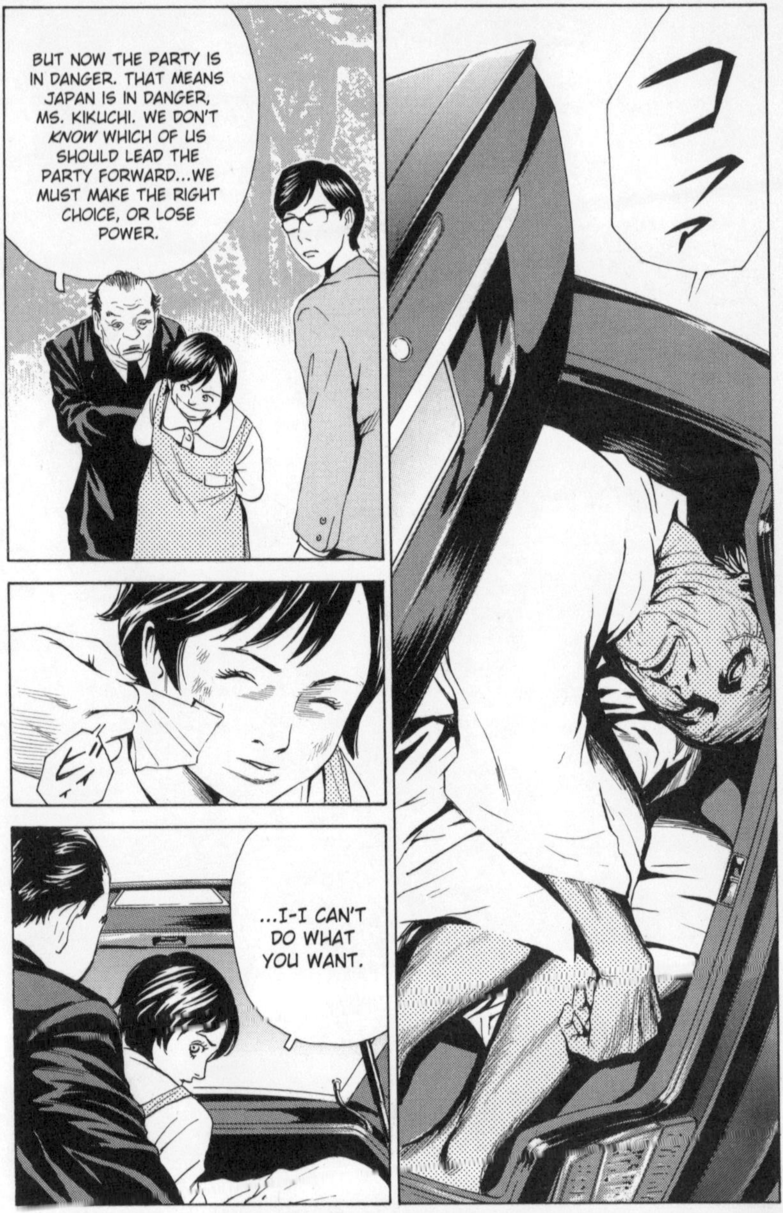
BUT NOW THE PARTY IS IN DANGER. THAT MEANS JAPAN IS IN DANGER, MS. KIKUCHI. WE DON'T *KNOW* WHICH OF US SHOULD LEAD THE PARTY FORWARD...WE MUST MAKE THE RIGHT CHOICE, OR LOSE POWER.
...I-I CAN'T DO WHAT YOU WANT.

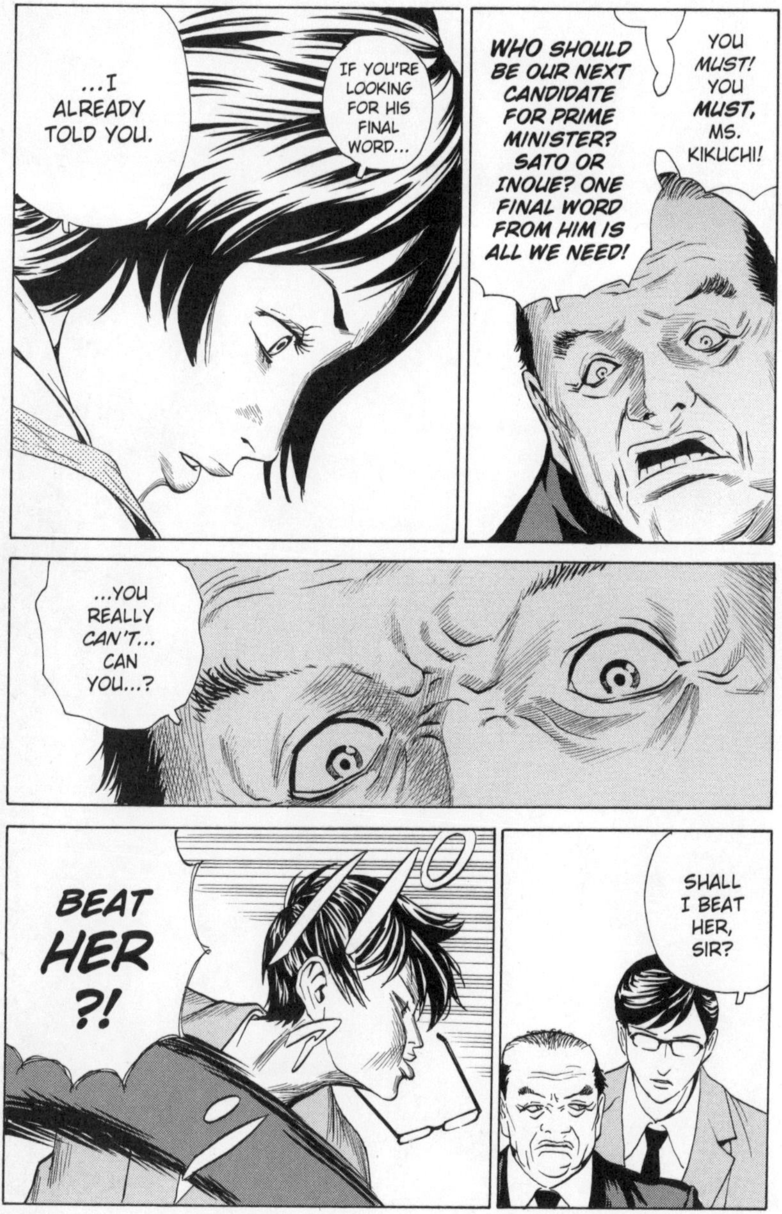
YOU MUST! YOU MUST, MS. KIKUCHI!
WHO SHOULD BE OUR NEXT CANDIDATE FOR PRIME MINISTER? SATO OR INOUE? ONE FINAL WORD FROM HIM IS ALL WE NEED!
IF YOU'RE LOOKING FOR HIS FINAL WORD...
...I ALREADY TOLD YOU.
...YOU REALLY CAN'T... CAN YOU...?
SHALL I BEAT HER, SIR?
BEAT HER ?!

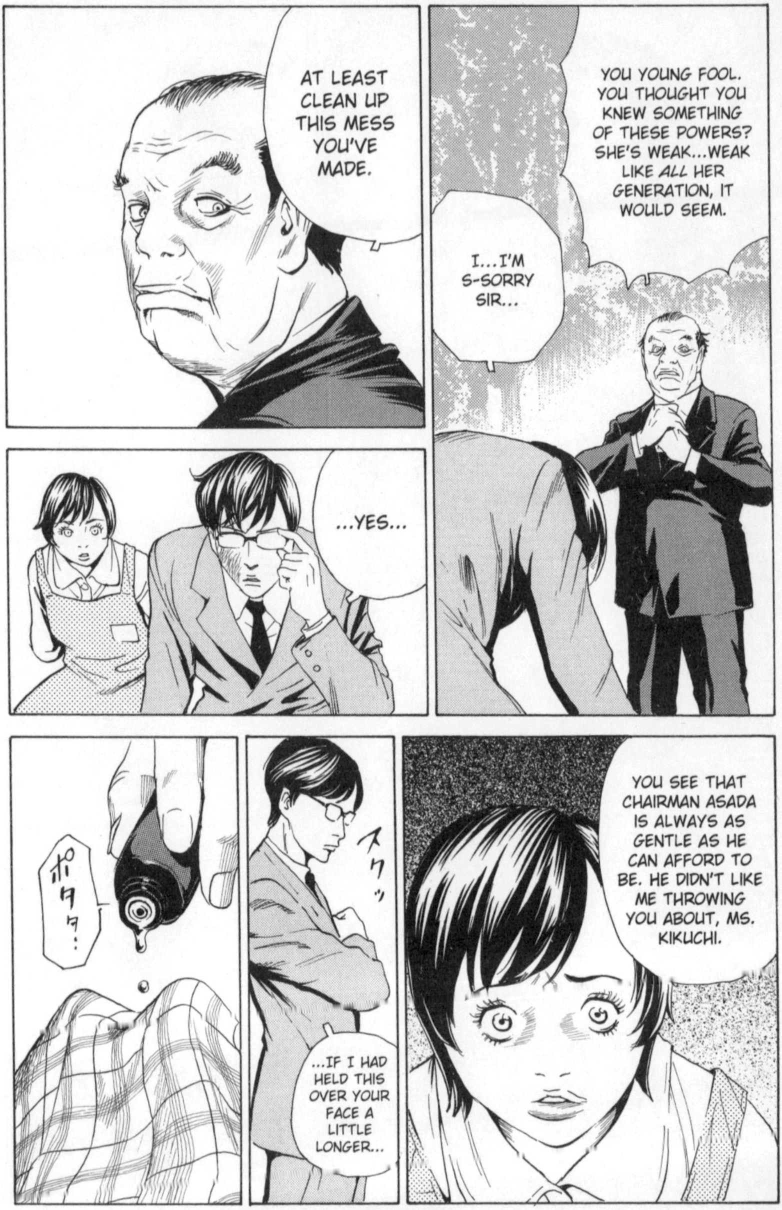
YOU YOUNG FOOL. YOU THOUGHT YOU KNEW SOMETHING OF THESE POWERS? SHE'S WEAK...WEAK LIKE *ALL* HER GENERATION, IT WOULD SEEM.
I...I'M S-SORRY SIR...
AT LEAST CLEAN UP THIS MESS YOU'VE MADE.
...YES...
YOU SEE THAT CHAIRMAN ASADA IS ALWAYS AS GENTLE AS HE CAN AFFORD TO BE. HE DIDN'T LIKE ME THROWING YOU ABOUT, MS. KIKUCHI.
スクッ
...IF I HAD HELD THIS OVER YOUR FACE A LITTLE LONGER...
ポタタ‥

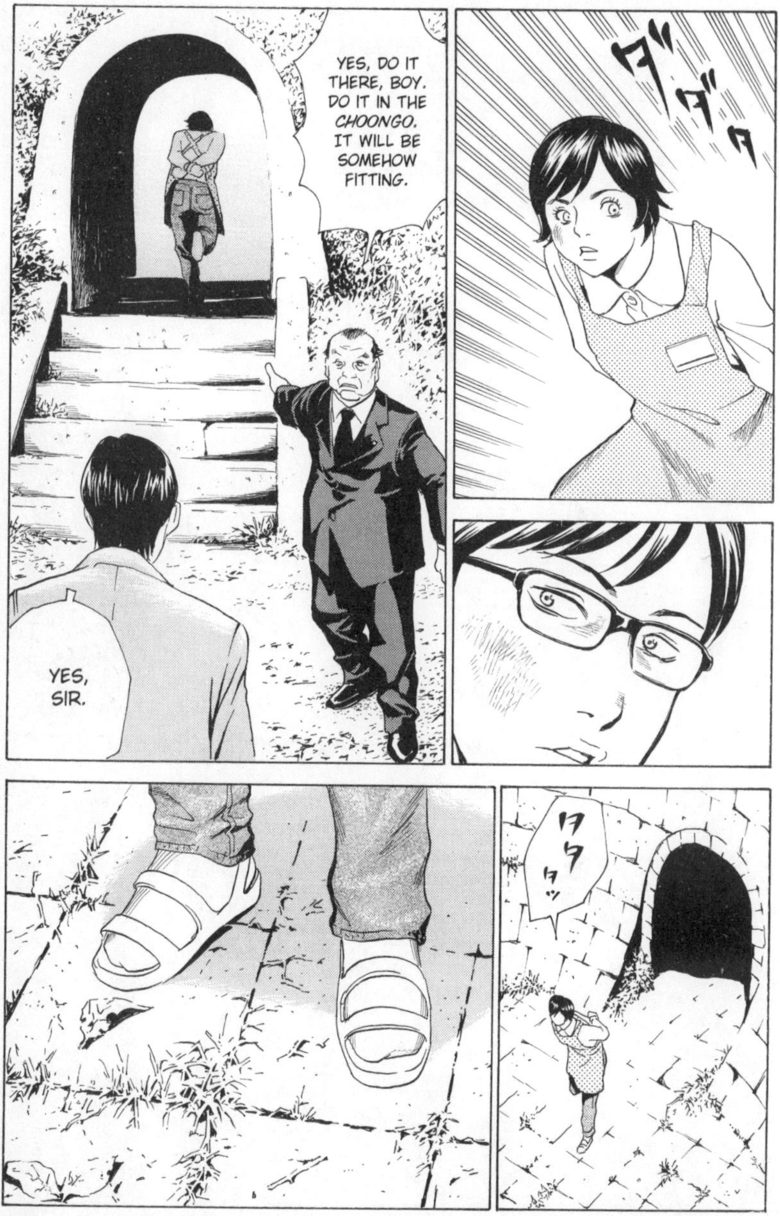
ダダタ
YES, DO IT THERE, BOY. DO IT IN THE *CHOONGO*. IT WILL BE SOMEHOW FITTING.
YES, SIR.
タタタッ

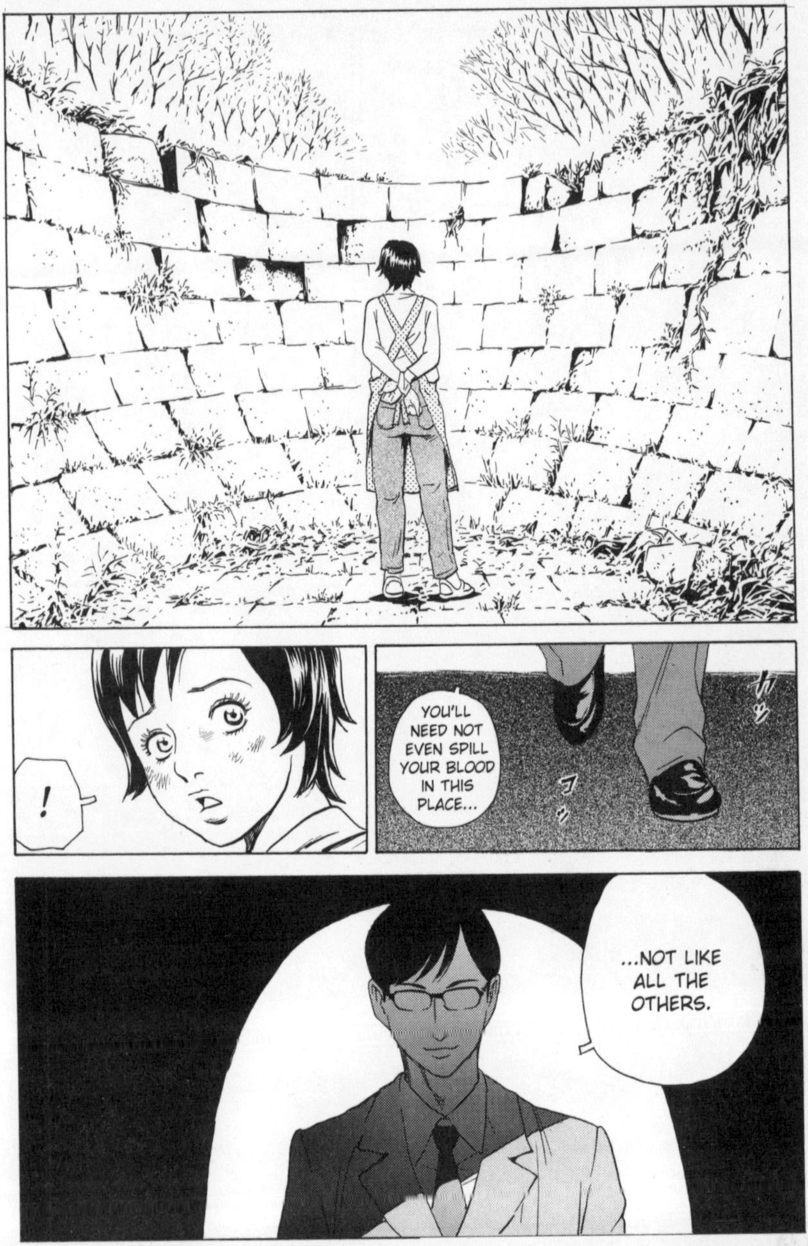
YOU'LL NEED NOT EVEN SPILL YOUR BLOOD IN THIS PLACE...
!
...NOT LIKE ALL THE OTHERS.

6th delivery: a certain situation—the end

NOW, LET'S JUST DO THIS PEACEFULLY ...
IT CAN'T BE!
!
...YES, *YES!* HE'S COME BACK. PROFESSOR, I KNEW YOU WOULDN'T FAIL US...
...SIR ...?
カチャ
カチャ

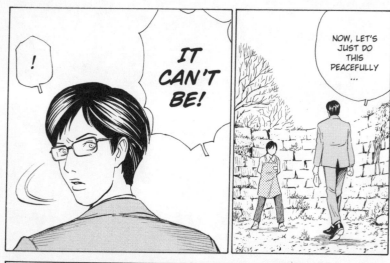

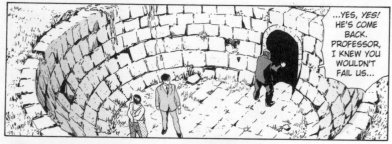

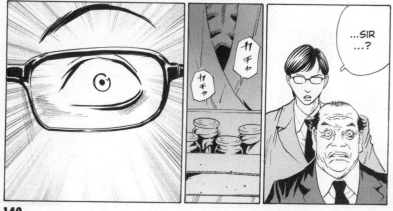

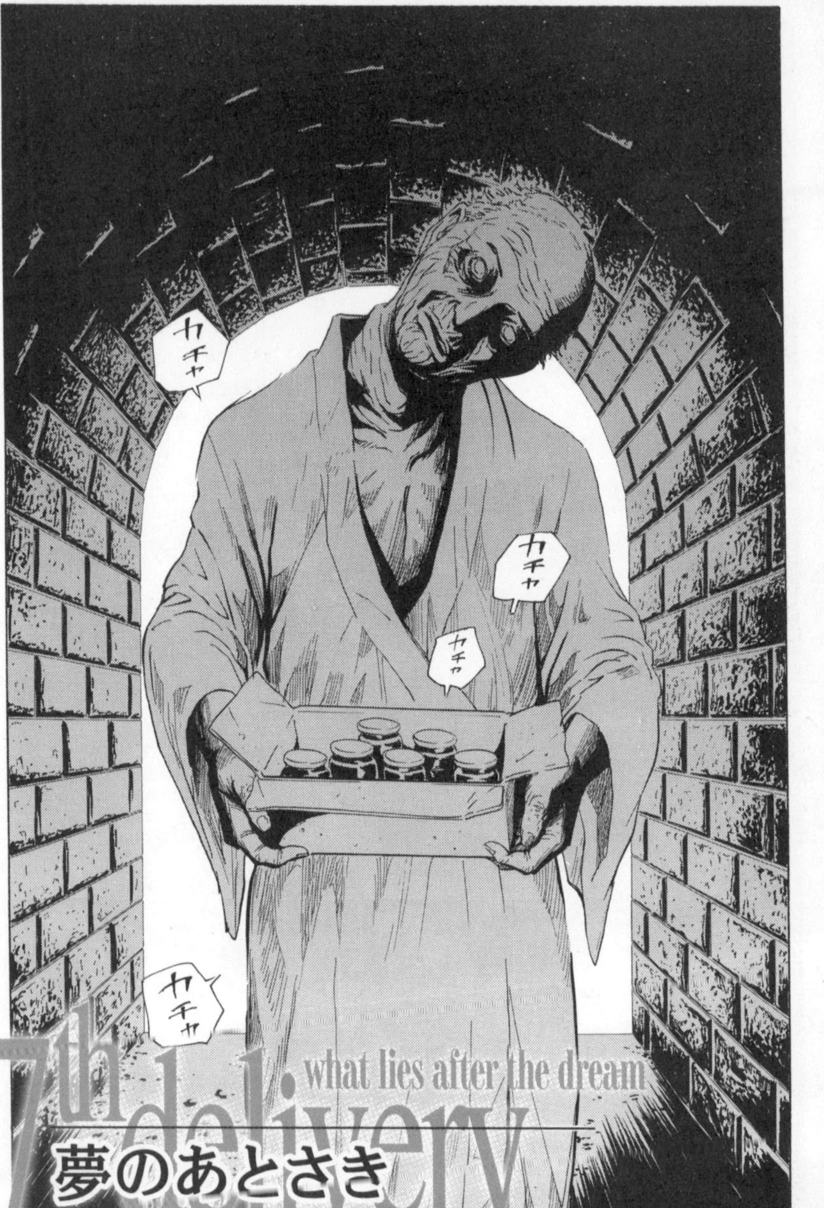
カチャ
カチャ
カチャ
カチャ

7th delivery
what lies after the dream
夢のあとさき

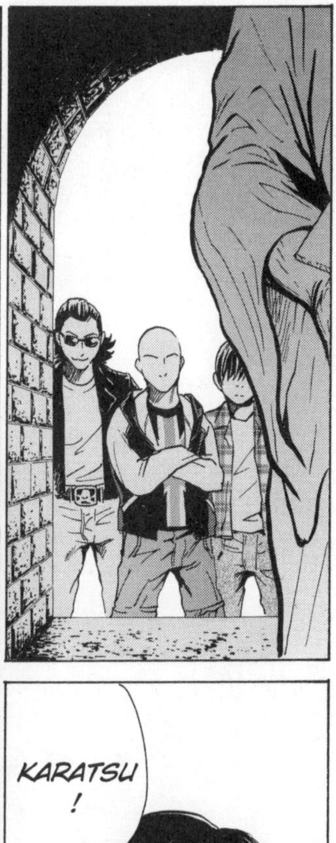

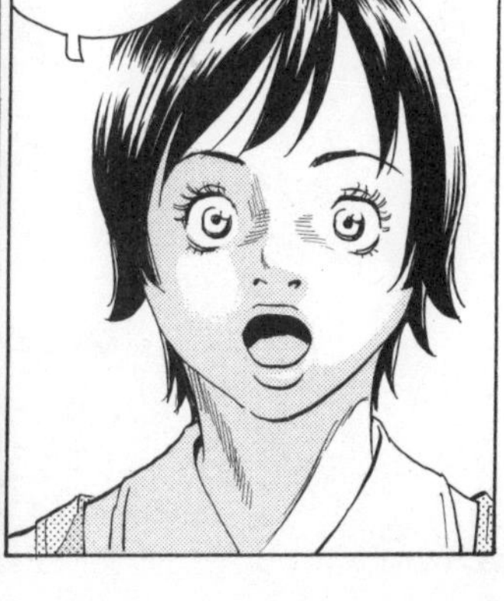
KARATSU
!

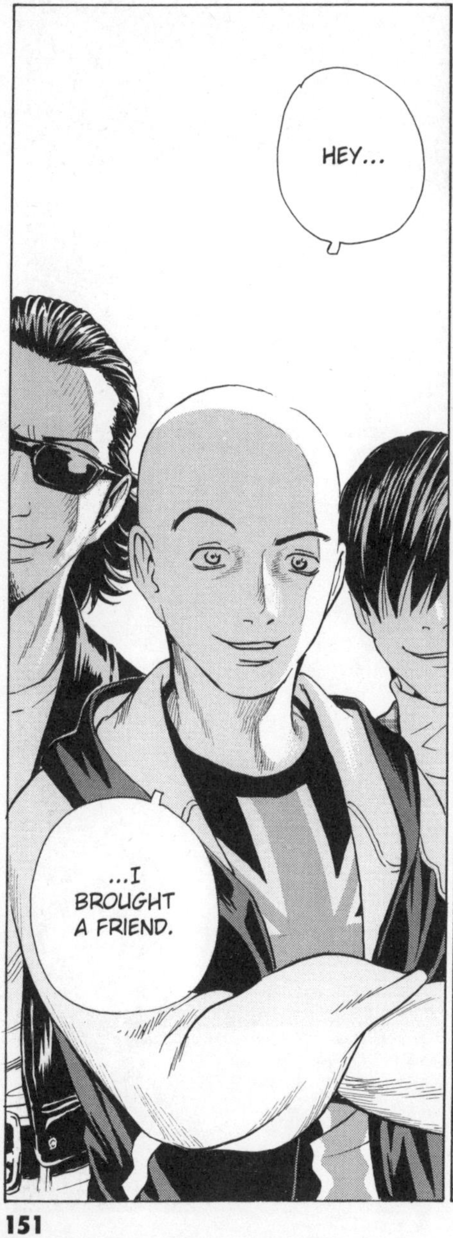
HEY...
...I BROUGHT A FRIEND.

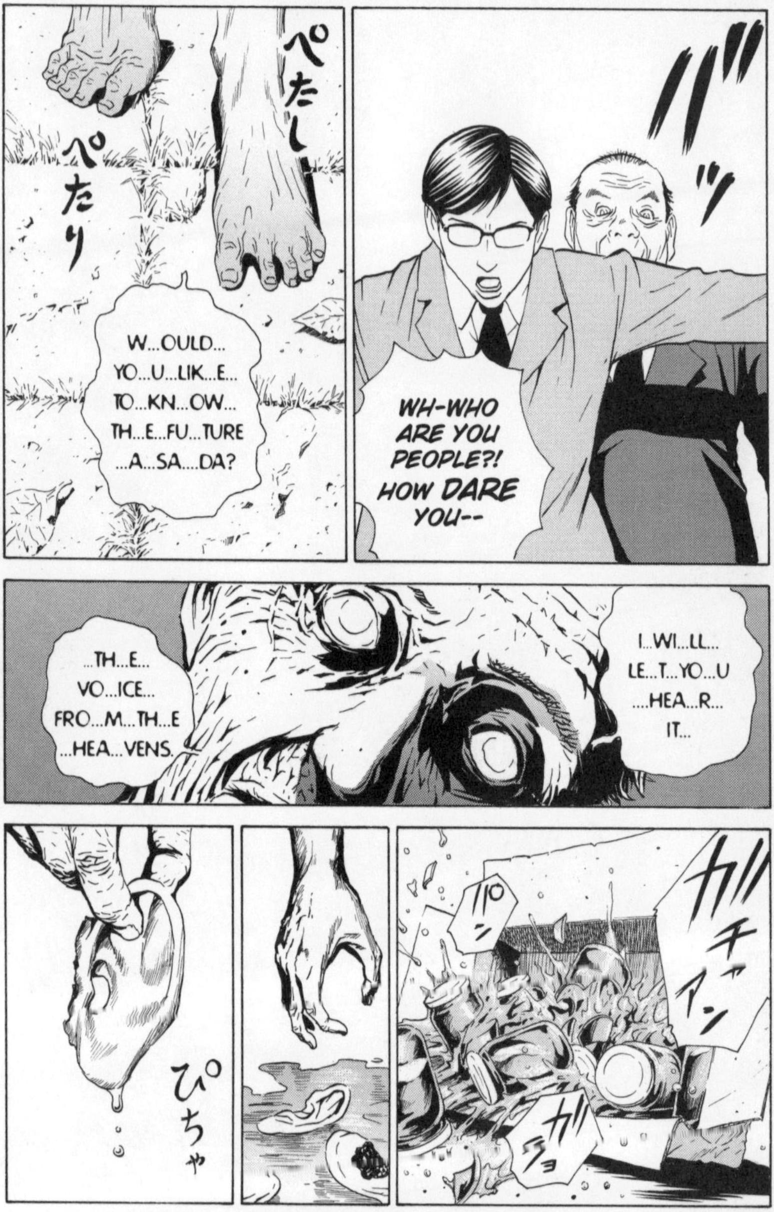
WH-WHO ARE YOU PEOPLE?! HOW DARE YOU--
ぺたし
ぺたり
W...OULD... YO...U...LIK...E... TO...KN...OW... TH...E...FU...TURE ...A...SA...DA?
I...WI...LL... LE...T...YO...U ....HEA...R... IT...
...TH...E... VO...ICE... FRO...M...TH...E ...HEA...VENS.
ガチャン
パリン
ぴちゃ

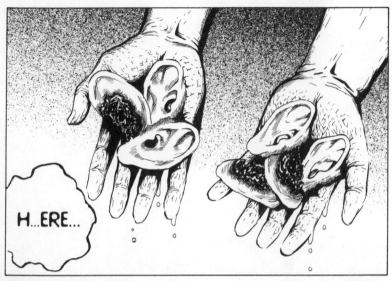

H...ERE...

LIS...TEN...

...HEAR.

ぴちゃり

くちゃ

I...
I...

...H...EAR...

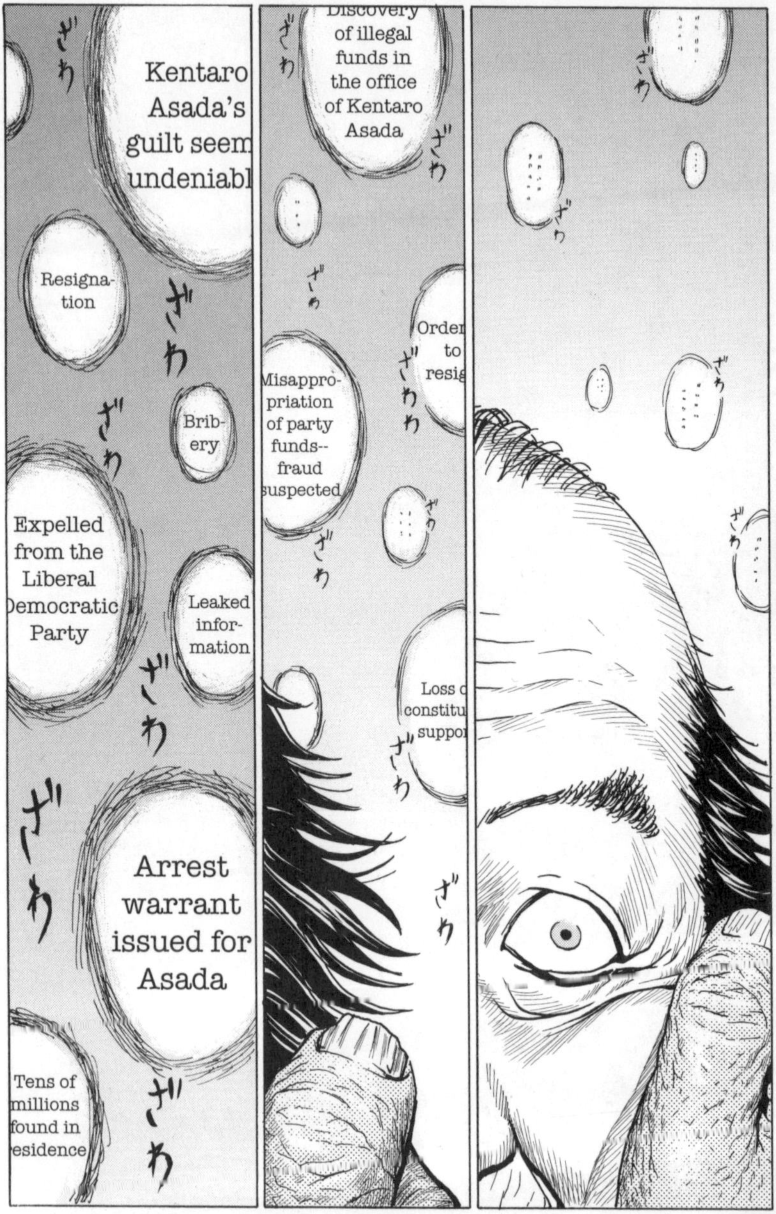
ざわ
ざわ
ざわ
ざわ
Discovery of illegal funds in the office of Kentaro Asada
ざわ
ざわ
Order to resig
ざわわ
Misappro-priation of party funds--fraud suspected
ざわ
ざわ
Loss c constitu suppor
ざわ
ざわ
ざわ
Kentaro Asada's guilt seem undeniabl
Resigna-tion
ざわ
ざわ
Bribery
Expelled from the Liberal emocratic Party
Leaked infor-mation
ざわ
ざわ
Arrest warrant issued for Asada
Tens of millions found in esidence
ざわ

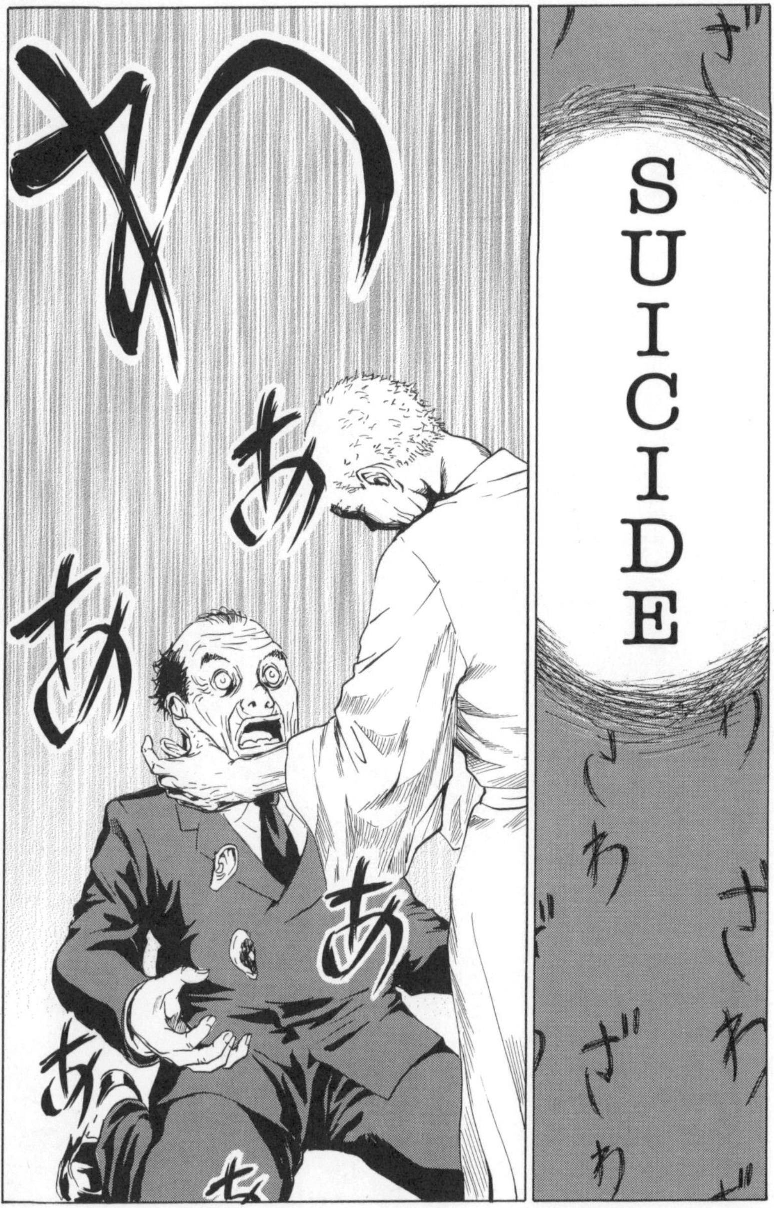
ざわ
SUICIDE
ざわざわ
ざわざわ
やあああ

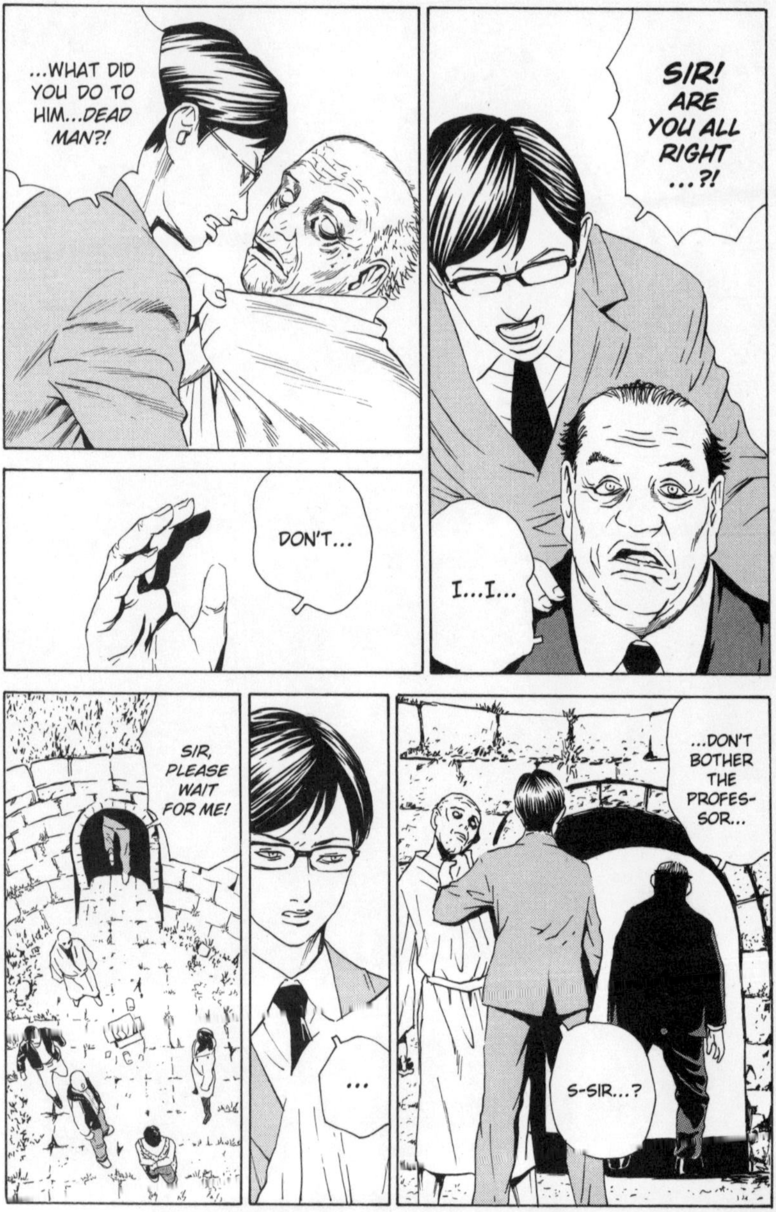
SIR! ARE YOU ALL RIGHT ...?!
I...I...
...WHAT DID YOU DO TO HIM...DEAD MAN?!
DON'T...
...DON'T BOTHER THE PROFES-SOR...
S-SIR...?
...
SIR, PLEASE WAIT FOR ME!

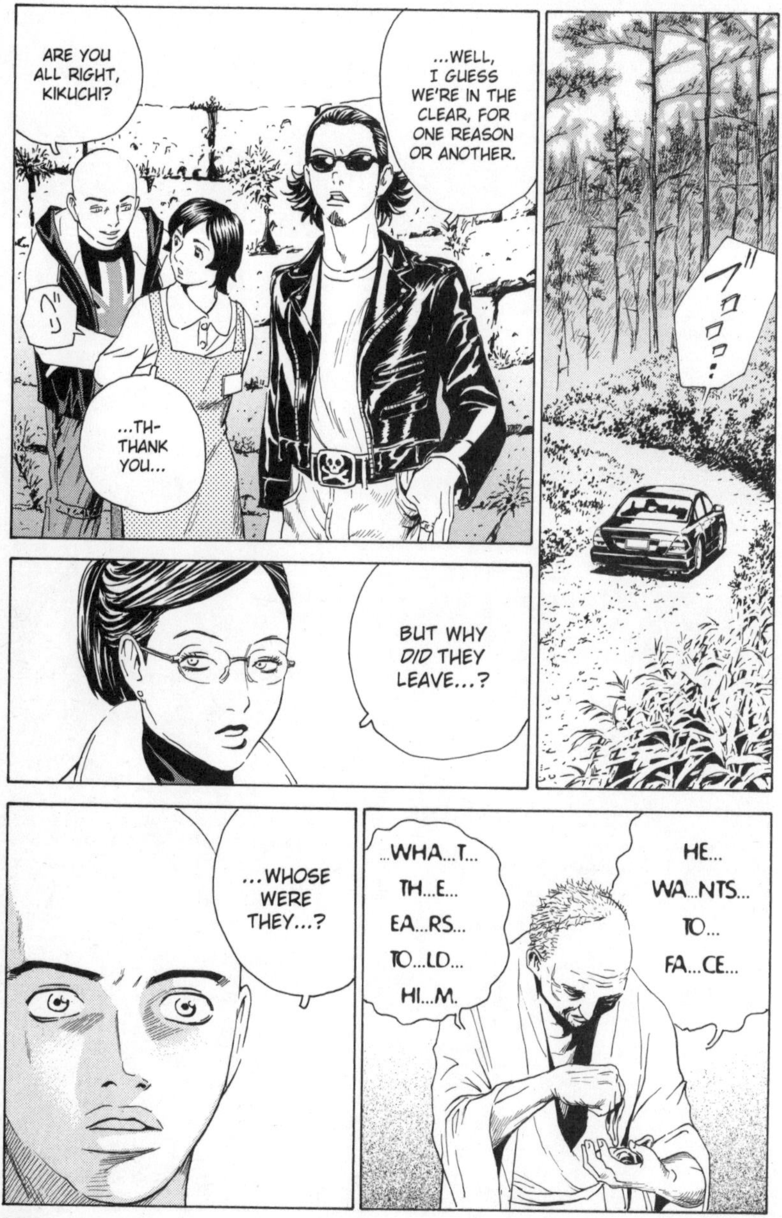
ブロロロ…
...WELL, I GUESS WE'RE IN THE CLEAR, FOR ONE REASON OR ANOTHER.
ARE YOU ALL RIGHT, KIKUCHI?
ベリ
...TH-THANK YOU...
BUT WHY *DID* THEY LEAVE...?
HE... WA...NTS... TO... FA...CE...
...WHA...T... TH...E... EA...RS... TO...LD... HI...M.
...WHOSE WERE THEY...?

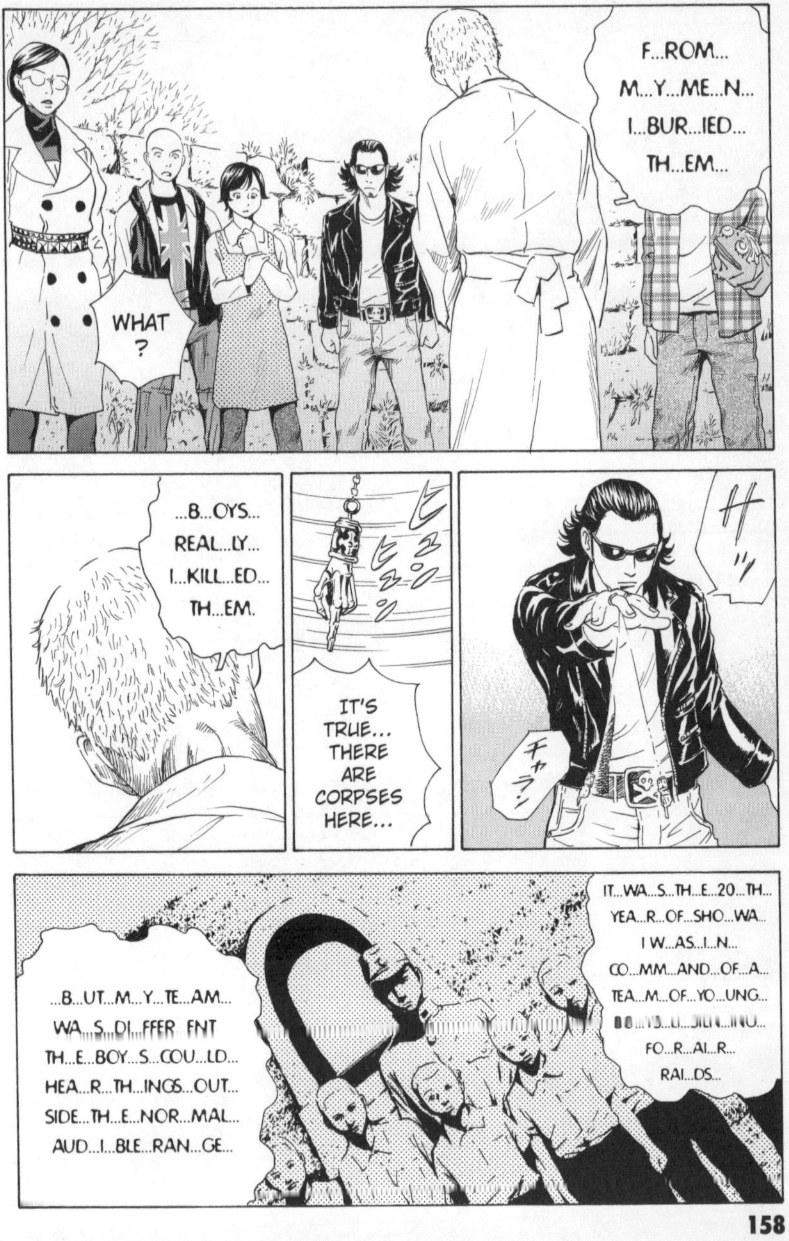
F...ROM...
M...Y...ME...N...
I...BUR...IED...
TH...EM...
WHAT
?
ハッ
チャラン
ヒュン
ヒュン
IT'S TRUE... THERE ARE CORPSES HERE...
...B...OYS...
REAL...LY...
I...KILL...ED...
TH...EM.
IT...WA...S...TH...E...20...TH...
YEA...R...OF...SHO...WA...
I W...AS...I...N...
CO...MM...AND...OF...A...
TEA...M...OF...YO...UNG...
FO...R...AI...R...
RAI...DS...
...B...UT...M...Y...TE...AM...
WA...S...DI...FFER...ENT
TH...E...BOY...S...COU...LD...
HEA...R...TH...INGS...OUT...
SIDE...TH...E...NOR...MAL...
AUD...I...BLE...RAN...GE...

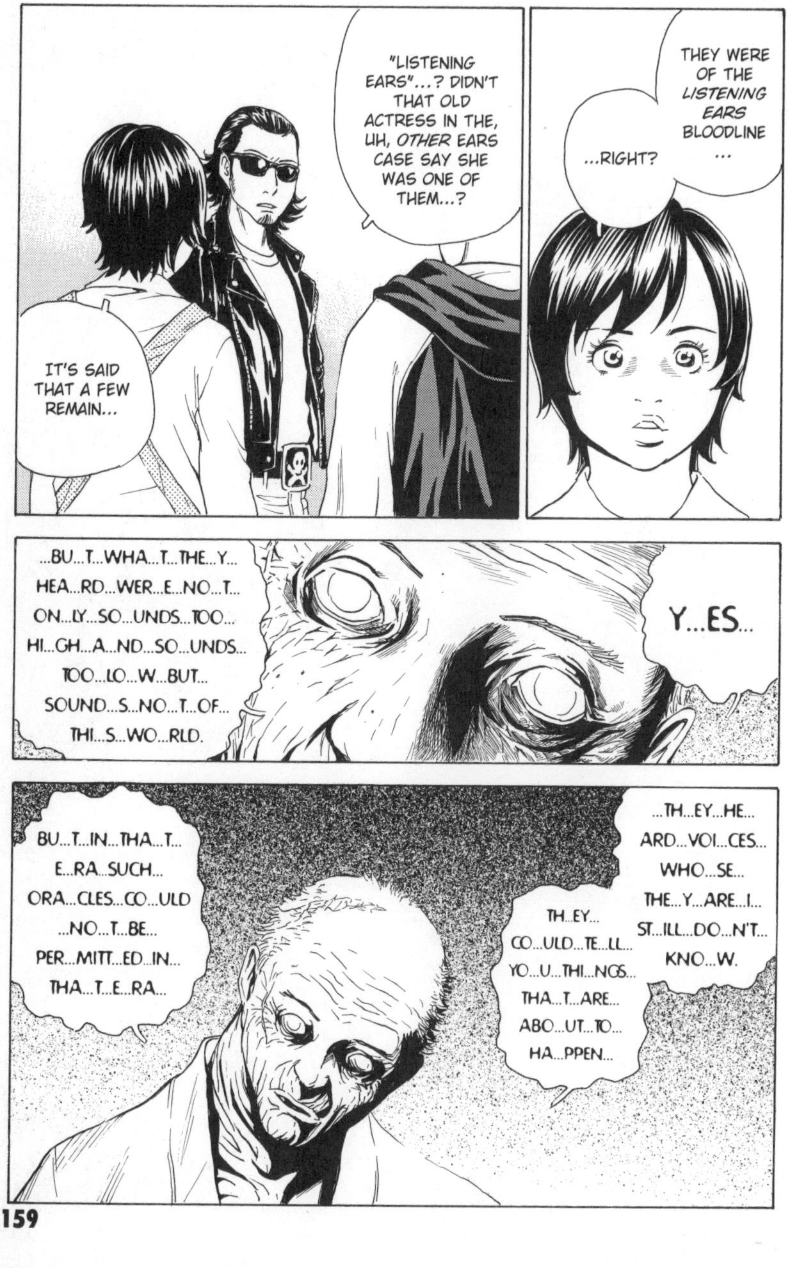
THEY WERE OF THE *LISTENING EARS* BLOODLINE ...
...RIGHT?
"LISTENING EARS"...? DIDN'T THAT OLD ACTRESS IN THE, UH, *OTHER* EARS CASE SAY SHE WAS ONE OF THEM...?
IT'S SAID THAT A FEW REMAIN...
Y...ES...
...BU...T...WHA...T...THE...Y... HEA...RD...WER...E...NO...T... ON...LY...SO...UNDS...TOO... HI...GH...A...ND...SO...UNDS... TOO...LO...W...BUT... SOUND...S...NO...T...OF... THI...S...WO...RLD.
...TH...EY...HE... ARD...VOI...CES... WHO...SE... THE...Y...ARE...I... ST...ILL...DO...N'T... KNO...W.
TH...EY... CO...ULD...TE...LL... YO...U...THI...NGS... THA...T...ARE... ABO...UT...TO... HA...PPEN...
BU...T...IN...THA...T... E...RA...SUCH... ORA...CLES...CO...ULD ...NO...T...BE... PER...MITT...ED...IN... THA...T...E...RA...

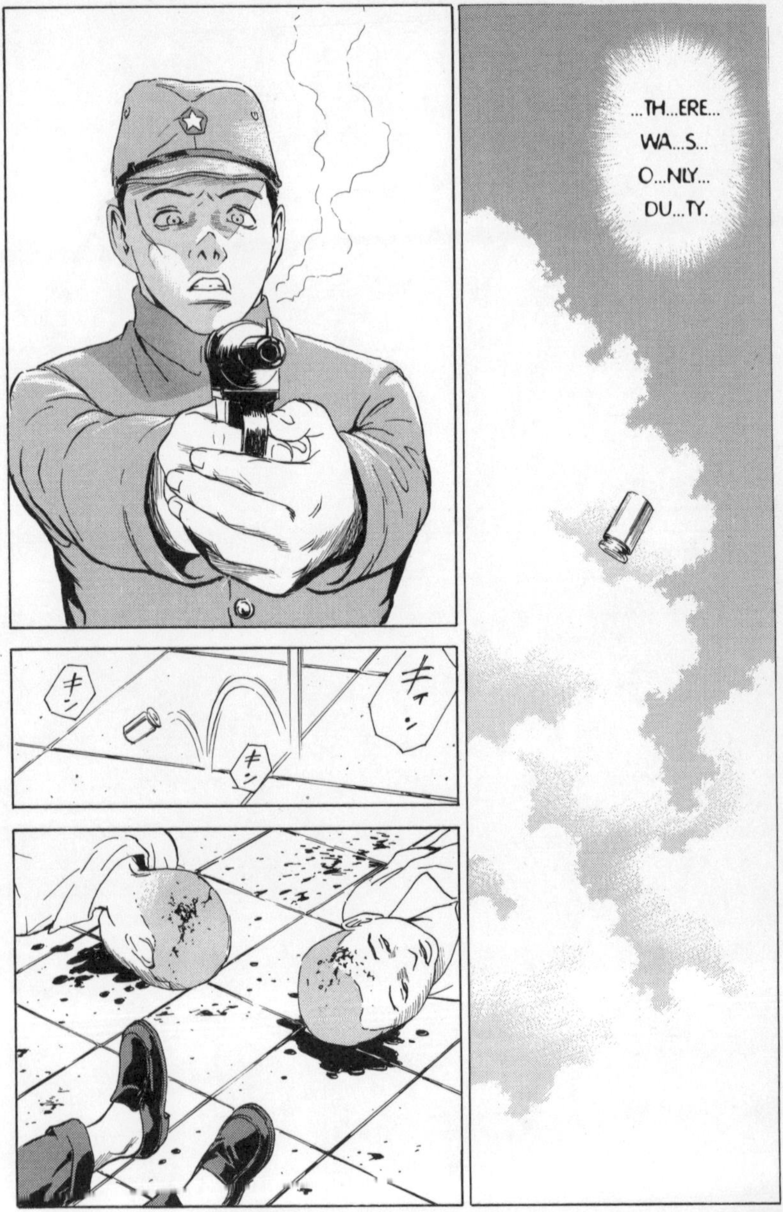
...TH...ERE... WA...S... O...NLY... DU...TY.
キィン
キン
キン

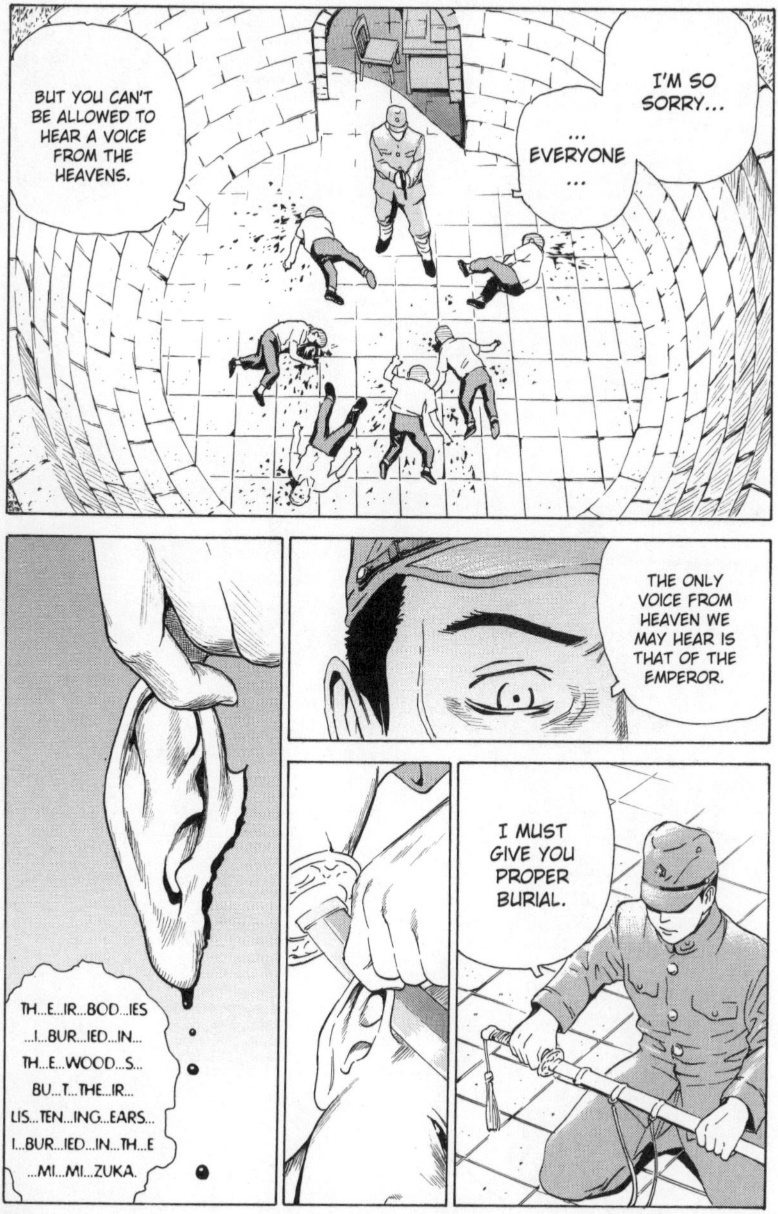
I'M SO SORRY...
... EVERYONE ...
BUT YOU CAN'T BE ALLOWED TO HEAR A VOICE FROM THE HEAVENS.
THE ONLY VOICE FROM HEAVEN WE MAY HEAR IS THAT OF THE EMPEROR.
I MUST GIVE YOU PROPER BURIAL.
TH...E...IR...BOD...IES ...I...BUR...IED...IN... TH...E...WOOD...S... BU...T...THE...IR... LIS...TEN...ING...EARS... I...BUR...IED...IN...TH...E ...MI...MI...ZUKA.

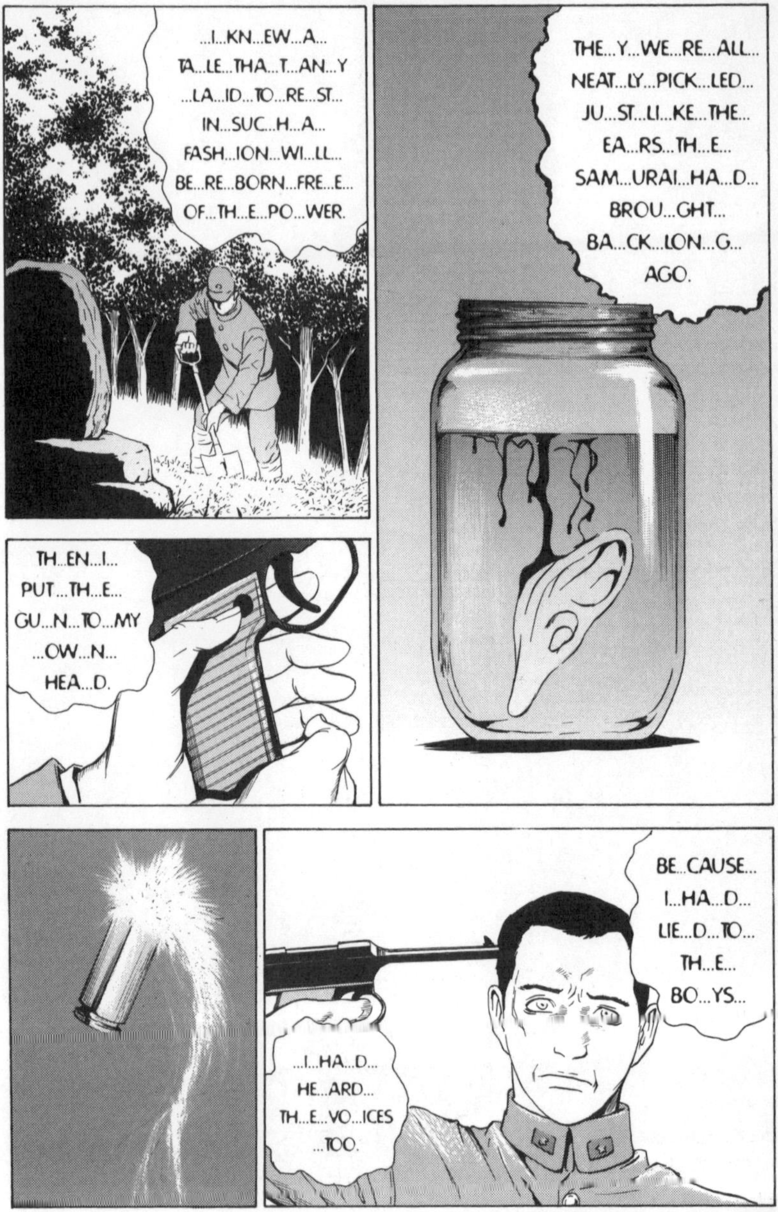
THE...Y...WE...RE...ALL... NEAT...LY...PICK...LED... JU...ST...LI...KE...THE... EA...RS...TH...E... SAM...URAI...HA...D... BROU...GHT... BA...CK...LON...G... AGO.
...I...KN...EW...A... TA...LE...THA...T...AN...Y ...LA...ID...TO...RE...ST... IN...SUC...H...A... FASH...ION...WI...LL... BE...RE...BORN...FRE...E... OF...TH...E...PO...WER.
TH...EN...I... PUT...TH...E... GU...N...TO...MY ...OW...N... HEA...D.
BE...CAUSE... I...HA...D... LIE...D...TO... TH...E... BO...YS...
...I...HA...D... HE...ARD... TH...E...VO...ICES ...TOO.

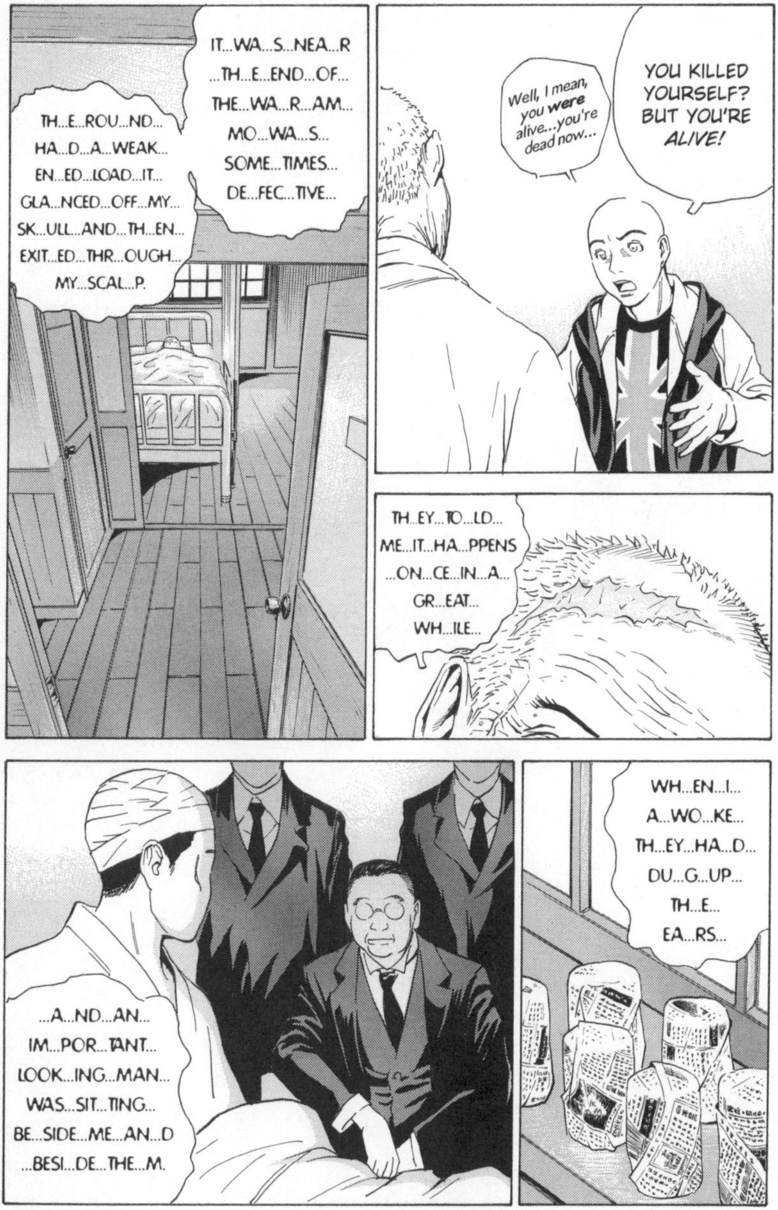
YOU KILLED YOURSELF? BUT YOU'RE *ALIVE!*
Well, I mean, you **were** alive...you're dead now...
TH...EY...TO...LD... ME...IT...HA...PPENS ...ON...CE...IN...A... GR...EAT... WH...ILE...
IT...WA...S...NEA...R ...TH...E...END...OF... THE...WA...R...AM... MO...WA...S... SOME...TIMES... DE...FEC...TIVE...
TH...E...ROU...ND... HA...D...A...WEAK... EN...ED...LOAD...IT... GLA...NCED...OFF...MY... SK...ULL...AND...TH...EN... EXIT...ED...THR...OUGH... MY...SCAL...P.
WH...EN...I... A...WO...KE... TH...EY...HA...D... DU...G...UP... TH...E... EA...RS...
...A...ND...AN... IM...POR...TANT... LOOK...ING...MAN... WAS...SIT...TING... BE...SIDE...ME...AN...D ...BESI...DE...THE...M.

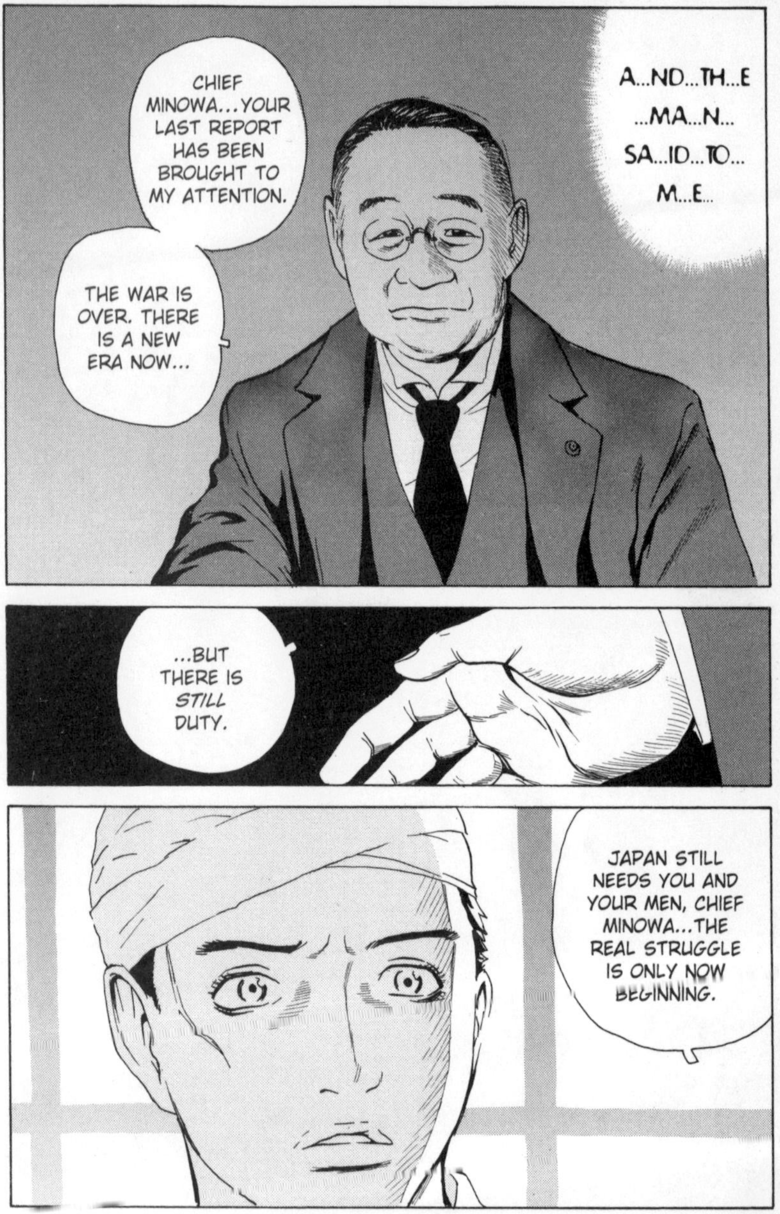
A...ND...TH...E ...MA...N... SA...ID...TO... M...E...
CHIEF MINOWA... YOUR LAST REPORT HAS BEEN BROUGHT TO MY ATTENTION.
THE WAR IS OVER. THERE IS A NEW ERA NOW...
...BUT THERE IS *STILL* DUTY.
JAPAN STILL NEEDS YOU AND YOUR MEN, CHIEF MINOWA... THE REAL STRUGGLE IS ONLY NOW BEGINNING.

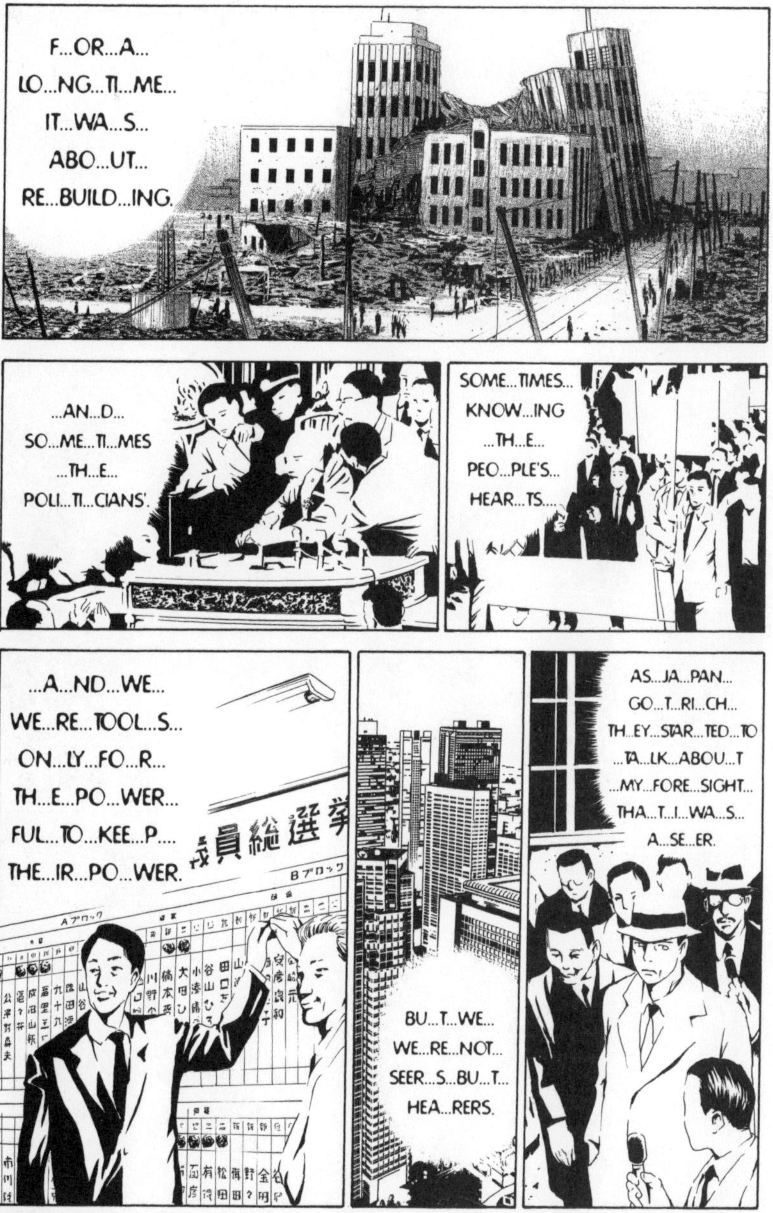
F...OR...A...
LO...NG...TI...ME...
IT...WA...S...
ABO...UT...
RE...BUILD...ING.
SOME...TIMES...
KNOW...ING
...TH...E...
PEO...PLE'S...
HEAR...TS....
...AN...D...
SO...ME...TI...MES
...TH...E...
POLI...TI...CIANS'.
AS...JA...PAN...
GO...T...RI...CH...
TH...EY...STAR...TED...TO
...TA...LK...ABOU...T
...MY...FORE...SIGHT...
THA...T...I...WA...S...
A...SE...ER.
BU...T...WE...
WE...RE...NOT...
SEER...S...BU...T...
HEA...RERS.
...A...ND...WE...
WE...RE...TOOL...S...
ON...LY...FO...R...
TH...E...PO...WER...
FUL...TO...KEE...P....
THE...IR...PO...WER.

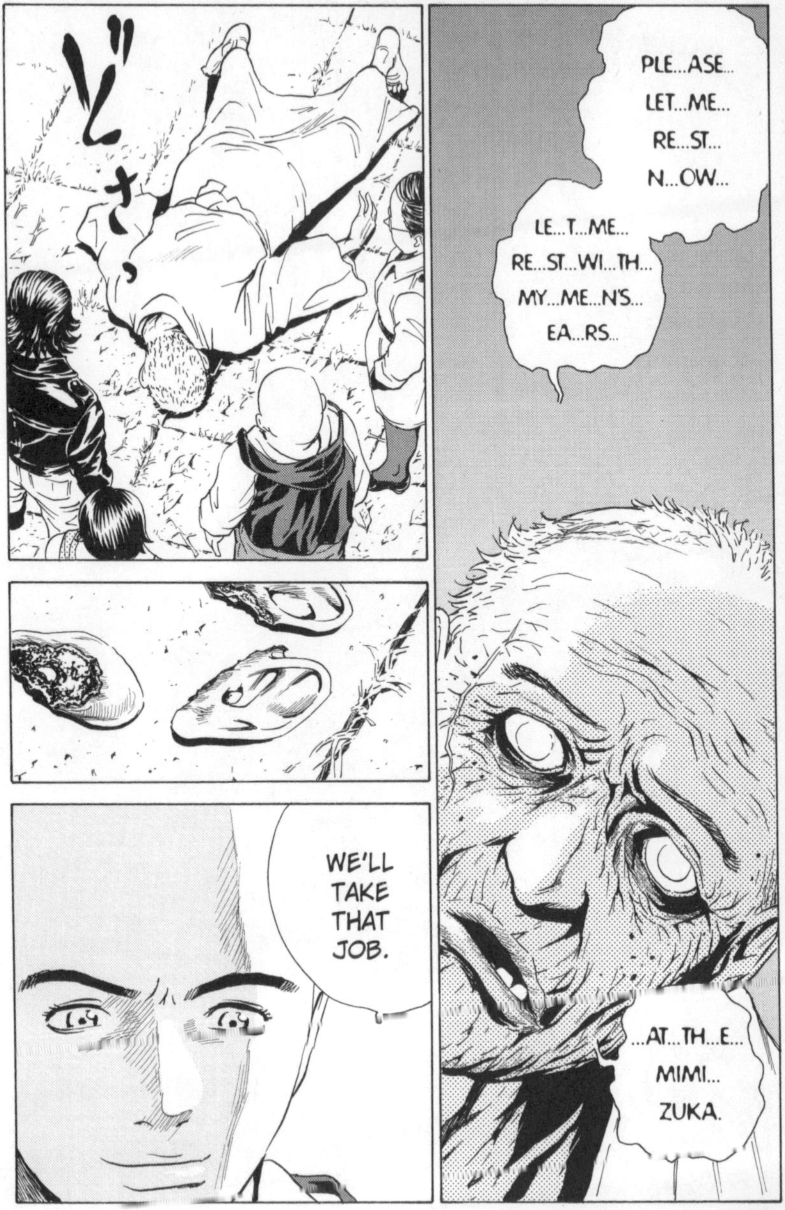
PLE...ASE... LET...ME... RE...ST... N...OW...
LE...T...ME... RE...ST...WI...TH... MY...ME...N'S... EA...RS...
...AT...TH...E... MIMI... ZUKA.
どさっ
WE'LL TAKE THAT JOB.

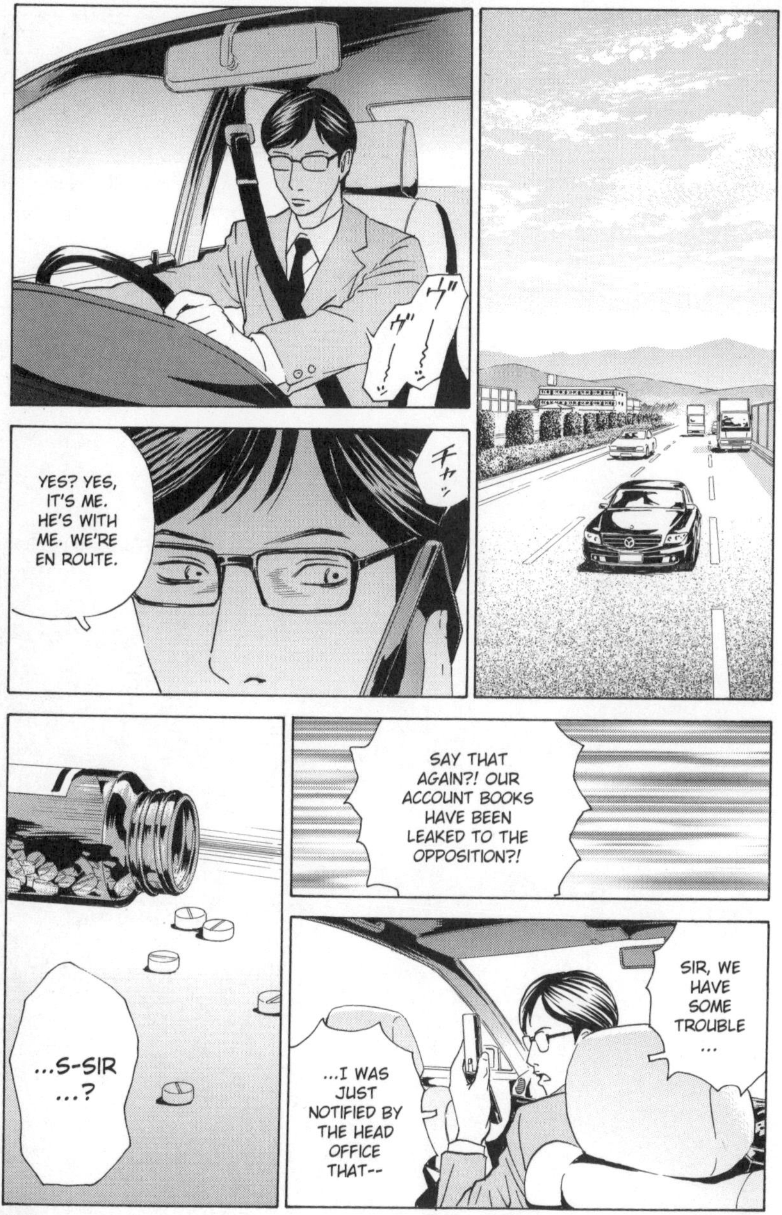
チャッ
YES? YES, IT'S ME. HE'S WITH ME. WE'RE EN ROUTE.
SAY THAT AGAIN?! OUR ACCOUNT BOOKS HAVE BEEN LEAKED TO THE OPPOSITION?!
SIR, WE HAVE SOME TROUBLE ...
...I WAS JUST NOTIFIED BY THE HEAD OFFICE THAT--
...S-SIR ...?

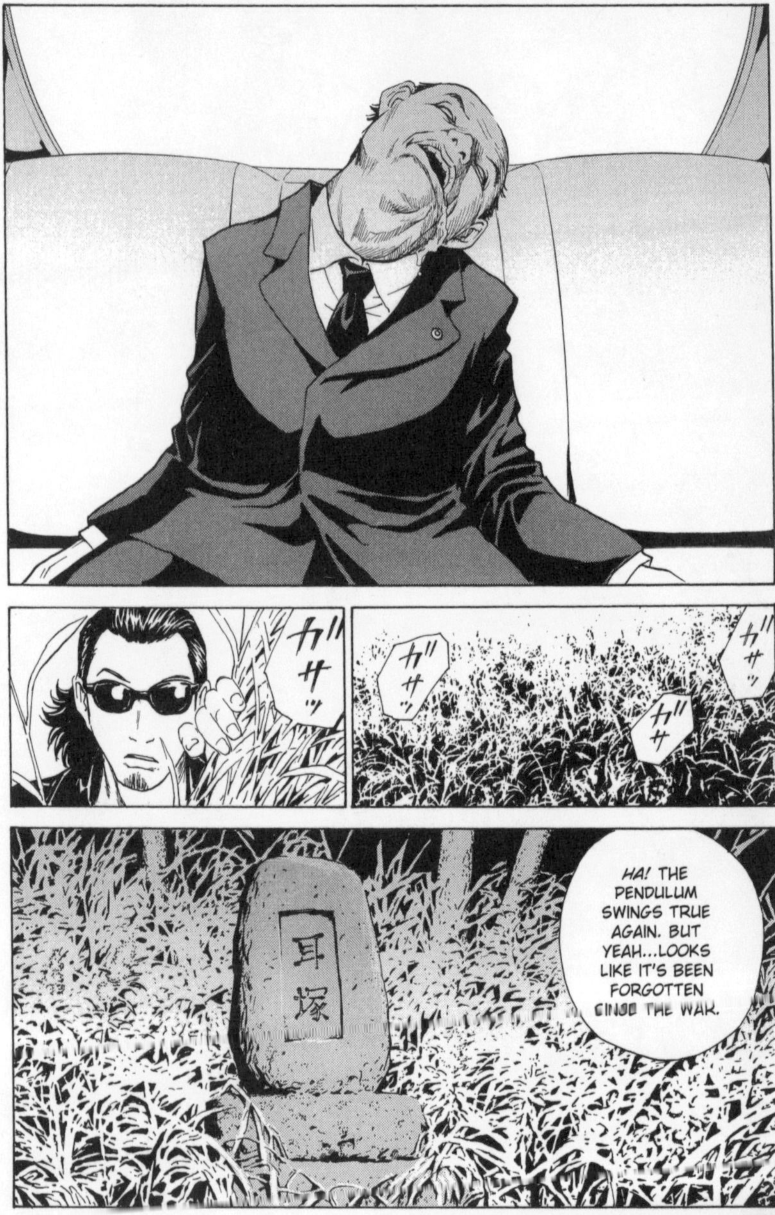
ガサッ
ガサッ
ガサ
ガサッ
耳塚
HA! THE PENDULUM SWINGS TRUE AGAIN. BUT YEAH...LOOKS LIKE IT'S BEEN FORGOTTEN SINCE THE WAR.

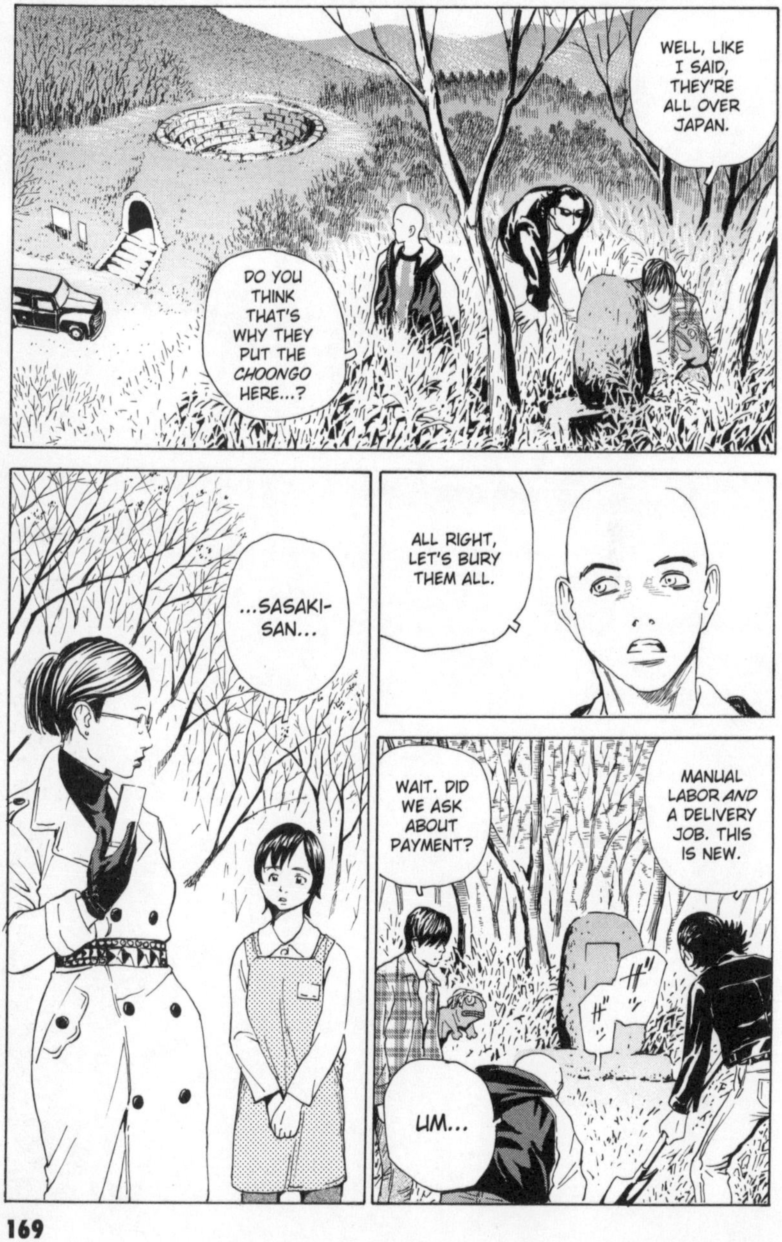
WELL, LIKE I SAID, THEY'RE ALL OVER JAPAN.
DO YOU THINK THAT'S WHY THEY PUT THE *CHOONGO* HERE...?
ALL RIGHT, LET'S BURY THEM ALL.
MANUAL LABOR *AND* A DELIVERY JOB. THIS IS NEW.
WAIT. DID WE ASK ABOUT PAYMENT?
UM...
...SASAKI-SAN...

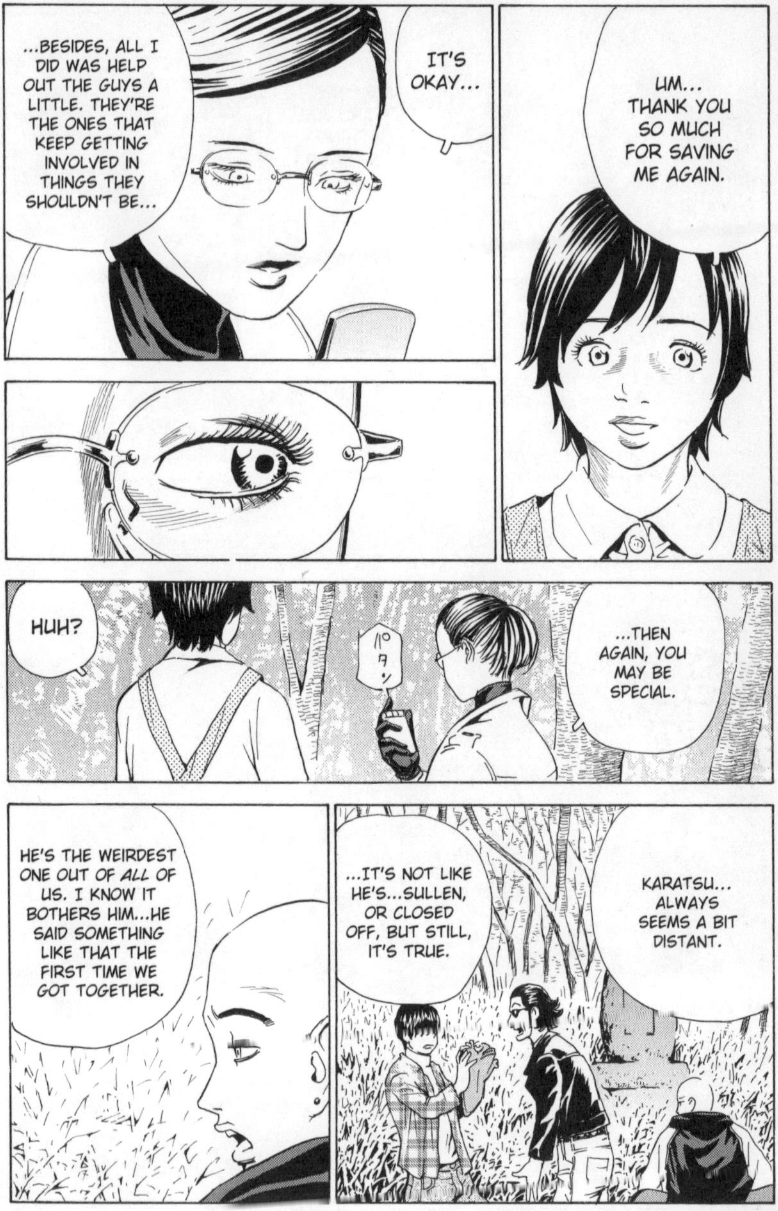
UM... THANK YOU SO MUCH FOR SAVING ME AGAIN.
IT'S OKAY...
...BESIDES, ALL I DID WAS HELP OUT THE GUYS A LITTLE. THEY'RE THE ONES THAT KEEP GETTING INVOLVED IN THINGS THEY SHOULDN'T BE...
...THEN AGAIN, YOU MAY BE SPECIAL.
パタン
HUH?
KARATSU... ALWAYS SEEMS A BIT DISTANT.
...IT'S NOT LIKE HE'S...SULLEN, OR CLOSED OFF, BUT STILL, IT'S TRUE.
HE'S THE WEIRDEST ONE OUT OF *ALL* OF US. I KNOW IT BOTHERS HIM...HE SAID SOMETHING LIKE THAT THE FIRST TIME WE GOT TOGETHER.

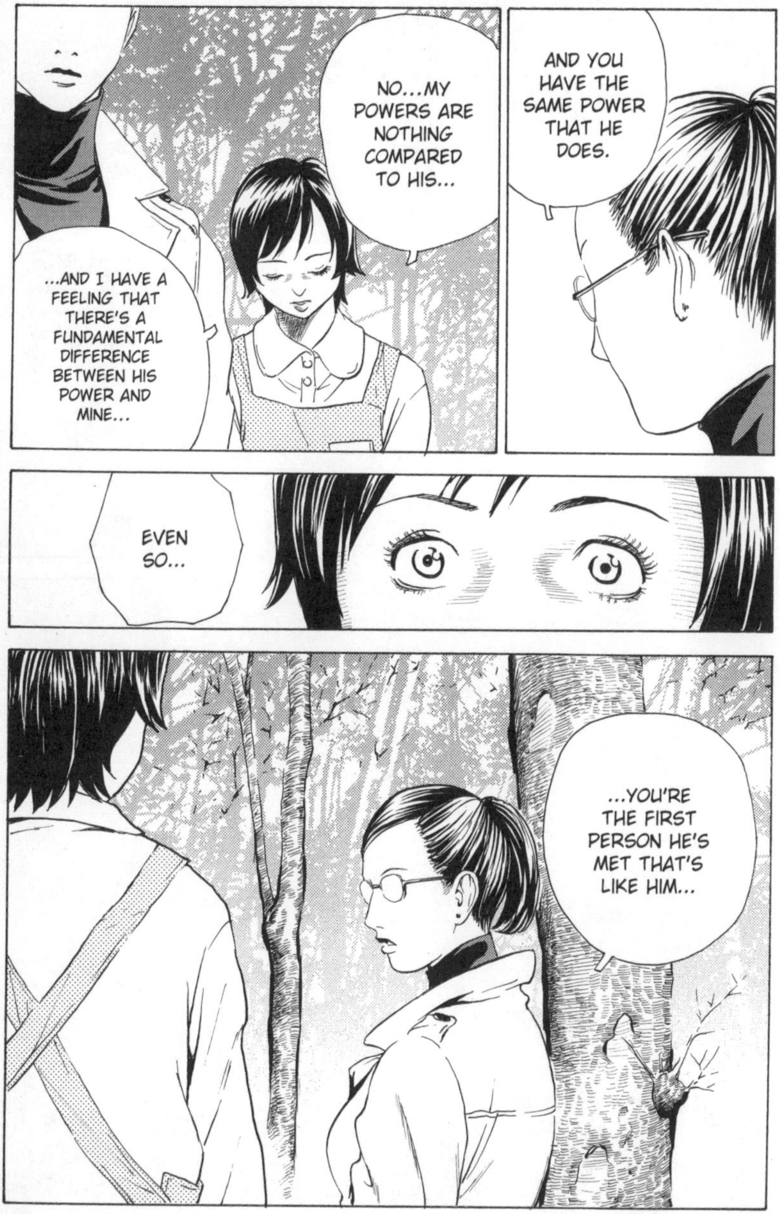
AND YOU HAVE THE SAME POWER THAT HE DOES.
NO…MY POWERS ARE NOTHING COMPARED TO HIS…
…AND I HAVE A FEELING THAT THERE'S A FUNDAMENTAL DIFFERENCE BETWEEN HIS POWER AND MINE…
EVEN SO…
…YOU'RE THE FIRST PERSON HE'S MET THAT'S LIKE HIM…

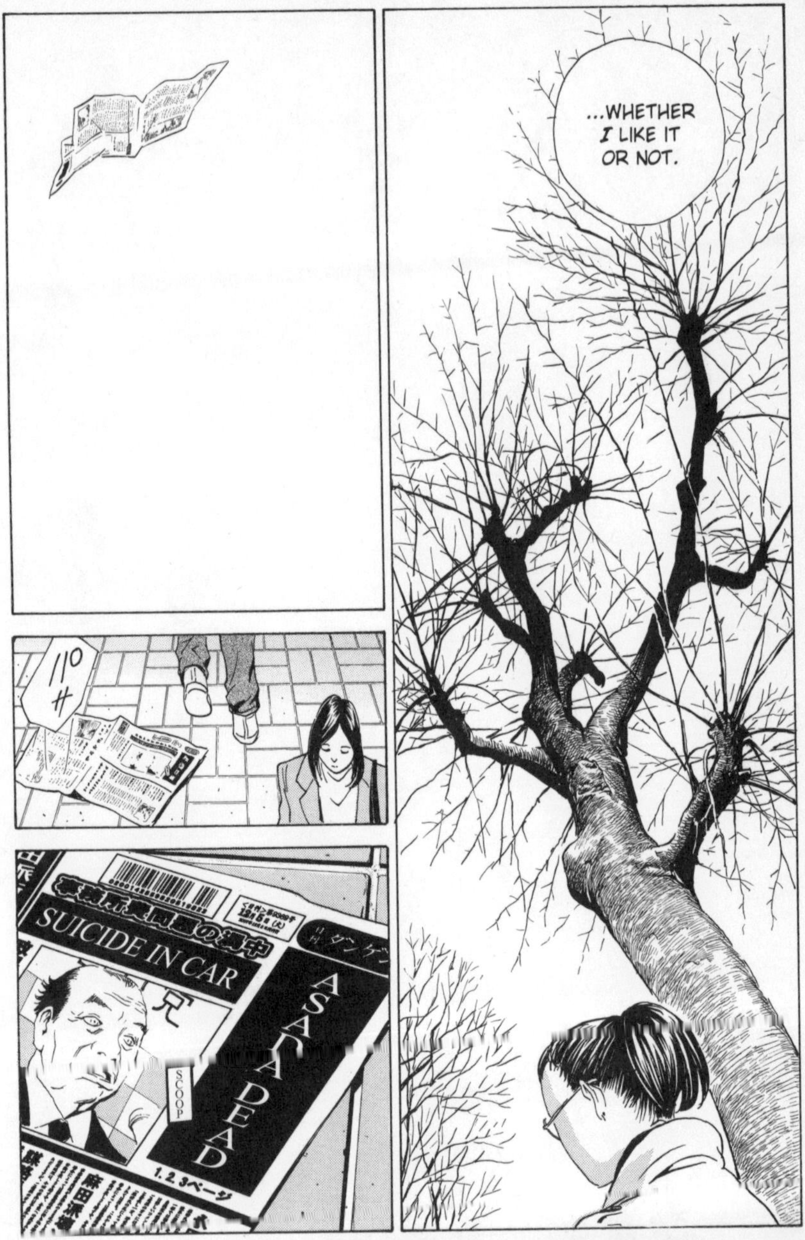
...WHETHER I LIKE IT OR NOT.
パサ
SUICIDE IN CAR
ASADA DEAD
SCOOP
1.2.3ページ

7th delivery: what lies after the dream—the end

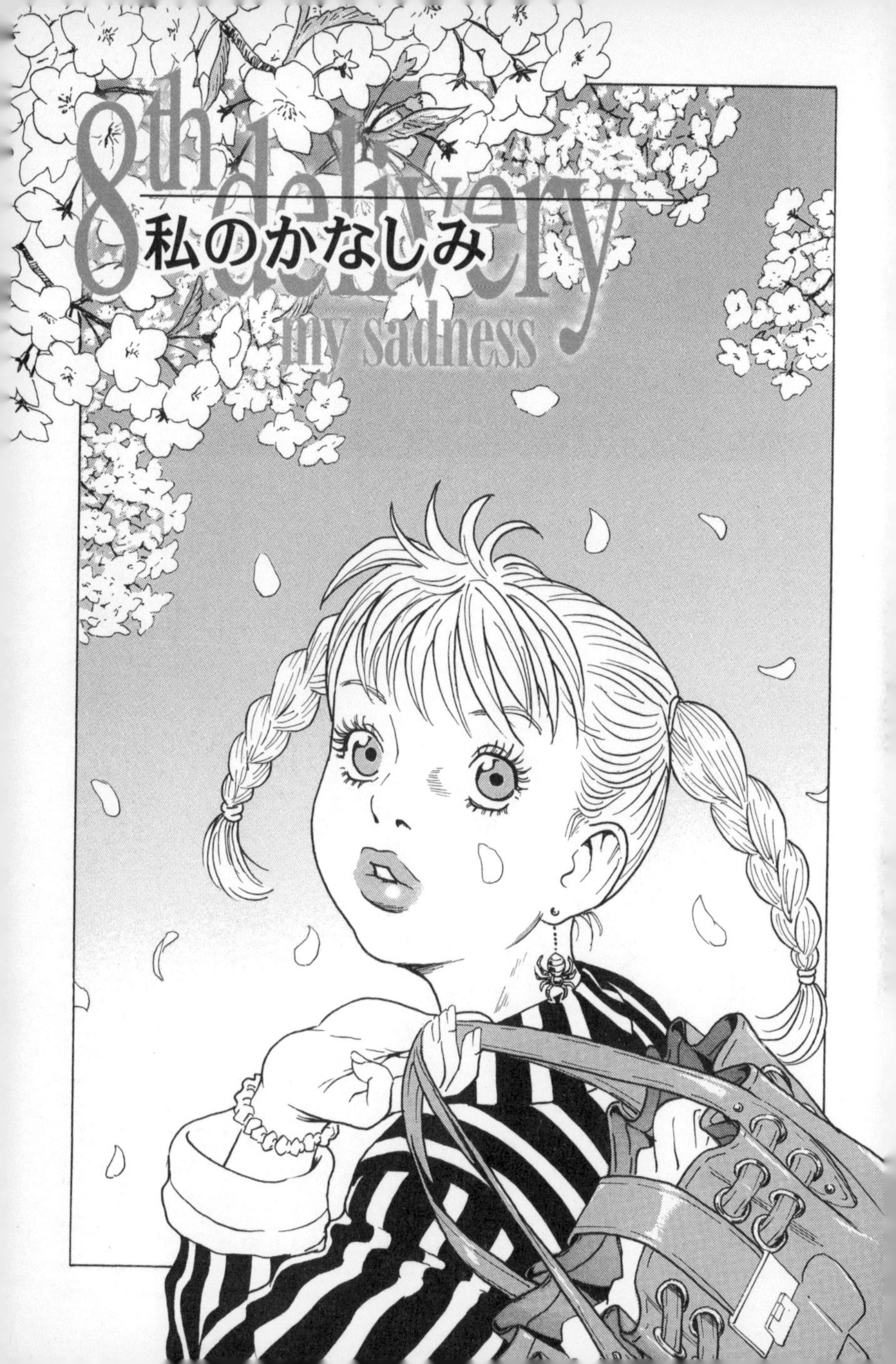
8th delivery
私のかなしみ
my sadness

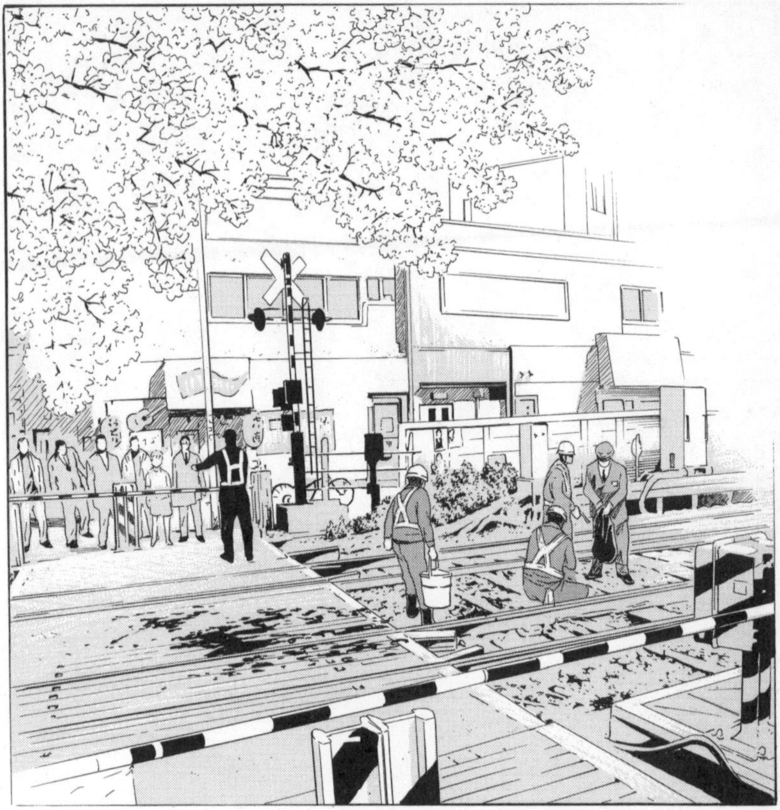

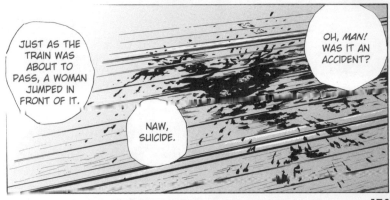

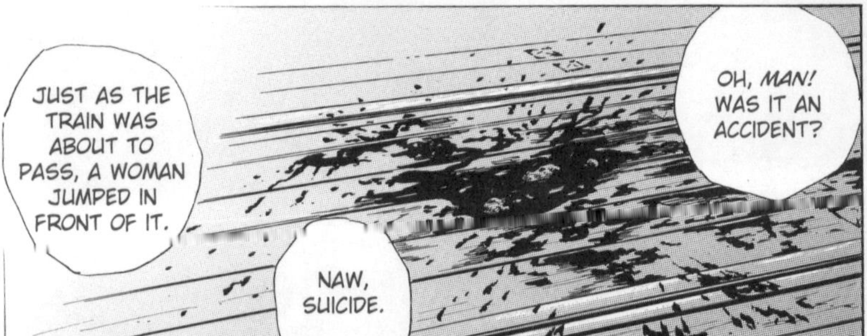
OH, *MAN!* WAS IT AN ACCIDENT?
JUST AS THE TRAIN WAS ABOUT TO PASS, A WOMAN JUMPED IN FRONT OF IT.
NAW, SUICIDE.

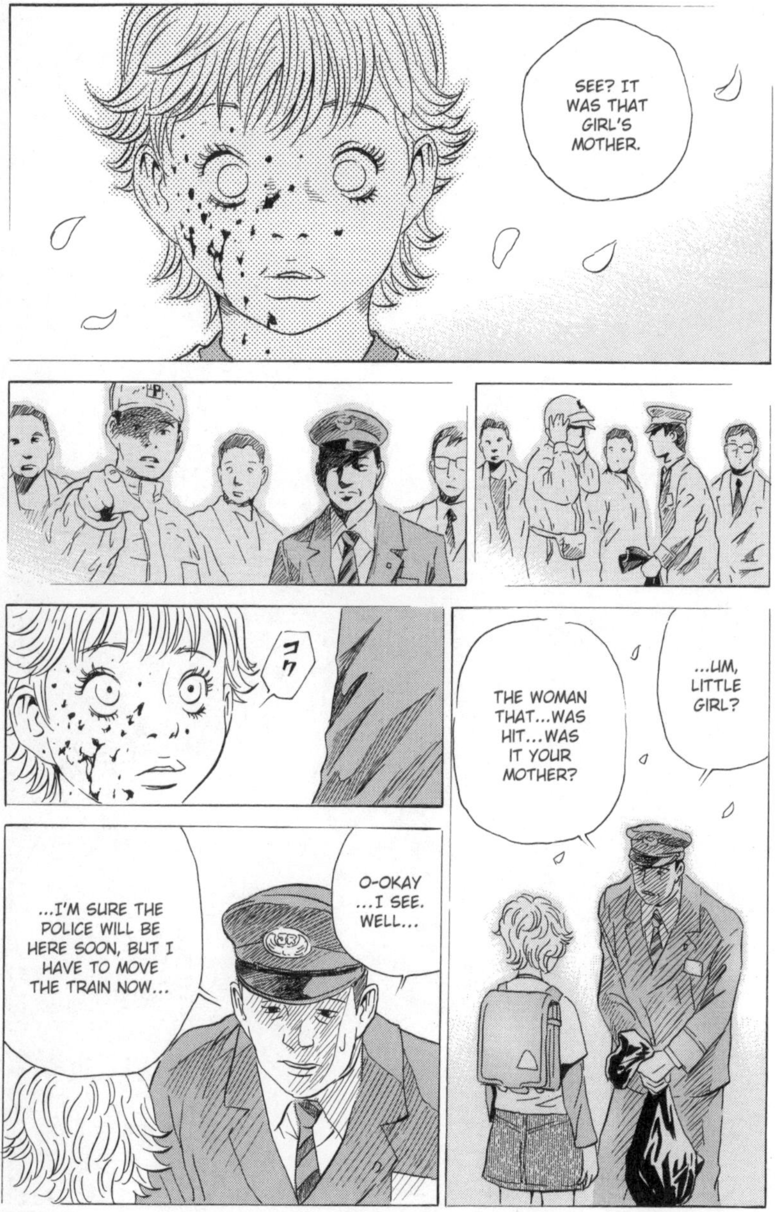
SEE? IT WAS THAT GIRL'S MOTHER.
...UM, LITTLE GIRL?
THE WOMAN THAT...WAS HIT...WAS IT YOUR MOTHER?
コク
O-OKAY ...I SEE. WELL...
...I'M SURE THE POLICE WILL BE HERE SOON, BUT I HAVE TO MOVE THE TRAIN NOW...

...huh?

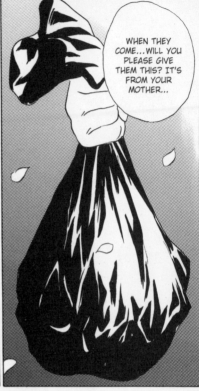

WHEN THEY COME...WILL YOU PLEASE GIVE THEM THIS? IT'S FROM YOUR MOTHER...

MY *mother?* B-BUT...

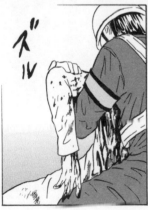

ズ
ル

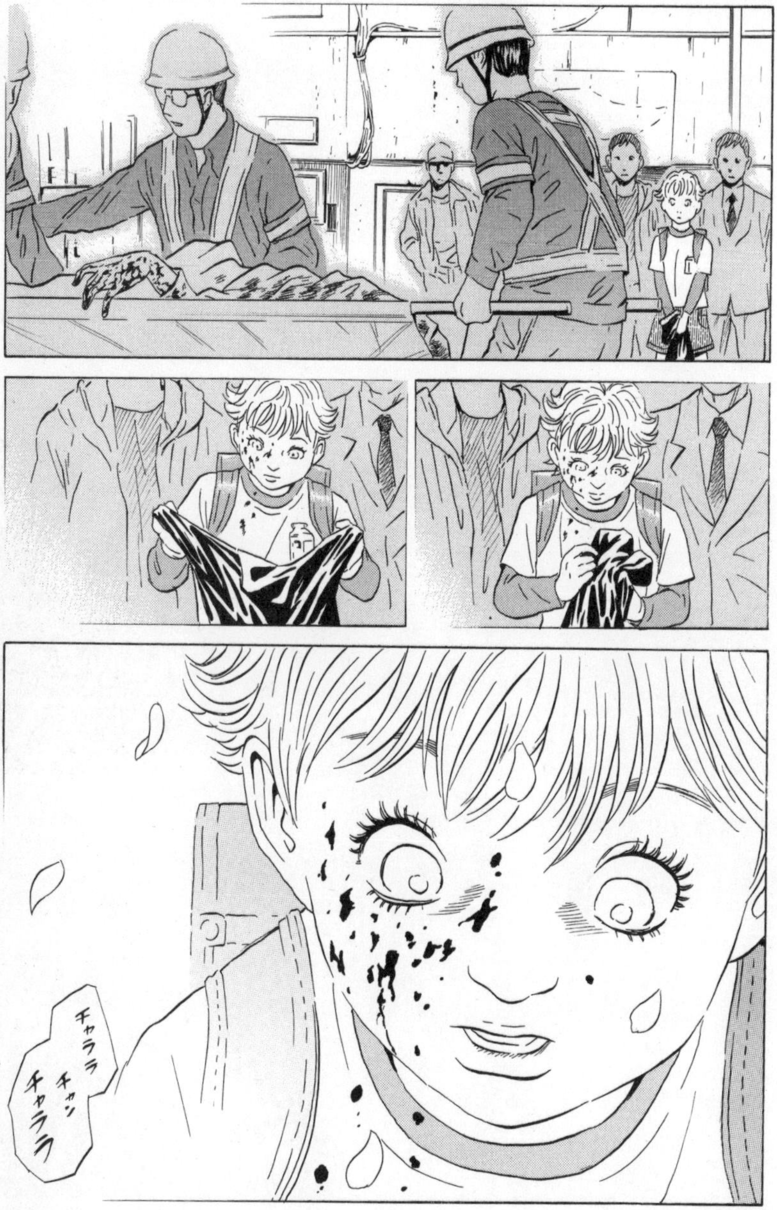
チャララ チャン チャララ

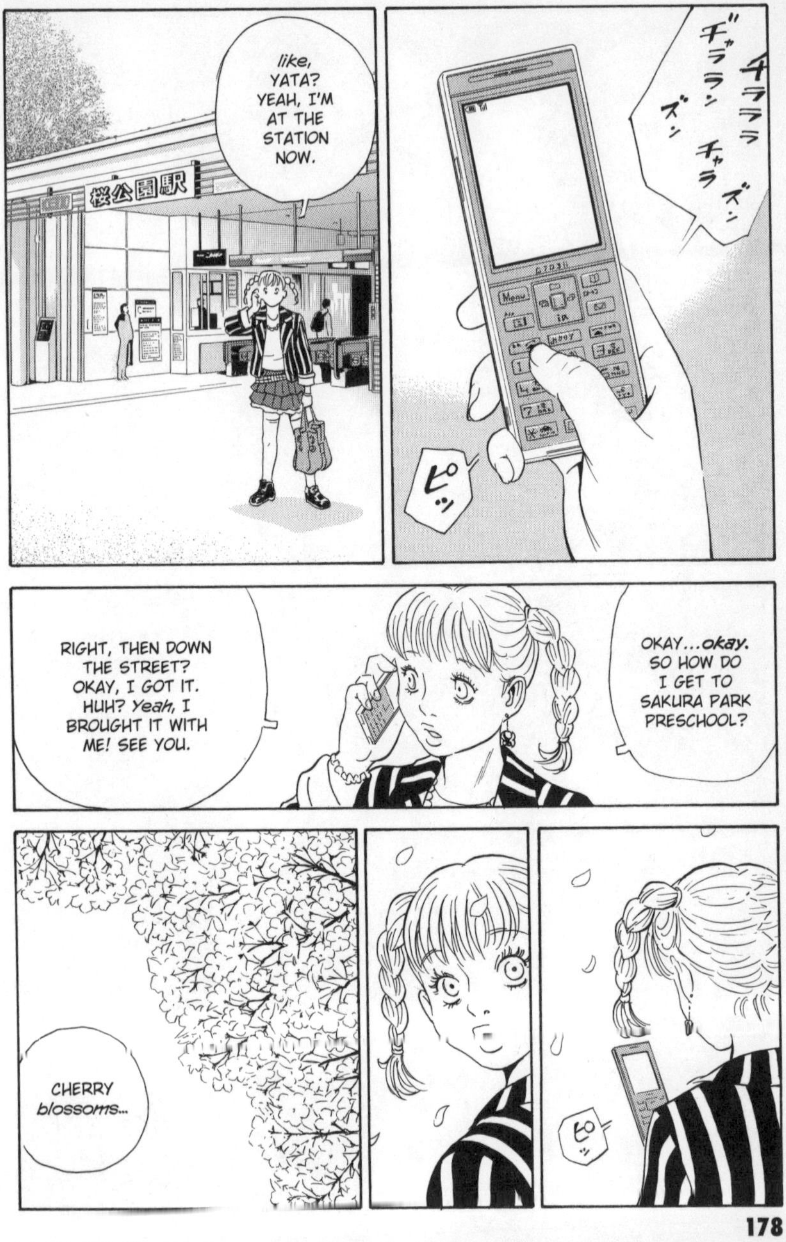

チャララ
ギャラン
ズン
チャラ
ズン
ピッ
桜公園駅
like, YATA? YEAH, I'M AT THE STATION NOW.
OKAY...*okay*. SO HOW DO I GET TO SAKURA PARK PRESCHOOL?
RIGHT, THEN DOWN THE STREET? OKAY, I GOT IT. HUH? *Yeah*, I BROUGHT IT WITH ME! SEE YOU.
ピッ
CHERRY *blossoms*...

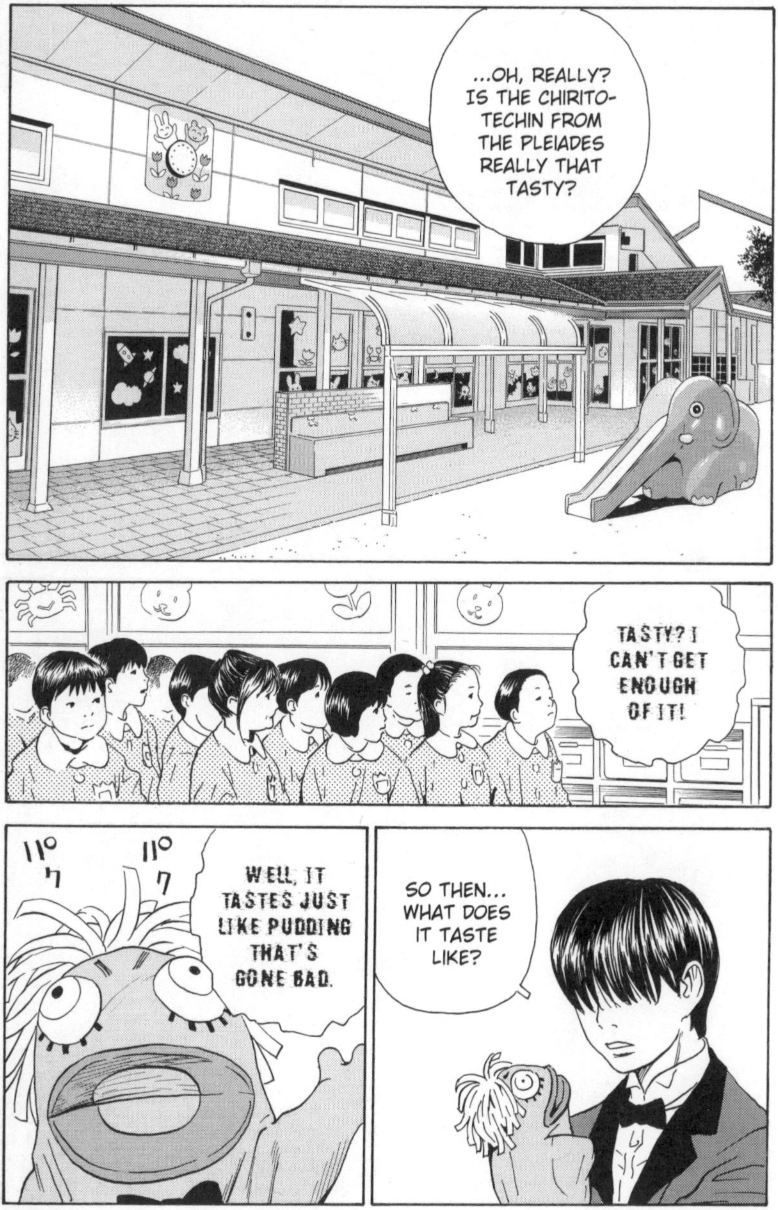
...OH, REALLY? IS THE CHIRITO-TECHIN FROM THE PLEIADES REALLY THAT TASTY?
TASTY? I CAN'T GET ENOUGH OF IT!
SO THEN... WHAT DOES IT TASTE LIKE?
パク
パク
WELL, IT TASTES JUST LIKE PUDDING THAT'S GONE BAD.

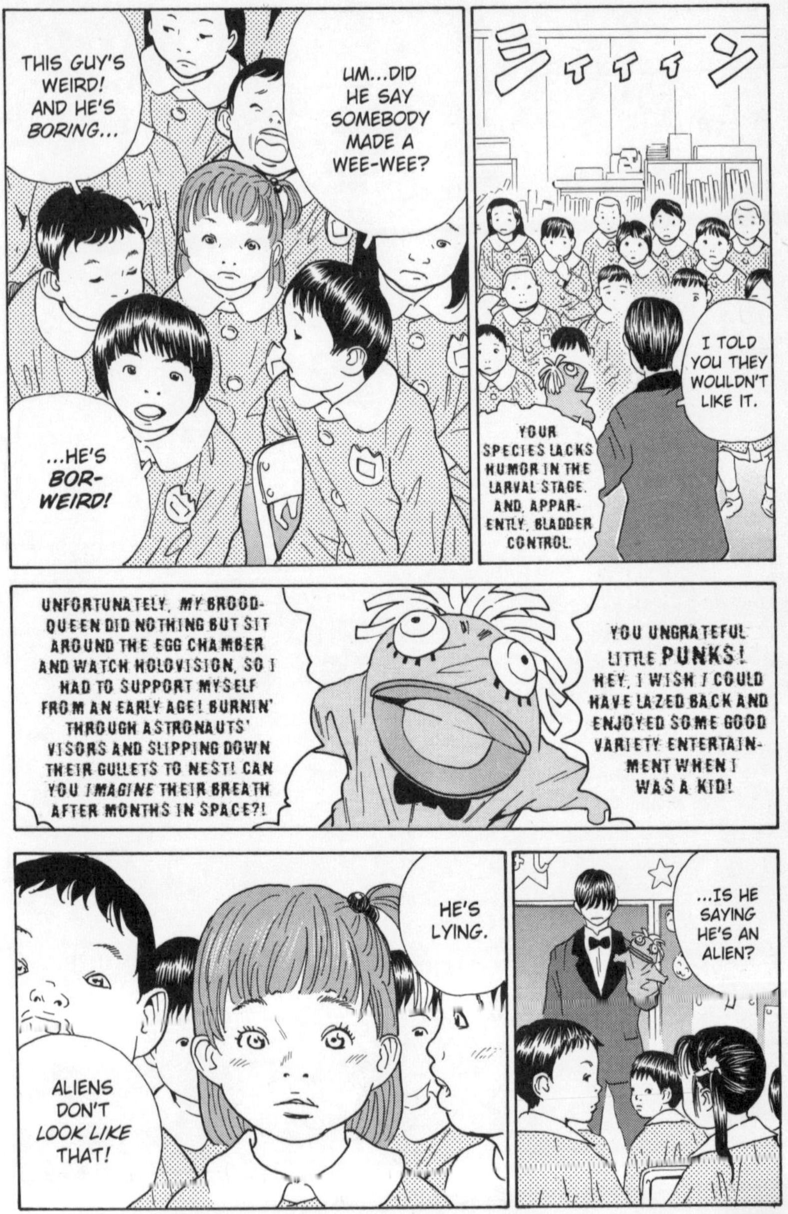
シィィィン
I TOLD YOU THEY WOULDN'T LIKE IT.
YOUR SPECIES LACKS HUMOR IN THE LARVAL STAGE. AND, APPARENTLY, BLADDER CONTROL.
UM...DID HE SAY SOMEBODY MADE A WEE-WEE?
THIS GUY'S WEIRD! AND HE'S *BORING*...
...HE'S ***BOR-WEIRD!***
YOU UNGRATEFUL LITTLE **PUNKS!** HEY, I WISH *I* COULD HAVE LAZED BACK AND ENJOYED SOME GOOD VARIETY ENTERTAINMENT WHEN I WAS A KID!
UNFORTUNATELY, *MY* BROOD-QUEEN DID NOTHING BUT SIT AROUND THE EGG CHAMBER AND WATCH HOLOVISION, SO I HAD TO SUPPORT MYSELF FROM AN EARLY AGE! BURNIN' THROUGH ASTRONAUTS' VISORS AND SLIPPING DOWN THEIR GULLETS TO NEST! CAN YOU *IMAGINE* THEIR BREATH AFTER MONTHS IN SPACE?!
...IS HE SAYING HE'S AN ALIEN?
HE'S LYING.
ALIENS DON'T *LOOK LIKE* THAT!

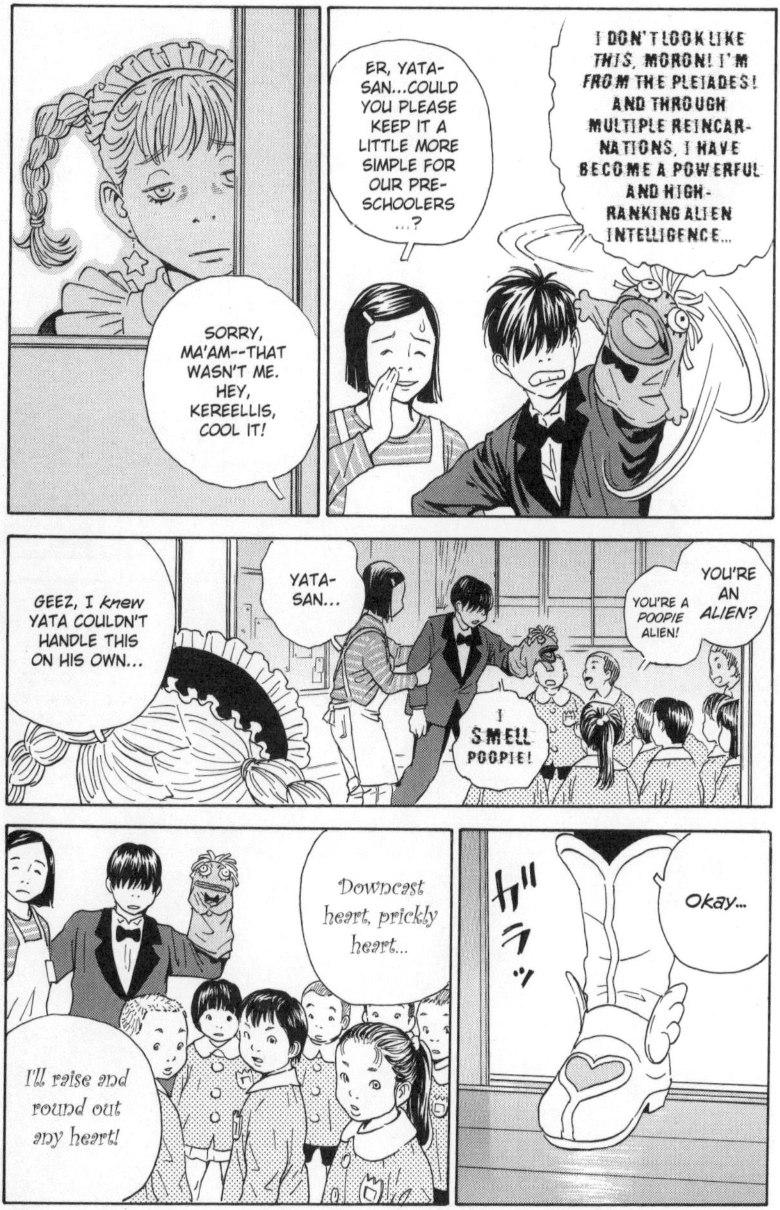
I DON'T LOOK LIKE THIS, MORON! I'M FROM THE PLEIADES! AND THROUGH MULTIPLE REINCARNATIONS, I HAVE BECOME A POWERFUL AND HIGH-RANKING ALIEN INTELLIGENCE...
ER, YATA-SAN...COULD YOU PLEASE KEEP IT A LITTLE MORE SIMPLE FOR OUR PRESCHOOLERS ...?
SORRY, MA'AM--THAT WASN'T ME. HEY, KEREELLIS, COOL IT!
YOU'RE AN ALIEN?
YOU'RE A POOPIE ALIEN!
I SMELL POOPIE!
YATA-SAN...
GEEZ, I knew YATA COULDN'T HANDLE THIS ON HIS OWN...
Okay...
ガラッ
Downcast heart, prickly heart...
I'll raise and round out any heart!

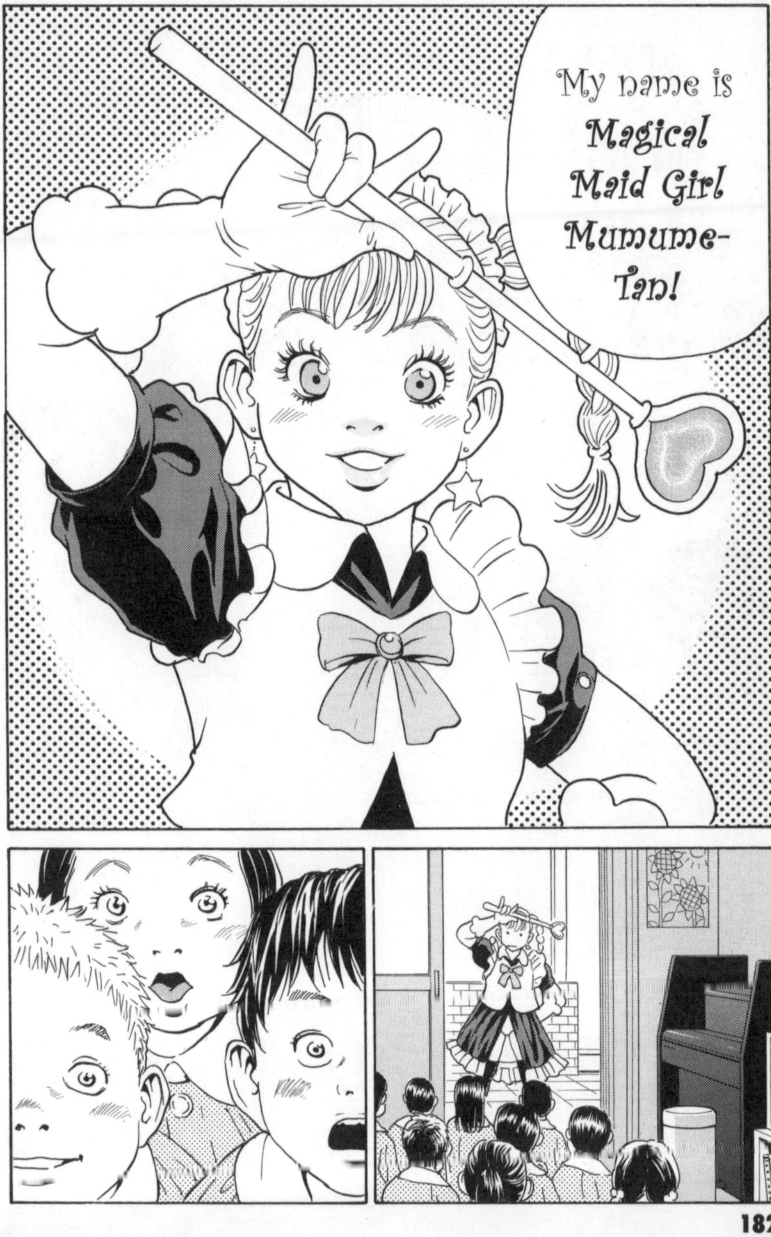
My name is Magical Maid Girl Mumume-Tan!

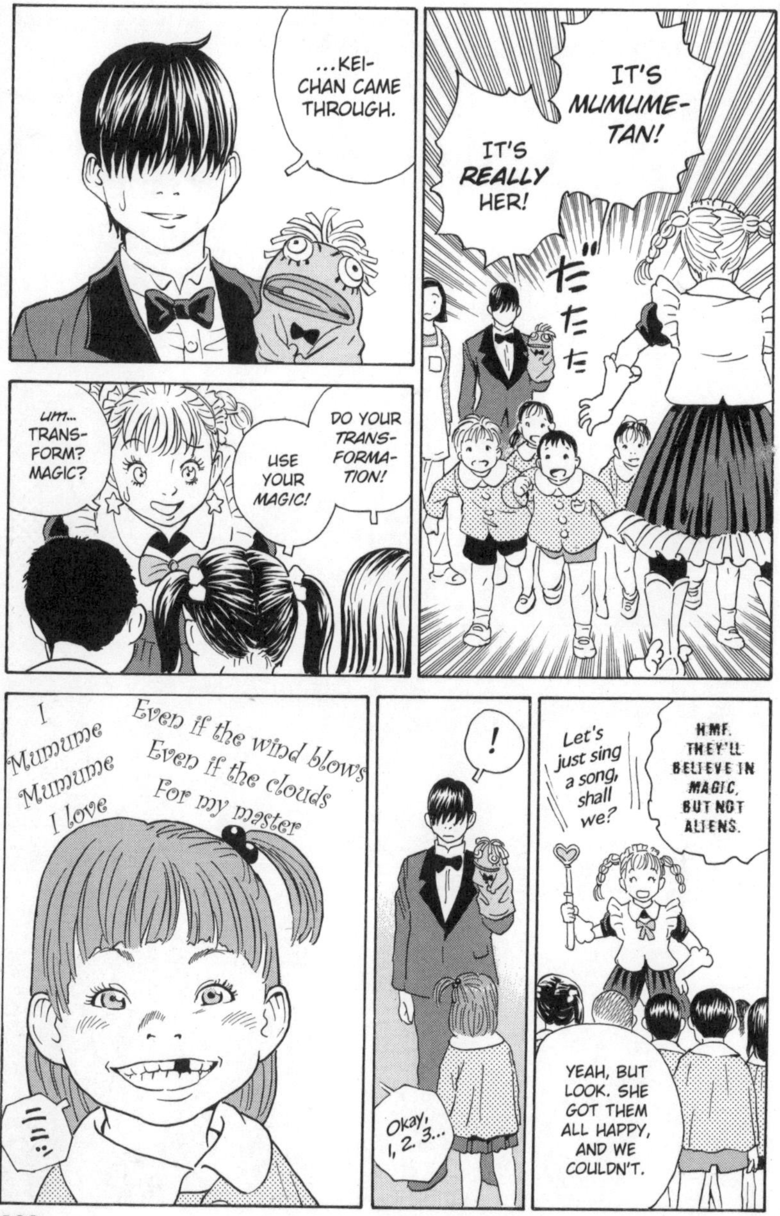
IT'S MUMUME-TAN!
IT'S REALLY HER!
だたたた
...KEI-CHAN CAME THROUGH.
DO YOUR TRANSFORMATION!
USE YOUR MAGIC!
um... TRANSFORM? MAGIC?
HMF. THEY'LL BELIEVE IN MAGIC, BUT NOT ALIENS.
Let's just sing a song, shall we?
YEAH, BUT LOOK. SHE GOT THEM ALL HAPPY, AND WE COULDN'T.
!
Okay, 1, 2. 3...
I Mumume Mumume I love
Even if the wind blows Even if the clouds For my master
!!!

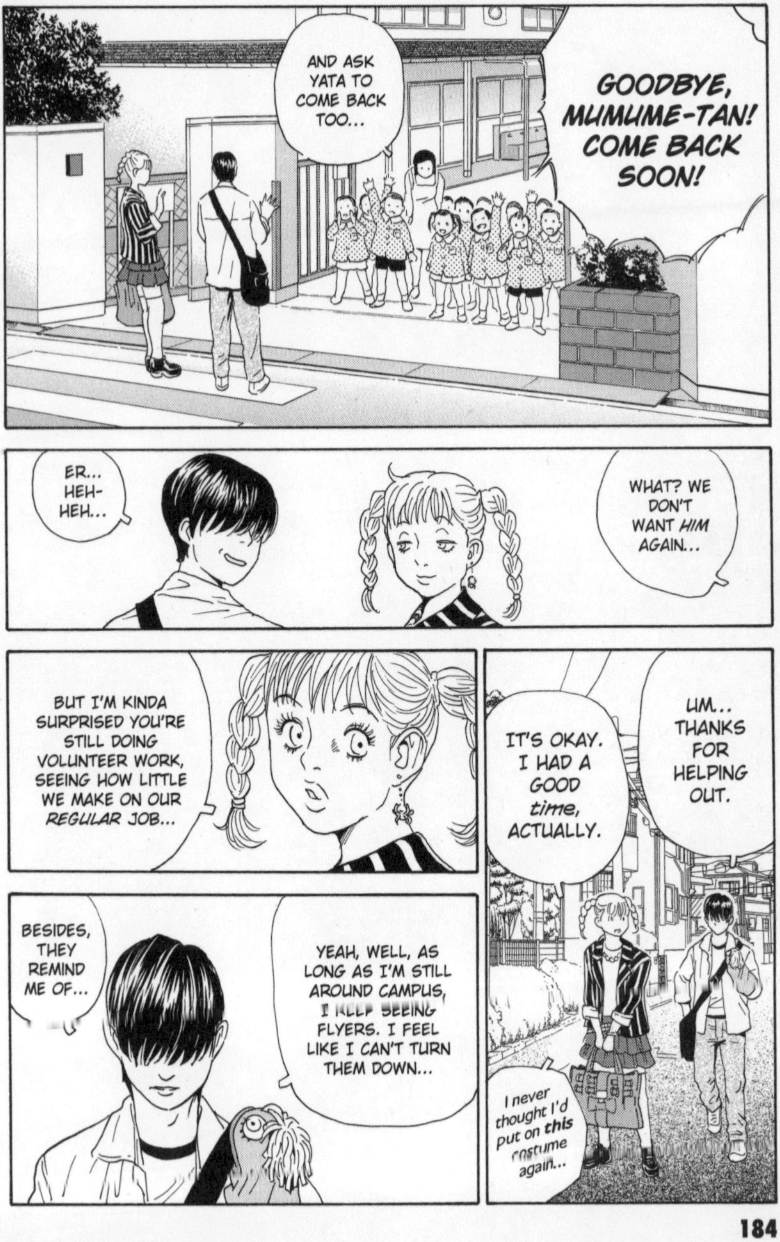
GOODBYE, MUMUME-TAN! COME BACK SOON!
AND ASK YATA TO COME BACK TOO...
WHAT? WE DON'T WANT *HIM* AGAIN...
ER... HEH-HEH...
UM... THANKS FOR HELPING OUT.
IT'S OKAY. I HAD A GOOD *time*, ACTUALLY.
I never thought I'd put on **this** costume again...
BUT I'M KINDA SURPRISED YOU'RE STILL DOING VOLUNTEER WORK, SEEING HOW LITTLE WE MAKE ON OUR *REGULAR* JOB...
YEAH, WELL, AS LONG AS I'M STILL AROUND CAMPUS, I KEEP SEEING FLYERS. I FEEL LIKE I CAN'T TURN THEM DOWN...
BESIDES, THEY REMIND ME OF...

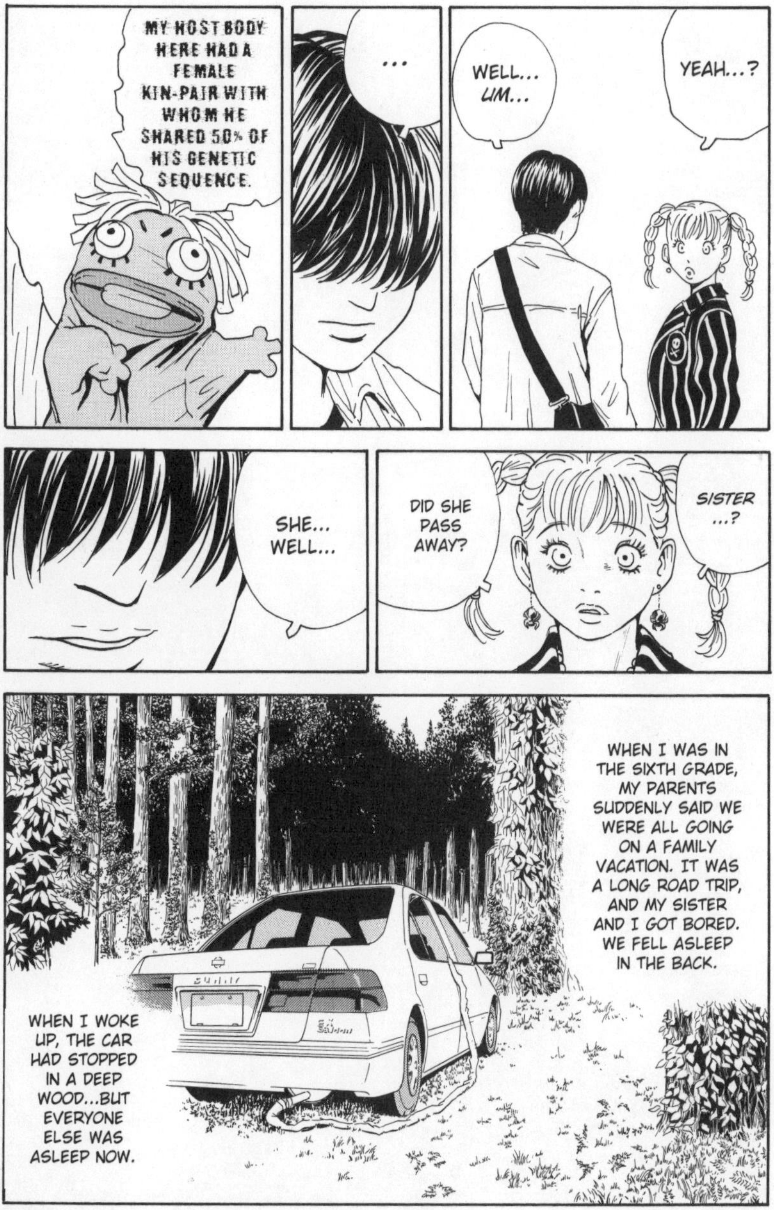
YEAH...?
WELL... UM...
...
MY HOST BODY HERE HAD A FEMALE KIN-PAIR WITH WHOM HE SHARED 50% OF HIS GENETIC SEQUENCE.
SISTER ...?
DID SHE PASS AWAY?
SHE... WELL...
WHEN I WAS IN THE SIXTH GRADE, MY PARENTS SUDDENLY SAID WE WERE ALL GOING ON A FAMILY VACATION. IT WAS A LONG ROAD TRIP, AND MY SISTER AND I GOT BORED. WE FELL ASLEEP IN THE BACK.
WHEN I WOKE UP, THE CAR HAD STOPPED IN A DEEP WOOD...BUT EVERYONE ELSE WAS ASLEEP NOW.

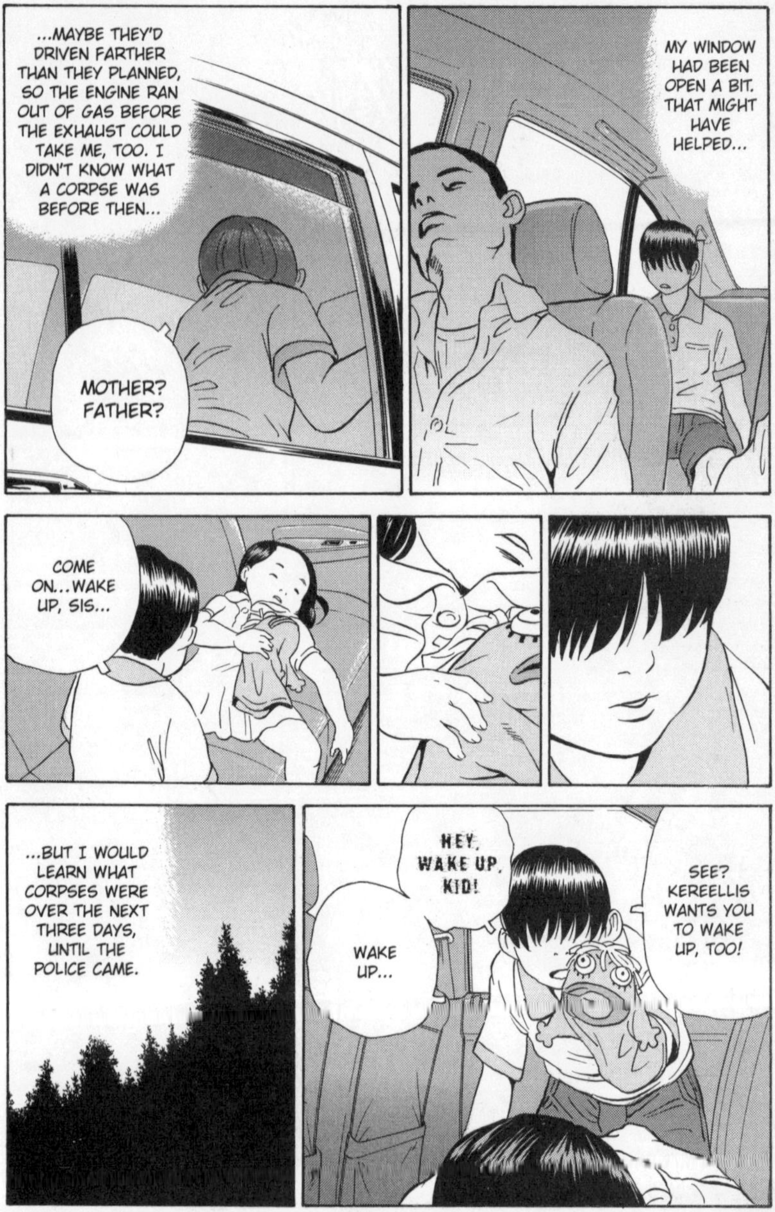
MY WINDOW HAD BEEN OPEN A BIT. THAT MIGHT HAVE HELPED...
...MAYBE THEY'D DRIVEN FARTHER THAN THEY PLANNED, SO THE ENGINE RAN OUT OF GAS BEFORE THE EXHAUST COULD TAKE ME, TOO. I DIDN'T KNOW WHAT A CORPSE WAS BEFORE THEN...
MOTHER? FATHER?
COME ON...WAKE UP, SIS...
SEE? KEREELLIS WANTS YOU TO WAKE UP, TOO!
HEY, WAKE UP, KID!
WAKE UP...
...BUT I WOULD LEARN WHAT CORPSES WERE OVER THE NEXT THREE DAYS, UNTIL THE POLICE CAME.

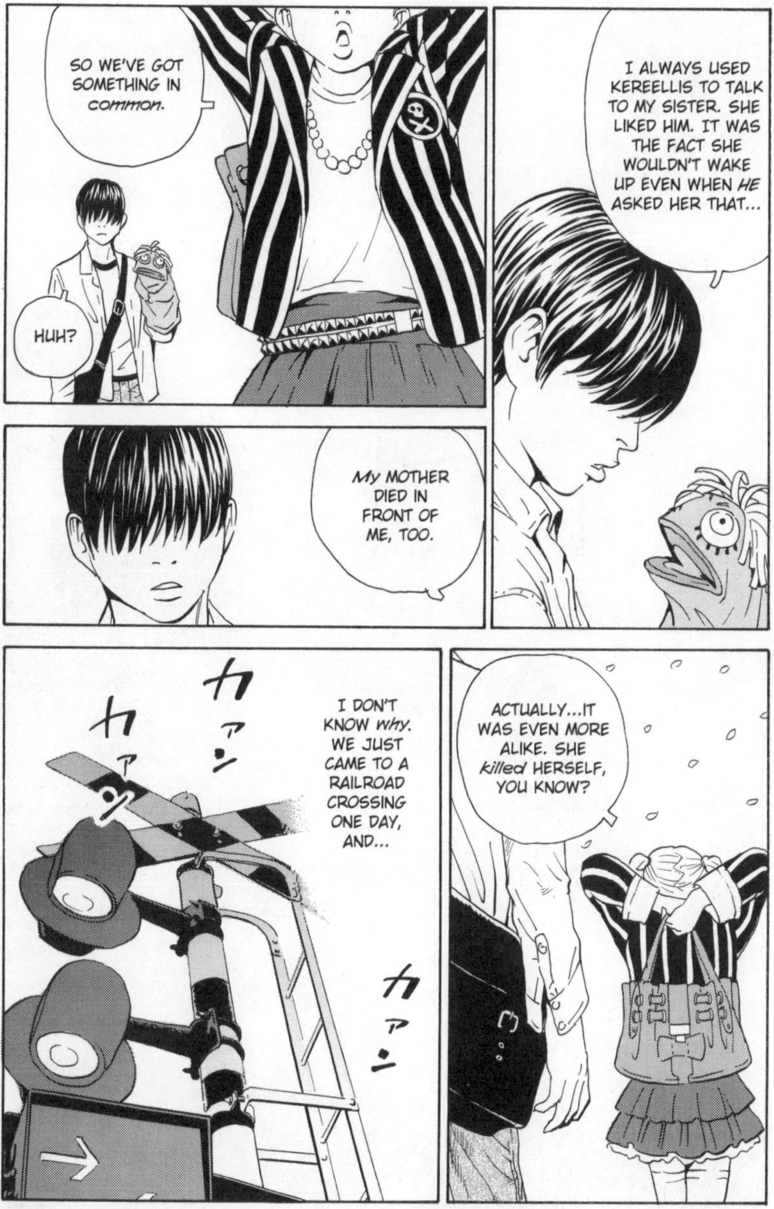
I ALWAYS USED KEREELLIS TO TALK TO MY SISTER. SHE LIKED HIM. IT WAS THE FACT SHE WOULDN'T WAKE UP EVEN WHEN *HE* ASKED HER THAT...
SO WE'VE GOT SOMETHING IN *common*.
HUH?
My MOTHER DIED IN FRONT OF ME, TOO.
ACTUALLY...IT WAS EVEN MORE ALIKE. SHE *killed* HERSELF, YOU KNOW?
I DON'T KNOW *why*. WE JUST CAME TO A RAILROAD CROSSING ONE DAY, AND...
カァン
カァン
カァン

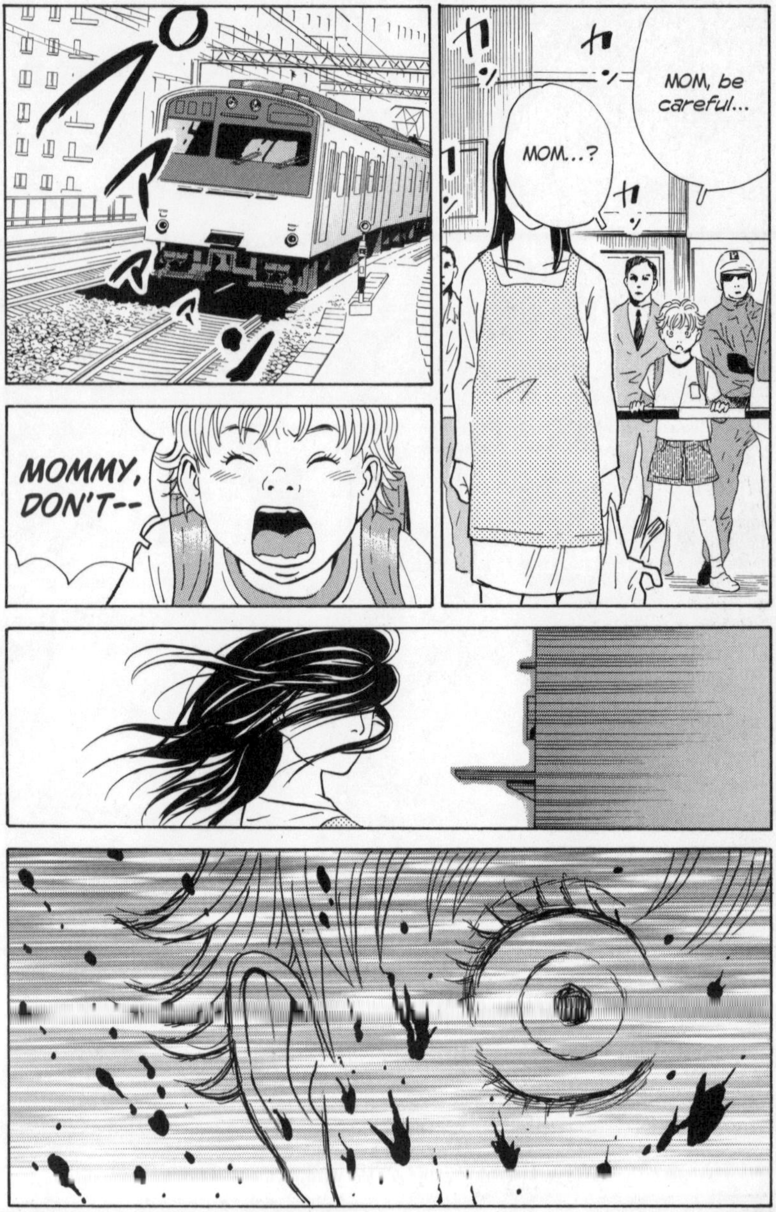
MOM, be careful...
カッ
MOM...?
カッ
カッ
パアアアン
MOMMY, DON'T--

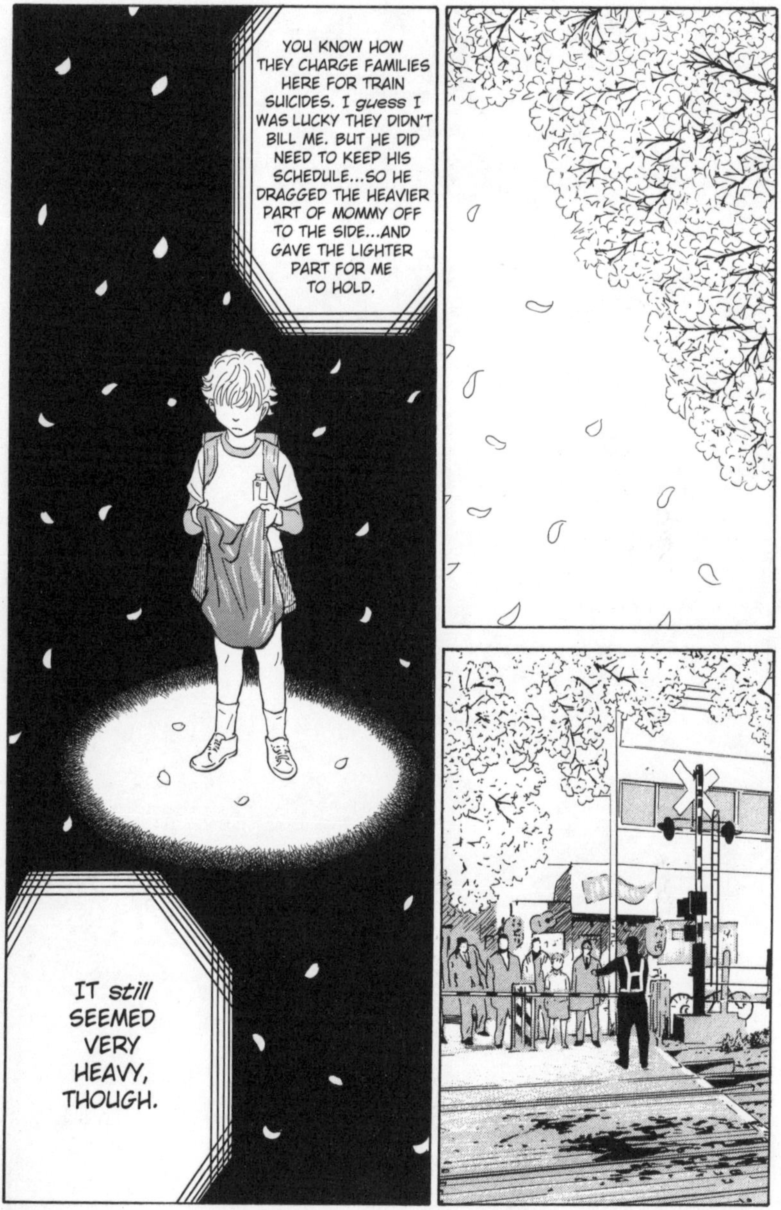
YOU KNOW HOW THEY CHARGE FAMILIES HERE FOR TRAIN SUICIDES. I *guess* I WAS LUCKY THEY DIDN'T BILL ME. BUT HE DID NEED TO KEEP HIS SCHEDULE...SO HE DRAGGED THE HEAVIER PART OF MOMMY OFF TO THE SIDE...AND GAVE THE LIGHTER PART FOR ME TO HOLD.
IT *still* SEEMED VERY HEAVY, THOUGH.

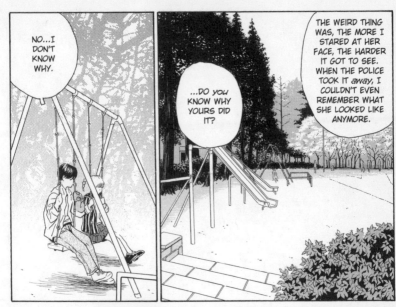

THE WEIRD THING WAS, THE MORE I STARED AT HER FACE, THE HARDER IT GOT TO SEE. WHEN THE POLICE TOOK IT *away*, I COULDN'T EVEN REMEMBER WHAT SHE LOOKED LIKE ANYMORE.
...DO *you* KNOW WHY YOURS DID IT?
NO...I DON'T KNOW WHY.
heh, I GUESS THIS IS THE FIRST TIME WE'VE TALKED ABOUT OUR FAMILIES...
I GUESS SO. EVEN THOUGH WE'VE KNOWN EACH OTHER A WHILE NOW...
HEY, MISTER! MISTER WITH THE ALIEN!
HUH? YOU'RE...
ニヒッ

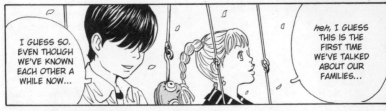

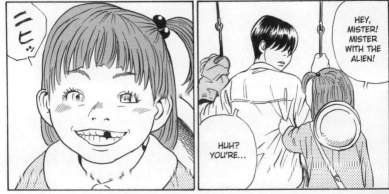

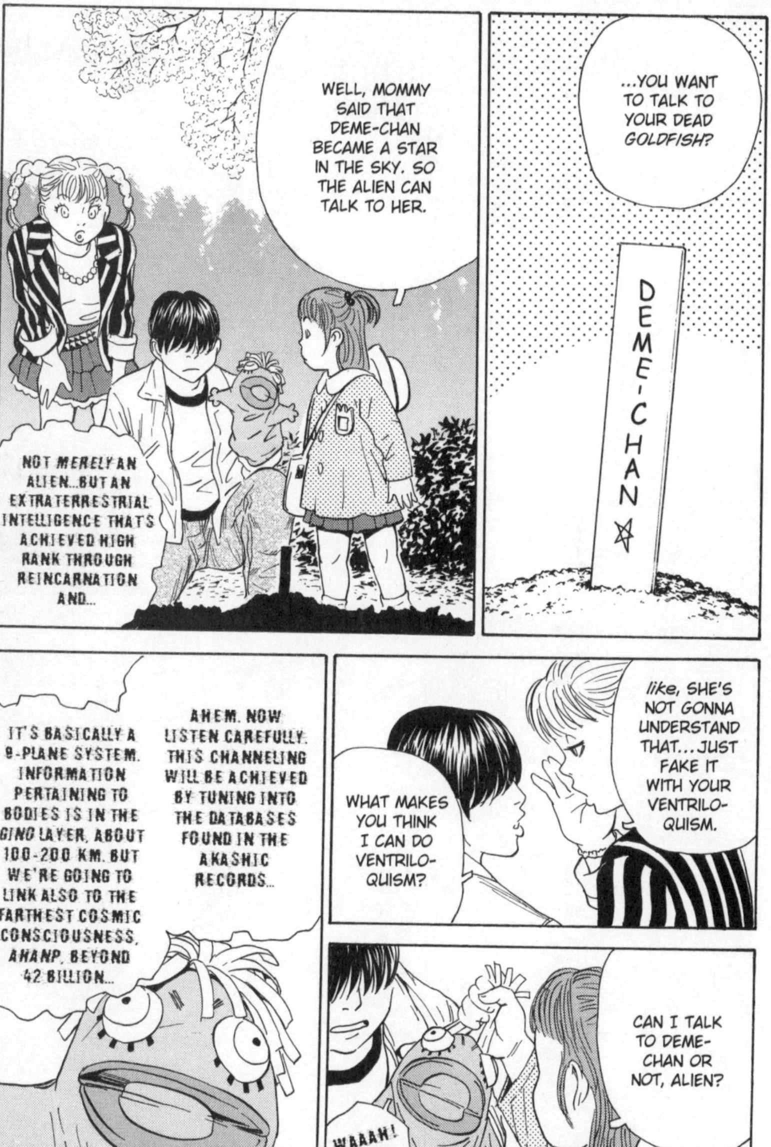
...YOU WANT TO TALK TO YOUR DEAD *GOLDFISH?*
DEME-CHAN
WELL, MOMMY SAID THAT DEME-CHAN BECAME A STAR IN THE SKY. SO THE ALIEN CAN TALK TO HER.
NOT *MERELY* AN ALIEN...BUT AN EXTRATERRESTRIAL INTELLIGENCE THAT'S ACHIEVED HIGH RANK THROUGH REINCARNATION AND...
like, SHE'S NOT GONNA UNDERSTAND THAT... JUST FAKE IT WITH YOUR VENTRILOQUISM.
WHAT MAKES YOU THINK I CAN DO VENTRILOQUISM?
CAN I TALK TO DEME-CHAN OR NOT, ALIEN?
WAAAH! STOP THAT!
AHEM. NOW LISTEN CAREFULLY. THIS CHANNELING WILL BE ACHIEVED BY TUNING INTO THE DATABASES FOUND IN THE AKASHIC RECORDS...
IT'S BASICALLY A 9-PLANE SYSTEM. INFORMATION PERTAINING TO BODIES IS IN THE *GINO* LAYER, ABOUT 100-200 KM. BUT WE'RE GOING TO LINK ALSO TO THE FARTHEST COSMIC CONSCIOUSNESS, *AHANP*, BEYOND 42 BILLION...

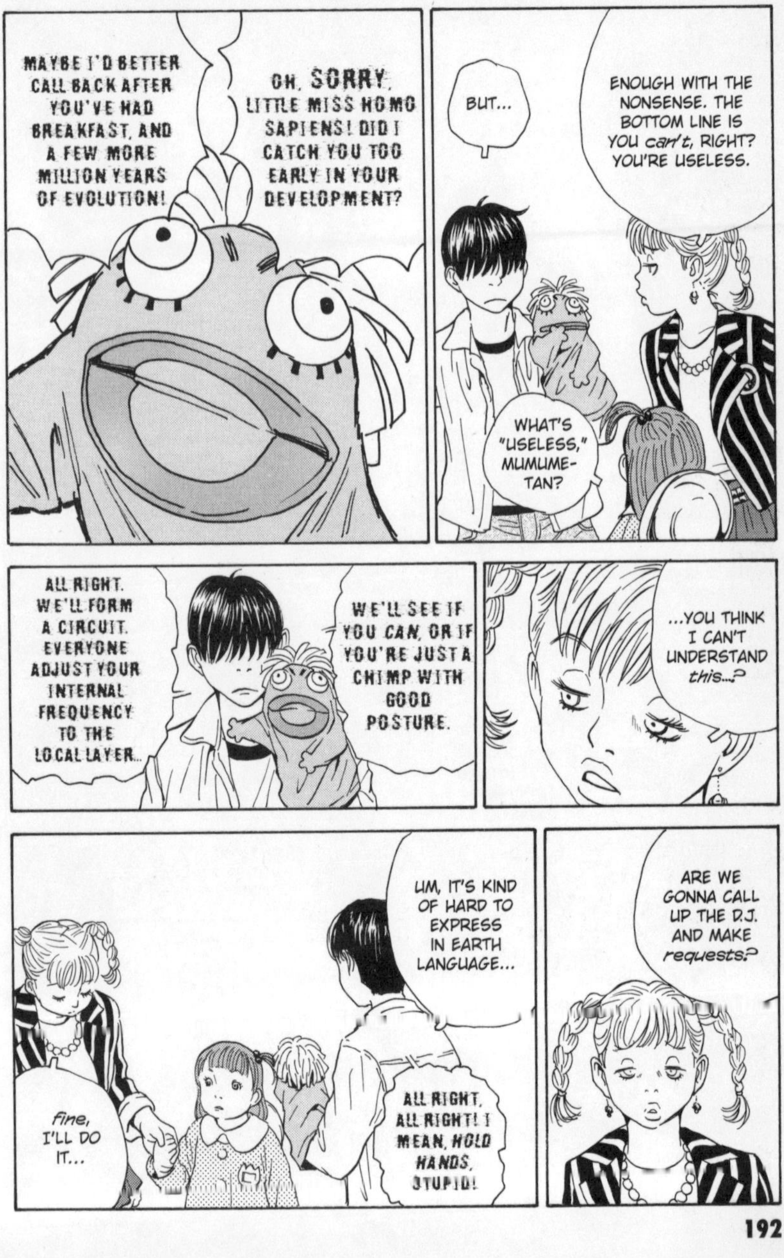
ENOUGH WITH THE NONSENSE. THE BOTTOM LINE IS YOU *can't*, RIGHT? YOU'RE USELESS.
BUT...
WHAT'S "USELESS," MUMUME-TAN?
OH, SORRY, LITTLE MISS HOMO SAPIENS! DID I CATCH YOU TOO EARLY IN YOUR DEVELOPMENT?
MAYBE I'D BETTER CALL BACK AFTER YOU'VE HAD BREAKFAST, AND A FEW MORE MILLION YEARS OF EVOLUTION!
...YOU THINK I CAN'T UNDERSTAND *this*...?
WE'LL SEE IF YOU *CAN*, OR IF YOU'RE JUST A CHIMP WITH GOOD POSTURE.
ALL RIGHT. WE'LL FORM A CIRCUIT. EVERYONE ADJUST YOUR INTERNAL FREQUENCY TO THE LOCAL LAYER...
ARE WE GONNA CALL UP THE D.J. AND MAKE *requests*?
UM, IT'S KIND OF HARD TO EXPRESS IN EARTH LANGUAGE...
ALL RIGHT, ALL RIGHT! I MEAN, *HOLD HANDS*, STUPID!
fine, I'LL DO IT...

OKAY... CONCENTRATE BUT DON'T THINK... FEEL THE WAVES...

Who are you— Bruce Lee?

YEAH, yeah...

OKAY.

MINDFULNESS, MAKINO! YOU TOO, LITTLE GIRL!

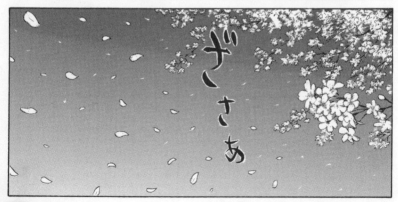

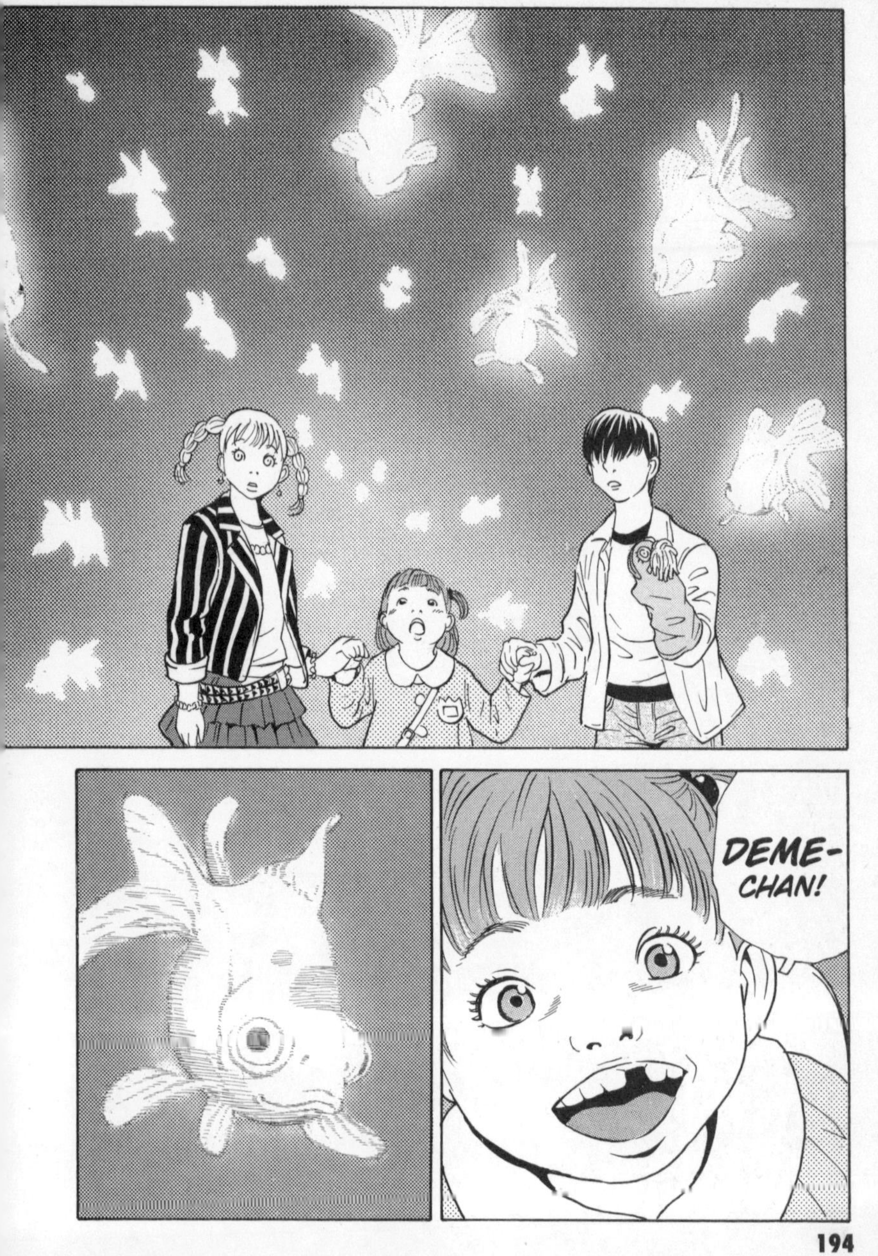
DEME-
CHAN!

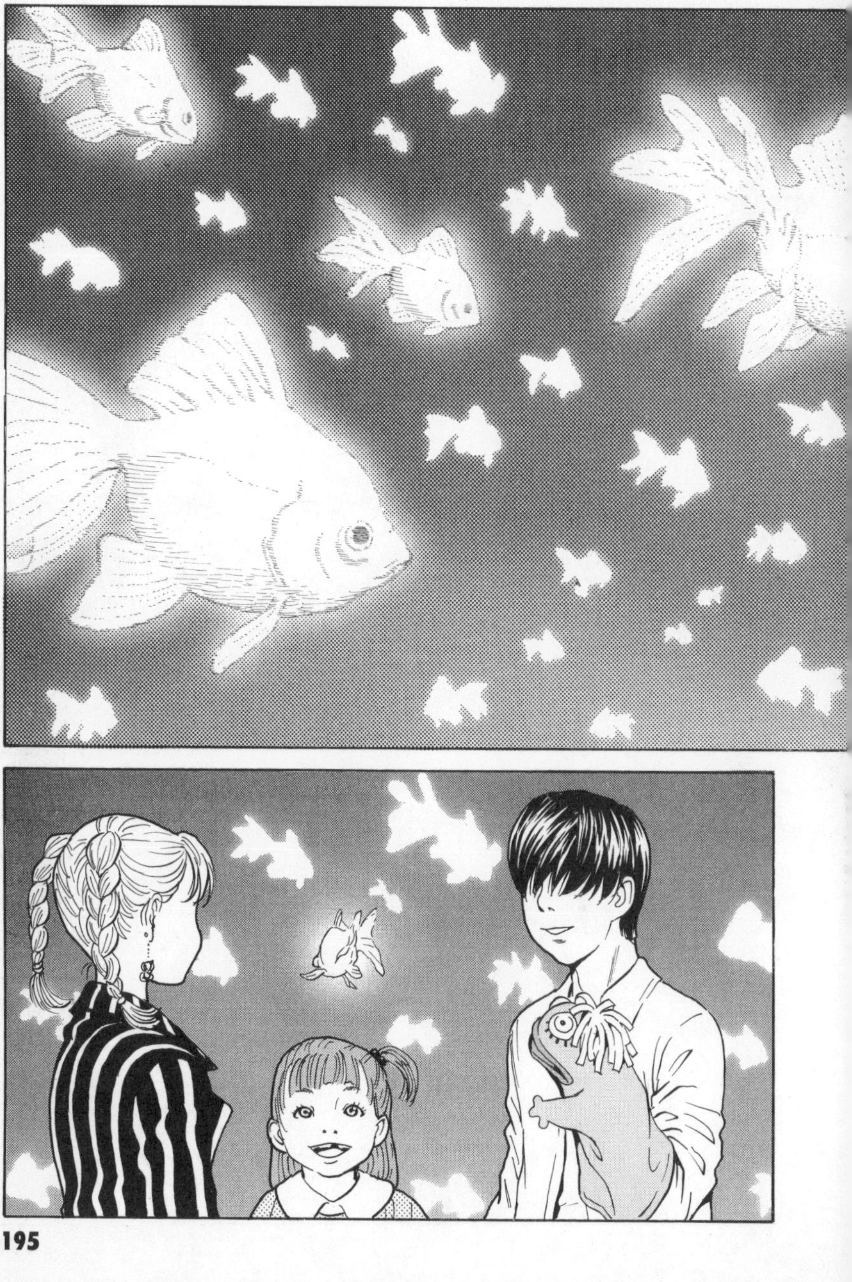

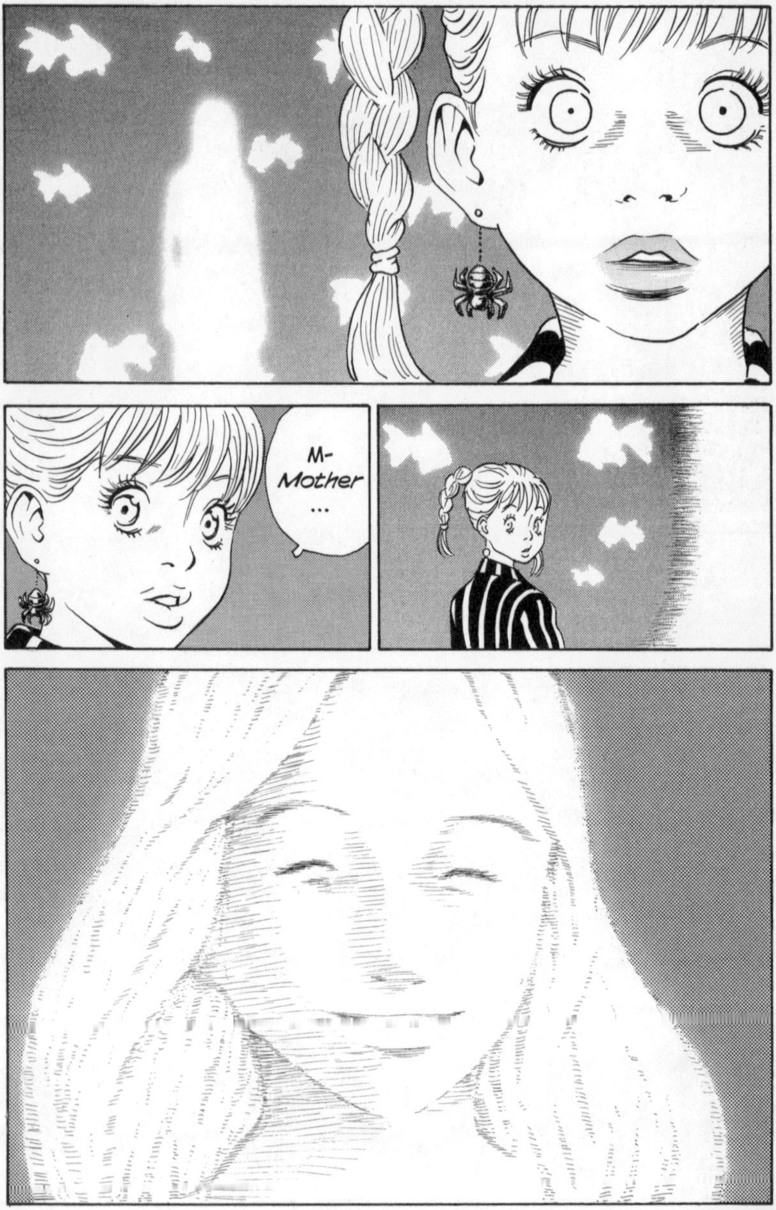
M-
Mother
...

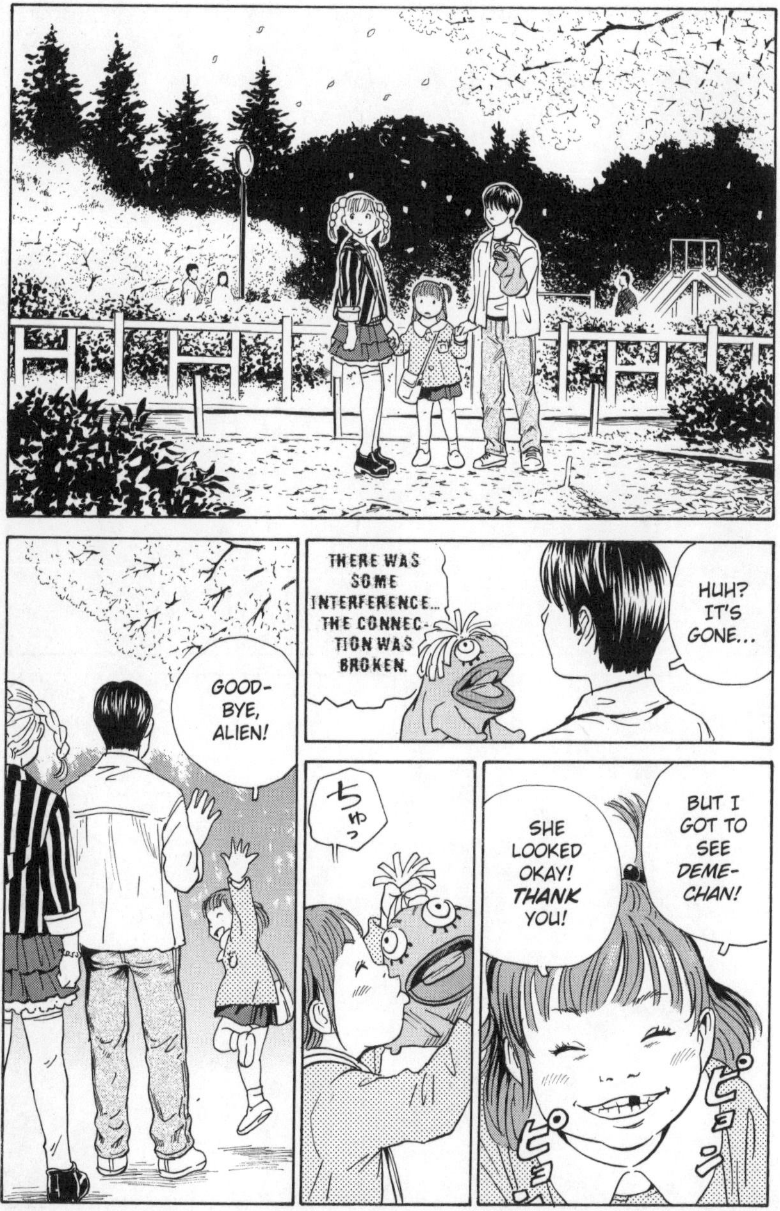
HUH? IT'S GONE...
THERE WAS SOME INTERFERENCE... THE CONNECTION WAS BROKEN.
BUT I GOT TO SEE DEME-CHAN!
SHE LOOKED OKAY! THANK YOU!
ピョン
ちゅっ
GOOD-BYE, ALIEN!

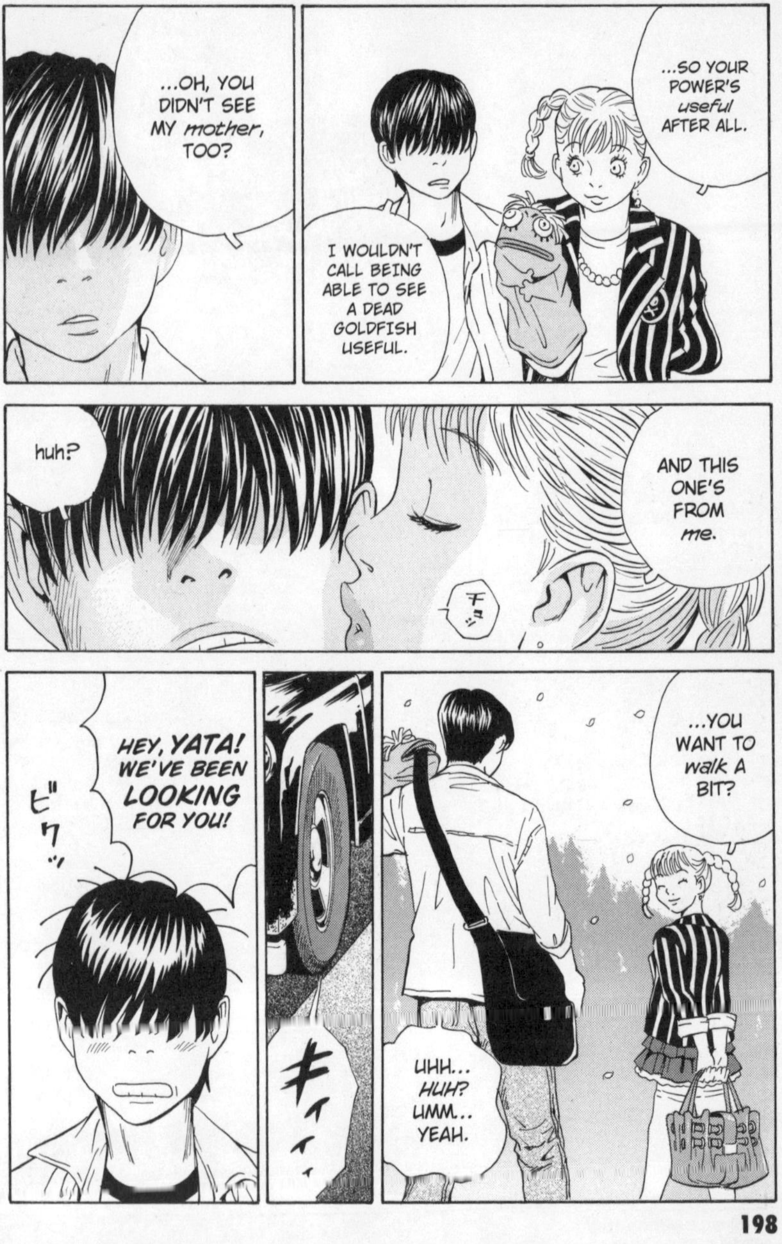
...SO YOUR POWER'S *useful* AFTER ALL.
I WOULDN'T CALL BEING ABLE TO SEE A DEAD GOLDFISH USEFUL.
...OH, YOU DIDN'T SEE MY *mother*, TOO?
AND THIS ONE'S FROM *me*.
チュッ
huh?
...YOU WANT TO *walk* A BIT?
UHH... *HUH?* UMM... YEAH.
キィィ
HEY, YATA! WE'VE BEEN LOOKING FOR YOU!
ビクッ

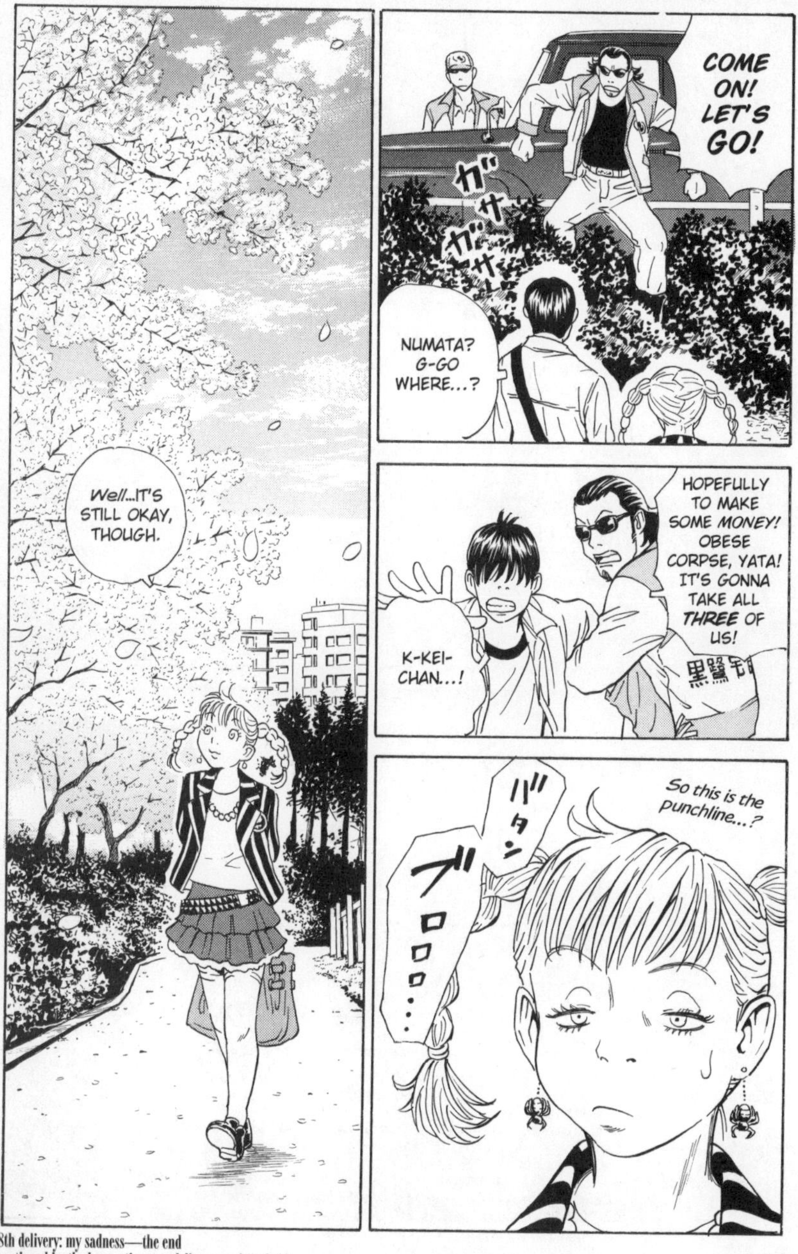
COME ON! LET'S GO!
ガサ
ガサ
NUMATA? G-GO WHERE...?
HOPEFULLY TO MAKE SOME *MONEY*! OBESE CORPSE, YATA! IT'S GONNA TAKE ALL *THREE* OF US!
K-KEI-CHAN...!
バタン
ブロロロ...
So this is the punchline...?
Well...IT'S STILL OKAY, THOUGH.

8th delivery: my sadness—the end
continued in *the kurosagi corpse delivery service* vol. 10

the KUROSAGI corpse delivery service

黒鷺死体宅配便

eiji otsuka 大塚英志 housui yamazaki 山崎峰水

designer **HEIDI WHITCOMB**
editor **CARL GUSTAV HORN**
editorial assistant **ANNIE GULLION**
publisher **MIKE RICHARDSON**

English-language version
produced by Dark Horse Comics

THE KUROSAGI CORPSE DELIVERY SERVICE VOL. 9
© OTSUKA Eiji Jimusyo 2008, © HOUSUI YAMAZAKI 2008. First published in
Japan in 2008 by KADOKAWA SHOTEN Publishing Co., Ltd., Tokyo. English
translation rights arranged with KADOKAWA SHOTEN Publishing Co., Ltd., Tokyo,
through TOHAN CORPORATION, Tokyo. This English-language edition ©2009 by
Dark Horse Comics, Inc. All other material ©2009 by Dark Horse Comics, Inc. All rights
reserved. No portion of this publication may be reproduced or transmitted, in any form
or by any means, without the express written permission of the copyright holders. Names,
characters, places, and incidents featured in this publication are either the product
of the author's imagination or are used fictitiously. Any resemblance to actual persons
(living or dead), events, institutions, or locales, without satiric intent, is coincidental.
Dark Horse Manga™ is a trademark of Dark Horse Comics, Inc. All rights reserved.

Published by
Dark Horse Manga
A division of Dark Horse Comics, Inc.
10956 SE Main Street
Milwaukie, OR 97222
darkhorse.com

To find a comics shop in your area,
call the Comic Shop Locator Service
toll-free at 1-888-266-4226

First edition: May 2009
ISBN 978-1-59582-306-9

1 3 5 7 9 10 8 6 4 2

PRINTED IN CANADA

DISJECTA MEMBRA

SOUND FX GLOSSARY AND NOTES ON KUROSAGI VOL. 9 BY TOSHIFUMI YOSHIDA
introduction and additional comments by the editor

TO INCREASE YOUR ENJOYMENT of the distinctive Japanese visual style of this manga, we've included a guide to the sound effects (or "FX") used in this manga. It is suggested the reader *not* constantly consult this glossary as they read through, but regard it as supplemental information, in the manner of footnotes, or perhaps one of those nutritional supplements, the kind that's long and difficult to swallow. If you want to imagine it being read aloud by Osaka, after the manner of her lecture to Sakaki on hemorrhoids in episode five of *Azumanga Daioh*, please go right ahead. In either Yuki Matsuoka or Kira Vincent-Davis's voice—I like them both.

Japanese, like English, did not independently invent its own writing system, but instead borrowed and modified the system used by the then-dominant cultural power in its part of the world. We still call the letters we use to write English today the "Roman" alphabet, for the simple reason that about 1,600 years ago, the earliest English speakers, living on the frontier of the Roman Empire, began to use the same letters the Romans used for their Latin language to write out English.

Around that very same time, on the other side of the planet, Japan, like England, was another example of an island civilization lying across the sea from a great empire—in this case, that of China. Likewise, the Japanese borrowed from the Chinese writing system, which then, as now, consisted of thousands of complex symbols—today in China officially referred to in the Roman alphabet as *hanzi*, but which the Japanese pronounce as *kanji*. For example, all the Japanese characters you see on the front cover of

The Kurosagi Corpse Delivery Service—the seven which make up the original title and the four each which make up the creators' names—are examples of kanji. Of course, all of them were hanzi first—although the Japanese did also invent some original kanji of their own, just as new hanzi have been created over the centuries as Chinese evolved.

(Note that whereas both "kanji" and "hanzi" are examples of foreign words written in Roman letters, "kanji" gives English speakers a fairly good idea of how the Japanese word is really pronounced—*khan-gee*—whereas "hanzi" does not—in Mandarin Chinese it sounds something like *n-tsuh*. The reason is fairly simple: whereas the most commonly used method of writing Japanese in Roman letters, the Hepburn system, was developed by a native English speaker, the most commonly used method of writing Chinese in Roman letters, called the Pinyin system, was developed by native Mandarin speakers. In fact Pinyin was developed to help teach Mandarin pronunciation to speakers of other Chinese dialects; unlike Hepburn, it was not intended as a learning tool for English speakers per se, and hence has no particular obligation to "make sense" to English speakers or, indeed, to users of the many other languages spelled with the Roman alphabet.)

Whereas the various dialects of Chinese are written entirely in hanzi, it is impractical to render the Japanese language entirely in them. To compare once more, English is a notoriously difficult language in which to spell properly, and this is in part because it uses an alphabet designed for another language, Latin, whose sounds are different (this is, of course, putting aside the fact the sounds of both languages experienced change over time). The challenges the Japanese faced in using the Chinese writing system for their own language were even greater, for whereas spoken English and Latin are at least from a common language family, spoken Japanese is unrelated to any of the various dialects of spoken Chinese. The complicated writing system the Japanese evolved represents an adjustment to these great differences.

When the Japanese borrowed hanzi to become kanji, what they were getting was a way to write out (remember, they already had ways to *say*) their vocabulary. Nouns, verbs, many adjectives, the names of places and people—that's what kanji are used for, the fundamental data of the written language. The practical use and processing of that "data"—its grammar and pronunciation—is another matter entirely. Because spoken Japanese neither sounds nor functions like Chinese, the first work-around tried was a system called *manyogana*, where individual kanji were picked to represent certain syllables in Japanese. A similar method is still used in Chinese today to spell out foreign names; companies and individuals often try to choose hanzi for this purpose that have an auspicious, or at least not insulting, meaning. As you will also observe in *Kurosagi* and elsewhere, the meaning behind the characters that make up a personal name are an important literary element of Japanese as well.

The commentary in *Katsuya Terada's The Monkey King* (also available from Dark Horse, and also translated by Toshifumi Yoshida) notes the importance that not only Chinese, but also Indian culture had on Japan at this time in history—particularly, through Buddhism. Just as in Western history at this time, religious communities in Asia were associated with learning, as priests and monks were more likely to be literate than other groups in society. It is believed

the Northeast Indian *Siddham* script studied by Kukai (died 835 AD), founder of the Shingon sect of Japanese Buddhism, inspired him to create the solution for writing Japanese still used today. Kukai is credited with the idea of taking the manyogana and making shorthand versions of them—which are now known simply as *kana*. The improvement in efficiency was dramatic: a kanji previously used to represent a sound, that might have taken a dozen strokes to draw, was now replaced by a kana that took three or four.

Unlike the original kanji they were based on, the new kana had *only* a sound meaning. And unlike the thousands of kanji, there are only 46 kana, which can be used to spell out any word in the Japanese language, including the many ordinarily written with kanji (Japanese keyboards work on this principle). The same set of 46 kana is written two different ways depending on its intended use: cursive style, *hiragana*, and block style, *katakana*. Naturally, sound FX in manga are almost always written out using kana.

Kana works somewhat differently than the Roman alphabet. For example, while there are separate kana for each of the five vowels (the Japanese order is not A-E-I-O-U as in English, but A-I-U-E-O), there are, except for *n*, no separate kana for consonants (the middle *n* in the word *ninja* illustrates this exception). Instead, kana work by grouping together consonants with vowels: for example, there are five kana for sounds starting with *k*, depending on which vowel follows it—in Japanese vowel order, they go KA, KI, KU, KE, KO. The next set of kana begins with *s* sounds, so SA, SHI, SU, SE, SO, and so on. You will observe this kind of consonant-vowel pattern in the FX listings for *Kurosagi* Vol. 9 below.

Katakana are generally used for manga sound FX, but on occasion hiragana are used instead. This is commonly done when the sound is one associated with a human body, but can be a subtler aesthetic choice by the artist as well. In *Kurosagi*

Vol. 9 you can see an example on 37.2, with the BUBAAA of Yuriri spitting, which in hiragana style is written ぶばあつ. Note its more cursive appearance compared to the other FX. If it had been written in katakana style, it would look like ブバアツ.

To see how to use this glossary, take an example from page 6: "6.1 FX: ZAAAAAA—sound of pouring rain." 6.1 means the FX is the one on page 6, in panel 1. ZAAAAAA is the sound these kana—ザアアアアア—literally stand for. After the dash comes an explanation of what the sound represents (in some cases, like this, it will be less obvious than others). Note that in cases where there are two or more different sounds in a single panel, an extra number is used to differentiate them from right to left; or, in cases where right and left are less clear, in clockwise order.

The use of kana in these FX also illustrates another aspect of written Japanese—its flexible reading order. For example, the way you're reading the pages and panels of this book in general—going from right to left, and from top to bottom—is similar to the order in which Japanese is also written in most forms of print: books, magazines, and newspapers. However, some of the FX in *Kurosagi* (and manga in general) read left to right. This kind of flexibility is also to be found on Japanese web pages, which usually also read left to right. In other words, Japanese doesn't simply read "the other way" from English; the Japanese themselves are used to reading it in several different directions.

As might be expected, some FX "sound" short, and others "sound" long. Manga represent this in different ways. One of many instances of "short sounds" in *Kurosagi* Vol. 9 is 7.5's PASA—パサツ. Note the small ツ mark it has at the end, which stands for the sound "tsu." In hiragana, such as 37.2, it looks like つ. The half-size "tsu" seen at the end of FX like this means the sound is the kind which stops or

cuts off suddenly; that's why 7.5 and 37.2 are written as PASA and BUBAAA, and not PASATSU and BUBAAATSU—you don't pronounce the "tsu" when used this way. Note the small "tsu" has another occasional use *inside*, rather than at the end, of a particular FX, where it indicates a doubling of the consonant sound that follows it.

There are three different ways you may see "long sounds"—where a vowel sound is extended—written out as FX. One is with an ellipsis, as in 91.5's GOSO. Another is with an extended line, as in 114.1's CHIII CHII KIII KII. Still another is by simply repeating a vowel several times, as in 59.1's OOOO. You will note that the CHIII CHII KIII KIIs in 114.1 each have a "tsu" at their end, suggesting an elongated sound that's suddenly cut off; the methods may be combined within a single FX. As a visual element in manga, FX are an art rather than a science, and are used in a less rigorous fashion than kana are in standard written Japanese.

The explanation of what the sound represents may sometimes be surprising, but every culture "hears" sounds differently. Note that manga FX do not even necessarily represent literal sounds. Such "mimetic" words, which represent an imagined sound, or even a state of mind, are called *gitaigo* in Japanese. Like the onomatopoeic *giseigo* (the words used to represent literal sounds—i.e., most FX in this glossary are classed as giseigo), they are also used in colloquial speech and writing. A Japanese, for example, might say that something bounced by saying PURIN, or talk about eating by saying MUGU MUGU. It's something like describing chatter in English by saying "yadda yadda yadda" instead.

One important last note: all these spelled-out kana vowels should be pronounced as they are in Japanese: *A* as *ah*, *I* as *eee*, *U* as *ooh*, *E* as *eh*, and *O* as *oh*.

2.1 The translator notes that all the chapter titles in Volume 9 are songs by Asami Kobayashi. She was active as a singer, actor, and model starting in the 1970s, until she retired in 1991. The title to the second chapter gets a little complicated. In the original Japanese, it is "Yume miru shanson ningyoo" (that's a long "ohhh" sound on the end, of course, rather than "oooh"), which literally translates to "the *chanson* doll that dreams" (*chanson* meaning *song* in French). This was a Japanese-language cover sung by France Gall of her own French-language original song, "Poupée de cire, poupée de son" ("doll of wax, doll of bran"—bran being a filling used in France for dolls; compare to the rice used in this story) that won the Eurovision Song Contest in 1965. French pop was, well, popular enough in Japan then (you'll recall that in *Masculin, féminin*, Chantal Goya mentions she's climbing the Japanese charts) to warrant the cover; Gall also recorded versions in German and Italian. Various artists have covered it in other languages. The song itself was written for Gall by *l'creep le plus extraordinaire* Serge Gainsbourg (and as a manga fan, the editor is no longer sure how he means that). The original French version has also been covered by The Arcade Fire and Belle and Sebastian. But "A Lonely Singing Doll" is used as the title here as this was the name of the English version, covered (also in 1965) by the UK singer Twinkle (whose own single "Golden Lights" you may possibly know from The Smiths' cover of it on *Louder Than Bombs*. And this is only the *first* note in "Disjecta Membra."

5 I love the fact that this is a *doll* version of Kereellis, who is, of course, in everyday life, a *puppet*.

6.1 **FX: ZAAAAAA**—sound of pouring rain

6.2 **FX/balloon: WIIIIN**—sound of elevator rising

6.3 **FX: KA KA**—sound of heels

6.4 **FX/balloon: PI**—turning off mobile phone

7.1 **FX: GACHA**—sound of a door opening

7.4 **FX/balloon: PACHI**—light switch being flipped

7.5 **FX/balloon: PASA**—sound of hair falling down out of hat

8.1 **FX/balloon: KII**—door creaking open

8.4 **FX: PUKA PUKA**—sound of doll floating/bobbing

8.5 **FX: PUKA PUKA**—sound of doll floating/bobbing. Note the retractable cover on the bathtub, intended to keep heat in and suds out (one washes outside the tub in Japan before soaking a *clean* body—in America, we just throw a little more chlorine in the hot tub).

9.1 **FX: DOSHA**—wet thud as trash bag hits ground

9.3 She actually said *wota no fan*; that she hates the "wota" kind of fan. It's been an affectation the last few years in Japan, especially on the image forum 2chan, to spell *otaku*—normally written オタク, o-ta-ku—as ヲタク, or *wo*-ta-ku. This was possibly inspired—or perhaps reflective of—Hideaki Anno's 2006 decision to spell the new *Evangelion* movies ヱヴァンゲリヲン, which is romanized as *Wevangeliwon*. This risks making Anno sound like Kim Jong-Il in *Team America: World Police*, but you will be relieved to hear it's still *pronounced* "Evangelion," just as *wota* and *wotaku* are still pronounced "ota" and "otaku." The effect is a little like the way one might choose in English to use the old-fashioned spelling *phantasy* for *fantasy* (as used, for example, in the game *Phantasy Star*). The *we* ("weh") sound has not actually existed in Japanese for centuries (English, too, used to sound quite different centuries ago; anyone who's ever heard *The Canterbury Tales* will be reminded of the Swedish Chef from *The Muppet Show*), and by the early twentieth century the kana for *we* had simply become a redundant form of *e* ("eh"), so it was officially discarded in the orthographic reforms following WWII. The *wo* ("woh") sound does still exist in dialect, although generally speaking it has the same value as *o* ("oh"), and in fact as early as 1996 *Evangelion* was spelling its famous bishie's name *Kaworu*, even though, yeah, yeah, it's just pronounced "Kah-oh-roo." Bear it in mind when you read *Neon Genesis Evangelion: The Shinji Ikari Raising Project*, also from Dark Horse, and one of those love comedies Numata is so apprehensive towards. Even a non-otaku (are there any left?) may be familiar with this kind of usage from Clint Eastwood's much-acclaimed recent film *Letters from Iwo Jima*; the *Iwo* is pronounced "ee-oh," not "ee-woh," but seeing as how it was WWII that made the place famous, it is the old romanization of *Iwo Jima* rather than the postwar *Io Jima* that has remained in the popular mind.

9.5   **FX/balloon: GACHA**—placing door chain

9.6   **FX/balloon: PACHIN**—locking deadbolt

10.1   **FX: PINPOON**—doorbell sound

10.2   **FX: PINPOON PINPOON PINPOON**—doorbell sounds

10.3.1   **FX/balloon: GACHA**—jiggling-door-handle sound

10.3.2   **FX/balloon: GACHA**—jiggling-door-handle sound

10.3.3   **FX/balloon: GACHA**—jiggling-door-handle sound

10.4   **FX/balloon: SUCHA**—picking up phone

11.3   **FX: BECHA PATA BECHA**—sound of something moving with a wet squishing sound

11.4   **FX/balloon: GATA**—sound of grate rattling

11.5   **FX: ZU**—sound of something sliding along

11.6   **FX: ZU ZU**—sound of something sliding along

14.5   **FX: SUCHA**—taking out pendulum

15.3   **FX: HYUN HYUN**—pendulum swinging back and forth

16.3   **FX/balloon: HYUN HYUN**—pendulum swinging

17.2   **FX/balloon: SU**—touching doll

17.5   **FX: SHAKIN**—pair of scissors opening up

17.6   **FX: BA**—grabbing doll

18.1.1   **FX/black: SA**—Makino reaching for doll

18.1.2   **FX/white: GURIN**—Yata's body twisting out of the way

18.3.1   **FX/top: GU**—Makino tugging

18.3.2   **FX/bottom: GUGUGU**—puppet tugging

18.4   **FX: BABII**—doll tearing

18.5   **FX/balloon: ZAAAA**—sound of rice pouring out

20.4 Actually she said *rajikaru, rajikaru!* By spelling *raji* in katakana and *karu* in hiragana, the original dialogue makes the English word *radical* into a trendy-sounding Japanese verb, taking advantage of the fact *aru* is a verb ending (one of several in Japanese). Dark Horse Director of Asian Licensing Michael Gombos points out that something comparable is done in Japanese by turning the English *jealousy* into *jeraru*, which can then, like *rajikaru*, be conjugated as if it were a Japanese verb for "to be jealous."

24.2 This is an unusual volume of *Kurosagi*, in that we run into something we rarely see in the story (in fact, we haven't seen it in the main story since vol. 1)— actual, you know, Buddhist priests. You may wonder why he gets a square title in English like *Reverend*, instead of something more cool you might associate with a Buddhist priest, like, say, *Brother*. But a term like *Reverend* is closer to what the sociology majors call *unmarked*, meaning it's seen as a default or normal term, because Buddhism is a default or normal religion in Japan. Indeed, it's very common for Buddhist priests in America to call themselves *Reverend*; like most community religious leaders, they want to be seen as, well, a normal member of the community. Buddhism still has a somewhat exotic image in American culture (that is, outside the small percentage of Americans who are raised in it)—the words *Buddhist priest* call to mind a monk leaping into the air, or the Dalai Lama. *Reverend* calls to mind the guy who chews you out for having brought a copy of *Trinity Blood*

to the youth retreat (I heard this anecdote at Kumoricon). But, as you may have noticed by now, being a Buddhist in Japan is like being a Baptist in the South. Except for minor differences in doctrine. I'd like to see the *Kurosagi* gang run into the wacky American versions of themselves, who went to Howard Payne University.

26.3 **FX: PARA PARA**—sound of rice grains falling out

27.2 The doll-blessing temple portrayed here is—you guessed it—based on a real one. Setsuko Kamiya wrote in the October 15, 2006, issue of the *Japan Times* (eight months before the story appeared in *Comic Charge* magazine) about the annual prayer and burning ceremony, held September 25, at the Kiyomizu Kannondo Temple in Tokyo's Ueno Park. The ceremony apparently evolved out of the practice of parents bringing their children to the temple for a blessing and leaving behind a doll at the temple to represent the child (or so that any bad influences would fall upon the doll, not the child). As time went on, this intersected with the Japanese love for dolls and figurines (an affection shared, of course, with many other cultures); people who didn't feel right about simply discarding such dolls started leaving them there alongside the dolls representing children.

27.5 **FX/balloon: JAN JYAKA JAN**—ring tone

29.1 **FX: TATA**—sound of keys being tapped

31.5 Japan (like much of the world) uses a 24-hour clock, a system in the U.S. associated with the military. However, whereas "24:00" means midnight in Japan, Michael Gombos notes it's not uncommon for Japanese schedules to give 1 AM as "25:00," 2 AM as "26:00," etc., when events run into the early morning hours. There's an interesting philosophy here—that time should be given as a person experiences it; that if they're still up at 1 AM, the day is going into "overtime" for *them*.

32.2 To paraphrase Chris Rock, idols love to *not know* shit. But I bet you wouldn't catch Shokotan acting the fool like this.

32.3 **FX/balloon: VWOOON VWOOON**—sound of cell phone vibrating

33.3 **FX: KA KO**—sound of footsteps

33.4 **FX: PURAN**—sound of doll dangling

33.6 **FX: KO**—footstep

34.1.1 **FX/balloons: CHIKI CHIKI**—blade clicking out

34.1.2 **FX/balloon: CHIKIN**—blade clicking into place

34.3 **FX/balloons: ZAKU ZAKU**—stabbing sound

34.4 **FX/balloon: CHAPUN**—sound of doll getting submerged

34.6 **FX/balloon: FU**—sound of lights turning off

34.7 **FX/balloon: BATAN**—door being closed

35.3 **FX/balloon: KACHA**—door being opened

35.4 **FX/balloon: PATAN**—door being closed

35.6.1 **FX/balloon: PACHI**—turning on lights

35.6.2 **FX: PA PAA**—fluorescent lights turning on

36.1 **FX/balloon: PICHOON**—sound of dripping faucet

36.2 **FX/balloon: CHAPU**—sound of an arm coming out of the water

36.3 **FX/balloon: BISHA**—soggy splashing sound

36.4 **FX: NUCHARI BICHA**—wet sloshing/splashing sound

37.1 **FX: KURU**—sound of Yuriri turning her head

37.2 **FX: BUBAAA**—spraying-water sound

37.3 **FX: BISHA PICHA**—sound of spray hitting doll

37.5 **FX/balloon: DOBICHA**—sound of doll hitting floor with a wet thud

38.1 **FX: DOKA DOKA DOKA**—stomping sounds

38.2 **FX/balloon: BAN**—door being banged open

39.5 **FX: GWOOOO**—sound of the car

40.2 **FX/balloon: PI**—hanging-up sound

41.2 **FX: KON KON**—knock knock

41.4 **FX: GA**—grabbing door

42.3 **FX: GA**—grabbing doorknob

42.4 **FX/balloon: MEKI**—sound of Kuro's hand getting smashed

43.1 **FX: GA GA**—fingers grabbing edge of door

43.3 **FX: GAKYAN**—door being ripped off hinge

44.2 **FX: KWOOOO**—sound of the air conditioner

46.6 **FX: SU**—placing hand on body

48.2 **FX/balloon: WIIIIN**—sound of sliding doors opening

48.3 **FX: KO KA**—sound of heels on floor

48.4 **FX: PI**—hanging up cell phone

49.1 **FX/balloon: GACHA**—opening door

49.4 FX/balloon: **PACHI**—turning on light

49.5 FX/balloon: **PASA**—hair falling down out of cap

50-51.1 FX: **GURIN**—head turning

50-51.2 FX: **MUKU**—getting-up sound

52.2.1 FX/balloon: **DOSA**—sound of doll falling over in the pyre

52.2.2 FX/small: **PACHI**—crackling flame

52.2.3 FX/small: **PACHI**—crackling flame

52.4 *Hanako* literally means *flower child*, although it don't have none o' them hippie connotations to it; in fact, it's a very traditional name— too traditional, perhaps—these days just plain *Hana* would be considered more cool.

53.4 Eiji Otsuka's feelings about otaku are, shall we say, nuanced. On one hand, he depicted as lulzworthy Comiket being nerve-gassed in *MPD-Psycho* Vol. 4. On the other, he manages to suggest a little empathy with a weak and sad specimen as seen in this story. Or rather, is it not so much empathy for the departed, as a certain distaste for the attitude of Yuriri, who, after all, like many idols, prospers by making a cult of personality out of herself (as evidenced by all the merchandise in 44.1), but then gets outraged when she attracts cultists? Karatsu's attitude seems to be that anyone who wants to make their living as an idol has no business insulting their fans for sending tributes. The headlines seen here seem to suggest everyone became happier when Yuriri dropped her Lolita act in favor of a bad-girl image instead, trumpeting her "*Transformation!*" and "*Sexy and Revealing Body!*" on a new tour for her fans, with mutual affection.

55 Is it just the editor's doujin-corrupt brain, or are Makino and Sasaki making eyes at each other? 'Cause otherwise, this could be, like, an early-eighties album cover. Actually, that would make it even *more* like an early-eighties album cover. The editor thinks the best part of Berlin's "Sex (I'm a . . .)" is when Terri Nunn says "*I'm a bi!*" and John Crawford does that chuckle.

58.3 FX: **BAWOOOO**—motorcycle sound

58.4.1 FX: **OOO**—wind/motorcycle sound

58.4.2 FX/balloon: **KURURI**—sound of head turning

59.1 FX: **OOOO**—wind/motorcycle sound

60.1 FX: **BAWOOON**—motorcycle sound

60.4 Note the mechanical traffic director, designed for high-speed roads where it would be too dangerous for a human signaler to do the job (at least, when Numata's about). As mentioned way back in vol. 1's "Disjecta Membra," note for 94.2–3, Japan's construction sector is far larger and more active than Japan's actual construction needs. The reason for this, as you might guess, is to give as many people as many jobs as possible. Besides the jobs that involve actually building something or tearing it down, every construction site also creates employment for an outer ring of people (often student or part-time workers—even Keiichi Morisato did it once in *Oh My Goddess!*) whose job it is to direct foot or vehicular traffic *around* the site. About ten years ago, the editor was rounding a building under construction in Tokyo, where a bracket-shaped path of cones led the pedestrian off the sidewalk, a few feet out onto the street away from the scaffolding, and then back onto the sidewalk again. There was a person to signal you as you entered the path, another as you made the first turn, another as you made the second turn, and then finally one to wave you out. All with those little lighted wands.On an American street construction site there might be a worker checking their text messages, but that's about it (at least one builder I saw on Burnside had an *Operation: Mindcrime* sticker on his hard hat—cool, but I was disappointed when I read Gore Vidal's *Lincoln* and found out that Portland's main drag was named for such a poor general).

60.5.1 **FX: BAKYAN**—sign breaking

60.5.2 **FX/balloon: GOKIN**—sound of car hitting signpost

60.6 **FX/balloon: SHUU**—sound of steam escaping

62.2 These are, as you might guess, all forum postings about the Riding Head, although the name given it in Japanese is *kubi dake raidaa*, literally "Head-Only Rider." *Kubidake* can also mean "complete devotion," appropriate enough, as we shall see. *Kannana* is the understandably shortened form of the highway officially known as the *Tokyo-to keikaku douro kansen sengai rokan jodai nana-go sen*, or "Line 7 of the major bypass for the Tokyo city building plan". . . or something like that.

62.5 **FX: BAN**—hitting-table sound

63.3 Note that there are supposedly already seventeen pages of archived postings about the Peeping Head available at

www.kubidakenozokima.jp.html (surprisingly, a nonexistent website). In panel 5, they're checking out the video on "YouTofu," a play on the definitely existing Japanese version of YouTube.

63.5 **FX/balloon: TSUUU KAKO**—sound of finger sliding down track pad then clicking

66.3 **FX: PAN PAN**—slapping feet

66.4 **FX: BATAAN**—slamming door. In the back are the Japanese versions of the Yuriri poster from 2nd Delivery, not to mention the "Go Ricefish!" banner from vol. 4, 1st Delivery. I like how they collect this stuff. It's kind of a pauper's version of the Batcave.

70.6 *"IIIIIII don't believe it! Thermop-tic camouflage!"* Note how at that moment in the movie (or manga) they can still *see* the Major as she disappears, but nobody thinks to actually *shoot* her. To paraphrase Dr. Evil, "No, no, I'm just going to stand here and watch as she gradually becomes completely invisible."

71.4 **FX: KATA**—standing-up sound

71.5 **FX: BASA**—spreading out fabric

71.6 **FX: GATA**—setting up projector

72.3 This "invisibility suit" really exists as depicted (and, just as depicted, is more like appearing transparent than invisible) and was first reported in world media in February of 2003, based on a demo version developed by Susumu Tachi and his team at Tokyo University. Dr. Tachi, who looks like a proper manga scientist, has his homepage at www.star.t.u-tokyo.ac. jp/~tachi/.

73.4 **FX/balloon: CHARAN**—dangling sound

74.4.1 FX: ZA—footstep

74.4.2 FX: ZA—footstep

74.4.3 FX: ZA—footstep

74.5 FX: GA—tripping sound

75.2 FX: SU—reaching down

76.3 FX: DON—putting hand down on body

77.4 FX/balloon: KACHA—clatter of the zipper

77.5 FX: BABIIIII—zipper being pulled

79.3 When I first saw the Riding/Peeping Head close-up on 65.1, I did think, *Hey . . . this guy looks like **Mamoru Oshii!*** But then, there's a lot of cats who look like Mamoru Oshii—in Japan, anyway. I didn't expect it to actually *be* a reference to him (you have to look closely at his ID, but the guy's name is in fact Mamoru Oshii—the only difference from the film director being that different kanji are used to spell his first name. The kanji in *Esuefu* make it sound like the name of a (fictitious) urban prefecture, but it's a pun on *SF*, i.e., science fiction. I really want to see Oshii's latest, *The Sky Crawlers*. I'm a little concerned because, unlike most Oshii films, the protagonists are teenagers, and there's already more than enough anime where the protagonists are teenagers. It's not about putting the youth of today down. It's about a thirty-eight-year-old otaku, faithful follower of the scene since age eleven, requesting some equity. Shit, man, since they rebooted the movie series, James Bond is now supposed to be the same age as Daniel Craig—forty. If he can still do all that stuff with the help of CG, surely an anime character can do it with the help of Production I.G.

79.5 FX: MUNYU—cheeks being pulled

81.1 The morpho butterfly, native to Latin America, has ultrafine, iridescent scales whose structure has been studied for various applications, including thin-film optics, and, increasingly, photonic-crystal fibers. As for what that really means, I majored in history, so I'm inclined to echo Numata's response.

82.1 FX: GASHI—grasping-hand sound

82.2 FX/balloon: JIJI—closing-zipper sound

82.3 FX/balloon: JI—zipper closing

82.5.1 FX/balloon: GON GATAN—hitting obstacles

82.5.2 FX/balloon: GASHAN—knocking cart over

83.2 FX: NUBO—head appearing out of nowhere

84.2 FX/balloon: CHARA—dangling-key sound

85.3 FX/balloon: JIII—closing-zipper sound

85.4 FX: PIII PIII—reverse warning beeps

85.6.1 FX/top: DON—impact sound

85.6.2 FX/middle: GO—hitting wall on the way down

85.6.3 FX/bottom: GOKI—sound of a bone breaking

86.1 FX: DOSA—sound of body hitting ground

87.3 FX: BAN—hitting table

89.1.1 FX/balloon: GATAN—pulling out drawer

89.1.2 FX/balloon: GARA GARA—dumping out contents

89.4 This is vol. 1 of the original *Oh! Invisible Man* (in Japanese, *Oh! toumeiningen*), which, as you might guess from its appearance, was a 1980s manga series that ran in Kodansha's *Monthly Shonen*

Magazine (today, home of the *Pumpkin Scissors* manga) for eleven volumes. Yasuhiro Nakanishi has revived it in recent years, switching publishers to Shueisha, where the sequel *Oh! Invisible Man 21* (21, after this oh-so-wonderful-thus-far century) ran in the biweekly *Super Jump* magazine for eight volumes (home of the immortal *Golden Boy*). When you have "Oh" beginning an exclamatory phrase, Japanese seem to like placing the exclamation point immediately after the exclamation itself, instead of at the end of the phrase. Thus you will often see in manga a foreigner being shown to say in English "Oh! My God," rather than "Oh My God!" Now, to the native English reader, that makes it look like the stress is being put on the "Oh!" which sounds a little unnatural, but the issue likely doesn't occur to the person reading in Japanese. Gombos sees in this the Japanese simply applying their own usage of exclamations at the beginning of a phrase to English (the original title of the manga *Oh My Goddess!* is *Aa megami-sama*, where the *Aa* is the exclamation). As usual, it's not like it was intended for native English readers to fret over. It's kind of like how you see people writing *ninjas*, applying English usage to Japanese (where there's no special plural spellings to words; whether it's one attacking you or a hundred, it's just *ninja*).

90.1 **FX/balloon: GACHA**—door opening

90.4.1 **FX: DOSA**—putting body down

90.4.2 **FX/balloon: JI**—starting to pull zipper

90.5 **FX: JIPAAAAA**—pulling zipper down

90.6 **FX: IIII**—zipper coming to a stop

91.3 **FX: SU**—disc floating out of hand

91.5 **FX: GOSO**—rummaging in pocket

92.1 **FX: BASHUUUU**—spraying sound

92.2 Of course no one, even in Japan, would be crazy enough to make a consumer product like this. Ha, ha, just kidding—it's real, of course. You can buy it at www.strap ya-world.com/products/10932.html. "Please don't spray directly to skin. It may cause burn wounds."

92.2.1 That was uncalled for. I'm an American; now excuse me while *I* go buy something safe and sensible, like a Desert Eagle Mark XIX chambered for .50 Action Express.

92.3.1 **FX: PISHI PISHI PISHI**—sound of the suit's surface hardening

92.3.2 **FX/balloon: PORO**—dropping disc

93.1 **FX/balloon: GA**—grabbing disc

93.2 **FX: BA**—putting disc into coat

93.3 **FX: BAAAAAAA**—spraying face

93.4 **FX: DATATATATA**—running down stairs

93.5 **FX: BAN**—slamming door

94.1 **FX: GYUGYUWOON**—car speeding off

94.2 **FX/balloon: PARIN**—glass breaking

94.3.1 **FX/balloon: DON**—sound of something landing on car

94.3.2 **FX: WOOOOO**—car speeding away

94.6 **FX: BAN**—hand hitting windshield

95.2.1 **FX/balloon: PAKI PAKI**—suit starting to flake away

95.2.2 **FX/balloon: PAKI**—suit falling apart

95.3.1 **FX/balloon: PAKI**—suit falling apart

95.3.2 **FX/balloon: PAKI**—suit falling apart

99.1 **FX/balloon: KAN KORON**—sound of sign clattering on the ground

99.2 **FX/balloon: PATAN**—broken sign falling to a stop

102 Oh, yeah, and have you ever wondered what's up with pages like this—and page 54, and similar pages in other volumes? 99.9% of the time, a manga comes out in Japan one chapter at a time in an anthology magazine, and only later gets collected to graphic novel (or not; if it remains uncollected, it's sometimes because no one liked it the first time, and sometimes because the material was unfinished or insufficient in length for a graphic novel—Kenji Tsuruta, Yoshiyuki Sadamoto, and Hiroaki Samura have all done great stuff for magazines that remains uncollected). *Kurosagi* runs in Kadokawa's *Comic Charge* biweekly magazine (or rather, it did, until the magazine's recent cancellation, but don't panic—it was *Kurosagi*'s third home, and Kadokawa has promised to find it a fourth). But, being an anthology manga magazine, any given chapter of *Kurosagi* naturally has to be laid out in a particular issue in a way that takes into account all the other manga sharing that issue. Notice how "4th delivery" ends, and "5th delivery" begins, both on the left-side page. That was how they had to fit into their respective issues, but it means you have to add a "blank" page like 102 when you collect them to a graphic novel. Like most manga magazines (and unlike most major-publisher U.S. comic books), only a very small percentage of *Comic Charge* consisted of ads—in a typical four-hundred-page issue there might be eight or nine interior pages (that is, not counting the outside or inside covers) of ads, and maybe five or six pages devoted to editorial matters (table of contents, reader giveaways, etc.)—meaning that it's over 95% actual manga content. You may be curious as to what the original *Kurosagi*-reader demographic was expected to buy. A survey of nine random issues of *Comic Charge* shows that for six of them, the inside-back-cover ad was taken out by a chain of circumcision clinics (recall *Even a Monkey Can Draw Manga*'s report on the great phimosis debate). In the ad, a handsome male model tries to free his head from a black turtle-neck pulled up to his nose, a struggle despite the help of two attractive women who are already hanging off each shoulder. Three issues out of the nine had back-cover ads for the Merrell Jungle Moc (and a fourth had it on the inside front cover). Other ads to appear included the Nintendo DS test prep for the TOEIC (Test Of English for International Communication) twice; also twice, the DVD release of the film *Walking My Life* (original Japanese title: *Zo-no senaka*, "The Back of the Elephant"—English-subtitled trailer at www.shochikufilms.com/movie/zou.html), and ads for Suntory Bitter & Sharp beer and Black Boss coffee in a can.

103.1 **FX: MEEN MEEN MEEN JEEWA JEEWA**—sound of cicadas

103.2 FX: MEEN MEEN MEEN—sound of cicadas

108.3 FX: FUSA—cloth being placed over face

108.4 FX/balloon: DON DON—banging on door

109.1 FX: GACHA—door opening

111.2 FX/balloon: KII KII—sound of squeaky wheels on a cart

112.1 FX: PAKU PAKU—puppet mouth flapping

112.2 FX: CHII CHII CHII—high-pitched, mosquito-like sounds

112.3 FX/balloon: KOSO—rustling under desk

112.4 FX: KACHA KACHA KACHA KACHA—pressing keys

112.5.1 FX: CHII CHII—high-pitched sounds

112.5.2 FX/balloon: KACHA—pressing keys

112.5.3 FX/balloon: TATATA—tapping on keys

112.6 FX: CHII CHII CHIII—high-pitched sounds

113.4 Makino's jacket, bearing a cheerful youth with an IV, says "Kizumono Kids," meaning "Injured Kids." It's kind of Junko Mizuno-ish, don't you think?

114.1 FX: CHIII CHII KIII KII—sounds

115.3 FX/balloon: CHARARAN CHARARA JA JA JAAN—ring tone

116.1 FX: CHIRA—glancing back at Sasaki

116.2 FX: NIKO—smile

116.4 FX/balloon: PI—hanging up cell phone

120.5 FX/balloon: GASA—taking out a newspaper-wrapped object

122.2 FX: GASA—opening up paper

123.4 FX: DAN—slamming hand down

124.3 FX/balloon: KACHA—door opening

124.6 FX/balloon: BATAN—closing door

125.1 FX: KA KA—sound of cane on floor

126.2 FX/balloon: WIIIN—sound of motorized car mirror tracking Kikuchi

126.4 FX: NNNH—sound of power window being lowered

130.1 Folklorist Kunio Yanagita, of course, is an influence Eiji Otsuka has paid tribute to since the first volume, including making him a Sherlock Holmes–like detective in vol. 6.

131.3 FX: SU—placing hand on body

132.1 FX: KACHA—footstep

132.6 FX: POTATA POTA—sound of falling droplets

133.1 FX: GA—grabbing sound

133.3 FX/balloon: BURAN—hand going limp

133.4 FX/balloon: CHARARA CHARARAN JAJAJAAAN—ring tone

134.1 FX: SUCHA—placing phone on ear

136.2 FX: TATATA TATA—tapping at keys

137.3 The screen relates that Keisuke Matsuzawa was born and lives in the Setagaya Ward of Tokyo (remember that Sasayama works for one of Tokyo's other wards, Shinjuku), went to Gakkan High, and attended Waseda University School of Law, with a stint at Tokyo Empire Bank after graduation. Waseda is often considered to be the second- or third-best university in Japan (battling for the rank with Keio)— and Michael Gombos went there, in case you doubt you're in good hands with Dark Horse Manga.

138.2 FX: KA KA—sound of heels

139.4.1 FX/balloon: KACHI KACHI—jar rattling

139.4.2 FX/balloon: KACHI—jar rattling

139.4.3 FX/balloon: KACHI—jar rattling

139.5.1 FX/balloon: KACHI—jar rattling

139.5.2 FX/balloon: KACHI KACHI—jar rattling

139.5.3 FX/balloon: KACHI—jar rattling

141.3 Radar was invented in the years just before WWII, but the war (understandably) greatly accelerated its development. Martin Favorite suggests that the critical issue in Japan's case seems to be that senior officers didn't grasp its importance until late in the war, and hence Japanese radar in 1945 remained as much as three years behind America's, (which was also using its advanced radar offensively, to help guide its bombs). A dramatic illustration of this difference is in the fact that on December 7, 1941, the Japanese naval air task force approaching Pearl Harbor was actually picked up by U.S. Army radar on Oahu (but dismissed as a false alarm), yet the attackers themselves had no radar! You can see a picture of a surviving *choongo* at www.outdoor.geocities.jp/kotetsu0213/dsc02802.jpg.

142.2.1 FX/balloon: JARI JARI—sound of tires on gravel

142.2.2 FX/balloon: JARI—sound of tires on gravel

142.3 FX/balloon: KII—door creaking open

143.1 FX: DOZA—Kikuchi hitting gravel

144.1 FX: KOFAA—sound of the truck being opened

145.5 FX: PAAAN—slap

146.4 FX: SUKU—standing-up sound

146.5 FX/balloon: POTATA—sound of droplets

147.1 FX: DADADA—running sound

147.4 FX/balloon: TATATA—running sound

148.2 FX: KO KA—footsteps

149.5.1 FX/balloon: KACHA—jar rattling

149.5.2 FX/balloon: KACHA—jar rattling

150.1.1 FX/balloon: KACHA—jar rattling

150.1.2 FX/balloon: KACHA—jar rattling

150.1.3 FX/balloon: KACHA—jar rattling

150.1.4 FX/balloon: KACHA—jar rattling

152.1 FX: BA—jumping in the way

152.2 FX: PETASHI PETARI—bare footsteps

152.4.1 FX/balloon: GASHAAN—breaking glass

152.4.2 FX/balloon: PAN—popping-jar sound

152.4.3 FX/balloon: GASHO—muffled shattering sound

152.6 FX: PICHO—dripping sound

153.4.1 FX: BICHARI—wet squishing sound

153.4.2 FX: KUCHU—wet pressing sound

154.1 FX: ZAWA ZAWA ZAWA ZAWA—distant murmuring sound

154.2 FX: ZAWA ZAWA ZAWAWA ZAWA ZAWA ZAWA—murmuring sound

154.3 FX: ZAWA ZAWA ZAWA ZAWA—loud murmuring sound

155.1 FX: ZAWA ZAWA ZAWA ZAWA—loud murmuring sound

155.2 FX: WAAAAAAAAAAA—scream

157.1 FX/balloon: BURORORO—car driving away

157.2 FX/balloon: BERI—ripping duct tape off

158.2.1 FX/balloon: SA—taking out pendulum

158.2.2 FX/balloon: CHARAN—sound of dangling chain

158.3 FX: HYUN HYUN—sound of pendulum swinging

160.3 FX/balloons: KYAN KIN KIN—sound of bouncing shell casing

164.1 This is the Shigeru Yoshida referred to in 119.5. Prime minister of Japan during most of the postwar U.S. occupation (1945–52), Yoshida laid the groundwork for the basic rules of Japanese policy ever since: concentrate on domestic economic development and leave defense to the United States. In *Modern Times*, conservative historian Paul Johnson compares Yoshida's role to that of Adenauer in Germany or de Gasperi in Italy; that is, a politician who can take credit for leading a former Axis power out of devastation and on the path to peace and prosperity. This seems fair enough, but Johnson also characterizes Yoshida as "a former diplomat and thus from the background closest to Anglo-Saxon traditions of democracy and the rule of law," whereas John Dower in *Embracing Defeat* views Yoshida as believing that "the Japanese people were not capable of genuine self-government"—the two views are not necessarily contradictory. The editor, by the way, thinks that because the *actual* America is full of *both* liberal and conservative people—and that's not likely to change anytime soon—it's a good idea to try to understand America by reading both conservative and liberal *interpretations* of its history. So, if you've read Howard Zinn's *A People's History of the United States*, try Paul Johnson's *A History of the American People* (the differences in phrasing between the two titles are themselves interesting), and vice versa. Note that the present (at least, as of March 2009—his ratings are dropping fast) prime minister of Japan, the famously manga-loving Taro Aso, is Shigeru Yoshida's maternal grandson.

166.2 FX: DOSA—corpse falling down

167.2 FX/balloon: VWOON VWOON—sound of cell phone vibrating

167.3 FX/balloon: CHA—placing phone on ear

168.2.1 FX/balloon: GASA—moving through foliage

168.2.2 FX/balloon: GASA—moving through foliage

168.2.3 FX/balloon: GASA—moving through foliage

168.3 FX/balloon: GASA—moving through foliage

169.3 FX/balloon: ZA ZA—digging sound

170.4 FX/balloon: PATAN—closing cell phone

172.3 FX/balloon: PASA—sound of newspaper landing on ground

175.5 FX/balloon: KOKU—nod

176.6 FX: ZURU—wet, dragging sound

177.4 FX/balloon: CHARARA CHAN CHARARA—ring tone

178.1.1 FX/balloon: CHIRARA JARARAN CHARA ZUN—ring tone

178.1.2 FX/balloon: PI—answering phone

178.4 FX/balloon: PI—hanging up

179.4 FX: PAKU PAKU—sound of puppet's mouth flapping

180.1 FX: SHIIIIN—sound of silence

181.4 FX: GARA—opening sliding door

183.1 FX: DADADA—kids running to Mumume-tan. A good reminder of the fact that many of the shows otaku lavish their, er, affection upon were technically directed at children; famous magical-girl series of the '90s such as *Sailor Moon* and *Cardcaptor Sakura* ran in *Nakayoshi* magazine, a shojo monthly (since 1954!) intended for readers in junior-high and elementary school. But with *Nakayoshi*'s circulation numbers having declined from 1.8 million in 1995 to 400,000 today, there is, of necessity, often more acceptance of the otaku element in marketing, with the perception that a contemporary magical-girl show such as *Futari wa Pretty Cure* (also a *Nakayoshi* title) is kept going in large part through otaku support (*vide* Kohta Hirano's plot to insert himself into the show in the back of *Hellsing* Vol. 7). The editor feels the idea that it's only otaku who sexualize this stuff is a *little* overstated; for example, it was quite possible to see a *Sailor Moon* routine at Japanese strip clubs in the mid-'90s, and they're not really an otaku thing. It's hard (*uh-huh-huh-huh*), you know, for me to properly express how much I like *Hellsing*. It's not so much conveying the intensity, as the proper tone. I'm not especially into vampires, Nazis, or the Alucard x Integra equation, so it's not like that. It's more like—in Howard Hibbett's *The Floating World in Japanese Fiction*, there's a woodcut reproduced from Ejima Kiseki's 1715 story "The Rake," where the rake, witnessing a dance at an inn, exclaims, "*It's so delightful I can hardly bear it!*" I'm that guy. By the way, in the same book, Hibbert shows a scene from Saikaku's *The Man Who Spent His Life in Love* of a man peeping on a bathing woman, suggesting not much has changed in Japanese pop culture these last three hundred years.

183.2 "Kei-chan," is it? If you'll recall, her full name is Keiko Makino.

183.6 **FX/balloon: NINI**—smirk

187.5 **FX: KAN KAN KAN**—warning bells

188.1 **FX: KAN KAN KAN KAN**—warning bells

188.2 **FX: PWAAAN**—train horn

190.5 **FX/balloon: NIHI**—smirk

191.5 The "Akashic Records" (from the Sanskrit *akasha*, "aether") refer to a supposed complete account of all human knowledge, past, present, and future, supposedly existing on another plane (also supposed to exist). The concept apparently arose in the nineteenth-century Theosophist movement and is very useful as an all-purpose plot device in fantasy and SF, sort of like orichalcum. Then again, it's possible that Kereellis is just *fucking with us*.

193.1 **FX/balloons: HO HO HO**—jogging man exhaling

193.5 **FX: ZAAA**—sound of wind through the trees

197.3 **FX: PYON PYON**—jumping up and down in happiness

197.4 **FX/balloon: CHU**—kiss

198.3 **FX/balloon: CHU**—kiss

198.5 **FX/balloon: KIII**—sound of brakes

198.6 **FX: BIKU**—twitch of fear

199.1 **FX: GASA GASA**—tromping through bushes

199.3 **FX/balloons: BAN BURORORO**—door closing and car driving away